Migration and Refugee Law

Principles and Practice in Australia

Third Edition

Migration and Refugee Law: Principles and Practice in Australia is a comprehensive overview of the legal principles governing the entry of people into Australia. This fully revised third edition provides an accessible analysis of the theory and practice of this complex and controversial area of the law. It considers the social and political context of migration and refugee law in devising innovative policies aimed at creating an equitable and rational immigration system.

Migration and Refugee Law: Principles and Practice in Australia combines an astute consideration of theory with the creation of practical policy solutions, and is therefore an essential resource for migration lawyers and agents, government employees, students, judicial officers and policymakers.

John Vrachnas was a full-time member of the Refugee Review Tribunal for more than ten years and currently practises as a solicitor in Victoria with a migration and refugee practice.

Mirko Bagaric is Professor of Law at Deakin University and has worked as a part-time member of both the Migration Review Tribunal and the Refugee Review Tribunal.

Penny Dimopoulos is completing a PhD in refugee law at La Trobe University.

Athula Pathinayake is Lecturer in Law at Deakin University. He has over seven years' experience practising in the migration field.

Migration and Refugee Law

Principles and Practice in Australia

Third Edition

John Vrachnas
Mirko Bagaric
Penny Dimopoulos
Athula Pathinayake

CAMBRIDGE
UNIVERSITY PRESS

CAMBRIDGE
UNIVERSITY PRESS

Shaftesbury Road, Cambridge CB2 8EA, United Kingdom

One Liberty Plaza, 20th Floor, New York, NY 10006, USA

477 Williamstown Road, Port Melbourne, VIC 3207, Australia

314–321, 3rd Floor, Plot 3, Splendor Forum, Jasola District Centre, New Delhi – 110025, India

103 Penang Road, #05–06/07, Visioncrest Commercial, Singapore 238467

Cambridge University Press is part of Cambridge University Press & Assessment, a department of the University of Cambridge.

We share the University's mission to contribute to society through the pursuit of education, learning and research at the highest international levels of excellence.

www.cambridge.org
Information on this title: www.cambridge.org/9781107623279

First published 2005
Second edition 2008
Reprinted 2010
Third edition 2012

Cover design by Jeni Burton
Typeset by Aptara Corp.

A catalogue record for this publication is available from the British Library

National Library of Australia Cataloguing in Publication data
Migration and refugee law : principles and practice in Australia / John Vrachnas . . . [et al.].
3rd ed.
9781107623279 (pbk.)
Includes index.
Emigration and immigration law – Australia.
Political refugees – Legal status, laws, etc. – Australia.
Asylum, Right of – Australia.
Vrachnas, John.
342.94083

ISBN 978-1-107-62327-9 Paperback

Additional resources for this publication at www.cambridge.edu.au/academic/planning

Contents

Table of cases

Abbreviations

MIEA	Minister for Immigration and Ethnic Affairs
MILGEA	Minister for Immigration, Local Government and Ethnic Affairs
MIMA	Minister for Immigration and Multicultural Affairs
MIMIA	Minister for Immigration and Multicultural and Indigenous Affairs

Cases

Table of statutes

Preface to the third edition

A defining aspect of national sovereignty is that nation states have the right to determine which people are permitted to come within their geographical borders. Individuals, like nations, appear to be inherently territorial. In addition to this, a defining aspect of many people's personhood (their core identity) is the place where they were born or live.

Despite the disparate range of interests and projects that individuals have and pursue, there are basic goals that communities invariably share. Thus, in Australia, the current generation (building on the work of earlier generations) has committed enormous resources to building state institutions (such as our political and legal system), hospitals, schools, roads and recreational and sporting amenities and facilities.

These common projects serve to entrench our feeling of community. We also come to share some fundamental values and beliefs.

Immigration policy and law is concerned with setting the parameters within which 'foreigners' (or 'aliens' as they are called in the Commonwealth Constitution) come to share our community, enjoy our resources and become exposed to our culture and values, whether permanently or for a shorter period. It is, thus, inherently controversial. Limits seemingly need to be placed on the numbers and types of people who can come to Australia.

This book examines the way in which Australia currently responds to this challenge. It is divided into two main sections. The first 11 chapters examine migration law. The next seven chapters look at refugee law. The dichotomy between migration and refugee law is nonexistent at a formal level. Refugee law and policy is in fact one branch of migration law. It involves three among over 150 available visas. Chapter 19 outlines the scope for 'merits review' and judicial review of decisions made in relation to migration or refugee visas.

However, substantively, there is a fundamental distinction between migration and refugee law. Migration law and policy is in essence concerned with what migrants can do for Australia. The principal objective in framing migration law is to let in people who will contribute something tangible to Australia. Australia seeks to attract people who will make the community richer or smarter.

Refugee law is the main exception to this principle. It focuses on what we as a community can do for a person fleeing serious harm, rather than what he or she has to offer us as a nation. Refugees make a significant contribution to the country, but this is an incidental outcome of refugee policy.

The differences between migration and refugee law are also to some extent reflected in the development and state of the law. Migration legislation is regulation-driven, and is highly fluid and constantly changing. Refugee law, though far less voluminous in terms of legislation, is imbued with many conflicting principles and interests.

The authors have incorporated into this third edition the numerous and significant changes to migration legislation and policy, as well as important developments in migration and refugee case law, that have occurred since the publication of the second edition in 2007.

The chapters dealing with migration law provide a detailed analysis of the major legislative provisions relating to the most widely utilised visa categories. The structure of these chapters reflects the fact that migration law is predominantly contained in Regulations. Each visa category has numerous legal criteria, but invariably has a 'signature' criterion (such as having a spouse for a spouse visa). This book does not look at all visa categories or at all criteria for the visa classes it does consider. While it focuses on the signature criteria, it does so with the caveat that the failure to meet any of the other criteria can prove fatal to a visa application.

Refugee law is derived from the Convention relating to the Status of Refugees which was completed at Geneva on 28 July 1951 as amended by the Protocol relating to the Status of Refugees done at New York on 31 January 1967 (the Refugees Convention). Article 1A(2) of the Refugees Convention defines a refugee as a person who:

> ... owing to a well-founded fear of being persecuted for reasons of race, religion, nationality, membership of a particular social group or political opinion, is outside the country of his nationality and is unable or, owing to such fear, is unwilling to avail himself of the protection of that country; or who, not having a nationality and being outside the country of his former habitual residence as a result of such events, is unable or, owing to such fear, is unwilling to return to it.

At the heart of this definition are the concepts of fear and persecution. Despite the apparent simplicity of these concepts, the interpretation of Article 1A(2) has proven to be fertile ground for legal and judicial analysis. Refugee law is littered with controversy regarding the meaning and scope of key terms in the definition, due in no small part to the history of the drafting of the Refugees Convention, and to the absence of a coherent doctrinal rationale underpinning it.

The chapters on refugee law provide an overview of existing legal principles in relation to the more unsettled areas of law (such as how persecution is defined) and suggest a way in which the law can be made more coherent and workable.

Chapter 18 analyses the fundamental failings of the Convention and suggests a more appropriate definition of a refugee.

This book is essentially concerned with the principles governing the manner in which non-citizens come to gain lawful access to Australia. The focus is not on how people come to lose this status or the legal process through which migration and refugee status is determined. This last area involves the entire ambit of administrative law and is another fertile source of jurisprudence. A treatment of this is beyond the scope of this book. However, for the sake of completeness, we provide an overview of these areas in Chapters 11 and 19 respectively.

Acknowledgments

Excerpts from Chapters 15 and 18 have been published elsewhere. Such sections as are reprinted are done so by permission. In this regard we are very grateful to the following journals:

The Bond Law Review: Mirko Bagaric & Penny Dimopoulos, 'The shifting meaning of persecution in Australian refugee law: how much must one suffer to be deserving of asylum?', (2003) 15 *The Bond Law Review*, 284–302.

The Canterbury Law Review: Mirko Bagaric & Penny Dimopoulos, 'Refugee law: time for a fundamental re-think – need as the criterion for assistance', (2003) 9 *The Canterbury Law Review* (NZ), 268–93.

The International Journal of the Sociology of Law: Mirko Bagaric & Penny Dimopoulos, 'Discrimination as the touchstone of persecution in refugee law', (2004) 32 *The International Journal of the Sociology of Law*, 310–34.

The authors' knowledge of refugee law has been greatly assisted by their training and experience at the Refugee Review Tribunal and in particular by the excellent publication by S. Haddad et al., *A Guide to Refugee Law in Australia* (RRT).

We also thank M. Saunders, S. Mullins and J. Gryle for allowing us to source and use extracts from the excellent online course: 'In Search of Australia: Historical Perspectives', developed for Central Queensland University. This assisted us greatly in the writing of Chapter 1.

Readers will note that the case citations in the book do not accord with those found in the various hard copy law reports. For reasons of expense and accessibility to readers, references to all cases which can be accessed on a free database are as per the citation in the electronic database. In relation to these cases, readers are referred to the Australasian Legal Information Institute database (a joint facility of UTS and UNSW Faculties of Law) at www.austlii.edu.au.

1

Historical context to migration

We will decide who comes to this country and the circumstances in which they come.

Former Prime Minister John Howard, 28 October 2001,
Liberal Party election launch

1.1 Introduction

It is not possible to understand the ongoing immigration debate and current immigration policy in Australia without some understanding of its genesis and development, particularly since white settlers first arrived in the late 18th century. Until late into the 20th century, issues that are fundamental to human diversity, particularly race and colour, were overt policy considerations that found their way, one way or another, into Australian legislation. Innate factors of birth and others of conscience, such as religion or political opinion, continue to figure in debate about who is entitled to live in Australia. In recent times, the debate has centred on 'boat people', and in the wake of the 11 September 2001 Al-Qaeda attacks on the United States, the issue of religion has been an undercurrent in the focus on terrorism.

The immigration debate is never far from the surface. When former Prime Minister John Howard made the statement quoted at the head of this chapter, it was nothing new. Similar expressions have been made by members of the judiciary and politicians of all hues since before Federation.

When the Labor Party was in the throes of completing a largely bipartisan overhaul of the migration legislation in the late 1980s, the then Immigration Minister, Senator Robert Ray, made a similar comment when he announced the Labor government's response to the Fitzgerald Report.[1] He told Parliament:

1 S. Fitzgerald, 'Immigration: A Commitment to Australia', *The Committee to Advise on Australia's Immigration Policies* (Canberra, AGPS, 1988).

> The Australian Government alone will determine who will be admitted to Australia consistent with laws enacted by the Federal Parliament to regulate immigration.[2]

Justice Isaacs summarised the early view of the High Court Bench when he held that:

> The history of this country and its development has been, and must inevitably be, largely the story of its policy with respect to population from abroad. That naturally involves the perfect control of the subject of immigration, both as to encouragement and restriction with all their incidents.[3]

His Honour was reflecting the opinion of the first Attorney-General of the Commonwealth, Alfred Deakin, who had argued:

> The most powerful force compelling the colonies towards federation has been the desire 'that we should be one people and remain one people without the admixture of other races'.[4]

As Kathryn Cronin has pointed out, 'Australia has consistently held fast to the principle that immigration must be controlled.'[5]

1.2 Historical developments[6]

1.2.1 The period before 1778

Australia was an ancient landmass when the first Australians, the ancestors of the Aborigines, arrived around 40 000 years ago. Nobody really knows why they came to Australia. In modern-day Australia, the concept of the immigrant may be misplaced when applied to Australia's first settlers. Nevertheless, since time immemorial, people have been motivated to migrate from one place to another for a vast array of reasons, such as seeking wealth and opportunity; finding freedom; escaping oppression, violence or natural disaster; pursuing adventure and discovery; exercising force and expanding territory; or reuniting with family or friends. In some cases, groups of slaves or convicts have been forced against their will to move to another location. In other cases, there might have been no particular reason, and settlement at a new location was the result of an accident such as being blown off course or having a trip interrupted by unforeseen or unavoidable circumstances.

2 Senate Hansard p. 3753: Ministerial statement made to the Senate on 8 December 1988.
3 *R v Macfarlane; Ex Parte O'Flanagan and O'Kelly* [1923] HCA 39 (23 August 1923), (1923) 32 CLR 518.
4 A. Markus, *A Fear and Hatred: Purifying Australia and California 1850–1901* (Sydney, Hale & Iremonger, 1979).
5 K. Cronin, 'A Culture of Control', in J. Jupp and M. Kabala (eds), *The Politics of Australian Immigration* (Canberra, AGPS, 1993), p. 84.
6 The following brief history, including extracts from other authors, is predominantly derived from the excellent online course 'In Search of Australia: Historical Perspectives' developed for the Central Queensland University by M. Saunders, S. Mullins and J. Cryle. In addition, it is partly compiled from a number of DIMIA Fact Sheets (Nos 4, 6 and 8).

Whatever the reason the first humans came to Australia, there has been an ongoing influx of migrants and visitors ever since, the migrants arriving in waves that have been influenced by both push and pull factors. By the time Europeans started arriving in Australia to settle, in the late 18th century, there were more than 250 000 Aborigines in Australia, living in hundreds of tribes in any areas that could provide adequate sustenance. Intense migration by European settlers during the following two centuries decimated that original population through disease, dispossession and cultural oppression, not to mention direct attack by white settlers.

It was the British colonial government that first formalised controls on the mode of entry to Australia. The north and northwest Australian coast and nearby northern islands had been visited by explorers and adventurers from various European colonial powers between the 16th and 18th centuries, largely in search of gold, silver and spices. Finding nothing of real promise and weighed down by the costs of distant exploration, those visitors did not settle in Australia. James Cook was the first to recognise the potential for settlement. Having been sent to Tahiti in 1769 to track the Transit of Venus across the sun in order to establish co-ordinates to be used in assessing the distance between the earth and the sun, he headed south, circumnavigated New Zealand and then headed west. He arrived at the southeast corner of Australia and then sailed north, charting the eastern coastline. He formally claimed the eastern part of Australia for the British Crown in 1770, first naming it New Wales and then later New South Wales.

1.2.2 Early white settlement – the first wave[7]

Six years later, in 1776, the British lost their American colonies in the War of Independence and needed to find new land that would be suitable for displaced loyal American colonists, and would meet the requirements of the British policy of transporting convicts in order to alleviate overcrowding in penal institutions. The colonists displaced in America largely returned to England or migrated to Canada and the West Indies. However, the British Crown determined the early course of white settlement and created the first wave of modern migration when it decided to send convicts to New South Wales. In the following decades, the British established and expanded a series of colonies significantly populated by transported convicts. The purpose of colonial expansion was partly to foster agriculture, particularly the wool industry, and partly to create trade in goods, such as sealskins and whale oil, but largely to protect territory and allay suspicion and fears of French intentions to claim Australia, particularly during and following the Napoleonic Wars. New colonies were established in Van Diemen's Land (now known as Tasmania), Victoria, South Australia and Western Australia, each with its own administration. Trade and national security remain factors that feed into immigration policies and programs.

7 See M. Dugan and J. Szwarc, *There Goes the Neighbourhood!* (Melbourne, Macmillan, 1984), pp. 192–94 for a clear chronological representation of waves of migration.

Contracts for transporting convicts were let to private ship owners, but following an unacceptably high incidence of death during the voyages to the new colonies, regulations were introduced to provide for adequate food and water, and a bonus was paid for safe delivery of prisoners. By 1802, the British Government had adopted a system of sending convicts twice a year in ships specifically designed for the purpose, under the direction of a Transport Board and commanded by Navy officers. After their arrival, some of the convicts worked on public projects and some were assigned as labour for free settlers. After serving part or all of their sentences, some were granted tickets of leave and could work for themselves, while others were emancipated and could also receive grants of land.

1.2.3 The first colonial emigration programs

At a time when the Industrial Revolution was causing dislocation in agricultural Europe, the growing colonies encountered labour shortages and, at the same time, the transportation system created imbalances between the numbers of convicts and free settlers and between men and women. The Crown set about redressing the shortages in its Australian colonies by establishing assisted migration schemes, often coupled with land grants or the release of Crown Land for auction, collectively described as the Wakefield principle and administered by the Colonial Office through Her Majesty's Colonial Land and Emigration Commissioners.[8] These schemes generally involved subsidised or free passage to the Australian colonies to counteract the attraction of America and Canada, which were far cheaper to reach.

In subsequent assisted migration schemes over the next few years, significant numbers of women from Ireland and England migrated, including many who had been poor or institutionalised; they were largely exploited by being put into menial domestic service after their arrival in Australia.

By the time the first wave of migration was coming to an end, towards the middle of the 19th century, many of the factors that are still considerations in immigration policy had already emerged, such as a need to meet short-term economic demands, family issues, the responsibilities of carriers and problems of settling into a new country.

1.2.4 The gold rushes and the second wave

A second wave of migration accompanied reduced transportation and consequent labour shortages in the 1840s and 1850s and the gold rushes provoked by the discovery of gold in 1851. During the 1850s, more than 600 000 immigrants arrived in Australia. Unlike the first wave, which was predominantly British and Irish, this wave of miners, merchants, tradesmen, manufacturers

8 State Records New South Wales: Concise Guide to the State Archives (H–K): Immigration, www.records.nsw.gov.au/cguide/hj/immig.htm.

and other entrepreneurs included significant numbers of non-British Europeans and a number of non-Europeans, particularly from China. It greatly increased the population of indentured Chinese labourers brought to Australia to meet labour shortages in the growing agricultural sector in the 1840s. By 1861, there were 40 000 Chinese in Australia. Many Chinese migrants came to Australia under what was known as the 'credit-ticket' system,[9] whereby Chinese merchants advanced money in exchange for an agreement to work overseas for a low fixed wage, or to make regular repayments of both loan and interest on the security of the emigrant's title to village land, or on the persons of his wife and children.

In the meantime, the assisted migration schemes continued and the earlier requirements to be married or to repay the loan advanced for passage were largely discarded, as illustrated in an article in the *Illustrated London News* of 12 August 1848 which reported on the imminent departure of an emigrant ship from London, bound for Moreton Bay:

> We should first explain that it is not as generally known as it should be, that the Government gives free passage (including food), to New South Wales and South Australia, to agricultural labourers, shepherds, female domestic and farm servants, and dairy maids; also, to a few blacksmiths, wheelwrights, carpenters, and other country mechanics...
>
> The conditions may be learned from 'The Colonisation Circular', issued by her Majesty's Colonial Land and Emigration Commissioners... emigrants must be of good character, and recommended for sobriety and industry.
>
> ... on their arrival, a Government Agent gives advice as to wages, and places where they will get work. No repayment is required. The full particulars are furnished at the Government Emigration office, 9, Park Street, Westminster, or by agents in most other large towns.
>
> ... [at the Emigration dépôt] the applicants [are] examined as to the state of their health by the surgeon appointed to the ship in which they are to embark...
>
> ... The passengers were agricultural laborers and artisans from various parts of England and Scotland, from the infant in its mother's arms to those in mid-life.[10]

The schemes were popular with the Irish escaping the potato famine and Scots escaping the Clearances, as well as other Europeans avoiding the privations brought by wars, religious repression and economic necessity, although the Australian colonies had serious competition from America and other colonies. Some of the schemes sought to encourage family reunion as well as the migration of skilled labour, as exemplified in the public notice taken from the *Belfast Banner* and published in Port Fairy (Victoria) in April 1858. It advertised:

> Persons wishing to bring their relatives and friends from the United Kingdom to Victoria can secure passages for them in vessels chartered by Her Majesty's Government, on the following conditions –

9 Chinese Heritage of Australian Federation 'Brief History of the Chinese in Australia', www.chaf.lib.latrobe.edu.au/education/history.htm.
10 ARTEMISIA London to Australia 1848, www.theshipslist.com/ships/australia/artemisia.htm.

1. The persons eligible for passages under these regulations are agricultural laborers of every kind, domestic servants, railway laborers, mechanics, and artisans, and their wives, children and near relatives. They must be in sound health, free from all bodily or mental defects, of good moral character, sober, industrious and accustomed to work for wages, at the occupation specified in the application forms . . .
9. Persons resident in Victoria, therefore, desirous of availing themselves of the advantages of these regulations should apply at the following offices . . . [23 offices around Victoria] . . . Form A should then be filled in by the applicant, signed by him, and left with the officer. He will then be informed of the amount required to be paid, and of the outfit [Form C]. So soon as the amount mentioned shall be paid to the Assistant Immigration Agent, or Receiver and Paymaster [as the case may be] the money, or a Treasury receipt for it, is to be sent to the Immigration Agent Melbourne, with the application forms [marked C] and a statement of the sums paid for passages and outfit. The Immigration Agent will then transmit a certificate for the persons nominated either to the office at which the money was paid, or to such address as the applicant may request. This certificate must be sent by the applicant to his friends in the United Kingdom.
10. Persons residing at a distance from any of the places not mentioned in the list appended to clause 9 may be supplied with the application form [A] at the nearest Post Office . . . which, after having been duly filled up and signed, should be transmitted to the Immigration Agent in Melbourne by whom every information will be furnished . . .
11. Should the persons nominated decline or be unable to emigrate the money paid towards their passages will be refunded to the depositor in this colony . . .
12. Should the applicant wilfully misrepresent particulars respecting the persons nominated, the deposits made towards the passages will be liable to forfeiture.
13. Persons resident in Victoria desirous of introducing female domestic servants, through the agency of their friends in the United Kingdom, will be allowed to do so upon depositing with the Immigration Agent in Melbourne, an amount in accordance with the scale set forth in the 4th clause of the regulations.[11]

1.2.5 Self-government and the 'White Australia' policy

With the granting of internal self-government through the *Australian Colonies Act 1850* (Imp.),[12] the regulation of entry to Australia was passed from colonial authorities in London to each colony, which administered its own immigration policies. The emerging colonial governments then started to introduce legislation that restricted entry to their respective colonies. The Victorian example is instructive. In 1855, the Victorian Parliament enacted legislation that restricted the number of Chinese permitted to land to one for every ten tonnes of a ship's cargo, and that required ship captains to pay a head tax of £10 on every Chinese migrant landing at a Victorian port.[13] That legislation also provided for taxes on Chinese residents to pay for their protection and supervision by Protectors

11 J. Fawcett, *Genseek*, www.hotkey.net.au/~jwilliams4/d5.htm.
12 13 & 14 Vict, c 59.
13 *Chinese Immigration Act 1855* (Vic).

on each goldfield, ostensibly in response to goldfield riots and the expression of blatant anti-Chinese sentiment. The head tax laws were a failure, as ship owners merely bypassed Victoria and landed their Chinese passengers in South Australia and New South Wales, from where they walked to the goldfields.

That law was repealed in 1857 but reinstated after a series of anti-Chinese incidents. It was then fortified with new legislation requiring adult Chinese males to produce a receipt for their entry tax and pay an additional residence tax of £1 every two months. The new Act included a clause that denied any Chinese miner the right to take legal action for the recovery of a mining claim, property or damages, giving European claim-jumpers virtual immunity.

The NSW government introduced similar legislation after the Lambing Flat riot in 1861, adding a clause that denied the Chinese the right to naturalisation. However, by 1867 the eastern colonies had repealed the discriminatory legislation. The sense of European superiority was never far below the surface, though, and it continued to manifest itself in various forms.

In the mid-19th century, the principles that inform modern immigration policy were continuing to evolve and expand. Chain-family migration and assisted passage were becoming commonplace, and nascent concepts of restriction of entry, family and economic sponsorship, fees paid in advance, payment of administrative fees, penalties for providing misleading information and the existence of migration agents had emerged.

1.2.6 After the gold rushes

The gold rushes ushered in the spread of population centres from the coast to inland areas. In their wake, and with the ensuing diminished opportunities in rural areas, a number of people left Australia. However, the majority stayed, providing labour and accelerating the death of the transportation system. Most of the Chinese population moved to urban areas and established occupations such as market gardening, retailing and other small business pursuits. They often worked for themselves or for each other, and while the pastoralists who had brought Chinese workers to Australia as cheap, indentured labour began to complain that they were demanding excessive wages, they were often willing to work for lower wages or in less desirable conditions than the European labourers. This led to confrontations with the emerging labour movement, particularly when Chinese labour was hired to break a miners' strike in 1873 and again a few years later to undercut seamen's wages, thereby contributing to the dismissal of many seamen and provoking the seamen's strike of 1878. There have been ongoing repercussions since those first days of antagonising the labour movement, as the movement has remained suspicious of migrants, seeing them as threats to both the availability and the conditions of employment.

In the meantime, other groups of non-Europeans had come to Australia, in relatively small but significant numbers. Pacific Islanders were in demand as cheap and competent seamen and were able to command higher wages when the gold rushes provoked labour shortages in shipping. When the cotton industry was established in Queensland in the 1860s and soon after replaced by the sugar industry, large numbers of Pacific Islanders were 'recruited' (many commentators say they were kidnapped) to work as indentured labour on plantations, despite protests from humanitarians, who saw the process as a new form of slavery, and the fears of the organised labour movement, which felt threatened by what it perceived as cheap, coloured labour.

Japanese divers had also migrated to parts of northern Australia to participate in the pearl industry, particularly from the mid-1880s. Unlike the Pacific Islanders, who remained subservient employees, the Japanese established themselves as owners of a majority proportion of pearling licences and luggers and were integral in establishing the colonies of Queensland and Western Australia as world leaders in the industry. They also had the diplomatic support of the Japanese government, potentially a major trading partner of the Queensland government, as evidenced by the signing of the Anglo-Japanese Treaty of 1894.

1.2.7 The Federation debates

In the two decades prior to Federation, sentiment against non-Europeans reached a crescendo, fanned by groups of exclusionists and nationalists, and led by prominent politicians aspiring to positions of power and influence in the Federation debates, including Henry Parkes and W. Russell. *The Centenary Companion to Australian Federation*[14] lists the arguments that were promoted in favour of restricting non-European immigrants:

- fears that people immigrating in large numbers who looked different and had different customs could 'contaminate' the white population and that people not familiar with British political traditions might undermine Commonwealth political systems;
- with the emergence of the Australian Labor Party in the 1890s, concern about the employment of cheap labour leading to a reduction in wages when the Commonwealth was formed; and
- the desire to prevent the racial conflict that had occurred in America.

The arguments at the end of the 19th century remain familiar at the beginning of the 21st: exaggerated migrant numbers; the fear of hordes of Asians gathering at Australia's doorstep; accusations that potential migrants are a fifth column of aliens who could make Australia militarily vulnerable; exaggerated tales of the occurrence of contagious disease, immorality, violence and crime among them; accusations by the labour movement that migrants are too compliant with the bosses; accusations by employers that migrants are too 'clannish' to provide a cheap and co-operative workforce; migrants being of 'inferior biological stock'. The perceived threats were symbolised in public stereotypes, especially

14 H. Irving (ed.), *The Centenary Companion to Australian Federation* (Melbourne, Cambridge University Press [CUP], 1999).

in illustrated newspapers, where the Chinese were portrayed as ghouls, Pacific Islanders were depicted as so debased and mentally degenerate that they could not control their 'vicious sexual passions', and the Japanese became the 'yellow peril'.

During the 1880s, most colonies reintroduced immigration restriction laws directed at the Chinese. Subsequently, following an agreement reached at an Intercolonial Conference in 1896, the restrictions were extended to cover other coloured races, although Queensland did not adhere to this agreement and continued to use indentured labour on the sugarcane fields in the face of a failing economy.

The 1891 census recorded a population (not including Aborigines, who were not recorded) of 3 174 392 people, including 2 158 975 born in Australia; 470 399 in England and Wales; 226 949 in Ireland; 123 818 in Scotland; 46 623 in Asia; 45 008 in Germany; 10 673 in the Pacific Islands; 10 121 in Sweden and Norway; 7472 in the United States; 6406 in Denmark; 4261 in France; 3890 in Italy; 3044 in Africa; 3027 in Canada; 2881 in Russia; 2086 in Switzerland; and 1639 in the Austro-Hungarian Empire. Asians and Islanders comprised around 50 000 people among a population of more than 3 million, but nevertheless, by the 1890s, the overwhelmingly predominant British population, supported by other Europeans, had engendered a national racial ideology that underpinned Australian immigration policy for the next 70 years or so.

In 1897, the Colonial Secretary, Joseph Chamberlain, assured the colonial premiers that he sympathised with their strongly held view that there should not be an influx of people alien in customs, religion and civilisation who would impact on the rights of the existing population to employment. When the Australian government passed its first laws in 1901, it implemented policies that reflected Australian nationalism in the late 1880s and 1890s, and the moves to restrict non-European immigration to most of the Australian colonies that dated back to the 1850s.

1.2.8 Federation and 'White Australia' legislation

The 1901 census recorded a population of 3 773 801 (again, not counting Aborigines) of whom 77 per cent were born in Australia and 18 per cent were born in Britain. One of the first Acts to be passed by the new Commonwealth government was the *Immigration Restriction Act 1901* (Cth). It was the cornerstone of a package of legislation that indicated the first federal government's comfort in implementing a policy that effectively discriminated on the basis of race and colour, and that became commonly known as the White Australia policy. The other parts of the statutory package were the *Pacific Islanders Labourers Act 1901* (Cth), which required that the bulk of Pacific Islanders be expatriated by 1907, and section 15 of the *Post and Telegraph Act 1901* (Cth), which provided that ships carrying Australian mail, and hence subsidised by the Commonwealth, should employ only white labour. It was followed by the *Contract Immigrants Act 1905*

(Cth), which required employers to show that they could not recruit suitable local employees and to demonstrate, in effect, that those they intended to recruit from overseas would not contribute to present or potential labour disputes.

Immigration policy and law in the new Federation of Australia was both restrictive and selective, designed to meet economic and political considerations, and founded on the accepted wisdom of a firmly established racial hierarchy. It set out negative criteria to exclude 'immigrants' (not defined in the legislation) rather than positive criteria for entry. The statutory mechanism restricting immigration could not be overtly based on race, as this was officially opposed by Britain and may have offended Britain's ally and Australia's trading partner, Japan. Instead, the filter used for prospective migrants was literacy, assessed by a dictation test. It was not a new idea, as similar legislation had been adapted from laws used in Natal in South Africa and introduced in Western Australia, New South Wales and Tasmania in the late 1890s.

Section 3 of the Immigration Restriction Act defined six classes of prohibited immigrants. Five of the effectively excluded classes were the poor, the insane, the diseased, the criminal and the immoral. The most effective restriction in section 3 enabled the government to exclude any person who 'when asked to do so by an officer fails to write out at dictation and sign in the presence of the officer, a passage of fifty words in length in a European language directed by the officer'. The officers exercised their discretion to administer the dictation test 805 times in 1902–03, with 46 people passing, and 554 times in 1904–09, with only six people being successful. After 1909, no person asked to take the dictation test passed and people who failed were refused entry or deported. The Act, frequently amended, remained in force until 1958.[15]

While the Commonwealth passed laws that restricted the categories of people to be admitted (or excluded), the states remained responsible for the selection of migrants, but they did not provide any assistance during the first five years of Federation. From 1906, the states offered assisted or free passage and some free land, and migration rose to high levels until it was halted by World War I.

1.2.9 Empire-building – the post-World War I wave

Following World War I, the Commonwealth assumed responsibility for selection of migrants and became the principal participant in the Empire Settlement Scheme, designed to 'redistribut[e] . . . the white population of the British Empire' by offering incentives – in the form of assisted passage – to immigrants and subsidised infrastructure and settlement projects to the Commonwealth and the states to provide employment and help 'absorb' the assisted British migrants.

The desire to preserve British culture was reflected in friction with non-British European groups who were perceived to be a threat to the local population. Significant numbers of Italian migrants came to work in the Queensland canefields,

15 To view a copy of the original Act, see www.foundingdocs.gov.au/places/cth/cth4ii.htm#history.

where they became the target of prejudice. While they were not subjected to serious violence, their numbers (about 25 000 in the 1920s) prompted the Australian government to restrict Italian immigration in the 1930s. On the Kalgoorlie goldfields, simmering resentment against Italians and Yugoslavs erupted into two days of violence at a lease known as Dingbat Flat in January 1934. Miners used shotguns, rifles, jam-tin bombs and dynamite to make their point at Dingbat Flat and then went on strike until the mining companies gave an assurance that no unnaturalised person would be given a job in the mines.

The Empire Settlement Scheme was suspended during the Great Depression and resumed in 1938, and it only came to a standstill with the advent of World War II. In the meantime, in a decision that ushered in an ongoing policy of receiving significant numbers of refugees, the government had agreed to take refugees who had escaped Nazi persecution and had made their way to various European centres. Over the next three years, Australia received about half of the agreed 15 000 refugees. In June 1940 the government also agreed to accept around 2000 civilians interned in England as enemy aliens, notwithstanding that they were mostly Jewish refugees, as well as 500 German, Austrian and Italian prisoners who were deemed dangerous or potentially dangerous to England's security. They travelled on HMT *Dunera*, which subsequently found infamy when three of the guards, including the commanding officer, were court-martialled after being convicted of mistreating their passengers.

1.2.10 Post-World War II

The period following World War II witnessed the largest wave of migration. The country had been bombed and threatened with invasion, many able people had been lost to war, others put training on hold and population growth had significantly decreased. Australian industry had run down, the country's economy was stressed and there were serious shortages in transport, energy resources, housing, schools and hospitals. There was insufficient infrastructure and labour to exploit resources. On the other hand, there was a large pool of skilled and unskilled workers in Europe who had been devastated by war and were seeking opportunities and security for themselves and their families.

In 1945, the new Labor government, under Ben Chifley, established the Department of Migration, with Arthur Calwell sworn in as the first Minister for Immigration. In promulgating his defence policy to 'populate or perish' in the face of 'the yellow peril', the Minister expressed the intention to keep Australia 'white'. Calwell became infamous for his statement that 'two wongs don't make a white' and for assuring the population that for every 'foreign' migrant there would be ten from the United Kingdom. His policy found resonance in public opinion, as historian G.C. Bolton has noted:

> A Melbourne survey of 1948 found that the majority of those interviewed were prepared to welcome only unrestricted English migration, although the Irish would be tolerated

> also. Germans, although wartime enemies, were preferred in limited quantities to Southern Europeans. Nearly half of those interviewed favoured a total ban on Italians, and more than half wanted to keep out all Jews and Negroes.

A formal immigration policy was established, with impressive target numbers – theses were needed to defend Australia and expand its infrastructure projects and manufacturing industries in the postwar period. Despite the government's express and overwhelming preference for British migrants, many difficulties arose to complicate the implementation of Calwell's agenda. Postwar shipping shortages, the early opposition of Winston Churchill to an exodus from Britain and United Nations' pressure to deal with large numbers of displaced persons in Europe interfered with plans to effect a massive migration from Britain to Australia. Once it became clear that large-scale British migration could not be attained, non-British Europeans, particularly southern Europeans, came to be acceptable as migrants.

Along with that wave of migration came the concept of 'assimilation', requiring those migrants to discard their birth cultures and languages and assimilate into what the government of the day perceived to be the 'Australian nationality'. There was no institutionalised racial discrimination such as that directed against non-Caucasians, but there was some ethnic discrimination as non-English speakers were directed into the lowest-paid jobs while the government that conducted the migration program failed to provide any meaningful language instruction.[16]

1.2.11 Dismantling the 'White Australia' policy

While the White Australia policy was not officially abandoned until 1973, successive governments took measures to dismantle it, or at least to remove the overtly racial aspects from it, in the face of a local anti-racist movement, international embarrassment and economic practicality. In 1949, the Liberal–Country Party Coalition accepted some non-European refugees and Japanese war brides; non-Europeans became eligible for citizenship in 1957 if they lived in Australia for 15 years (reduced to five years in 1966), their immediate relatives could obtain permanent entry, and highly qualified people could stay indefinitely on temporary permits. The dictation test was abolished when the *Immigration Restriction Act 1901* (Cth) was repealed and replaced by the *Migration Act 1958* (Cth).

In 1967, a watershed referendum resulted in an overwhelming vote to grant Aborigines formal equality. In the same year, the Labor Party's racist old guard, led by Arthur Calwell, was ousted by a new leadership under Gough Whitlam. Around the same time, the policy of assimilation was replaced by 'integration', which did not require migrants to jettison their cultures to become 'Australian'. After Whitlam took office in 1972, he formally ended the White Australia policy with an announcement in the House of Representatives in May 1973 that

16 See J. Collins, Chapter 1, 'Migrant Hands in Many Lands' and Chapter 2, 'Australia's Post-war Immigration Experience', *Migrant Hands in a Distant Land: Australia's post-war immigration*, 2nd edn (Sydney, Pluto Press Australia, 1991).

denounced 'racialism'. His government introduced the concept of multiculturalism to replace the policy of assimilation, a concept that was subsequently taken up by conservative governments. More money was dedicated to welfare for migrants and ethnic councils were established. Over time, various governments began to address 'settlement' issues and established more expansive and sophisticated policies and programs to assist migrants to Australia.

Since the early 1970s, Australia has had a more or less bipartisan and non-racial migration program, although this is not to say that differences between the parliamentary parties and commentators do not exist. The ongoing immigration debate demonstrates that some views of immigration are informed by racial prejudices and that some of the stakeholders in that debate are willing to exploit racism if they perceive that they can thus gain an advantage.

The central plank of migration law during the postwar period has been the *Migration Act 1958* (Cth). Until major reform in 1989, it provided the basic machinery to empower the Minister for Immigration and Immigration Department officers to grant, cancel or revoke visas (granted overseas) and entry permits (granted onshore, including to arriving visa-holders) as an exercise of discretion. The exercise of those powers was guided by a series of policy manuals authored by the Immigration Department and not subject to parliamentary scrutiny, but subject to alteration at the Minister's direction. That discretionary regime and the failure to provide adequate avenues of review for disgruntled applicants came under increasing criticism, particularly from several of the committees that had been established to review administrative decision-making processes, including the Administrative Review Council, the Human Rights Commission and the Committee to Advise on Australia's Immigration Policies (CAAIP, which produced the 'Fitzgerald Report').

1.3 The modern immigration debate

The immigration debate has waxed and waned. It attracted a lot of public attention and raised the ire of many people when the emerging policy of multiculturalism came under fire from Geoffrey Blainey in the late 1970s and early 1980s, ostensibly on the grounds of economic difficulties creating conflict between migrants (particularly Asians) and Europeans.[17] Blainey records one of the comments he made in November 1983 at the National Press Club, a comment that more or less reiterates what some judges and politicians have stated:

> We should continue to welcome a variety of Asian immigrants, but they should come on our terms, through our choosing, and in numbers with which our society can cope.[18]

17 Recounted in G. Blainey, Chapter 2, 'The Controversy Begins', *All for Australia* (Sydney, Methuen Hayes, 1984), pp. 21–35.
18 ibid., p. 24.

The following March, Blainey made a speech at Warrnambool in Victoria, stating, among other things:

> An increasing proportion of Australians seem to be resentful of the large numbers of Vietnamese and other south-east Asians, who are being brought in, have little chance of gaining work, and are living – through no fault of their own – at the taxpayer's expense.[19]

The speech attracted a large amount of media attention and contributions by politicians speaking about the 'Asianisation of Australia' – a term Blainey states was coined by the then-Minister for Immigration and misunderstood by the public as Blainey's own when it became headline news.[20] Blainey claims he was then unfairly attacked by the proponents of multiculturalism as a racist throwback to the White Australia policy.[21] The 'Asianisation' debate generated a lot of comment, much of it blatantly racist.[22]

One of Blainey's strongest academic critics was Andrew Markus. He argued that Blainey created a false impression about the numbers of Asians by pointing to a high percentage of a particular immigration intake, when the actual Asian proportion of the population was 2 per cent. He added that Blainey misrepresented comments by Labor Minister Bill Hayden about the growth of the Australian population over a period of 200 years and claimed that there was a secret policy that ran counter to publicly announced immigration principles. Finally, Markus argued that Blainey's use of the term 'Surrender Australia' was alarmist and emotive.[23] He expressed the view that Blainey's 'colourful writing on the subject . . . encourages the very prejudice it discusses'.[24]

Another critic of Blainey was Jock Collins, who directed much of his criticism at the then Opposition Leader and former Prime Minister, John Howard. In *Migrant Hands in a Distant Land*,[25] Collins accused the then Opposition Coalition of flirting with a repudiation of the policy of multiculturalism, and accused Howard of 'playing the "prejudice card"' and expressing the desire to reduce Asian immigration if Australia's 'social cohesion' came under threat.[26] Collins also damned the Fitzgerald Report[27] with faint praise, stating that most of its conclusions were sensible but, among other things, it fell 'into the danger of pandering to, rather than combating, entrenched attitudes of racism and prejudice in

19 ibid., p. 25.
20 ibid., pp. 30–31.
21 ibid., pp. 34–35.
22 There is a large collection of materials on the Australian Nationalism Information Database – see www.ozemail.com.au/~natinfo.
23 A. Markus, '1984 or 1901? Immigration and some "lessons" of Australian History', in A. Markus and M.C. Ricklefs (eds), *Surrender Australia? Essays in the study and uses of history: Geoffrey Blainey and Asian immigration* (Sydney, George Allen & Unwin, 1985), pp. 10–35, particularly pp. 30–32.
24 ibid., p. 32.
25 J. Collins, Chapter 13, 'New Developments in the Immigration Debate', *Migrant Hands in a Distant Land*, pp. 301–19.
26 ibid., Preface and pp. 286, 302–03.
27 See footnote 2.

Australia', 'echoes the views that multiculturalism is divisive... [and]... panders to the views of the Blaineys, [Bruce] Ruxtons and [Ron] Caseys'.[28]

Collins went on to argue that the new areas of debate that emerged from the Fitzgerald Report related to the impact of immigration on the economy and the environment, and rejected the view that migration is a cause of problems in either of those areas.[29] As mentioned above, political developments in the new century have again focused some attention on race and religion in the immigration debate, with much of that attention being directed at human rights issues surrounding the detention of 'boat people' from the Middle East and Afghanistan.

The debate has not been confined to the desirability of refugees. A key election issue in the 2010 election debate was whether or not we should have a 'Big Australia'. While Kevin Rudd was Prime Minister Australia increased its immigration quota to around 300 000 people. When Kevin Rudd was deposed as Prime Minister by Julia Gillard, a key point of differentiation between the two leaders was that Gillard rejected the notion of a big Australia, instead advocating a 'sustainable' Australia. This resulted in a significant reduction in the immigration quota. This was a move that was supported by the federal Liberal Opposition, although there was no consensus among the parties regarding the extent to which the immigration quota should be reduced.

28 J. Collins, Chapter 13, 'New Developments in the Immigration Debate', *Migrant Hands in a Distant Land*, pp. 288–89.
29 ibid., p. 308.

2

Immigration control: An overview

2.1 Constitutional foundations

The Commonwealth Constitution has provided the Australian Parliament with the power to make laws about immigration and emigration in section 51(xxii) and the power to make laws about naturalisation and aliens in section 51(xix). Argument has also been made that a third source of constitutional power to legislate about migrants might be found in section 51(xxix), relating to external affairs.[1] The Australian High Court has generally given those powers a broad interpretation on the basis that it is an inherent right of sovereign states to determine when, or if, a non-citizen (generally referred to as an 'alien' as a consequence of the language of section 51(xix)) of the state can enter the country, the conditions under which that person can remain and the circumstances that require departure.

Thus, when the appellant in *Robtelmes v Brenan*[2] sought to have the order for his deportation pursuant to section 8 of the *Pacific Islanders Labourers Act 1901* (Cth) overturned on the basis that there was no constitutional power to deport him, he did not attract the sympathy of the court, notwithstanding his argument that he should at least be returned to the place from which he was recruited, as otherwise he would be imprisoned. Chief Justice Griffith predicated his finding on the following view:

> Now, there can be no doubt that, to use the words of the Judicial Committee of the Privy Committee in the case of *The Attorney-General for Canada v Cain and Gilhula*, decided on 30th July last, 'one of the rights preserved by the supreme power in every State is

1 See *Re Patterson; Ex parte Taylor* [2001] HCA 51 per Gummow and Hayne JJ, [257].
2 [1906] HCA 58 (2 October 1906).

> the right to refuse to permit an alien to enter that State, to annex what conditions it pleases to the permission to enter it, and to expel or deport from the State, at pleasure, even a friendly alien, especially if it considers his presence in the State opposed to its peace, order, or good government, or to its social or material interests' . . .
>
> The Commonwealth Parliament has power to make whatever laws it may think fit 'for the peace, order, and good government' of the Commonwealth with respect, among other things, to 'naturalization and aliens'. The power to make such laws as Parliament may think fit with respect to aliens must surely, if it includes anything, include the power to determine the conditions under which aliens may be admitted to the country, the conditions under which they may be permitted to remain in the country, and the conditions under which they may be deported from it. I cannot, therefore, doubt that the Commonwealth Parliament has under that delegation of power authority to make any laws that it may think fit for that purpose; and it is not for the judicial branch of the Government to review their actions, or to consider whether the means that they have adopted are wise or unwise.

In respect of the argument that the appellant would be imprisoned as soon as he was deported, His Honour found:

> The most serious difficulty suggested was, however, that the deportation of a person from Australia will necessarily, owing to the geographical position of the Commonwealth, result in the imprisonment of the person deported beyond the territorial jurisdiction of the Colony. That is no doubt true, and it is equally clear that the legislature of the Commonwealth cannot make any laws which have effect as laws beyond its own territorial limits, that is to say three marine miles from the coast . . . The deporting State has no authority beyond its own borders. All it can do is to extrude the alien. What becomes of him afterwards is for him, not for them. It may be that it would be unreasonable to take him against his will to some place which is not his own home, but the remedy must be sought elsewhere.

Barton J asked himself 'Has the Commonwealth power to legislate in this connection?' and answered by finding:

> It is not necessary, I think, to determine that question upon any notion of absolutely inherent right in the Commonwealth, because there are powers given under the Constitution, which have been referred to in argument, and which seem to me sufficient to cover the matter. Those are the powers – particularly with reference to aliens – in the 19th sub-section of sec. 51, and also possibly the power in sub-sec. 26, and I think much more clearly the powers as to immigration and external affairs in paragraphs 27 and 29. As to three of those powers I am of opinion that they may be well exercised by legislation of this kind and that as, under the decision of the Privy Council in *Hodge v The Queen*, the powers given are plenary within their ambit, it is within these powers to pass legislation, however harsh and restrictive it may seem, and as to that it is not the province of a Court of Justice to inquire, where the law is clear. This legislation, I think, is perfectly competent within the meaning of three at least of those four powers. The right to deport is the complement of the right to exclude; the right to exclude is involved in the right to regulate immigration. The right to prescribe the conditions upon which persons may remain and reside within this Commonwealth is included in that power to regulate immigration by Statute. Equally undeniable is the right to legislate with respect to aliens, and as to the power of external affairs, just like the

> others, the authority to legislate, as I think, also exists, and it is possible to legislate effectively under that power with respect to the exclusion or deportation of subjects of other powers, always premising that the legislation for the purpose is assented to by the Crown, and becomes the proper exercise of delegated authority. I think that, if the power to legislate exists with respect to the conditions of entry or residence of the subjects of civilised powers, it would be idle to attempt to deny that it is also included with respect to Pacific Islanders. I am of opinion, therefore, that the Commonwealth has power to legislate in this connection.

In the same case, O'Connor J held that:

> It is apparent, therefore, that when in the division of powers between the States and the Commonwealth, this power of making laws for the peace, order, and good government of Australia, in regard to aliens and to immigration and emigration, was conferred on the Parliament of the Commonwealth, it was intended to confer the power in the fullest extent that was necessary for its effective exercise.

As Crock states, there is little argument that the immigration power of the Constitution permits making laws about entry to Australia and the 'absorption' (or otherwise) of migrants into the community.[3] In recent times, however, most of the significant cases relate to deportation and have turned on the argument that the constitutional powers did not permit the *Migration Act 1958* (Cth) to extend either to former migrants who were British subjects eligible for citizenship, or to long-term permanent residents who had been 'absorbed' into the Australian community and who could not therefore be properly described as 'aliens'.

In the case of *Pochi v MacPhee*,[4] the plaintiff had arrived in Australia as a 20-year-old in 1959. His application for citizenship had been approved in 1975 but he was not notified and did not take the requisite oath. His deportation was ordered in 1978 after he was convicted in 1977 of supplying Indian hemp and sentenced to two years in prison.

The plaintiff submitted a technical argument that the *Migration Act 1958* (Cth) was unconstitutional because the *Australian Citizenship Act 1948* (Cth) had the effect that some persons who were in truth British subjects did not have the status of British subjects under the latter Act, and were therefore aliens within the meaning of the *Migration Act 1958* (Cth), but were not aliens within the meaning of section 51(xix) of the Constitution. Gibbs CJ, delivering the majority decision, observed:

> . . . the Parliament can in my opinion treat as an alien any person who was born outside Australia, whose parents were not Australians, and who has not been naturalized.

In regard to the argument that Mr Pochi had been absorbed into the Australian community, the Chief Justice found:

> 11. . . . s. 51(xix) provides ample power to enact legislation providing for the deportation of aliens. The question whether the immigration power would extend to the

3 M. Crock, *Immigration and Refugee Law in Australia* (Sydney, Federation Press, 1998), p. 21.
4 [1982] HCA 60 (22 October 1982).

> case of an immigrant who has become absorbed into the community – a question on which opinions in this Court have in the past been divided – does not arise when the immigrant is an alien . . .
>
> 12. The argument was put in another way by submitting that the fact that the plaintiff has become totally absorbed into the Australian community meant that he is no longer an alien. This argument is impossible to maintain. It was well settled at common law that naturalization could only be achieved by Act of Parliament . . . a person's nationality is not changed by length of residence or by an intention permanently to remain in a country of which he is not a national. There are strong reasons why the acquisition by an alien of Australian citizenship should be marked by a formal act, and by an acknowledgement of allegiance to the sovereign of Australia. The *Australian Citizenship Act* validly so provides.

The judicial view that only citizens are not subject to the 'aliens power' and that citizenship could only be gained by a formal act of naturalisation was strongly approved in the subsequent High Court case of *Nolan v Minister for Immigration and Ethnic Affairs*[5] and the Federal Court case of *Kenny v Minister for Immigration, Local Government and Ethnic Affairs*.[6] Moreover, in *Kenny*, Gummow J made it clear that the Commonwealth's power to legislate with respect to aliens validly extended to non-citizens outside Australia, as well as those inside its borders. To emphasise that the Constitution has an off-shore application, Gummow J went so far as to add that even if the aliens power did not extend to people outside Australia, the external affairs power contained in section 51(xxix) probably would.

More recently, however, the High Court has been divided on the issue of who is or is not an alien, particularly as that issue relates to British subjects.[7] The division has largely arisen from the minority decision of Gaudron J in *Nolan*, where her Honour argued that Nolan was a British subject when he arrived in Australia in the 1960s, as were all Australian citizens at that time, and that therefore he was not an alien; and that, as nothing had occurred to transform his status from non-alien to alien, he was not caught by the aliens power in the Constitution.[8] That argument has found some resonance in more recent High Court judgments,[9] although there has been no real agreement about precisely when non-alien British subjects became, in Australian law, aliens.

The cases illustrate a shift in thinking with respect to membership of the Australian community, from the concept that British subjects were not aliens to the notion that membership of the community is conferred through citizenship. That is reflected in legislative amendments. The issue of absorption was resolved by Parliament when it shifted the constitutional basis of the *Migration Act 1958* to

5 [1988] HCA 45 (13 September 1988).
6 (1993) 442 FCR 330.
7 See *Re Patterson; Ex parte Taylor* [2001] HCA 51; and *Shaw v MIMA* [2003] HCA 72 (9 December 2003).
8 (1993) 442 FCR 330, [14].
9 See, for example, *Singh v Commonwealth of Australia* [2004] HCA 43 (9 September 2004) per McHugh J, [139] and *Shaw v MIMA*, above n 7 per Kirby J, [113].

the 'naturalisation and aliens' power contained in section 51(xix) of the Constitution. The shift took effect on 2 April 1984 by way of the *Migration Amendment Act 1983* (Cth). The *Migration Act 1958* (Cth) from then on referred to 'non-citizens' rather than 'immigrants' thereby removing the issue of 'absorption', because the only way non-citizens cease to be non-citizens is by acquiring Australian citizenship. The effect of the amendment was that persons who had overstayed their visas for more than five years would be rendered prohibited non-citizens only if they had not been absorbed into the Australian community prior to 2 April 1984. After that date, the status of 'immigrant' was to become irrelevant for the structure of the Principal Act.

That amendment does not necessarily have retrospective operation. However, while there is some judicial disagreement about when a non-citizen British subject might be treated as a non-alien, there is ample authority to demonstrate that non-citizens (both British and non-British) who arrived after 2 April 1984 retain their status as non-citizens until the formal grant of citizenship and, regardless of how long they have lived in Australia, are subject to the *Migration Act 1958* (Cth). As such, they are also subject to the requirement of the Act that they hold a visa or become unlawful non-citizens subject to detention and removal.

The recent High Court case of *Minister for Immigration and Multicultural and Indigenous Affairs v Nystrom*[10] confirmed that even 'absorbed' migrants do not become citizens unless they apply for, and are granted, citizenship. Nystrom was a Swedish citizen who arrived in Australia as a four-week-old baby in 1974 and had never left the country. He was automatically granted both a Transitional (Permanent) Visa and an Absorbed Person Visa, by the operation of law, in September 1994. That gave him permanent residence, but he never applied for citizenship. In 2004, the Minister for Immigration made a decision pursuant to section 501(2) of the *Migration Act 1958* (Cth) to cancel his Transitional (Permanent) Visa on character grounds. This rendered Nystrom an 'unlawful non-citizen' and liable to removal from Australia pursuant to section 198 of the Act. While the legal issues to be determined centred on the power to deport and the power to cancel a visa and remove its holder, the court was unanimous in confirming that non-citizens remain aliens, regardless of their history of residence. The state of the law was succinctly put in a citation from *Re Minister for Immigration and Multicultural Affairs; Ex parte Te*,[11] in which Gleeson CJ said:

> Treating absorption into the community as relevant to the status of alienage is inconsistent with earlier judicial views as to the width of par (xix) compared with par (xxvii) . . . In my opinion, it is wrong in principle. For reasons already discussed, while absorption reflects the fact that an activity of immigration has come to an end, it may co-exist, and commonly co-exists, with a legal status of alienage. Resident aliens may be absorbed into the community, but they are still aliens.[12]

10 [2006] HCA 50, 8 November 2006.
11 [2002] HCA 48, 7 November 2002.
12 at [141].

Nystrom's case contains an excellent summary of the legislative history of the absorption issue and the deportation power.

2.2 The control model

Since Australia was first settled, colonial and then federal governments have always stuck to the principle that they have a sovereign right – and, indeed, a duty – to control immigration.[13] It sounds unremarkable, but it is interesting to note that the British government did not impose restrictions of entry and residence in Britain until the mid-19th century, well after it selected convicts for transportation to Australia and introduced assistance programs for people it wished to encourage to move to Australia. As discussed in the previous chapter, the need to control who crosses Australian borders has a significant basis in fear and anxiety about the composition of the Australian community. It is also underpinned by the need for proper planning and budgeting in the implementation of a sophisticated migration and settlement program.

The introduction in 1989 of a new legislative regime controlling the exclusion, entry, stay and removal of non-citizens of Australia is a codified refinement of the control model that had been in place since first settlement. While the *Migration Act 1958* (Cth) remains the source of power, the Migration Regulations[14] provide the procedural mechanism for how that power is to be administered and, as subordinate legislation, are relatively easy to amend in response to new policy developments or judicial interpretation. In effect, the current legislative system is now driven by subordinate legislation that has reduced the scope for the exercise of discretion in administrative decision-making, and reduced the scope for judicial intervention, in relation to migration and refugee matters.

2.3 The advent of current migration legislation

Under increasing pressure in the 1970s, successive governments took legislative measures to improve the quality and accountability of administrative decision-making, including by introducing of *Administrative Decisions (Judicial Review) Act 1977* (Cth) and establishing the Federal Court and Administrative Appeals Tribunal. Some members of the judiciary, particularly the newly established Federal Court, added their own criticism of immigration decision-making procedures to the criticisms that had been identified by the committees. Eventually many of the recommendations of the Fitzgerald Report were taken up and the *Migration Act 1958* (Cth) was radically reformed in 1989. The policy manuals that had informed decision-makers were codified in the Migration Regulations

13 See, generally, K. Cronin, 'A Culture of Control', in J. Jupp and M. Kabala (eds), *The Politics of Australian Immigration* (Canberra, AGPS, 1993), p. 84.
14 Made under the *Migration Act 1958* (Cth), s 504.

1989, with a view to establishing a fairer, more certain, open and accountable system for both applicants and decision-makers.[15]

2.4 The amended *Migration Act 1958* (Cth) and new Migration Regulations

The amended *Migration Act 1958* (Cth) provided that a visa or entry permit must be granted if the criteria were met, and refused if they were not met. The Migration Regulations 1989 set out an exhaustive list of visas and entry permits and all the criteria that needed to be met before any particular visa or entry permit could be granted.

Both the Act and the Migration Regulations have undergone many significant amendments since 1989. The *Migration Reform Act 1992* (Cth)[16] established a statutory two-tiered merits review procedure for most departmental migration decisions by the Migration Internal Review Office (MIRO) and the Immigration Review Tribunal (IRT – now the Migration Review Tribunal – MRT). The first level was an internal review conducted by officers of the Department of Migration, and the second level was independent of the department. Nevertheless, the new review procedures excluded independent review of decisions based on humanitarian/refugee claims. It also established the Refugee Review Tribunal (RRT) as an external and independent review authority; it was the equivalent of the IRT for refugee decisions.

In addition, the *Migration Reform Act 1992* (Cth) introduced a detailed statutory code of procedures for most primary decisions, and created a migration-specific judicial review scheme by replacing the *Administrative Decisions (Judicial Review) Act 1977* (Cth) and section 39B of the *Judiciary Act 1903* (Cth) with Part 8 of the *Migration Act 1958* (Cth). The new judicial review scheme excluded grounds of judicial review such as the grounds of natural justice, unreasonableness and relevant and irrelevant considerations. This occurred as a result of a perception by the government and the department that the Federal Court was using these grounds as a means to engage in merits review. That has been a common complaint of Ministers in charge of the immigration portfolio.[17] While Part 8 became the sole source of the Federal Court's jurisdiction to review migration decisions, the High Court retained its original jurisdiction to review administrative decisions under section 75 of the Constitution.

Subsequently, in 2001, still concerned that the Federal Court was engaging in merits review, the government introduced a privative clause into Part 8 of the *Migration Act 1958* (Cth), in an attempt to oust the Federal Court's jurisdiction in migration matters. Section 474 of the Act provided that a 'privative clause

15 See the recommendations of the Fitzgerald Report.
16 No. 184, 1992.
17 See, for example, Hon Philip Ruddock MP, MIMA 'Democratic Governance: Improving the Institutions of Accountability', Discussion Paper No. 68, September 1999.

decision' (effectively, nearly all decisions made to grant, refuse or cancel visas by the RRT, the MRT and the AAT) is 'final and conclusive', that it cannot be challenged in any court, and that it 'is not subject to prohibition, mandamus, injunction, declaration or certiorari in any court on any account'.

In the case of *Plaintiff S157/2002 v Commonwealth of Australia*,[18] the High Court held that section 474 was constitutionally valid. Nevertheless, the court determined that a decision involving a jurisdictional error was legally not a decision at all; that it was therefore not a 'decision' made under section 474; and that, consequently, it was not protected as a privative clause decision by that section.[19]

The regulatory scheme was significantly amended in 1993 and again on 1 September 1994. Those amendments brought about changes to the law and policy underlying migration processes. Some of the more significant changes are:

- the legal basis of entry to and stay in Australia and the status under the Act of non-citizens were simplified so that the 'visa' replaced the 'entry permit' and 'entry visa' as the sole authority to travel to, enter and/or remain in Australia;[20]
- a non-citizen without a visa was defined as an 'unlawful non-citizen' who must be detained;[21]
- a system of bridging visas was created to allow non-citizens to maintain lawful status in specified circumstances;[22]
- the procedures for immigration clearance were codified;[23] and
- codes of procedure relating to the making of certain decisions under the Act were established to provide decision-makers (including administrative review decision-makers) with clear guidance on how to make fair decisions.[24]

The *Migration Act 1958* (Cth) remains the source of power and the Migration Regulations continue to provide the procedural mechanism for how that power is to be administered and, with few exceptions, exhaustive criteria for all visa classes and subclasses.

18 [2003] HCA 2 (4 February 2003).
19 [2003] HCA 2 (4 February 2003), per Gleeson CJ, [37–38] and per Gaudron, McHugh, Gummow, Kirby and Hayne JJ, [75–76, 83].
20 *Migration Act 1958* (Cth), ss 29–30.
21 *Migration Act 1958* (Cth), see ss 13–14 and 189.
22 See Chapter 9, 'Bridging visas'.
23 *Migration Act 1958* (Cth), Part 2, Division 5.
24 *Migration Act 1958* (Cth), Part 2, Division 5; see, for example, Part 2, Division 3, Subdivision AB.

3

Basic migration legislation and policy

The basic tools of trade for people wanting to understand migration law are the *Migration Act 1958* (Cth), the Migration Regulations 1994 and the Minister for Immigration's policy guidelines (Procedures Advice Manual [PAM3]). The last is a crucial component for guidance in providing the evidence needed to satisfy each criterion for a particular visa and in applying or assessing the law. Equally crucial is the necessity to have up-to-date statutory and policy materials, as the Migration Regulations are the subject of constant amendment.

3.1 The legislative framework and relationship between the Act and the Regulations

The impetus for legislating about migration derives from the policy of the government of the day. Notwithstanding some disagreement between the two major political parties, there is a largely bipartisan policy, based on a view that there should be a formal immigration policy that is beneficial to Australia. To that end, the policy seeks to address long- and short-term economic needs and interests; the needs of individuals and families who have previously migrated; and an international commitment to humanitarian settlement. It implements its policy by controlling who can enter and remain within Australia's borders.

The vehicle used to control entry and stay is the *Migration Act 1958* (Cth). Its preamble is unequivocal:

> An Act relating to the entry into, and the presence in, Australia of aliens, and the departure or deportation from Australia of aliens and certain other persons.

Its objects are spelled out in section 4:

1. The object of this Act is to regulate, in the national interest, the coming into, and presence in, Australia of non-citizens.
2. To advance its object, this Act provides for visas permitting non-citizens to enter or remain in Australia and the Parliament intends that this Act be the only source of the right of non-citizens to so enter or remain.
3. To advance its object, this Act requires persons, whether citizens or non-citizens, entering Australia to identify themselves so that the Commonwealth government can know who are the non-citizens so entering.
4. To advance its object, this Act provides for the removal or deportation from Australia of non-citizens whose presence in Australia is not permitted by this Act.

3.1.1 Entry, stay and departure

As discussed in the previous chapter, it is recognised that the powers of the *Migration Act 1958* (Cth) extend to all non-citizens. Section 5 of the Act defines a migration zone for the purposes of its application and section 42 requires that all non-citizens (with some specified exceptions) must have a visa to travel to Australia. Sections 13 and 14 provide that all non-citizens who are in Australia and hold a current visa are lawful non-citizens and those who do not hold a current visa are unlawful non-citizens. Section 189 requires that unlawful non-citizens must be detained and section 198 provides for the removal of detainees who do not change their status to lawful non-citizens by obtaining a visa.

3.1.2 The nature of a visa

Division 3 of Part 2 of the Act sets out provisions relating to what a visa is (section 29); that a visa can be permanent or temporary (section 30); and that visas are categorised into classes (section 31). Section 31(3) has a vital link between the Act and the Regulations in providing that '[t]he regulations may prescribe criteria for a visa or visas of a specified class . . . ' Apart from a few visas that have specific criteria set out in the Act,[1] detailed criteria for the grant of visas are prescribed in the Regulations and the Schedules attached to the Regulations.

3.1.3 Circumstances and conditions of visa grants

Division 3 goes on to provide that visas may only be granted in specified circumstances and under certain conditions,[2] and that, with a few exceptions, a

1 *Migration Act 1958* (Cth), ss 32–38B.
2 *Migration Act 1958* (Cth), ss 40 and 41 and Migration Regulations 1994, Sch. 8.

non-citizen can only enter Australia as the holder of an effective visa.[3] The specified circumstances and the conditions relating to visas are generally set out in the Schedules to the Regulations.

3.1.4 Controlling the numbers

Sections 84 and 85 give the Minister for Immigration the power to suspend dealing with applications for visas of a specified class until a day specified in a Commonwealth Gazette notice, and to determine (also by Gazette notice) the maximum number of visas granted in a given visa class for a specified financial year. In addition, the number of points required to meet qualifications for points-tested visa classes can be quickly altered by Gazette notice as a means of fine-tuning numbers in the migration program.[4]

3.2 The structure of the Migration Regulations

The Migration Regulations 1994 commence with a table of provisions, followed by alphabetical and numerical indexes of visa subclasses. There are then five Parts containing general regulations dealing with:

- definitions[5] and general information about visas, including:
  - administration of visa processing;[6] and
  - sponsorship requirements and some special provisions relating to domestic violence;[7]
- special provisions relating to student visas;[8]
- general provisions relating to criteria for classes and sub-classes of visas,[9] to the circumstances of grant and conditions of visas,[10] to provision for New Zealand and Norfolk Island passport-holders to enter Australia without requiring a visa,[11] to time limits for determining protection visa applications,[12] to the making of applications for visas, and ancillary issues,[13] plus cancellation, refusal and revocation of visas;[14]
- procedures on entry;[15]

3 *Migration Act 1958* (Cth), s 42.
4 *Migration Act 1958* (Cth), s 93 and Migration Regulations 1994, regulation 2.26.
5 Migration Regulations 1994, regulations 1.03–1.15G. Regulation 1.12A was omitted with effect from 14/09/2009 by SLI 2009, 203 (which amended SLI 2009, 115).
6 Migration Regulations 1994, regulations 1.16–1.19.
7 Migration Regulations 1994, regulations 1.20 (renamed Sponsorship not applicable to Division 3A of Part 2 of the Act with effect from 14/09/2009)–1.27. Regulations 1.20A–1.20IA, 1.20LA–1.20UH were omitted by SLI 2009, 115 with effect from 14/09/2009.
8 Migration Regulations 1994, regulations 1.30 and 1.40–1.44.
9 Migration Regulations 1994, regulations 2.01–2.03.
10 Migration Regulations 1994, regulations 2.03–2.05.
11 Migration Regulations 1994, regulation 2.06.
12 Migration Regulations 1994, regulation 2.06AA.
13 Migration Regulations 1994, regulations 2.07–2.40. The Assurance of Support requirement – regulation 2.07AJ – was omitted by SLI 2009, 116 with effect from 01/07/2009.
14 Migration Regulations 1994, regulations 2.41–2.55.
15 Migration Regulations 1994, regulations 3.01–3.31.

- merits review of decisions other than decisions relating to refugee status;[16]
- decisions relating to refugee status (Refugee Review Tribunal and decisions relating to protections visas);[17]
- service of documents;[18] and
- miscellaneous matters.[19]

Following the general Regulations, there are 12 schedules and sub-schedules. These contain clauses (for example, 101.1), sub-clauses (for example, 101.1(1)) and items (for example, item 4007). These are described in more detail in the Readers Guide and summarised as follows:

- **Schedule 1:** Sets out the various classes of visa that are prescribed in the Regulations. It is divided into four parts, dealing with permanent visas, temporary visas, bridging visas and protection, refugee and humanitarian visas. It prescribes the requirements for making a valid visa application, including the approved form on which an application for each class must be made, the applicable fee (if any) and other requirements regarding when an application can be combined, where the application must be made and where the applicant must be at the time of application.
- **Schedule 2:** This Schedule is divided into Parts, which reflect the various subclasses that are prescribed in Schedule 1. Each subclass is identified by a unique three-digit numeric code (for example, 103) and a descriptive label. The subclasses appear in numeric order and the clauses related to each subclass are organised in a standard way, as follows:
  - xxx1: Interpretations limited to the subclass. General definitions are in Part 1.
  - xxx2: Primary criteria, including some criteria that must be satisfied at the time of application and other criteria that must be satisfied at the time of decision. Some are fully expressed and others are listed as four-digit code numbers that start with 3, 4 or 5 (for example, 3002, 4006, 5009). The texts for such criteria are then set out in full in other Schedules.
  - xxx3: Secondary criteria. These criteria must be satisfied by applicants who are the members of the family unit of a person ('member of family unit' is defined in Regulation 1.12) who satisfies the primary criteria.
  - xxx4: Circumstances applicable to grant. This will list any special circumstances that must be satisfied at the time a visa is granted.
  - xxx5: When visa is in effect. This provides details about the period of time the visa permits a person to remain in Australia and about the period during which the holder may travel to and enter Australia.
  - xxx6: Conditions that are either set out in full or listed as four-digit numbers that start with 8. They may be expressed to be mandatory or

16 Migration Regulations 1994, regulations 4.01–4.27A.
17 Migration Regulations 1994, regulations 4.28–4.37.
18 Migration Regulations 1994, regulations 4.38–4.40.
19 Migration Regulations 1994, regulations 5.01–5.44.

discretionary. Where a condition is listed by number, this is a reference to a condition explained in Schedule 8.

- **Schedule 3:** This Schedule sets out the complete text for the additional criteria that may be applicable to unlawful non-citizens and certain bridging visa holders.
- **Schedule 4:** This Schedule sets out the various prescribed public interest criteria, including matters such as the applicant's character, health, and potential to overstay.
- **Schedule 5:** Special Return Criteria. This Schedule sets out the additional criteria that certain persons must satisfy before they will be granted permission to travel to Australia. The criteria are usually imposed for offences committed against migration legislation and specify that in certain circumstances individuals must have applied for a visa only after a set period has elapsed since they left Australia.
- **Schedule 5A:** Evidentiary requirements for student visas.
- **Schedule 5B:** Evidentiary requirements for student visas – secondary applicants.
- **Schedule 6:** General Points Test – Qualifications and Points. The calculation of the points score is governed by Division 2.6 of Part 2 of the Regulations (applies only to applications made before 1 July 1999).
- **Schedule 6A:** General Points Test – Qualifications and Points (applies only to applications made after 1 July 1999). Regulation 2.27A was amended with effect from 1/10/2006 to add the additional requirement that the applicant's visa application had to be made before 1/10/2006.
- **Schedule 7:** Business Skills Points Test – Attributes and Points.
- **Schedule 8:** Visa Conditions.
- **Schedule 8A**: Omitted by SLI 2009, 289 with effect from 09/11/2009.
- **Schedule 9:** Special Entry and Clearance Arrangements, related to identification on entry.
- **Schedule 10:** Prescribed Forms (not concerned with forms for application for a visa).
- **Schedule 11:** Memorandum of Understanding (relating to certain Vietnamese refugees who had already been resettled in China).
- **Schedule 12:** Exchange of Letters (regarding Sino-Vietnamese refugees).

Each visa has a signature criterion. For instance, spouse visas require that the applicant and sponsor are spouses. 'Spouse' is the subject of a lengthy definition. However, meeting that definition does not ensure a successful application. Failure to meet requirements for a valid application (such as using the prescribed form and lodging it at the correct address) will result in rejection at the outset. For onshore applicants, not having the correct immigration status will preclude a successful application. As well, there are numerous public interest criteria (PIC) that must be met by the applicant and any members of the applicant's family unit. Even members of the family unit who are not included in the application are sometimes required to meet PIC requirements. Failure to meet one of those criteria can result in failure of the application. The point to be made is that each criterion is as important as the other, as the inability to meet a criterion, even though it does not appear important next to the signature criterion, is usually fatal for the application.

As an example of what is needed in an application for a particular visa, people who apply for a spouse visa in Australia apply for both a provisional visa and a permanent visa. Although the latter is not determined for two years, the applications are made at the same time. In addition to the signature criterion of a spouse relationship between the applicant and the sponsor, there are cross-references to 15 definitions and five other visa classes or subclasses.

3.3 Visa class/visa subclass

An application must be made for a class of visa. In the Regulations, classes are set out in Schedule 1 and comprise one or more subclasses. A subclass contains a set of criteria prescribed in Schedule 2 in the form of a 'recipe card'.[20] An application for a visa of a particular class entitles the applicant to be considered against the criteria for all the subclasses within that class. A decision to grant a visa of a class signifies that the requirements for the grant of a visa of that class have been met. Where there is more than one subclass in the class, this means that the requirements of at least one subclass have been met. A decision to refuse to grant a visa of a class means that the requirements for the grant of a visa of that class have not been met.

3.4 Gazette notices

Not all of the relevant law is contained in the Act and Regulations. Those pieces of legislation provide for many matters to be prescribed or specified by notice in the Commonwealth Gazette. A few examples are the pool and pass marks for points-assessed visa classes, numbers and dates for capping visa classes or suspending processing, specifying regional authorities for the purposes of some economic visas, listing 'skilled occupations', 'occupations requiring English' and 'migration occupations in demand', listing countries whose passport-holders are

20 In the following form:
- xxx.1 INTERPRETATION.
- xxx.2 PRIMARY CRITERIA.
- xxx.21 Criteria to be satisfied at time of application.
- xxx.22 Criteria to be satisfied at time of decision.
- xxx.3 SECONDARY CRITERIA.
- xxx.31 Criteria to be satisfied at time of application.
- xxx.32 Criteria to be satisfied at time of decision.
- xxx.4 CIRCUMSTANCES APPLICABLE TO GRANT.
- xxx.5 WHEN VISA IS IN EFFECT.
- xxx.6 CONDITIONS.
- xxx.7 WAY OF GIVING EVIDENCE.

eligible for electronically issued visas (known as Electronic Travel Authorities or ETAs), listing assessment levels for students and so on.

3.5 Ministerial policy and departmental policies and procedures

While decision-makers are required to apply the relevant law, that law is not always clear, particularly as it often changes. In addition, not all the procedures for determining a visa application are set out in the legislation or Regulations. To address real and perceived areas of possible uncertainty, the Minister and the department have established policies and procedures to provide their own interpretation of imprecise laws as an aid to decision-makers. These are contained in Ministerial Directions authorised under section 499 of the Act and in the Departmental Procedures Advice Manual (PAM). The latter is updated by Migration Series Instructions (MSIs) that are, over time, incorporated into the PAM. The current edition is PAM3.

The Ministerial Directions relate to diverse matters and must be followed by decision-makers as a matter of law. The PAM provides detailed guidance and assistance for decision-makers in assessing applications made under the *Migration Act 1958* (Cth), and while it is not legally binding, it is generally followed. Courts will generally only intervene in the application of policy if that policy is inconsistent with the law or its application would cause an injustice in a particular case.[21] In the matter of *Minister for Immigration, Local Government and Ethnic Affairs v Gray*,[22] French and Drummond JJ said:

> Ministerial policy is not to be construed and applied with the nicety of a statute. Policies are not statutory instruments. They prescribe guidelines in general, and not always very precise, language. To apply them with statutory nicety is to misunderstand their function. On the other hand, where the existence and content of such a policy is to be regarded as a relevant fact which the Tribunal is bound to consider, a serious misconstruction of its terms or misunderstanding of its purposes in the course of decision-making may constitute a failure to take into account a relevant factor and for that reason may result in an improper exercise of the statutory power. If a decision-maker, not bound to apply policy, purports to apply it as a proper basis for disposing of the case in hand but misconstrues or misunderstands it so that what is applied is not the policy but something else, then there may be reviewable error. In a limiting case a policy may be so broadly stated as to cover all considerations properly brought to bear on the exercise of the discretion. In such a case misconstruction of the policy may reduce to misconstruction of the statute or misunderstanding of its purpose.

The legal nature of PAM3 was described by Gray J in *El Ess v Minister for Immigration & Multicultural & Indigenous Affairs*[23] as follows:

21 *Drake v MIEA (No. 2)* (1979) 2 ALD 674.
22 (1994) 50 FCR 189, at 208.
23 [2004] FCA 1038, [45].

PAM3 is intended by its own terms to be nothing more than procedural and policy guidance to officers applying the Migration Act and the Migration Regulations. See *Xie v MIMA* [2000] FCA 230 (2000), 61 ALD 641 at [28]–[29] and *Soegianto v MIMA* [2001] FCA 1612 at [15]–[16]. PAM3 does not have the effect of a direction pursuant to s 499 of the Migration Act, which would bind a person or body having functions or powers under the Migration Act as to the performance of those functions or the exercise of those powers. Because the PAM3 guidelines are not binding on a decision-maker, they cannot be relevant considerations, in the sense of considerations that the decision-maker is bound by legislation to take into account. See *Minister for Aboriginal Affairs v Peko Wallsend Ltd* (1986) 162 CLR 24 at 39–40 per Mason J, with whom Gibbs CJ and Dawson J agreed. A failure to apply the guidelines may have significance in establishing some error on the part of a decision-maker, but it is not of itself a jurisdictional error.

3.6 How to locate visa criteria

Identifying the appropriate visa for a particular applicant generally involves a process of first identifying a description of the most likely visa, and then methodically considering the criteria that are set out in Schedules 1 and 2. This process can be divided into the following steps:[24]

- Find the relevant visa class in the alphabetical or numerical list of visas in the Readers Guide at the commencement of the Regulations. That will provide a referral to the appropriate subclass in Schedule 2;
- identify the criteria for the particular subclass set out in Schedule 2;
- check the definitions of terms. There is a list of defined terms in the Readers Guide of the Regulations. Most are in the definitions sections of the Act and the Regulations, but some that are specific to a particular clause are in particular visa subclass sections of Schedule 2 or sections of other schedules. Then clarify unclear definitions by referring to policy documents;
- check all references to other schedules or Gazette notices;
- go to Schedule 1 to find information on relevant forms, fees, place of lodgment and any other eligibility requirements;
- check to see if there are any policy directions that might affect processing or assessing the application.

24 J. Burn and A. Reich, *The Immigration Kit – A Practical Guide to Australia's Immigration Law*, 6th edn (Sydney, Federation Press, 2001), p. 30.

4

The visa system and application procedures

4.1 Validity of visa applications

As described in the previous chapter, the *Migration Act 1958* (Cth) provides that non-citizens must only travel to and enter Australia with a visa. Otherwise they will be refused entry or, if they manage to enter, will be unlawful non-citizens, and subject to removal. For the purposes of obtaining a visa, section 45 requires non-citizens to apply for a visa of a particular class, section 47 imposes a duty on the Minister to consider valid applications, and section 65 provides that the Minister, having considered a *valid* application for a visa, must grant the application if satisfied it meets the relevant criteria, including health criteria and other statutory requirements, and must refuse it if not so satisfied.

Section 46 establishes conditions for the validity or invalidity of a particular visa application, largely by way of providing that the regulations may prescribe criteria to be satisfied for an application to be valid (see regulation 2.07 and Schedule 1). In brief, a valid application must be made on the approved form and in accordance with the directions on the form; be for a specified class of visa; provide correct information; and be lodged at the specified place. The applicant must have paid the appropriate visa application charge (if any) and must not be prevented by legislation from making the application or an entitlement to the particular visa. These rules are reflected in Schedule 1, which sets out the prescribed form; the visa application charges; the place and mode of lodgment; how members of the applicant's family unit might be included; and often, where the applicant must be at the time of lodging the application.

The rigour of that statutory scheme can result in seeming injustice. For instance, in the matter of *Argente v Minister for Immigration*,[1] the applicant lodged an application for a visa class DE (Skilled Australian Sponsored Overseas Student) on 8 January 2002. On 11 February, the DIMIA (now DIAC) decision-maker (the delegate) informed the applicant that the application was invalid because (i) the application was not accompanied by evidence that during the 12 months immediately before the day on which the application was made the Australian Federal Police had completed a check of criminal records in relation to the applicant and (ii) the application was not accompanied by adequate evidence of the relationship between the applicant and his sponsoring aunt. On 3 February 2002, the applicant provided a police certificate dated 18 January 2002 and on 18 February 2002 the applicant's solicitor wrote advising, among other things, that it was not possible to submit a birth certificate of the applicant's mother (the sponsor's sister) as birth certificates were destroyed during the Japanese occupation of the Philippines during World War II.

The Minister's argument was that the delegate correctly refused to consider the application because it was not valid as satisfactory evidence of a police check and evidence of the relationship to the sponsor did not accompany the application, as required by sub-section 47(3) of the Act. The applicant argued that he was in an impossible position. He was required to apply for a class DE while he held a substantive visa. His visa was valid until 16 January 2002 and he had to apply before that date. He had applied for a police certificate prior to that date but had not received it and he could not obtain a birth certificate for his mother because it did not exist. Phipps FM found:

> [11] Unreasonableness, natural justice and jurisdictional error were argued. Unfortunately, if there was unreasonableness or unfairness in the situation it does not affect the decision the delegate made and was compelled to make . . .
>
> [14] The situation may be one where form prevails over substance. Evidence of a police check conducted 364 days prior to the date of the application would satisfy the requirement. An applicant might have committed and been convicted of serious criminal offences during the following 363 days yet the police check requirement would be satisfied. On the other hand, the applicant produced evidence of a police check which showed he had no criminal convictions at all, up to the date of the application and beyond. Unfortunately, while what might be thought to be the substance the requirement had been satisfied, the requirement is specific and unambiguous. The police check must be completed during the 12 months immediately before the date when the application is made. The result may be a triumph of form over substance (*Ibrahim v MIMA* [2002] FCA 1279, Wilcox J), but if the item in the schedule to the regulations has a clear and unambiguous requirement which must be satisfied, it must be satisfied.
>
> [15] The position with evidence that the sponsor was the applicant's aunt is the same.

1 [2004] FMCA 252 (30 April 2004).

A visa application not only has to comply with regulatory requirements, it must also be made in accordance with the directions on the approved form.[2] This issue arose in the context of the Federal Court determining whether or not the RRT was able to review decisions where the initial applications for protection visas were made on the relevant form, which instructed applicants to 'answer ALL questions', to 'tell us below everything about why you think you are a refugee' and, in answering the questions in the form, to indicate if any events referred to relate to a Convention ground or any other reason. In the matter of *MIMA v 'A'*,[3] the Full Federal Court considered a visa application on which the visa applicant had responded to various questions about his reasons for claiming to be a refugee by stating that 'I will be forwarding a statutory declaration detailing my claims for refugee status soon in response to questions 36–40.' The Minister's delegate made a decision before the statutory declaration was submitted, effectively on the basis that the applicant had not made any claims. The court found that the failure to answer the substantive questions on the form was a failure to comply with the directions on the form and consequently rendered the initial application invalid.

A further consequence of that decision was that the visa applicant was not barred from making another application for a protection visa by the operation of section 48A, which provides that a person whose application for a protection visa has already been refused cannot make a further application unless the Minister determines (under section 48B) that section 48A does not apply. In this case, the court found that the initial decision was not a decision for the purposes of section 48A.

The decision in *MIMA v 'A'* and similar cases where visa applicants stated that they would lodge further submissions later but failed to lodge the promised statements led to a series of determinations that addressed the meaning of 'substantial compliance' with regulation 2.07(3) for the purposes of section 25C of the *Acts Interpretation Act 1901* (Cth). In *Yilmaz v MIMA*,[4] the visa applicant had not completed the application form but had provided a previously flagged statement to the delegate, notwithstanding that it was signed two days before the delegate made the decision and posted on the date the decision was made, but was received after the decision had been signed. The majority held that an application for a protection visa that omits essential information from Form 866 is not necessarily incurably invalid. Spender and Gyles JJ (Marshall J dissenting) held that the RRT had acted within its jurisdiction and powers in affirming the delegate's decision. Both Spender and Gyles JJ took the view that had the appellant's statutory declaration of 13 October 1997 been received by the Department prior to the delegate's decision on 15 October 1997, the appellant would have made a valid application for a protection visa. The delegate then would have had power, under section 65 of the *Migration Act 1958* (Cth), to grant or refuse to grant the

2 Migration Regulations 1994, regulation 2.07(3).
3 [1999] FCA 1679 (3 December 1999).
4 [2000] FCA 906 (14 July 2000).

application. Their Honours went on to hold that, by virtue of section 415(1) of the Act, the RRT had the same powers as the delegate. Spender J explained why, in these circumstances, there would have been a valid application:

> . . . when a person seeking a protection visa submits an 'application' which, in respect of the claims for protection under the Refugees Convention, notes 'statement to follow', it is not at that time a valid application. It is inchoate. The duty of a delegate of the Minister is not to consider it: s 47(3) of the Act.
>
> If, before the making of the decision of the delegate, the promised information is supplied, in my opinion the amalgam of the original document with the claims foreshadowed in it, and the document expressing the claims that had been foreshadowed, constitutes a valid application, and the delegate is to exercise the powers referred to in s 65 of the Act in relation to it.
>
> As a matter of common sense, it seems to me that an application based on grounds which are said to be 'to follow' is not complete until those grounds have been supplied.[5]

The approach taken in *Yilmaz* was approved of by Bennet J in *SZECD v MIMI*,[6] where her honour held:

> The weight of authority supports the approach of *Yilmaz*; that is, that missing information can complete an invalid application when submitted to the department or to the tribunal. A delegate's decision, which involved consideration of an invalid application, is an 'RRT-reviewable' decision.

In *MIMA v Li; MIMA v Kundu*,[7] the two different visa applicants had failed to complete the visa application form but had applied for review of the delegate's refusals and had submitted to the RRT the materials that had been flagged in their initial visa application. The Full Federal Court found there had been no substantial compliance with the requirements of regulation 2.07(3), that their applications were rendered invalid at the time of lodgment by the operation of section 46(1)(b) of the *Migration Act 1958* (Cth) and the Minister was precluded from considering them by the operation of section 47(3). It further found that the invalid applications were not remedied by the supply of additional information to the Tribunal, particularly as the effect of regulation 2.10(1)(b)[8] was that the additional information had to be supplied to an office of Immigration rather than the Tribunal. Whereas in *Yilmaz* it had been held that section 415(1) of the Act permitted the RRT to review, on the merits, a decision of the Minister's delegate where a valid application for a visa had been lodged (albeit after the date of the delegate's decision), the circumstances in *Li* are distinguished by the fact that the promised information was never lodged at an office of Immigration and a valid application was not made. The court held that:

> Section 415(4) of the Migration Act makes it clear that the RRT cannot make a decision not authorised by the Migration Act or the regulations. A decision to refuse a visa

5 [2000] FCA 906 (14 July 2000), [19]–[21].
6 (2006) 227 ALR 656, 26.
7 [2000] FCA 1456 (18 October 2000).
8 [2000] FCA 1456 (18 October 2000), [81].

> where no valid application for a visa has been made is a decision not authorised by the Migration Act or the regulations. The fact that the Migration Act preserves an unauthorised decision by a delegate, so as to make it subject to review by the RRT, does not confer on the RRT greater powers than a delegate could ever have properly exercised in relation to an invalid application.

The courts, then, needed to determine what 'substantial compliance' meant, as various arguments were made that the information presented on the application form for a protection visa was inadequate. For instance, in *Bal v MIMA*[9] the applicant had stated in response to Question 36 (which asks why he left his country):

> I have been repeatedly and severely tortured by police because of my political opinion and because I am Kurdish, and because I am a Christian. Detailed statement follows.

He answered the remaining questions on the form relating to his claims by stating 'see Q36'. The Full Federal Court canvassed relevant jurisprudence and held that:

> 36. Section 25C of the *Acts Interpretation Act 1901* (Cth) provides:
>
> 'Where an Act prescribes a form, then, unless the contrary intention appears, strict compliance with the form is not required and substantial compliance is sufficient.'
>
> The section applies to the Regulations as if they were an Act (subs 46(1) of the *Acts Interpretation Act*).
>
> 36. Although Form 866 is not prescribed by the Act or the Regulations, it has been accepted that a 'substantial compliance' requirement is applicable to it; cf *Wu v Minister for Immigration & Ethnic Affairs* (1996) 64 FCR 245 ('*Wu*') at 279 per RD Nicholson J, with whom Jenkinson J agreed; *MIMA v 'A'* per Merkel J at [43]; *Shahabuddin* at [16].
>
> 37. In *Nie*, the applicant stated in his application form that he feared persecution by the Chinese Communist Party because of a 'blemish in [his] political life'. He gave no further particulars but stated that a submission would 'be provided soon'. Heerey J held the application to be a valid one because the applicant had made it clear that he feared persecution on the ground of political opinion. Similarly, Mr Bal made it clear that he feared persecution on, inter alia, the ground of political opinion.
>
> 38. In *Shahabuddin* the applicant gave more detail of the 'political opinion' ground on which he relied, stating that he had been a member of the Bangladesh Freedom Party and adding that a 'statement would be sent very shortly'. Katz J followed Hill J in *Nader* at [4] and Tamberlin J in *Myint* at [15], in holding that substantial compliance was to be assessed by reference to the purpose of the form in eliciting the applicant's claim to be a refugee within the Convention and that the questions posed in the form were only guidelines to that end. Accordingly, so his Honour held, it was not necessary to be able to distil from the applicant's responses, answers to all questions on the form.
>
> 39. We agree with the approach taken to the notion of 'substantial compliance' in the present context by Heerey J in *Nie* and Katz J in *Shahabuddin*, outlined above. (See

9 [2002] FCAFC 189 (14 June 2002).

too, *Wu* at 280 per RD Nicholson J; *MIMA v 'A'* per Merkel J at [43], [44]; *Li v MIMA* [2000] FCA 421 (Heerey J) at [49].)

40. Was there substantial compliance in the present case? In the answer he gave to Question 36 and his cross-references to that answer in his responses to Questions 37, 38, 39 and 40 in Form 866, Mr Bal was answering those questions as follows:

> (Q37) that what he feared would happen to him if he returned to Turkey was that he would suffer repeated and severe torture by the police;
>
> (Q38) that those who he thought might 'harm/mistreat' him if he went back were the Turkish police;
>
> (Q39) that the reasons he thought that they would 'harm/mistreat' him if he went back to Turkey were his holding of a political opinion, his being Kurdish and his being a Christian;
>
> (Q40) that he did not think the Turkish authorities would protect him because, in the past, those authorities, the Turkish police, had been his torturers.

Also Question 6(e) asked Mr Bal whether he had been asked to leave any country, to which he replied, relevantly:

> 'I have been repeatedly told under torture, to leave Turkey by Turkish police.'

42. In sum, Mr Bal made it clear that he claimed to satisfy the Convention definition of a refugee on the basis that he had a well-founded fear of persecution at the hands of the Turkish police for reasons of religion, membership of a particular social group and political opinion, in particular, by reason of his being a Kurd and a Christian. While this was only the 'bare bones' of Mr Bal's claims, and while they were in fact fleshed out by him later in ways which were not implied in the sparse statement he elected to include in his application for the visa, this did not prevent that application from having substantially complied with the requirement of the Act and Regulations that he complete Form 866. It was sufficient that he claimed to have a well-founded fear of persecution by the Turkish police by reason of the three Convention grounds he identified.

In the matter of *Ali Shahabuddin v MIMA*[10] the applicant did not answer the six 'core' questions on the form, but had made the following statement:

> . . . [I] was a member of Bangladesh Freedom Party. Due to my political opinion I was ousted from the country. A number of my political leaders are arrested by the Present government. On the name of Mujib's trial, they would hang our leaders. Heads/workers like me are in deep trouble [sic]. That's why I left my motherland. (A statement would be sent very shortly.)

No further statement was provided. The Federal Court discerned that the applicant was making a claim that he feared persecution for reasons of political opinion if he returned to Bangladesh and held that the protection visa application was valid as there was substantial compliance with the form. It held that the six core questions were guidelines for the purpose of eliciting claims and, alternatively, if it was a statutory requirement to answer those questions to achieve substantial

10 [2001] FCA 273 (23 March 2001).

compliance, the questions could be answered *impliedly*, as had occurred in the application before the court. On the other hand, in *Zanaj v MIMA*,[11] the applicant said she had left Albania to 'visit and study the market' and otherwise had stated that she was 'afraid of getting killed' in response to questions that were unrelated to that answer. The court held that this was a non-responsive answer to the questions which resulted in the omission of essential information, and therefore the form had not been completed according to its directions.

Despite the court rulings, the department's PAM3 advises decision-makers that:

> Notwithstanding the requirements of regulation 2.07(3) to complete the application form 'in accordance with any directions on it', a partly completed form can be accepted as a valid application unless seriously deficient in information.[12]

4.2 Procedures for dealing with visa applications

Sections 51A–64 establish a code of procedure that is expressed to be 'an exhaustive statement of the requirements of the natural justice hearing rule in relation to the matters it deals with'.[13] The procedures relate to visa applications that are considered by the Minister or a delegate, but do not apply to sponsorship or nomination applications, nor to review applications, which are the subject of other provisions of the legislation.

In nearly all cases, the visa applicant must communicate in writing[14] and has the right to provide information at any time prior to a decision to grant or refuse to grant a visa being made.[15] The Minister or delegate is required to take into account all the proffered information and may ask the applicant to provide further information and, in order to ensure procedural fairness, the Minister must provide adverse information in some circumstances and provide an opportunity for the applicant to respond to that information within prescribed periods.[16] While the Act purports to establish an exhaustive code of procedure, the High Court has found that the common law rules of natural justice still apply: *Re MIMA; Ex parte Miah*.[17] In that case, the applicant for a protection visa had claimed, among other things, that he feared persecution by the Bangladesh Nationalist Party (BNP) if he returned to Bangladesh. That party was in power when he applied for the protection visa but had been voted out by the time the delegate decided the application. One of the reasons the delegate refused the application was that the BNP had lost power. The applicant was not invited to comment on the change in circumstances, apparently on the basis that it was

11 [2000] FCA 1766 (8 December 2000).
12 Generic Guidelines section 34 – What is a valid application.
13 See *Migration Act 1958* (Cth), s 51A(1).
14 Migration Regulations 1994, regulation 2.13.
15 *Migration Act 1958* (Cth), s 55.
16 *Migration Act 1958* (Cth), ss 56–58 and 61.
17 [2001] HCA 22 (3 May 2001).

not 'relevant information' for the purposes of section 57, which requires, among other things, that such information 'is specifically about the applicant or another person and is not just about a class of persons of which the applicant or other person is a member'. The majority (Gaudron, McHugh and Kirby JJ) found that the Minister or delegate is obliged to accord procedural fairness to an applicant notwithstanding the code of procedure established by the provisions of Part 2, Division 3, Subdivision AB of the Act. In the applicant's case, the rules of procedural fairness required that the delegate inform him that he was intending to rely on the information concerning a change in government, and give the applicant the opportunity to comment. As French CJ, Gummow, Hayne, Crennan and Kiefel JJ explained in *Saeed v Minister for Immigration and Citizenship*,[18] whether or not Subdivision AB relevantly and validly limits or extinguishes the obligation to accord procedural fairness requires a clear expression of intention to do so by the legislature.[19] The majority in *Re MIMA; Ex parte Miah* found no such intention.[20]

Section 65 requires the Minister to grant the visa if satisfied that all statutory requirements are met (and to refuse it if they are not), and section 66 obliges the Minister to notify the applicant of the decision and provide reasons if the application is refused. Section 67 provides that the visa is granted by 'the Minister causing a record of it to be made' and section 68 provides that the visa comes into effect once it is granted, subject to any other commencement date that may have been specified. Section 71 of the Act makes provision for ways of giving evidence that a visa is in effect. In nearly all cases, the prescribed manner of giving such evidence is by a visa label attached to a passport, as required by regulation 2.17, which also specifies information that must be included on the label.

4.3 Restrictions on visa applications

It was pointed out in the previous chapter that numbers can be controlled by the operation of sections 84, 85 and 93. In addition, visas can be refused or cancelled on character grounds (section 501) and some of the public interest criteria of Schedule 4 impose bans on granting visas to former visa-holders who fall within specified 'risk factor' categories – people who have breached visa conditions or had their visas cancelled, for instance. Others of these categories are built through a statistical analysis of how other passport-holders of that country have (or have not) complied with visa conditions, and movement records of persons who have remained in Australia after the expiry of the period they were authorised to under their visa. The Minister will also have regard to other characteristics, including gender and age group, occupation, marital relationship and the class of visa

18 [2010] HCA 2010.
19 [2010] HCA 2010, [25].
20 *Re MIMA; Ex parte Miah* [2001] HCA 22, [90].

being applied for,[21] and will use these to assess the likelihood that a particular applicant might remain in Australia after their visa has expired. As well, the special return criteria of Schedule 5 impose bans on former visa-holders who have been the subject of deportation orders, or been removed, or had their visas cancelled on character grounds.

The ability to refuse visa applications supplements the requirements, discussed above, that visa applications must be in the prescribed form and comply with the relevant procedural criteria to be valid. In addition, the legislation also has mechanisms that operate to restrict the making of valid applications, including restrictions on making onshore visa applications set out in Schedule 3 to the Regulations.[22]

Sections 46A and 46B prevent 'offshore entry persons' and 'transitory persons' (essentially undocumented arrivals at places excised from the migration zone) from making valid onshore visa applications while they are deemed unlawful non-citizens. This is to conform with the government policy of refusing entry to undocumented boat people.[23] Sections 91E, 91K and 91P also restrict applications for protection visas by people who have protection under the Comprehensive Plan of Action (CPA) made in Geneva in 1989 to deal with Indo-Chinese asylum-seekers; by people who have protection in prescribed 'safe third countries';[24] by holders of safe haven visas, such as the Albanians who arrived during the attacks by Serbian forces; and by people who have nationality or other rights of entry and residence in third countries. That is an issue that is dealt with in the chapters concerning refugees.

Section 48 restricts the type of visa that a person who has previously had a visa application refused or a visa cancelled (under sections 109, 116, 134, 137J or 137Q) can make an application for (commonly called the 'second application bar'), and section 48A, as discussed in the case of *MIMA v 'A'* above, restricts the making of an application for a protection visa by a person who has previously applied for the same visa (also known as the 'further application bar'). Section 48B provides for the Minister to exercise a personal and non-compellable discretion to waive that restriction. In practice, case managers assess whether the information provided by a person pursuant to section 48B falls within the Minister's Guidelines, and determine whether or not to refer a section 48B application to the Minister. The Federal Court has found that the Minister's discretion is not a 'decision' that is judicially reviewable, notwithstanding that the matter was

21 Migration Regulations 1994, Sch. 4, 4011(2). Note that the Minister has revoked the Instrument Number IMMI 08/033, signed on 12 May 2008, specifying risk factor groups for the purposes of paragraph 4011(2)(b) of Schedule 4 to the Migration Regulations on 15 May 2009 by a Gazette notification. Since then, a new instrument has not been reintroduced.

22 Sch. 3 – Additional Criteria Applicable to Unlawful Non-Citizens and Certain Bridging Visa Holders.

23 But s 46A(2) allows the Minister to lift this bar. The High Court in *Plaintiff M61/2010E v Commonwealth of Australia* (11 November 2010) decided that the Minister's discretion is not compellable, but once the Minister decided to consider this discretion the Minister had to comply with the law affording procedural fairness to the applicant. As s 46A(7) does not compel the Minister to exercise the relevant power, a mandamus will not be available to the applicant.

24 Migration Regulations 1994, regulation 2.12A prescribes PRC (People's Republic of China).

not referred to the Minister by the relevant case officer.[25] A further restriction is the imposition of a condition that the visa-holder may not apply for further visas while in Australia.[26] Those restrictions can be waived by the Minister in prescribed circumstances.[27] Regulation 2.05 then provides:

> (4) For subsection 41(2A) of the Act, the circumstances in which the Minister may waive a condition of a kind described in paragraph 41(2)(a) of the Act are that:
> (a) since the person was granted the visa that was subject to the condition, compelling and compassionate circumstances have developed:
> (i) over which the person had no control; and
> (ii) that resulted in a major change to the person's circumstances; and
> (b) if the Minister has previously refused to waive the condition, the Minister is satisfied that the circumstances mentioned in paragraph (a) are substantially different from those considered previously; and
> (c) if the person asks the Minister to waive the condition, the request is in writing.
>
> (4A) However, the Minister must not waive:
> (a) in relation to a Subclass 020 Bridging B visa granted to a person who is an applicant for a Subclass 462 (Work and Holiday) visa – condition 8540; and
> (b) in relation to a Subclass 462 (Work and Holiday) visa – conditions 8503 and 8540.
>
> (5) For subsection 41(2A) of the Act, further circumstances in which the Minister may waive condition 8534 in relation to a visa are that the holder of the visa:
> (a) has, after holding a student visa to which condition 8534 applies, been granted:
> (i) a Subclass 497 (Graduate – Skilled) visa; or
> (ii) a Subclass 010 (Bridging A) visa or a Subclass 020 (Bridging B) visa associated with the Subclass 497 (Graduate – Skilled) visa application; and
> (b) has not, after holding a student visa to which condition 8534 applies, been granted a protection visa.
>
> (5A) For subsection 41(2A) of the Act, further circumstances in which the Minister may waive condition 8534 in relation to a visa are that the holder of the visa:
> (a) has completed the course for which the visa was granted; and
> (b) has a genuine intention to apply for a General Skilled Migration visa.
>
> (6) For subsection 41(2A) of the Act, further circumstances in which the Minister may waive condition 8534 in relation to a visa are that the holder of the visa is a registered nurse, or satisfies the requirements for registration as a registered nurse, in Australia.

The Federal Court has considered the meaning of Regulation 2.05(4)(a). In *Auva'a, in the matter of an application for a Writ of Prohibition and Certiorari and Declaratory and Injunctive Relief against Vanstone*,[28] Dowsett J held that:

25 *Bedlington v Chong* [1997] 1416 FCA (15 December 1997).
26 *Migration Act 1958* (Cth), s 41(2)(a), 46(1A) and Migration Regulations 1994, Sch. 8, Items 8503, 8534 and 8535.
27 *Migration Act 1958* (Cth), s 41(2A).
28 [2003] FCA 1506 (18 December 2003).

8. In subreg 2.05(4), the word 'circumstances' is used with three different meanings. In the introductory part of the sub-regulation, the word is used to describe collectively the conditions which will enliven the first respondent's power to waive a relevant condition. The word is then used in par 2.05(4)(a) to describe '*compelling and compassionate*' factors which must have developed since the issue of the visa. In subpar 2.05(4)(a)(ii), the word is used to describe the whole of the relevant person's position, presumably to the extent that it is relevant to the issue of a visa. The '*compelling and compassionate circumstances*' must themselves result in a '*major change*' to the person's 'overall' circumstances. This requirement seems to contemplate a comparison of the relevant person's position prior to the issue of the visa with his or her position as a result of the '*compelling and compassionate*' circumstances . . .

15. The allegedly compelling and compassionate circumstances which '*developed*' after the visa was granted appear to have been that:

- the prosecutrix entered Australia on 4 April 1999 on a one-month visitor's visa;
- she has remained in Australia since that time;
- her parents have sold the house in Samoa;
- having arrived in Brisbane she thought that she could 'stay forever' and was unaware of the 8503 condition;
- in early 2002 she fell pregnant;
- the child was presumably born in December 2002;
- the prosecutrix married on 13 July 2002;
- her husband has no family in Samoa;
- the prosecutrix has never worked in Samoa; and
- the prosecutrix does not believe that she or her husband can obtain employment in Samoa.

16. For the purposes of the regulation, the '*compelling and compassionate circumstances*' may involve only one factor which is, itself, a relevant '*major change*' or causes such a change. Alternatively, more than one such factor may inter-act to bring about that result. In either case, the '*compelling and compassionate*' factor or factors may produce such result by inter-acting with other aspects of the relevant person's situation. It is not necessary that all factors, the combined effect of which produces the '*major change*', should satisfy subreg 2.05(4). It is only necessary that the relevant combination does so. However that question may depend upon whether individual factors satisfy the requirements contained in the sub-regulation.

17. The prosecutrix's complaint of denial of procedural fairness relates only to the rejection of her claims that she believed that she could remain in Australia permanently and that she was not aware of the 8503 condition. It seems that her belief that she was entitled to remain in Australia permanently arose at or after her entry into Australia, that is after the issue of the visa. However, this belief was based entirely upon assumptions made by her. There is no evidence to suggest that any other person misled her or encouraged her to form this view. It was open to her at any time to seek advice or to consult the department. She chose to rely upon her uninformed assumptions. Her belief was therefore a matter over which she had complete control. In any event such belief did not result in any change in the prosecutrix's circumstances. She was at no time entitled to permanent residence. As was pointed out by O'Loughlin J in *Thongpraphai v MIMA* (2000) FCA 1590 at [12], it is possible that the prosecutrix's realisation of her misapprehension was a '*developing*' circumstance. However, that circumstance did not contribute to any material change in her overall position.

In interpreting the term 'compelling and compassionate circumstances' in the case of *Terera v Minister for Immigration and Multicultural and Indigenous Affairs*,[29] Kenny J considered a matter where the applicant was a 5-year-old child who had come to Australia as a visitor with a 'no further application' condition endorsed on his visa. His mother had arrived earlier as a student and had subsequently married an Australian citizen. She and her spouse requested that the condition be removed from the child's visitor visa so that he could be included in their application for a partner visa. In finding that the delegate had made a jurisdictional error in addressing the parents' circumstances rather than the child's, her Honour found:

> 25. In *Thongpraphai v MIMA* [2000] FCA 1590 at [21], O'Loughlin J held that the words 'compelling and compassionate' in reg 2.05(4)(a) 'call for the occurrence of an event or events that are far-reaching and most heavily persuasive'. In a general sense, this is probably correct, although, for my part, I prefer not to put any exegetical gloss, by way of explanation, on the plain words of reg 2.05(4)(a). When a visa-holder requests the Minister, or Ministerial delegate, to waive a 'no further stay' condition imposed on his or her visa, then the question for the decision-maker will be whether, in the particular case, compelling and compassionate circumstances have developed since the visa was granted, over which the visa-holder has no control and resulting in a major change to his or her circumstances. Whether the decision-maker finds that these circumstances exist will depend entirely upon the facts of the case under consideration, particularly the circumstances of the individual visa-holder.
>
> 26. This is well illustrated by the decision by *Nguyen v MIMA* (2001) 109 FCR 169 ('*Nguyen*'). In *Nguyen*, the applicant entered Australia from Vietnam on 2 June 2000 on a business visa subject to condition 8503. The following month he married an Australian citizen and, six days later, applied for a spouse visa. His claim that the condition was invalid was treated by the Minister's delegate as a request for waiver, and the request was refused. Dealing with the visa-holder's contention that his marriage entitled him to the waiver of the condition, Marshall J said at 173 that '[t]he fact of a marriage to an Australia citizen without more . . . can rarely if ever constitute an event which is a compelling or compassionate circumstance'. The case presently before the Court is, however, entirely different from the situation in Nguyen and cannot be dealt with in this straightforward manner.
>
> 27. There are few in Australia who would dispute that amongst the greatest needs for a young child is the benefit of a nurturing family . . . It appeared from the letter of 15 January 2002, which was written by Janet Terera and Jerram Simonsen on the applicant's behalf, that between the applicant's arrival in Australia and his meeting with Mr Simonsen and his reunion with his mother, his mother (who was his sole remaining biological parent) and her husband-to-be decided to bring the five-year-old applicant under their joint care and protection and within their new family in Australia. It goes almost without saying that this decision was one of profound significance for the child.
>
> 28. This was the matter placed before the delegate in January 2002. On any natural reading of the letter of 15 January 2002, the couple not only informed the decision-maker that they were to marry but that, since his arrival in Australia, they had decided

29 *Terera v Minister for Immigration and Multicultural and Indigenous Affairs* [2003] FCA 1570; 135 FCR 335.

and now desired to include the five-year-old boy in his mother's application for migration to Australia, in order to incorporate him within their family. It will be recalled that, in the letter, the applicant's mother and her husband-to-be specifically asked the delegate to 'waive this [8503] condition to enable our son to stay here with us in Australia (while we lodge this application) and attend primary school . . . ' I do not think that it was open to doubt that, upon reading the letter of 15 January 2002, the delegate was asked to determine whether the inclusion of a five-year-old orphan in a family under the care of his remaining parent and a person desiring to be his new father constituted 'compelling and compassionate circumstances' for him. It was plainly open to the delegate to decide that such were the circumstances that had developed since the applicant was granted the visa. As already noted, it could scarcely be said that these circumstances were under the child's control or, indeed, that they would not result in a major change for him.

29. As the respondent's counsel submitted at the hearing, in deciding whether these circumstances had 'developed' in the relevant period, the delegate was entitled to have regard to the fact that only a little more than two weeks had elapsed since the visa had been granted and the waiver application made. It was also open to him to take the view that, having regard to the information sent to him from Harare (assuming it to be reliable in the relevant particulars) and the letter of 15 January 2002 (assuming it to be written in good faith), there had been an important development in the circumstances affecting Chengetai, in that his mother and her husband-to-be had decided to provide him with their parental care and that, having regard to his age, the significance of this development, so far as the child was concerned, was such as to constitute 'compelling and compassionate' circumstances, within the meaning of reg 2.05(4)(a).

4.4 Family members

In most visa categories (apart from protection visas, bridging visas and most visitor visas), provision is made in the relevant item of Schedule 1 for members of the family unit to be 'combined with' the application of the principal applicant. Regulation 1.12 defines members of a family unit as follows:[30]

(1) Subject to subregulations (2), (2A), (6) and (7), a person is a member of the family unit of another person (in this subregulation called the family head) if the person is:
- (a) a spouse or de facto partner of the family head; or
- (b) a dependent child of the family head or of a spouse or de facto partner of the family head; or
- (c) a dependent child of a dependent child of the family head or of a spouse or de facto partner of the family head; or
- (e) a relative of the family head or of a spouse or de facto partner of the family head who:
  - (i) does not have a spouse or de facto partner; and
  - (ii) is usually resident in the family head's household; and
  - (iii) is dependent on the family head.

30 Subregulations 1.12(2) to 1.12(8) qualify this definition in relation to temporary student visas; the definition of contributory parent, contributory aged parent; the definition of distinguished talent visas; Employee Nomination visas; and business and skilled visas.

Where Schedule 1 permits family members to be included in a visa application, the commensurate part of Schedule 2 will contain criteria that members of the family unit must meet. Generally, all members of the family unit, whether or not included in an application for permanent residence, are required to meet the health requirements. This is described as the 'one fails, all fail' criteria. PAM3 states the policy as follows:

> 28.1. For certain visas, Schedule 2 *primary* criteria require all members of the family unit to satisfy certain prescribed criteria in order for *any* family unit member (including the applicant who needs to satisfy primary criteria) to be granted a visa (as an example, see clause 103.227).

'One fails, all fail' applies even to some subclasses that do not allow all family members to be visa applicants:

> 28.2. Schedule 2 'one fails, all fail' criteria (where applicable) apply to all members of the family unit, whether visa applicants or not and regardless of whether they are currently residing with the applicant who needs to satisfy primary criteria . . .
>
> 28.4. Failure of any member of the family unit to satisfy these prescribed criteria means that:
> - the applicant who needs to satisfy primary criteria cannot do so and, it follows
> - neither this applicant nor any member of their family unit satisfies Schedule 2 requirements for visa grant.[31]

4.5 Sponsorship and assurance of support

Many visa categories require that the visa applicant have a sponsor. Most commonly, sponsorship is relevant in applications by family members of an Australian permanent resident or citizen and in employer-sponsored or nominated categories.

4.5.1 Family sponsors and assurers

Regulation 1.20 defines a sponsor as 'a person . . . who undertakes the obligations stated in subregulation (2) in relation to the applicant'.

In general, a sponsor must be: over 18; an Australian citizen, permanent resident or an eligible New Zealand citizen (see 4.7, below); and related to the applicant in the way specified for the class of visa for which the applicant has applied, although in the Partner, Prospective Marriage, Remaining Relative, Carer and Parent visa classes there is provision for another person to sponsor where the person who would normally do so is under 18.

All approved sponsors of applicants for permanent visas are obliged to assist the applicant with accommodation and financial assistance for two years after the grant of the visa or the holder's first entry into Australia, and in some cases to

31 PAM3: Div. 1.2/reg. 1.12.

assist the applicant to attend English classes. If the application is for a Prospective Marriage visa, subclass 300, the sponsor is obliged to accept responsibility for all the applicant's financial obligations while in Australia, ensuring that the applicant complies with relevant Australian laws and that the applicant complies with all conditions of their visa.

As well as sponsors having the obligations mentioned above, most permanent resident categories have provision for an assurance of support, either as a 'required' (mandatory) criterion or as a requirement to be imposed at the decision-maker's discretion. PAM3 describes the Assurance of Support Scheme as 'a response to concerns that certain persons settling permanently in Australia are potentially substantial users of Australia's health and welfare system'.[32] It obliges assurers, by law, to repay to the Australian government some of the health and welfare costs incurred in providing support to the assured persons during their first two years of settlement in Australia, with that period being extended to ten years for people granted Parent and Contributory Parent visas.[33] Regulation 2.38 sets out the payments, benefits and allowances that are recoverable from an assurer. In addition, Regulation 2.39 requires assurers to lodge a bond with the government, before the decision on the application is made, that is retained for the period of the assurance of support and is the first source of reimbursement should the applicant receive payments from any of the listed health and welfare schemes.

Sponsorship applications and assurances of support must be made on the approved forms and are assessed by DIAC. If the assessment officer has doubts about the sponsor's capacity to fulfil the sponsorship obligations and the visa category criteria do not require a mandatory assurance of support, the case officer may impose a requirement that the visa applicant provide a discretionary assurance of support. Assurers are also assessed for their capacity to meet the statutory obligations to which they have committed.

4.5.2 Employer sponsors

There are special provisions for employer-sponsored visas, although the sponsors of permanent residence applicants are not required to fulfil the statutory obligations or undertakings given by sponsors in the family migration stream. Rather, they are required to demonstrate that they have a need for a paid employee who is highly skilled and that there is no suitable Australian citizen or permanent resident to fill the position. To that end, they require approval from the department to be a standard business sponsor.

32 PAM3: Div. 2.7.

33 Migration Regulations 1994, regulation 2.36(1). Assurance of support is defined in regulation 1.03. The assurer can be the sponsor or any other person. An assurance of support is mandatory for some visas (such as remaining relative and contributory parent), and discretionary for others (such as spouse). From 1 July 2004, approvals of assurances of support rest with the Department of Family and Community Services, not the Department of Immigration and Citizenship (DIAC). Thus, decisions to reject assurances of support are reviewable by the AAT, not the MRT.

'Standard business sponsor' is defined under regulation 1.03. The 2-step test provides: the person is an approved sponsor, as defined in section 5(1) of the Act as a person who has been approved by the Minister under section 140E; and whose approval has not been cancelled under section 140M, or ceased to have effect under section 140G; or a person who is a party to a work agreement.[34] Division 2.12, regulation 2.58 provides a number of classes of sponsor in relation to which a person may be approved as a sponsor: inter alia, a standard business sponsor. The person is approved as a sponsor in relation to the standard business sponsor class by the Minister under subsection 140E(1) of the Act. This section provides that the Minister must approve a person as a standard business sponsor if the prescribed criteria are satisfied. However, a person who is party to a work agreement is not required to apply for approval as a sponsor and is not required to be approved as a sponsor in relation to a class of sponsor.

After approval of the sponsor and then the nomination comes the visa application. The relevant visa application is for a Temporary Business Entry Class UC visa, subclass 457 Business (Long Stay). For this visa, the applicant can rely on definitions under repealed regulations, including the definition of 'occupation' under 1.20G, 1.20GA, 1.20GB and 'approved business nomination' under 1.20H, provided the approval has not ceased to have effect (1.20H(5)) and is in force immediately prior to 14 September 2009. Although the approvals for the sponsorship and the nomination are conditions precedent to the approval of the visa application, in practice the latter can be made concurrently with the two other applications.

4.6 Special classes of person

The migration legislation makes provision for New Zealand citizens to be given some preference and/or concessions by way of the creation of some dedicated visa subclasses – for instance, the Subclass 444 (Special Category) visa and the Subclass 861 (Skilled – Onshore Independent New Zealand Citizen) visa – and the capacity to be sponsors of family members in the family migration stream. In most cases, a sponsor from New Zealand must be an 'eligible New Zealand citizen', defined as:[35]

> . . . a New Zealand citizen who:
>
> (c) at the time of his or her last entry to Australia, would have satisfied public interest criteria 4001 to 4004 and 4007 to 4009; and
>
> (d) either:
>
> (i) was in Australia on 26 February 2001 as the holder of a Subclass 444 (Special Category) visa that was in force on that date; or

34 Migration Regulations 1994, regulation 2.76/Division 2.18 defines 'work agreement' for the purpose of the Act.

35 Migration Regulations 1994, regulation 1.03.

(ii) was in Australia as the holder of a Subclass 444 visa for a period of, or periods that total, not less than 1 year in the period of 2 years immediately before 26 February 2001; or

(iii) has a certificate, issued under the *Social Security Act 1991*, that states that the citizen was, for the purposes of that Act, residing in Australia on a particular date.

If a New Zealand citizen does not fall within the definition of 'eligible New Zealand citizen' he/she can apply for permanent residence under any of the general categories that are applicable to all applicants or under one of the categories that is specific to New Zealanders.[36]

Some of the legislation also makes provision for specific groups of people: criminal justice visas, for instance, can be issued for people to face trial in Australia or to act as witnesses at trial,[37] and enforcement visas can be issued to non-citizens on foreign boats outside the migration zone when a fisheries officer has reasonable grounds to believe that the boat has been used, is being used or is intended to be used in the commission of a fisheries detention offence and 'detains' those on board.[38]

4.7 Third-party sources of decision-making power

There are several matters in which the decision-maker assessing a visa application (usually the Minister's delegate or a Member of the Migration Review Tribunal) is obliged to accept as fact conclusions that have been drawn by external parties. These include the assessment of health by Commonwealth medical officers or panel doctors appointed by DIAC for the purpose of making health assessments; the acceptance of an assurance of support by the Secretary of the Department of Family and Community Services; the assessment of skills by the relevant assessing authority; the sponsorship of certain business visa applicants by an appropriate State/Territory authority; certificates from Health Services Australia that assess the level of impairment of sponsors in carer visas; and statutory declarations concerning domestic violence made by competent persons. The decision-maker does not have the power to investigate those findings but may, in some cases concerned with health issues, have the power to waive the negative effects of them.

4.8 The DIAC decision-making process

DIAC issues a checklist for decision-makers, to guide them through the complexities of the statutory and policy requirements they need to address in processing an application for a visa, the most recent being as follows:

36 For example, class 861 Skilled – Onshore Independent New Zealand Citizen; class 862 Skilled – Onshore Australian-sponsored New Zealand Citizen; and class 863 Skilled – Onshore Designated Area-sponsored New Zealand Citizen.

37 *Migration Act 1958* (Cth), s 38.

38 *Migration Act 1958* (Cth), s 38A.

PAM3 Generic Guidelines A

Granting Visas – Lawful Decision Making Checklist

CHECKLIST SUMMARY

About the summary

This section summarises the requirements for a visa application decision to be lawful. It is a summary only – relevant sections elsewhere in this document give more information.

Delegation

Check you are a delegate and so have the power to make the decision under section 29 and section 65 of the Act.

Valid application

Check there is a valid visa application under section 46 of the Act and Regulations Schedule 1.

Apply the law

Apply the relevant migration law in the Act and the Regulations. The prescribed criteria for visas, in Schedule 2 of the Regulations, set out the basic rules for your decision.

There are also a few overriding matters, in provisions in the Act or the Regulations, that prevent the grant of a visa (even if prescribed criteria are met). Section 65(1)(a)(iii) and section 65(1)(a)(iv) of the Act operate as a checklist of most of these matters. See also Granting visas – Summary of legislative requirements.

Remember, a matter will be relevant only if it relates to the prescribed criteria or to the provisions that prevent grant.

Apply the policy

Apply any relevant policy.

Policy is a relevant consideration that will assist, in particular, in interpreting and applying the prescribed criteria and provisions.

Policy must be taken into account but should not be applied in an inflexible way. Remember, it is only the requirements of the Act and Regulations that must be met.

If policy requirements for grant of a visa are not met, consider whether the case should be one for grant outside policy. But if you believe a case is one for grant outside policy, you should normally contact the relevant policy area for further advice to assist you in making your decision.

Ascertain the facts

Obtain all the facts or evidence that you need. If you are seeking further information from the applicant, section 56 and section 58 of the Code of Procedure in the Act allow you to:

- specify to the applicant how you want his or her response (e.g. by writing, at interview, or by telephone)
- ask the applicant to respond or attend the interview within prescribed time limits, set out in regulation 2.15, so that decision making times are not 'strung-out'.

Make sure the information you seek (or the questions you ask at interview) will cast light on the prescribed criteria.

Test the evidence.

Test the 'facts' or evidence for relevance to prescribed criteria and reliability/credibility.

Remember, when you are recording your decision you should be able to discuss why you give certain weight to, or accept or reject, key evidence.

Procedural fairness

Check whether you must invite the applicant to comment on information under section 57 of the Act dealing with the Code of Procedure.

Section 57 of the Act applies in relation to information [other than non-disclosable information as defined in section 5(1) of the Act] where:

- the information would be the reason for refusing the visa and
- it is specifically about the applicant or another person and
- it was not given by the applicant for the purpose of the application.

(cont.)

Remember to:

- specify how you want the applicant to respond and within what prescribed time limits and
- ensure, as far as is reasonably practicable, that the applicant understands why the information is relevant to your consideration of the application.

See also the *Migration Legislation Amendment (Procedural Fairness) Act 2002* – Implications for decision makers.

Make findings of fact

Make your findings of fact against the relevant migration law, that is, the prescribed criteria for the class/subclass of visa, or the provisions that prevent grant.

Consider the issues in a comprehensive manner – explore both sides of a case.

Do not ignore evidence that is inconvenient.

Consider whether more than one finding of fact, or inference, is possible. If so, indicate why you preferred the finding you came to.

Make sure there is evidence for your findings – you should be able to refer to highly relevant evidence in your decision record.

Do not act under direction

Exercise your decision making power in an independent and personal manner.

Do not make a decision at the direction of another person.

Record the decision

Record your decision. A decision record should make it clear whether your decision is to grant or to refuse the visa and set out your reasoning process with reference to the prescribed criteria. It should include your name, position number and the date of the decision.

For refusal decisions:

Section 66(2) of the Act spells out notification requirements (and hence what you need to record). You must specify:

- which criterion was not satisfied. Be careful not to suggest that the applicant met all other criteria if these were not assessed or
- which provision in the Act or the Regulations prevented grant and
- give the reasons why the criterion was not satisfied (or why the provision prevented grant), spelling out your findings against the criterion/provision, and referring to highly relevant evidence. [This is not required for those offshore cases for which there is no merit review right.]

When setting out your reasons:

- use plain language that makes it clear what you are doing, e.g. 'I find that...', 'I accept that...', 'I reject that...', 'I acknowledge that...', 'I took into account that...', 'I found this to be irrelevant...'
- if you are referring to the criterion, use the specific wording of the criterion – do not substitute other words, which might indicate that you did not really understand or apply the correct legal test.

Avoid language that:

- is vague or ambiguous, e.g. 'it appears...'
- is negative such as to suggest bias, e.g. 'this reflects poorly on the applicant'
- suggests the case has not been given an individual assessment on the merits, e.g. 'this is a typical claim'.

Notify the applicant

Notify the applicant of the decision. For refusal decisions, notification requirements are set out in section 66(2) of the Act. Remember, you must:

- spell out which criterion/provision was not met and the reasons why (your decision record should contain these details)
- if there is a merit review right: advise the applicant that the decision may be reviewed and provide details on who can seek review, when, and where.

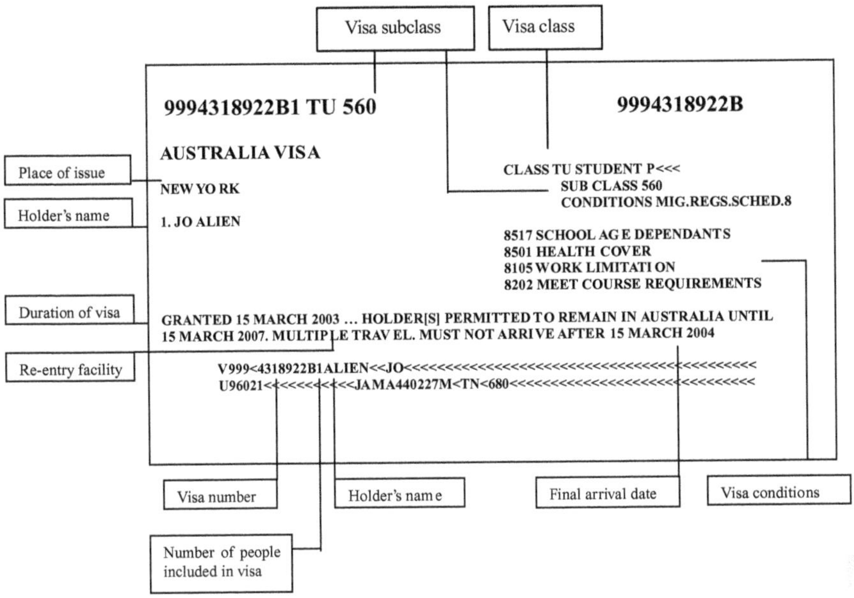

Figure 4.1 Visa label

4.9 Evidencing the visa

If the relevant Part of Schedule 2[39] does not specify the way of giving evidence, it may be done by a label affixed to the passport, or an imprint stamped in the passport by an officer, or a document. In the vast majority of cases, however, visas are evidenced by a visa label, a little smaller than the size of a page in a passport, and glued to such a page in a valid passport. The information that must be disclosed on a visa label is set out in regulation 2.17, and includes the applicant's name, the class (2-letter code relevant to Schedule 1) and subclass of visa (3-digit code relevant to Schedule 2), the visa number, the place of issue and date of grant, the final date for entry to Australia and the expiry date of the visa, whether it is for single or multiple entries, and any conditions relating to members of the holder's family unit, health insurance, work, study and further stay after the visa expires.

4.10 Visa Entitlement Verification Online (VEVO)[40]

This is an online facility run by DIAC for organisations to check the visa entitlements of a visa-holder. This facility is not available for organisations outside

39 Section 71 of the Act provides the regulations may provide the way in which evidencing the visa is given.
40 www.immi.gov.au/e_visa/vevo.htm, accessed 11 February 2011.

Australia (they cannot register) or for Australian passport-holders. Only the registered organisations[41] have access to this facility.

Employers and labour supply companies are the most common users of this facility. They can confirm a visa-holder's entitlement to work in Australia when such a person is in Australia permanently or temporarily.

Education providers are also noted beneficiaries of this facility as they can check the study entitlement of a visa-holder (student). Certain other organisations may also need to check visa-holder entitlements, and to check whether a person is in Australia permanently or temporarily.

Individuals can also use VEVO to ascertain their own visa details.

An advantage of VEVO is that a person no longer needs a visa label in their passport and can verify their status online.

41 Employers and labour suppliers, educational institutions, licensing authorities, commercial or government organisations to check residence status, government organisations to check immigration status, migration agents, Medicare Australia.

5

Family and interdependency migration and other Australia-based visas

5.1 Overview

The migration legislation provides for several categories of family migration on the basis that the visa applicant is a relative (within a defined degree) of the sponsor or has an interdependent relationship with the sponsor. That is, the visa categories in the family stream are predicated on a relationship, and each visa necessarily involves two parties, namely the applicant and the applicant's sponsor or nominator. In addition, the visa application might include members of the applicant's family unit. In general, the latter are not required to meet all criteria for a particular application and are not the subject of discussion in this chapter. They are assessed on the basis that they are, in fact, members of the family unit and meet secondary criteria related to health and character requirements, as alluded to in the previous chapter (at 4.5).

The visa subclasses for applicants migrating from overseas under the family categories are: Partner (100); Child (101); Adoption (102); Parent (103); Aged Dependent Relative (114); Remaining Relative (115); Carer (116); Orphan Relative (117); Designated Parent (118); and Contributory Parent (143). Most of these family stream visas for migrants from abroad have an equivalent visa for onshore applicants: Partner (801); Child (802); Aged Parent (804); Aged Dependent Relative (838); Remaining Relative (835); Carer (836); Orphan Relative (837); and Contributory Aged Parent (864).

For people already in Australia who want to change their status to permanent residence, the visa applicant, in most cases, must hold a substantive visa without a 'no further stay' condition (Schedule 8, Item 8503), although that condition can be waived in certain 'compelling and compassionate' circumstances. Generally, the applicant must meet the same criteria as an offshore applicant. In some cases, higher threshold criteria have been added to the criteria that apply to applications made onshore. For instance, parents who apply onshore must be 'aged' (eligible for an age pension) at the time of the application. Onshore applicants who do not hold a substantive visa may be able to lodge valid applications in restricted circumstances, depending on the visa subclass being sought and/or the reason their substantive visa expired without having been renewed. The requirements for such applicants are set out in Schedule 3 of the Regulations. On the other hand, an onshore applicant may get some practical advantages over an offshore applicant: an onshore applicant for a spouse visa, for instance, may get a bridging visa to stay in Australia till DIAC makes a decision.

There are further visa categories that cater for offshore applicants who intend to formally marry their sponsor after the initial application is lodged, either after they arrive in Australia – Prospective Marriage (300) – or after the application is lodged but before it is decided – Partner (Provisional) (309). In each case, once the marriage is formalised, the applicant joins the spouse stream of visa applicants.

For applications made prior to 1 September 2007 there were provisions for family members to sponsor relatives who have the necessary skills to enter Australia in the skills stream of visas: Skilled – Australian-sponsored (138); and Skilled – Designated Area-sponsored (Provisional) visa, subclass 496 (which commenced on 1 July 2006 as a subclass of the Skilled – Designated Area-sponsored (Provisional) (class UZ) visa and replaced the Skilled – Designated Area-sponsored (139) permanent resident visa. For subclass 138 applications, the familial relationship increases the number of points an applicant must obtain to pass the points test that is a criterion for being granted the visa. For subclass 139 visas, the relationship contributes to the policy aim of directing skilled persons to areas designated by the government as needing, among other things, people with employment skills. Holders of that visa are eligible to satisfy the criteria for the grant of a Sponsored – Designated Area-sponsored (Residence)(class CC) (883) visa if they hold the visa 496 for at least two years, comply with its conditions, live in a designated area for at least two years (except for short absences for business or recreation purposes) and work full-time in a designated area for at least 12 months.

Applicants who meet the criteria for each visa subclass are not automatically granted a visa, as they may fall within the operation of the capping provisions of sections 85–86 of the Act and be directed into a queue pending a final approval. Capping provisions do not apply to spouses, de facto partners and dependent children,[1] including applicants for orphan relative visas (subclasses 117 and 837). Section 87A also provides exemption from the capping provision for applicants who fail to meet health or character criteria due to circumstances beyond their control that have arisen since they were placed in the queue.

1 *Migration Act 1958* (Cth), s 87.

The Minister for Immigration and Citizenship capped the number of subclass 138 and 139 visas for the 2009–10 financial year at 546.[2] All other outstanding visa applications have been taken not to been have made, and the visa application charge has been refunded.[3] The subclass 138 and 139 visas have now been superseded by subclass 176 (Skilled – Sponsored).[4]

5.2 Sponsorship, assurances of support and bonds

5.2.1 Sponsorship

The general role of sponsors is the subject of regulation 1.20 (see 4.5 in the previous chapter). In all family visa categories, the sponsor must be an Australian citizen or permanent resident or an eligible New Zealand citizen. Regulations 1.20J and 1.20K impose some restrictions on sponsors of applicants for partner, prospective partner, and remaining relative visas. In some categories, the sponsor must be 'settled'. Regulation 1.03 defines 'settled' as meaning lawfully resident in Australia for a reasonable period. PAM3 states:

> Under policy, two years (as at time of visa application) is generally considered to be a 'reasonable period'. However, when assessing whether or not a person is 'settled', each case is to be considered on an individual basis with regard given to the facts of the case, such as extended periods of temporary residence.[5]

Partner visas require the applicant and sponsor to be of opposite sexes.[6] Regulation 1.15A was substituted to provide that the Minister will consider all the circumstances of the relationship in relation to an application for a partner visa. The requirement that only people of the opposite sex can meet the definition of spouse was unsuccessfully challenged by a homosexual couple under the *Sex Discrimination Act 1984* (Cth). The Federal Court found that neither the appellant nor his partner was treated less favourably than a person of the opposite sex might be treated in the same circumstances. The court found that:

> It is not correct to say that either Mr Rohner or Mr Biondi Tineo was, by reason of his sex, treated less favourably than, in similar circumstances, a person of the opposite sex would have been treated. For a female visa applicant, as for a male, a 'spouse' is a person of the opposite sex. Discrimination by reason of the sex of the person with whom one has a relationship is not discrimination on the ground of one's sex. It must be borne in mind that, for the purpose of an application for a visa in subclass 410, each of the two people concerned – the one claiming to satisfy the primary criteria and the other claiming to meet the secondary criteria – is treated as a separate applicant: see particularly 410.311. In each case, the relevant question is whether that applicant is discriminated against by reason of his or her sex, not that of the other applicant.[7]

2 IMMI 10/023, signed 24 June 2010.
3 PAM3: Sch. 2, Visa 138, Latest Changes.
4 Direction No. 48, Order of consideration – certain skilled migration visas, signed 14 July 2010.
5 PAM3: Div. 1.4 – Form 40 sponsors and sponsorship, s 16.1.
6 *Marriage Act 1961* (Cth), s 5 – definition of 'marriage', *Migration Act 1958* (Cth), s 5F.
7 *Rohner v Minister for Immigration and Ethnic Affairs* [1997] 1202 FCA (7 November 1997).

That decision was upheld on appeal,[8] where Keifel J, writing the leading judgment, held that:

> The circumstance which mirrors the example put forward by the appellants is one where a male applicant had a female partner. In neither case does the operation of the Migration Regulations differentiate between a male and female applicant. They are treated the same.
>
> An effect of regulation 1.15A is to discriminate, but the less favourable treatment is directed to couples of the same sex. The reason, apparent from the regulations, for that less favourable treatment is because of their relationship, which is to say the result of their decision as to their sexual practice. The regulations reflect some policy, but it is not necessary to comment upon the appropriateness of it in these times. The discrimination effected by the regulation is not, however, because of an applicant's sex. It is because of the nature of their relationship and the sex of their partner.

That does not mean that same-sex couples are excluded from the regulatory regime. For the purposes of a de facto relationship under section 5CB of the Act the Minister must consider all circumstances, including the financial aspects of the relationship: joint ownership of assets, joint liabilities, and other legal obligations and financial commitments. The Minister shall also consider the responsibility to the household, including children (if any); the aspects of the relationship, if they represent to others as being in a de facto relationship; and the duration of the relationship, including the length of time living together and the degree of emotional support they draw from each other.[9] Therefore they can extend to relationships between friends who are mutually dependent and cohabit but are not in a same-sex marriage-like relationship.

Spouse and de facto relationships do not involve a blood relationship. In each of the other visa categories listed above, however, the sponsor must be a blood relative who is an Australian citizen or permanent resident, or an eligible New Zealand citizen (see section 4.6). There are exceptions for some categories, and in limited circumstances, where the sponsor can be a relative by marriage, usually the spouse of the Australian blood relative of the visa applicant.

In some categories, the relationship between the applicant and sponsor is self-explanatory, as it goes to the core of the application: for instance, in the case of spouse parent and child visas. In others, the sponsor must be a 'relative', which is defined in Regulation 1.03 as:

> (i) a close relative; or
> (ii) a grandparent, grandchild, aunt, uncle, niece or nephew, or a step-grandparent, step-grandchild, step-aunt, step-uncle, step-niece or step-nephew.

The same regulation defines a 'close relative' as:

> (a) the spouse or de facto partner of the person; or
> (b) a child, parent, brother or sister of the person; or
> (c) a step-child, step-brother or step-sister of the person.

8 *Rohner v MIMA* [1998] 1006 FCA (24 August 1998).
9 Regulation 1.09A.

5.2.2 Assurances of support and bonds

All family visas have provision for an assurance of support. In all categories except partner, prospective partner and child visas, the assurances are mandatory. In contributory parent categories, they are more onerous than for other categories. In addition, the assurer must arrange payment of a social security bond (see Chapter 4 at 4.5.1).

5.3 Partner visas

In providing visas for life partners, the legislation provides for onshore and offshore visa categories that take into account engaged couples, de jure and de facto spouses and same-sex partners. The relevant visas are as follows:

- **Partner (Migrant) (class BC)**[10]
- Subclass 100 (Partner)[11]
- **Partner (Residence) (class BS)**[12]
- Subclass 801(Partner)[13]
- **Partner (Provisional) (class UF)**[14]
- Subclass 309 (Partner (Provisional))[15]
- **Partner (Temporary) (class UK)**[16]
- Subclass 820 (Spouse)[17]
- **Prospective Marriage (Temporary) (class TO)**[18]
- Subclass 300 (Prospective Marriage).[19]

A condition of Prospective Marriage visas is that the parties have met and are known to each other personally (clause 300.214). PAM3 states:

> Policy would intend that the parties have met as adults.
>
> The onus is on the applicant and their *prospective spouse* to provide satisfactory evidence of having met in person. Written correspondence or contact by phone, fax or the Internet *does not* constitute having 'met' [emphasis added]. The parties must have met even if an Australian court has given permission to marry.[20]
>
> [Emphasis in original.]

That requirement raises some significant issues for migrant groups that have a culture of arranged marriages, including the recent large intake of refugees from the Middle East and Afghanistan. The problem is partially ameliorated by the policy on minors:

10 Sch. 1, Item 1129.
11 ibid.
12 Sch. 1, Item 1124B.
13 ibid.
14 Sch. 1, Item 1220A.
15 ibid.
16 Sch. 1, Item 1214C.
17 ibid.
18 Sch. 1, Item 1215.
19 ibid.
20 PAM3: Sch. 2, Visa 300, 3.1.

> If the parties have met but not as adults, officers should require a higher level of proof that the parties are 'known to each other'.
>
> To gauge the extent to which the parties are known to each other, officers may wish to consider evidence such as:
>
> - evidence of contact that shows the development of the relationship
> - whether the relationship is traditionally or culturally appropriate within the circumstances of the applicant and their *prospective spouse* and
> - interviews with both the applicant and their *prospective spouse* (if appropriate).[21]

That policy still precludes arranged marriages among members of the extended family where the parties have not met, but it is traditional for them to marry.

Applications for partner visas have more or less the same criteria and procedures.

The following commentary largely addresses the law as it relates to partner visa applications, but insofar as it discusses the assessment of the relationship between the applicant and sponsor and the domestic violence provisions, it applies equally to de facto relationships, unless there is an expression to the contrary or differences are apparent from the context.

In each visa category, there is some restriction on sponsors who have sponsored a previous applicant, although the restriction can be waived in compelling circumstances.[22] Provided there is no such restriction, the applicant applies for permanent residence at the outset but, if successful, is first granted a temporary visa that permits him/her to reside in Australia until the permanent visa application is determined. That final consideration is not given until two years after the initial application was lodged, and success is contingent on the relationship continuing, with exceptions where the sponsor has passed away and for victims of domestic violence. In spouse cases, there is an added exception where the relationship has ended but there is a dependent child involved with whom the applicant has a legal relationship. In addition, the two-year period can be abridged for people in a long-term partner relationship, defined in regulation 1.03 as:

> . . . a relationship between the applicant and another person, each as the spouse or de facto partner of the other, that has continued:
>
> (a) if there is a dependent child (other than a step-child) of both the applicant and the other person – for not less than 2 years; or
>
> (b) in any other case – for not less than 5 years.

In that case, subclause 801.221(6A) allows a visa 801 to be granted within the two-year period provided the couple were already in a long-term partner relationship when the application was made.

In order to satisfy a decision-maker that a married relationship exists, the applicant must demonstrate that:

21 PAM3: Sch. 2, Visa 300, 3.2.
22 Regulation 1.20J(1) and (2).

- they are married to each other under a marriage that is valid for the purpose of the Act: Migration Act section 5F(2)(a);
- the couple have a mutual commitment to a shared life as husband and wife to the exclusion of all others: Migration Act section 5F(2)(b);
- the relationship is genuine and continuing: Migration Act section 5F(2)(c);
- they live together (Migration Act, section 5F(2)(d)(i); or do not live speratly apart on a permanent basis (section 5F(2)(d)(ii).

Regulation 1.15 provides matters that must be considered when considering an supplication for a partner visa. These include:

- The financial aspects of the relationship (regulation 1.15A(3)(a)), including: any joint ownsership of real estate or other major assets (i); any joint liabilities (ii); the extent of any pooling of financial resources (iii); whether one person owes any legal obligation in respect of the other (iv); and the basis of any sharing of day-to-day household expenses (v).
- The nature of the household (regulation 1.15A(3)(b)), including: any joint responsibility for the care and support of children (i); the living arrangements (ii); and any sharing of the responsibility for housework(iii).
- The social aspects of the relationship (regulation 1.15A(3)(c)), including: whether the persons represent themselves to other people as being married to each other (i); the opinion of the persons' friends and acquaintances about the nature of the relationship (ii); and any basis on which the persons plan to undertake joint social activities (iii).
- The nature of the persons' commitment to each other (regulation 1.15A(3)(d)), including: the duration of the relationship (i); the length of time during which the persons have lived together (ii); the degree of companionship and emotional support that the persons draw from each other (iii); and whether the persons see the relationship as a long-term one (iv).

Similar requirements apply to de facto relationships. While de jure spouses rely on a formal marriage, de facto applicants must demonstrate that they have lived together for at least the 12 months before the application is lodged, unless they can demonstrate compelling and compassionate circumstances warranting an abridgment of that period. There is also an age requirement for de facto partners: both the applicant and their Australian partner must have turned 18.[23] In that regard, PAM3 states:

> In assessing whether or not there are compelling and compassionate circumstances, decision makers are to take into account the circumstances which the Minister considered to be compelling and compassionate, including but not limited to applicants who have a dependent child of the relationship.[24]

There is a further exception to the 12-month rule, under regulation 2.03A(4)(a). It is available to holders of a permanent humanitarian visa who had informed

23 PAM3: Div. 2.1/reg. 2.03A.
24 PAM3: Div. 2.1/reg. 2.30A, s 7.

DIAC of their de facto relationship prior to the grant of that visa. In this case, the minimum age requirement – both parties being 18 years old when the current visa application is made – must still be met.[25]

In regard to valid marriages, section 12 of the *Migration Act 1958* (Cth) provides, in effect, that marriages recognised under the *Marriage Act 1961* (Cth) are recognised for the purposes of the Migration Act. Marriages that are solemnised and recognised under foreign laws are generally recognised under the *Marriage Act 1961* (Cth) (subject to: real consent being given by both spouses; neither partner already being in a valid marriage with another party; the spouses not being within a prohibited relationship; and spouses being of marriageable age).

There is no legal requirement that love or romance is a necessary component of a genuine marriage[26] and the departmental policy guidelines include procedural guidelines for assessing whether or not persons are in a married relationship as described in section 5F of the Act, and are thus each other's spouses as defined in section 5F(1) of the Act, having regard to:[27]

- the requirements of s 5F(2) of the Act; and
- the factors prescribed in regulation 1.15A for the purposes of s 5F(3) of the Act – financial aspects; the nature of the household; the social aspects; and the nature of the commitment.

There are also provisions for arranged, proxy and customary marriages that are more prevalent outside Australia. PAM3 informs decision-makers that in the case of arranged marriages:

> 9.1 The fact that a marriage may have been arranged by relatives, friends or marriage brokers does not affect recognition of the marriage (under the Marriage Act or migration law) unless one of the parties has not given 'real consent' to the marriage... Although an arranged marriage may be recognised under migration law, officers are expected to take particular care in assessing whether the marital relationship meets requirements 5F(2)(b) and (c) of the Act (i.e. a genuine, on-going, mutually-exclusive marital relationship).[28]

In cases of marriage by proxy, the stated policy is that:

> 10.1... the law of the country where the marriage was solemnised (i.e. where the marriage celebrant authorised the marriage) permits consent to be given by proxy; and the marriage was solemnised in accordance with that law; and both parties gave real consent to the marriage.

In respect of customary marriages, the policy requirements are:

> 11.1 Marriages solemnised (in or outside Australia) in accordance with customary or religious practices may not necessarily be recognised as valid under the laws of the country where the ceremony was performed. If not recognised as valid, the relationship should be assessed against s 5CB 'de facto relationship' provisions.

25 ibid.
26 *R v Cahill* (1978) 2 NSWLR 453 at p. 458.
27 PAM3: s 5F – Spouse.
28 ibid.

For the purposes of these provisions, the concept of 'real consent' is taken from section 23B of the Marriage Act: that is, there will not be 'real consent' of either of the parties if consent was obtained by fraud, if a party was mistaken as to the identity of the other or the nature of the ceremony, or if a party was mentally incapable of understanding the nature and effect of the ceremony.

Integral to the definition of 'spouse' is a requirement that each party has given real consent to the relationship, that the visa applicant and sponsor 'have a mutual commitment to a shared life as husband and wife to the exclusion of all others', and that 'the relationship between them is genuine and continuing'. That requirement has its genesis in section 5 of the *Marriage Act 1961* (Cth), where marriage is defined as 'the union of a man and a woman to the exclusion of all others, voluntarily entered into for life'. It has been adopted and adapted by the Federal Court, and is established in the test set out in the leading joint judgment of the Full Court in *Minister for Immigration, Local Government and Ethnic Affairs v Dhillon*,[29] where the court stated:

> The primary judge referred in his reasons to the concept of marriage in Australian law, citing the remarks of Street CJ in *R v Cahill* (1978) 2 NSWLR 453 at p. 458. As his Honour there pointed out, people enter marriages with a variety of purposes and motives, hopes and anticipations, so that it is not possible to classify some purposes etc, as according to what may be described as 'community expectations'. It is not necessarily inconsistent with a genuine marriage relationship that it was entered into by one or both parties with a view to material benefit or advancement, as for example, with the hope of becoming eligible to reside in a particular country. The true test, we would suggest the only test, is whether at the time at which the matter has to be decided it can be said that the parties have a mutual commitment to a shared life as husband and wife to the exclusion of others.[30]

There are many considerations that go to an assessment of the genuineness of a marriage. In the case of *Simpson v Minister for Immigration and Ethnic Affairs*,[31] the court considered the significance of the sexual relationship between spouses – in this case the spouses had given conflicting accounts of the frequency of their sexual activity. In arriving at a conclusion that the decision-maker had not made an error of law in finding that the marriage was not genuine, partly on the basis of the conflicting evidence of the spouses, the court held:

> It was not determinative for an ultimate finding of 'genuine, continuing relationship' that the parties either had sex on one occasion or on frequent occasions in the four weeks they were together. Marriage relationships can be genuine and continuing whether the spouses have frequent sex, little sex, or no sex at all. It would be wrong, and an error of law, to presuppose some standard of frequency of sexual contact and use that as

29 (Northrop, Wilcox and French JJ), 8 May 1990, No. WAG 26 of 1989 FED No. 200 (published on AustLII Federal Court decisions database).
30 *Minister for Immigration, Local Government and Ethnic Affairs v Dhillon*, 8 May 1990, No. WAG 26 of 1989 FED No. 200, [10].
31 Heerey J, 29 July 1994, No. G717 of 1993 FED No. 591/94 (published on AustLII Federal Court decisions database).

> a criterion to determine whether or not a marriage relationship was genuine and continuing.[32]

That case has also been cited as authority for the proposition that evidence that post-dates the application date may, in appropriate circumstances, be taken into account in assessing whether or not there was a genuine marriage at the date of the application. The court found:

> Events which occurred after 27 September 1991 [the application date] may bear on the question as to whether there was a genuine, continuing relationship at that date. One such event is the lack of communication between the spouses about a major misfortune. The weight to be put on such a circumstance is a matter for the decision-maker. The fact that Mr Simpson told his wife that he was in hospital but not the exact nature and cause of his disablement may tend to show there was no existing genuine, continuing relationship between them and accordingly there had not been such a relationship on 27 September 1991 – there being no intervening event to suggest the disruption of a genuine, continuing relationship at the earlier date. On the other hand, this non-disclosure may be explicable on human grounds of reticence or embarrassment on Mr Simpson's part. But those considerations are questions of fact for the decision-maker. It cannot be said as a matter of law that the circumstances of the accident and the applicants' communication about it were irrelevant to the particular decision-making function.[33]

That finding is consonant with the finding of the court in *Bretag v Minister for Immigration, Local Government and Ethnic Affairs*,[34] where O'Loughlin J stated:

> 'It is clear, of course, that the Tribunal was entitled to have regard to evidence that dealt with the relationship between Mr Bretag and the applicant and between Mr Bretag and Leanne subsequent to 28 January 1990 for the purposes of testing the claimed relationship between the applicant and Mr Bretag as at that date and as at the date of the application for [permanent residence] – 7 February 1990. But the evidence of the subsequent history is only relevant so long as it 'tends logically to show the existence or non-existence of facts relevant to the issue to be determined': *Minister for Immigration and Ethnic Affairs v Pochi* (1980) 4 ALD 139 at p. 160 per Deane J.[35]

Since then, the considerations that go into testing whether or not a relationship is genuine and continuing have been incorporated into the Migration Regulations 1994 and the *Migration Act 1958* (Cth). In assessing the relationship, regulation 1.15A obliges the Minister to '. . . have regard to all of the circumstances of the relationship, including, in particular . . . ' various specified circumstances relating to (a) the financial aspects; (b) the nature of the household; (c) the social aspects; and (d) the nature of the persons' commitment to each other.

32 *Simpson v the Minister for Immigration and Ethnic Affairs*, 29 July 1994, No. G717 of 1993 FED No. 591/94, [17].
33 *Simpson v the Minister for Immigration and Ethnic Affairs*, 29 July 1994, No. G717 of 1993 FED No. 591/94, [8].
34 29 November 1991, No. S G72 of 1991 FED No. 755 (published on AustLII Federal Court decisions database).
35 *Bretag v Minister for Immigration, Local Government and Ethnic Affairs*, 29 November 1991, No. S G72 of 1991 FED No. 755, [12].

The importance of regulation 1.15A(3) was addressed by the Full Federal Court in *MIMA v Asif*.[36] In that case the decision-maker was found to be biased largely because he failed to take into account information from third parties, relying on his conclusion that the applicant was not truthful. The court noted that:

> 22.... reg 1.15A(3) identifies classes of evidence from sources other than the applicant which are logically relevant to proving his state of mind on those issues and compels the decision-maker to have regard to such classes of evidence: sub-reg (3) provides that, 'in forming an opinion for the purposes of par 1(b) .... in relation to an application for a visa of sub-class... 820... the Minister **must** have regard to all the circumstances of the relationship including, in particular...', the various considerations set out in that sub-regulation.

Subsequently, in *Nassouh v MIMA*[37] the Federal Court clearly confirmed that regulation 1.15A(3) sets out mandatory considerations for decision-makers in forming an opinion as to whether a married relationship or de facto relationship exists between two persons. It does not follow that that list of considerations is exhaustive, and decision-makers must consider other circumstances brought to their notice by the applicant and/or sponsor pursuant to section 54 of the Act, which requires that the Minister consider all the information in the application.

PAM3 goes on to provide evidentiary guidelines for assessment. They are also useful in providing some sort of guidance for applicants, sponsors and witnesses who make declarations on behalf of the applicant, in terms of the type of information that could be included in statements that decision-makers consider to be relevant:

> 37. Financial aspects:
>
> reg. 1.15A(3)(a)
>
> Examples of major assets would include but are not restricted to:
> - joint loan agreements for real estate (including residential property and leases), cars, major household appliances
> - operating joint bank accounts: evidence that the accounts have been operating with reasonable frequency would be given more weight that just opening such accounts
> - pooling of financial resources in respect of major financial commitments
> - legally binding financial obligations that one party owes to another: for example, as guarantor for a loan and
> - the basis of sharing day-to-day household expenses.
>
> 38. Nature of the household
>
> reg. 1.15A(3)(b)
>
> The living arrangements may be evidenced by (but are not restricted to):
> - joint residential receipts
> - joint utilities accounts (electricity, gas, telephone)
> - correspondence addressed to either or both parties at the same address

36 [2000] FCA 228 (7 March 2000).
37 [2000] FCA 788.

- shared responsibility for care and support of children and
- joint ownership of residential property.

39. Social aspects of the relationship

reg. 1.15A(3)(c)

Officers may be satisfied on the basis of some or all of the following:
- evidence that the relationship has been declared to other government bodies and commercial/public institutions and authorities and acceptance of these declarations by these bodies
- statements of parents, family members, relatives, friends and other interested parties: statements in the form of statutory declarations are preferred as, under policy, they carry more weight (the form for this purpose is 888)
- joint membership of organisations or groups, documentary evidence of joint participation in sporting, social or other activities and
- joint travel and plans for the future.

40. The nature of the commitment

reg. 1.15A(3)(d)

Officers should regard this as requiring an assessment of the degree of the parties' commitment to each other, taking into account:
- knowledge of each other's personal circumstances (this could include background and family situation, which could be established at interview)
- evidence of intentions that the relationship will be long term – the extent to which the parties have combined their affairs and
- the terms of the parties' wills, life insurance policies and/or superannuation policies – policies in each other's favour provide some evidence of an intention that the relationship is permanent.

If parties who are (or until recently, were) living separately claim that their separation is (or was) not permanent, officers need to consider their reasons for the (temporary) separation.

There are exceptions to the success of a spouse application being contingent on a continuing relationship at the time of the final decision. For offshore applicants (but not those applying in Australia), the relevant provisions only apply if the applicant has already been granted a provisional visa. If that visa has not yet been granted, the application will be refused once the changed circumstances come to the decision-maker's attention, regardless of the applicant's circumstances. On the other hand, if the exception provisions do apply, the grant of permanent residence can be made before the expiry of the usual two-year period.

The most common exception arises where the applicant and/or a dependent child of the applicant and/or the sponsor has been the victim of domestic violence. The Regulations create some difficulty in the area of domestic violence as they remove an assessment of the fact that violence has occurred from the decision-maker to a 'competent person' (defined in a list of professionally qualified health/social work/welfare practitioners in regulation 1.21) and require that statutory declarations by those persons have a particular content. That has been the subject of some substantial judicial commentary. The policy aim of the Regulations was adverted to by Lindgren J stated in *Doan v MIMA*,[38] where he stated:

> I have set the provisions out at some length in order to emphasise the concern of the Regulations to ensure that a visa applicant should not enjoy the benefit of the subject exception to the general requirement that there be a genuine and continuing married relationship at the time of the decision unless the domestic violence directed against the visa applicant by the spouse be sufficiently serious and be clearly proved, by appropriate means, to have occurred.

In the Federal Court case of *Du v Minister for Immigration and Multicultural Affairs*,[39] Mathews J held that:

> The Regulations are in quite specific and peremptory terms. It is not sufficient compliance, in my view, with these Regulations for a competent person simply to note the consistency between a person's presentation and their account of domestic violence, or even the occurrence of domestic violence. The Regulations require that the competent person express an opinion in very specific terms, namely, as to whether relevant domestic violence as defined in reg 1.23 has been suffered by a person.
>
> This involves not only an opinion that past acts of violence have occurred but also an assessment of the state of mind of the alleged victim. None of this has been complied with here.

Sundberg J approved that proposition in *Alin v Minister for Immigration and Multicultural Affairs*.[40] In *Meroka v MIMA*[41] Ryan J, setting aside a decision of the Tribunal, posited:

> 32. In my view, it is not sufficient for an applicant to adduce statutory declarations from two 'competent persons' each of which recites the possession of an opinion that relevant domestic violence has been suffered by the applicant. Regulation 1.26(f) imposes the additional requirement that each statutory declaration must set out the evidence on which the competent person's opinion is based. The only purpose which can be imputed to the drafter who inserted that requirement is to provide an opportunity for objective examination of the evidence on which the opinion was based. Thus, if the competent person, in purporting to comply with Reg 1.26(f), were to refer to 'evidence' which was quite unrelated to whether relevant domestic violence had been suffered by the applicant, the alleged victim could not be 'taken' pursuant to Reg 1.23 to have suffered domestic violence.
>
> 33. That is not to say that the Minister (or the Tribunal) can substitute for that of the 'competent person', his or its own opinion of whether domestic violence has been suffered. Operation can be denied to Reg 1.23 only if the description of the nature of the violence experienced or the evidence set out by the competent person is incapable, as a matter of law, of affording a basis for an opinion that relevant domestic violence

38 [2000] FCA 909 (6 July 2000), [22].
39 [2000] FCA 1115 (2 August 2000), [18]–[19].
40 [2002] FCA 979 (7 August 2002).
41 [2002] FCA 482 (19 April 2002).

> has been suffered by an applicant and has been committed by the person identified by the competent person as the perpetrator . . .
>
> 34. . . . the statement of opinion by a competent person will not cause the applicant to be taken to have suffered domestic violence if the description of the nature of the violence, or the evidence on which the express or implied statement of opinion is said to be based, reveals that the competent person misconceived what the definition required for the formation of the requisite opinion.

The operation of domestic violence regulatory provisions (in this case, subclause 801.221(6) relating to an onshore application) was described by Wilcox J in *Ibrahim v Minister for Immigration and Multicultural and Indigenous Affairs*.[42] His Honour noted that the Member had correctly understood the findings of Ryan J in *Meroka v MIMA*:[43]

> 36. . . . In particular, [the Member] appreciated that authority required him to refrain from determining whether or not Mr Ibrahim had suffered domestic violence at the hands of Ms Saleh; his task was only to determine the sufficiency of the statutory declarations supplied by Mr Ibrahim; if there were statutory declarations by two competent people that complied with the requirements of reg 1.26 (and a statutory declaration by Mr Ibrahim under reg 1.25), that was enough.
>
> 37. . . . respectfully agree with Ryan J that this is what is intended by the Regulations. It leads to a curious result. The statutory declarations of the competent persons must state the competent person's opinion that relevant domestic violence has been suffered by the visa applicant (reg 1.26(c) and (d)) and must name the person who, in the competent person's opinion, is the perpetrator of the violence (reg 1.26(e)). However, once that is done, it seems immaterial if these opinions are based entirely on statements made to the competent person by the visa applicant or they lack any apparent credibility.

Justice Wilcox then went on to state:

> 40. The regulatory regime is a triumph of form over substance. Paragraph 801.221(6) creates an exception to the general rule that an application for a subclass 801 visa must continue to be supported by the applicant's spouse. It does so, no doubt, on the humanitarian ground that it would further victimise a victim of domestic violence if a breakdown of the spousal relationship, which may be the result of, or associated with, the domestic violence, thereby disqualified the victim from obtaining the visa to which she or he would otherwise have been entitled. However, although the relevant exception is expressed in para 801.221(6)(c) by reference to a factual situation ('has suffered domestic violence committed by the nominating spouse'), Division 1.5 of the Regulations precludes the visa decision-maker investigating the facts. If the appropriate statutory declarations are provided by the visa applicant, domestic violence 'is taken' to have been suffered by the visa applicant at the hands of the nominating spouse, even if the opinions stated in the statutory declarations lack any discernible cogency. If the visa applicant fails to obtain appropriate statutory declarations, by the required two competent persons, the visa application has to be refused. This is so even if the decision-maker is totally satisfied that the applicant has suffered domestic violence at the hands of his or her spouse.

42 [2002] FCA 1279 (18 October 2002).
43 [2002] FCA 482 (19 April 2002).

The effect of the domestic violence provisions, taking into account the statutory interpretations of the Federal Court, is set out in many MRT decisions, including that of *Cerff, Stephen Cyril*,[44] where the Member stated:

> 32. The domestic violence provisions require that the visa applicant would have continued to meet the requirements of subclause 801.211(2), (3), (4), (5) or (6) that he met at time of application except that the relationship is no longer continuing, and he has suffered domestic violence committed by the nominator.
>
> 33. Division 1.5 contains special provisions relating to domestic violence. Regulations 1.21 to 1.23 define relevant terms and set out when a person is taken to have suffered domestic violence.
>
> 34. The domestic violence provisions are extremely broad. All that is required of a person claiming domestic violence is the evidence of a kind referred to in Migration Regulation 1.23 and 1.24. Regulation 1.26 deals with statutory declaration made by competent persons.
>
> 35. The effect of regulation 1.23 is that once this evidence is produced there is no scope in the Regulations for any further inquiries. The Tribunal is not within power to examine the circumstances that lead to the events that are said to constitute domestic violence. The Tribunal's assessment in the matter under review is therefore limited to whether statutory declarations were made by 'competent persons' as defined and whether the statutory declarations conform to the requirements prescribed by the regulations.
>
> 36. A statutory declaration under regulation 1.26 must be made by a competent person and must set out the basis of the competent person's claim to be a competent person for the purposes of Division 1.5. It must state that, in the competent person's opinion, relevant domestic violence (within the meaning of paragraph 1.23(2)(b)) has been suffered by a person. It must name the persons who, in the opinion of the competent person, has suffered and committed that relevant domestic violence. It must set out the evidence on which the competent person's opinion is based. Competent persons are defined in regulation 1.21.

The meaning of the term 'domestic violence' has also been the subject of judicial scrutiny. In *Cakmak v Minister for Immigration and Multicultural and Indigenous Affairs*,[45] the Full Federal Court determined that it required physical violence or the threat of physical violence. That decision was distinguished in *Sok v Minister for Immigration & Multicultural & Indigenous Affairs*,[46] where the Full Court found that the findings in *Cakmak* were not part of the *ratio decidendi* of the decision and so there was no requirement to follow them. In *Sok*, the male applicant described his life as a being totally dominated by his spouse and her family, who took his wages and monitored his every move. His spouse gambled all of his earnings and savings, demanded he obtain a large sum from his mother and threatened to report him to DIMIA so that he would be deported if he defied her. (Go to p. 16 of the decision for a description of the violence.) In the leading judgment

44 [2003] MRTA 4549 (30 June 2003).
45 [2003] FCAFC 257 [60]–[62].
46 [2005] FCAFC 56 (11 April 2005).

of Branson J, Her Honour found that determining the meaning of 'violence' was the central issue in the case. She concluded:

> 27. I conclude that the better view of the true meaning of regulation 1.23(2)(b) is that the '*violence*' there referred to is not restricted to physical violence. It seems to me that this conclusion accords with notions of fairness and with what may be assumed to be the policy lying behind regulation 1.23(1)(g). Without wishing in any way to diminish the horror of physical violence, it seems unlikely, in my view, that it was intended that while a person who had experienced an act of physical violence at the hands of his or her spouse might be able to bring himself or herself within regulation 1.23(1)(g), a person who had suffered the psychological violence of, for example, being compelled by non-physical means to be complicit in the sexual abuse of a child would necessarily fall outside the regulation.

There are further exceptions to the requirement that the spouse relationship be continuing at the time of the final decision. Again, they are not applicable to offshore applicants whose application for a provisional visa has not been finalised. The death of the sponsor is one of those exceptions but does not automatically result in the application being approved. In such cases, the visa applicant must show that the relationship was genuine and continuing at the time of death and would have continued but for the death of the sponsor. In those circumstances, decision-makers will take into account the considerations that apply to assessing the nature of the relationship at that time. In addition, in regard to the applicant forming a new relationship, PAM3 states:

> It is policy that applicants cannot satisfy this criterion if they have since formed a new spouse relationship (*de jure* or *de facto*). In other words, they are taken to no longer satisfy the 820.211 criterion that requires the decision maker to be satisfied that the applicant would have continued to be the partner of the sponsoring partner.[47] The widowed partner also needs to demonstrate that he/she 'has developed close business, cultural or personal ties in Australia'. In that regard, PAM3 sets out the policy guidelines, which have a seemingly low threshold, such as property ownership, membership and participation in or contribution to arts, literature, music or cultural groups, regular and ongoing contact with relatives or close friends.[48] Nevertheless, those requirements may still present significant difficulties for newcomers to Australia.

A further exception to the requirement that relationships be ongoing applies in spouse cases where the relationship has ceased but the applicant has formal legal rights or obligations in regard to a child.[49]

5.4 Other family visa categories

The following commentary seeks only to address significant criteria that are peculiar to each subclass of visa.

47 PAM3: Sch. 2, Visa 820, 19.4.
48 PAM3: Sch. 2, Visa 820, 19.5.
49 Sch. 2, clause 820.221(3)(b)(ii).

5.4.1 Children

Visas for children are divided into three categories: those for applicants ordinarily regarded as children of the visa applicant who is sponsoring them, including stepchildren and children previously adopted; children adopted by an Australian citizen or permanent resident after the sponsor obtained citizenship or residence; and orphan relatives. The relevant visa classes are:

- **Child (Migrant) (class AH)**[50]
- Subclass 101 (Child)[51]
- Subclass 102 (Adoption)[52]
- Subclass 117 (Orphan Relative)[53]
- **Child (Residence) (class BT)**[54]
- Subclass 802 (Child)[55]
- Subclass 837 (Orphan Relative).[56]

5.4.1.1 Child (subclasses 101 and 802)

Applicants for a child visa can be a natural child or a stepchild or an adopted child, and all must meet the definition of 'dependent child' (regulation 1.03). That is, they must be (i) children under 18; or (ii) children 18 and over[57] who are still dependent; or (iii) children 18 and over who have a disability that incapacitates them for work due to the total or partial loss of their bodily or mental functions. Sponsors must demonstrate that they have the legal right or consent of others, with the right to determine where the applicant lives.[58] Dependent children cannot be married, engaged or in full-time employment. If they are over 18, they must be undertaking a full-time course of study leading to an award of professional, trade or vocational qualification, or commence studies within 6 months (or a reasonable time after) completing secondary school.[59] Under regulation 1.03 there is no test for dependency for minor children, but children over 18 and still claimed to be dependent must meet the definition of 'dependent' in regulation 1.05A. In essence, that requires that they are financially reliant on the sponsoring parent for basic needs.

Adult children with a disability that incapacitates them for work meet the definition of dependent child for that reason. However, adult or minor children with a disability will most likely encounter problems meeting the health criteria (see previous chapter, section 4.5). In such circumstances, applicants for a child

50 Sch. 1, Item 1108.
51 ibid.
52 ibid.
53 ibid.
54 Sch. 1, Item 1108A.
55 ibid.
56 ibid.
57 Limited to 25 years old by subclause 101.211(1)(b). It should be noted, however, that the age restriction is peculiar to the child visa subclass and that, in other visa applications, dependency of children of principal visa applicants is determined by the application of the definition in regulation 1.05A, which does not have an age restriction.
58 Sch. 4, criterion 4017.
59 Sch. 2, clause 101.213(1)(c); PAM3: Sch. 2, Visa 802, 12.2.

visa are entitled to seek a health waiver[60] on the basis that granting the visa is unlikely to result in undue cost to the Australian community or undue prejudice to the access to health care or community services of an Australian citizen or permanent resident.

5.4.1.2 Adoption (subclasses 102 and 802)

A child who has been adopted and was a member of the sponsor's family unit before the sponsor became a permanent resident is sponsored for a child visa. Children adopted after the sponsor became a permanent resident must apply for an adoption visa (102) if they are offshore. For onshore applicants, adoption falls within the child subclass 802 visa.[61]

All adoptions must be approved by the relevant overseas authorities and recognised under Australian law. The overseas authorities must also approve the departure of the child for the purpose of custody and adoption by the Australian sponsor parent. The definition of 'adoption' in regulation 1.04 provides that adoptions can be formal or customary, although in the latter case DIAC warns decision-makers that 'it is extremely rare for a customary adoption to sever the legal ties between the child and their pre-adoption parents, [and] the pre-adoption parent will almost always retain custody rights in respect of a customarily adopted child'.[62] That undermines the requirement that the adopter has a parental role and parental rights. The definition also requires that the adoption take place before the child reaches 18 years old. Thus if the child was older, the adoption will not be recognised as such for the purposes of migration law.

The issue of adoption most frequently arises in assessing whether 'adopted' children are members of a primary applicant's family unit. The fact that formal adoption is theoretically available does not exclude the possibility that a child might have been adopted by custom. In the MRT matter of *Sam, Sophy*,[63] the Tribunal set out the relevant claims as follows:

> 34. The parties claim that although legal adoption was available in Cambodia when the primary visa applicant assumed responsibility for the secondary visa applicants in 1996, the practice in the villages was not to make legal arrangements, because the only important issue was that someone would care for orphaned children. They claimed that the secondary visa applicants had no other relatives to care for them, that the primary visa applicant had been living in their father's house since before they were born, and that he agreed to care for them before their father died from Malaria in 1996. The parties stated that the primary visa applicant and the secondary visa applicants all lived with Thoen Thoek until the review applicant travelled to Cambodia in 1999, and then the children remained with Thoen Thoek only during the school week. They stated that the children cooked their own simple meals whilst staying with Thoen Thoek in 1999 and the review applicant cooked for them when they stayed at the farm with the primary visa applicant. The review applicant stated that this arrangement meant

60 Sch. 4, criterion 4007(2).
61 Sch. 2, clause 802.213.
62 PAM3: Div. 1.2/reg. 1.04, Adoption, s 13.1.
63 [2004] MRTA 475 (29 January 2004).

that the primary visa applicant did not need to give Thoen Thoek any money for the children's care.

35. The review applicant stated that the primary visa applicant continues to be personally and financially responsible for the secondary visa applicants, which results in some detriment to herself and their Australian child because he will need to visit them regularly and send more money than they can afford to spare whilst she is not working.

The Member then considered the evidence provided by the primary applicant in the context of the definition of adoption and found:

37. The Tribunal takes into account the evidence provided by the parties, most particularly the evidence given by the review applicant at the Tribunal hearing. The Tribunal accepts that, although formal adoption would have been available in Cambodia after the primary visa applicant assumed responsibility for the secondary visa applicants, local practice in his village in Battambang Province was not to make any formal arrangements. The Tribunal also accepts that the secondary visa applicants have no other relatives in Cambodia to care for them, that the arrangement with Thoen Thoek was a logical and practical solution to the primary visa applicant's childcare problems after his foster father died, and that their placement with Mr Hok is no longer suitable. The Tribunal finds that there are no other parental figures in the secondary visa applicants' lives, and accepts that the arrangements for the children's care by Thoen Thoek and by Mr Hok have been made on behalf of the primary visa applicant as foster care placements only.

38. The Tribunal finds that the primary visa applicant *customarily adopted* the secondary visa applicants when he assumed parental care for the then five and seven year old children after the death of their natural father in 1996.

For countries that are party to the Convention on Protection of Children and Cooperation in Respect of Intercountry Adoption 1993 (the Adoption Convention) or have a bilateral adoption agreement with Australia, arrangements for adoption are made through the relevant state welfare authorities in Australia that have responsibility for adoption. Among other things, those authorities approve prospective adoptive parents. As a matter of policy, they do not permit prospective adoptive parents to choose a particular child. Rather, they approve prospective parents on the basis that they will be allocated a child by one of the agencies approved under the auspices of the Adoption Convention or bilateral agreement.

The Federal Court has discussed the policy reasons in regard to adoption in the matter of *EC v Minister for Immigration and Multicultural and Indigenous Affairs*.[64] In that case, the sponsoring Australian relatives were both Australian citizens, living in Australia, and had adopted the child by a court order of the Vanuatu Supreme Court issued in April 2003. They sought a Child (Migrant) (Class AH) visa in July 2003. That class includes the subclasses of Child (101), Adoption (102) and Orphan Relative (117). Kenny J recorded:

64 [2004] FCA 978 (29 July 2004).

> 13.... the Tribunal found (and it is not disputed) that the adopted child could not satisfy subclause 101.211(1)(c), because she was neither the 'natural child' or 'step-child' of the adoptive parents... nor had she been adopted by a person who satisfied the description in par (ii), since her adoptive parents were Australian citizens at the time of her adoption...
>
> 14. The Tribunal also found (and it is no longer disputed) that the adopted child could not meet the criteria in subclause 102.211(2) because, at the time of application, neither of the adoptive parents had been residing overseas for more than 12 months.

In considering an argument that the applicant met the criteria for an adoption visa (102) her Honour observed:

> 31. In Australia, the laws of the respective States and Territories make provision for foreign and inter-country adoptions, although the Commonwealth is also necessarily involved because of the obligations it has assumed under international instruments and its other responsibilities, including those with respect to immigration.
>
> 32. Broadly speaking, the States and Territories have similar regimes with respect to foreign adoptions...
>
> 33. The State and Territory 'twelve month' residence provisions are reflected in subclause 102.211(2) of Sch 2 of the Regulations.
>
> 34.... The criteria in clause 102.211(3) and (4) of Sch 2 of the Regulations reflect the Commonwealth's recognition of the arrangements made by the States and Territories with respect to inter-country adoptions, as well as its international responsibilities.
>
> 35. The need to regulate inter-country adoptions in order to protect children is recognised by international instruments to which Australia has subscribed. The Adoption Convention, which entered into force for Australia on 1 December 1998, and the United Nations Convention on the Rights of the Child, which entered into force for Australia on 16 January 1991 (see art 21), recognise that, although inter-country adoption may provide a child with the benefit of a permanent family where none is available in his or her birth country, inter-country adoption may also give scope for trafficking in children and create conditions for their abandonment:... amongst other things, the Adoption Convention defines internationally agreed minimum standards for inter-country adoption.
>
> 36. Some of the relevant criteria for a subclass 102 (Adoption) visa were introduced in response to Australia's adoption of the Adoption Convention...
>
> 37. Other criteria for a subclass 102 (Adoption) visa also reflect the Commonwealth's recognition of the need to regulate inter-country adoptions in order to protect the interests of children who may be affected by such adoptions. In summary, the State, Territory and Commonwealth legislative provisions that deal with inter-country adoptions recognise that arrangements for such adoptions should be such as to ensure that the adoption is in the best interests of the child.

In considering the fact that the applicant had been adopted a few months before the application was made and the ensuing argument that the parents were therefore 'relatives' for the purpose of sponsoring an orphan relative (see below), the court found:

> 37. If it were possible for a person to become a 'relative' or 'Australian relative' merely by obtaining an adoption order in a foreign jurisdiction and, by this means, to fulfil the condition in clause 117.211(b), the visa provisions that are designed to assist in the regulation of inter-country adoptions could be readily circumvented. I reject the applicant's submission that reg 1.14(c) would safeguard the best interests of a child in a manner equivalent to the more stringent criteria for a subclass 102 (Adoption) visa.

In cases where the state welfare authorities are not involved, sponsors must have lived overseas for at least 12 months before lodging the application for the child they have adopted, and they must demonstrate that they did not live overseas for the purpose of circumventing the requirements for entry to Australia of adopted children. That 12-month period can be abridged for onshore applications because of compelling or compassionate circumstances,[65] although PAM3 does not provide guidance for what those particular circumstances might be.

5.4.1.3 Orphan relative (subclasses 117 and 837)

'Orphan relative' is defined in regulation 1.14. The person must be a 'relative' of the sponsor (see 5.2, above), must not have a spouse or de facto partner, must be under 18 years old, and cannot be cared for by either parent because each of them is either dead, permanently incapacitated or of unknown whereabouts. It must also be in the best interests of the applicant to grant the visa. PAM3 states: 'The child is not an orphan relative if there is at least one parent alive whose whereabouts are known and who is not permanently incapacitated.'[66] It is not sufficient that the parents are unwilling to care for the child or have relinquished custody to the Australian relative if they have the capacity to care for the child. In some circumstances, it may be more appropriate to apply for this visa rather than an adoption visa.

The Federal Court has considered the interpretation of orphan relative in *EC v Minister for Immigration and Multicultural and Indigenous Affairs*.[67] The MRT Member had found that the application must fail, as: 'the "Australian relative" link to the visa applicant under clause 117.211 in this case must exist other than as a consequence of the adoption . . . ' In respect of the argument that the MRT Member was mistaken in finding that the applicant did not meet the definition of orphan relative for that reason, the court noted:

> 26. As counsel for the applicant acknowledged, the adopted child in this case cannot satisfy clause 117.211(a) because she cannot satisfy the definition of 'orphan relative' in reg 1.14. As already noted, it was her contention that the adopted child satisfies clause 117.211(b) since she was not an orphan relative 'only because' the sponsoring Australian relative had adopted her. The submission was that the adopted child could not satisfy the definition of 'orphan relative' in reg 1.14 'only because', following her

65 Sch. 2, clause 802.213(5)(b)(ii).
66 PAM3: Div. 1.2/reg. 1.14.
67 [2004] FCA 978 (29 July 2004) per Kenny J.

adoption, she could not satisfy paragraph (b) of this definition since her adoptive parents, who were within the definition of 'parent' in reg 1.03, were not dead, permanently incapacitated or of unknown whereabouts.

27. I reject this submission. It is not correct to say that the adopted child is not an orphan relative 'only because' she has been adopted. If the applicant and his wife had not adopted her, then she would have no relevant relationship with them. When clause 117.211(b) is read with clause 117.211(a), the meaning of clause 117.211(b) is patent. Clause 117.211(b) applies where the visa applicant would be 'an orphan relative of an Australian relative of the applicant' if he or she had not been adopted by that Australian relative. The adopted child would not have been an 'orphan relative' of either adoptive parent but for her adoption, because, but for her adoption, she would not be 'a relative' of either of them and could not satisfy reg 1.14(a)(iii).

29.... paragraph (b) of clause 117.211 provides for the situation where an adoption *prevents* a person satisfying the definition of 'orphan relative' and not for the circumstance where an adoption *enables* a person to satisfy the definition of 'relative' but not 'orphan relative'.

30. Further, the construction for which the applicant contends would defeat the object of the provisions for subclass 102 (Adoption) visas, which form part of the Commonwealth, State and Territory arrangements for foreign and inter-country adoptions.

5.4.2 Parents

The quota for parent visas is small compared with the number of applications and therefore there is a long waiting list. However, some provision is made to have an application expedited if the applicant is willing to contribute to potential health and welfare costs. In addition, onshore applicants must reach an age eligibility threshold before they can successfully meet the criteria. The relevant visa classes are:

- **Parent (Migrant) (class AX)**[68]
- Subclass 103 (Parent)[69]
- **Aged Parent (Residence) (class BP)**[70]
- Subclass 804 (Aged Parent)[71]
- **Contributory Parent (Migrant) (class CA)**[72]
- Subclass 143 (Contributory Parent)[73]
- **Contributory Aged Parent (Residence) (class DG)**[74]
- Subclass 864 (Aged Parent)[75]
- **Contributory Parent (Temporary) (class UT)**[76]

68 Sch. 1, Item 1124.
69 ibid.
70 Sch. 1, Item 1124A.
71 ibid.
72 Sch. 1, Item 1130.
73 ibid.
74 Sch. 1, Item 1130A.
75 ibid.
76 Sch. 1, Item 1221.

- Subclass 173 (Contributory Parent (Temporary))[77]
- **Contributory Aged Parent (Temporary) (class UU)**[78]
- Subclass 884 (Contributory Aged Parent (Temporary))[79]
- **Designated Parent (Migrant) (class BY)**[80]
- Subclass 118 (Designated Parent)[81]
- **Designated Parent (Residence) (class BZ)**[82]
- Subclass 859 (Designated Parent).[83]

The category of visas for 'Designated Parents' (subclasses 118 and 859) are for applicants for an Aged Parent visa (subclass 113 under now repealed legislation) lodged between 1 November 1998 and 30 March 1999 and have a very restricted application. Those categories are not discussed in this chapter.

Parent visas are contingent on a child/parent relationship. However, the mere fact of a parental relationship with the sponsor is a necessary but not a sufficient requirement for success. Parents of sponsors cannot succeed in their application unless they demonstrate that they pass the balance of family test, defined in regulation 1.05. Parents in the non-contributory categories must meet the test both at the time of application and at the time of decision, whereas those in the contributory categories only need to meet it at the time of decision. The definition has three basic, alternative tests: (i) all the applicant's children are lawfully and permanently resident in Australia (or eligible New Zealand citizens); (ii) the applicant parent must have as many or more children permanently resident in Australia than abroad; or (iii) more children are permanently resident in Australia than in any single overseas country. Thus, children who are citizens or have permanent resident status but live abroad are not counted as Australian residents; nor are children who are not permanent residents but have lived in Australia for a lengthy period.

For the purposes of the balance of family test, the applicant's children include those of a former spouse who were born before or during the former marriage.[84] On the other hand, children who have been removed from the exclusive custody of the applicant (other than in consequence of marriage) and certain children registered as refugees or otherwise victims of human rights abuses and unable to be reunited with the family in another country are not considered for the test. As well, stepchildren who were 18 years old when the parent applicant became the spouse of that child's parent are not taken into account if the applicant is permanently separated or divorced from the child's parent, or the latter is deceased.

There are two major visa categories for parents of Australian residents or citizens or eligible New Zealand citizens. They are the parent and contributory

77 ibid.
78 Sch. 1, Item 1221A.
79 ibid.
80 Sch. 1, Item 1111A.
81 ibid.
82 Sch. 1, Item 1111B.
83 ibid.
84 Migration Regulations 1994, regulation 1.05(1)(a).

subclasses. To encourage applications for the contributory classes, the government caps numbers available for the non-contributory classes at a much lower level than the contributory classes. At the time of writing, there are 1000 visa places under the parent category, with an approximate wait of 20 years, and 7500 under the contributory parent category – the wait time is estimated at approximately 18 months for new applicants. Those applicants have been screened and meet all the substantive visa criteria other than the provision of an assurance of support.

The salient distinction between the two major categories is that contributory parents make significant contributions to potential health and income support payments the government might need to make, through means of high visa application charges. Those charges are set out in Schedule 1, Items 1130 and 1130A. In addition to the usual first instalment, there is a second instalment of $37 965. The payments can be defrayed by the applicant first obtaining a temporary visa that remains current for two years,[85] in which case the second instalment is $15 185, and then paying $13 745 when the permanent visa is granted.

For offshore applicants,[86] the parental relationship with the sponsor is a threshold criterion. For onshore applicants[87] an age threshold is added, as the applicant must also be an 'aged parent' – defined as 'a parent who is old enough to be granted an age pension under the *Social Security Act 1991*'.[88] The child of the applicant in all parent categories must be 'settled' in Australia.[89]

These categories permit non-blood relatives to sponsor applicants, so that if the child sponsor of the parent cannot meet relevant sponsorship requirements, a settled spouse, close relative or guardian, or a community organisation, can assume sponsorship obligations. All parent categories require that an assurance of support be provided, as well as a bond for each applicant included in the application, payable as a condition of the grant of the permanent visa.[90] The assurance is for two years in the non-contributory categories and ten years in the contributory categories, with correspondingly differential bonds.

5.4.3 Aged dependent relatives (subclasses 114 and 838)

As the visa name expresses, and according to the definition of the term in regulation 1.03, an aged dependent relative must be 'dependent' on the sponsor, 'aged'

85 Subclass 173 if offshore and 884 if onshore.
86 Subclasses 103, 143 and 173.
87 Subclasses 804, 884 and 864.
88 Migration Regulations 1994, regulation 1.03.
89 Regulation 1.03 defines 'settled' as meaning lawfully resident in Australia for a reasonable period. In this subclass of visa, the policy guideline is two years.
90 For comments on assurances and bonds see Chapter 4 at 4.5.1.

and a 'relative' of the sponsor.[91] They must also be single, have been dependent on the sponsor for a reasonable period and remain dependent, and the sponsoring relative must be 'settled' or, if the blood relative is not settled, the settled, cohabiting spouse of the relative can be the sponsor.

The definition of dependent, discussed above, relates only to financial reliance of the applicant on the sponsor. That is an issue of fact, determined on the evidence provided by the applicant. In regard to what constitutes a 'reasonable period' for the purposes of dependence, the policy guidelines provide a different 'reasonable period' from the period that a sponsor is 'settled' for sponsorship purposes. PAM3 states:

> Under policy specific to this provision, a reasonable period is taken to be three years.
>
> It is always open for officers to decide that dependency has existed for a 'reasonable period', being less than three years, if otherwise satisfied that the applicant has received from the Australian relative ongoing support (consistent with the policy guidelines above on dependency).[92]

5.4.4 Remaining relatives (subclasses 115 and 835)

A remaining relative[93] is the last relative outside Australia of a parent, brother, sister, stepparent, stepbrother or stepsister of the applicant who is an Australian citizen, an Australian permanent resident or an eligible New Zealand citizen and is usually resident in Australia.

Until 1 November 2005, there was a gloss that related to the definition of an 'overseas near relative'. If a visa applicant had no more than three overseas near relatives and those they did have usually resided in third countries (not being Australia), those relatives did not count if there had not been any contact between the applicant and/or the applicant's spouse and the overseas near relative/s for a reasonable period before the application.[94] Following litigation over the meaning of the definition as it then stood,[95] the government perceived that the interpretation of the definition had been diluted and did not meet its policy requirements. It simplified the definition by removing those aspects that related to relatives who resided in third countries and contact with such relatives. Since 1 November 2005, the statutory definition of remaining relative reads:

> 1.15 (1) An applicant for a visa is a *remaining relative* of another person who is an Australian citizen, an Australian permanent resident or an eligible New Zealand citizen if the applicant satisfies the Minister that:

91 All those terms are defined in regulation 1.03 and described earlier in this chapter.
92 PAM3: Div. 1.2/reg. 1.03/Aged dependent relative, s 5.4.
93 Defined in regulation 1.15.
94 Under policy as it then existed, three years: PAM3: Div. 1.2/reg. 1.15, s 18.2.
95 *Scargill v MIMIA* [2003] FCAFC 111 (3 June 2003); *Bagus v MIMA* NG 873 of 1992 FED No 334/94 (31 May 1994); *MIMIA v Hidalgo* [2005] FCAFC 192 (22 August 2005).

(a) the other person is a parent, brother, sister, step-parent, step-brother or step-sister of the applicant; and
(b) the other person is usually resident in Australia; and
(c) the applicant, and the applicant's spouse or de facto partner (if any), have no near relatives other than near relatives who are:
  (i) usually resident in Australia; and
  (ii) Australian citizens, Australian permanent residents or eligible New Zealand citizens; and
(d) if the applicant is a child who:
  (i) has not turned 18; and
  (ii) has been adopted by an Australian citizen, an Australian permanent resident or an eligible New Zealand citizen (the *adoptive parent*) while overseas:

[and] at the time of making the application, the adoptive parent has been residing overseas for a period of at least 12 months.

(2) In this regulation:

near relative, in relation to an applicant, means a person who is:
(a) a parent, brother, sister, step-parent, step-brother or step-sister of the applicant or of the applicant's spouse (if any); or
(b) a child (including a step-child) of the applicant or of the applicant's spouse (if any), being a child who:
  (i) has turned 18 and is not a dependent child of the applicant or of the applicant's spouse (if any); or
  (ii) has not turned 18 and is not wholly or substantially in the daily care and control of the applicant or of the applicant's spouse or de facto partner (if any).

Whether or not a person or their near relative is 'usually resident' in Australia depends on the actual physical residence of the person, meaning where the person eats and sleeps and has their 'settled or usual abode' and whether that person has the firm intention to reside in that country (to make that their usual home).[96] As PAM3 emphasises:

> A person's usual residence is *not* to be determined by a test relying on that person's historic ties and citizenship, nor by whether or not that person holds a permanent visa for that country.[97]

5.4.5 Carer (subclasses 116 and 836)

In general, the carer visa is for relatives in Australia who are unable to care for themselves and unable to obtain adequate care from relatives who are resident in Australia or from appropriate health or community services. 'Carer' is defined in regulation 1.15AA. The definition is predicated on the sponsor having a 'medical condition' that will continue for at least two years and necessitate direct assistance in attending to the practical aspects of daily life. The sponsor must

96 See *Scargill*'s case, footnote 98.
97 PAM 3: Div. 1.2/reg. 1.15/remaining relative, s 8.1.

be certified as having a specified impairment rating after a medical assessment by Health Services Australia. While it conducts a medical assessment, there is nothing to prevent an applicant or sponsor providing medical reports about the sponsor's condition for consideration by Health Services Australia. Regulation 1.15AA(4) provides that 'Impairment Tables means the Tables for the Assessment of Work-related Impairment for Disability Support Pension in Schedule 1B to the *Social Security Act 1991*.' That is, Health Services Australia assesses the impairment rating. Regulation 1.15AA(3) provides that the assessment must be taken as correct in applying the criteria for the carer visa. It is a fact that the decision-maker must take into consideration in applying the relevant criterion.

The carer visa replaced the former special need relative visa on 1 December 1998. It provides for a much more restricted band of needs than its predecessor, which was not determined by a third party such as Health Services Australia making an assessment. 'Special need relative' was defined in regulation 1.03, and while the part of the regulation relating to that definition has now been repealed, there are still a number of cases arising for determination according to that definition. The amendment to the Regulations appeared to be in response to a perceived exploitation of the definition of 'special need relative'. Nevertheless, the carer visa categories remain the subject of significant litigation.

In that respect, courts have paid some close attention to the following part of the current definition in regulation 1.15AA(1):

> (e) the assistance cannot reasonably be:
>
> (i) provided by any other relative of the resident, being a relative who is an Australian citizen, an Australian permanent resident or an eligible New Zealand citizen; or
>
> (ii) **obtained** from welfare, hospital, nursing or community services in Australia; and
>
> (f) ... the applicant is willing and able to **provide** to the resident substantial and continuing assistance of the kind needed under subparagraph (b)(iv) or paragraph (d), as the case requires. [Emphasis added.]

For instance, Finn J commented in *Rafiq v Minister for Immigration & Multicultural & Indigenous Affairs*[98] that:

> My own view is that it is clear that, in purporting to apply the subparagraph 1.15AA (1)(e)(i) criterion, the Tribunal asked and answered the wrong question. Having found that the applicant's sister both provided assistance to her mother when the applicant was not available to provide it and was apparently 'available' when the applicant was providing support, the Tribunal concluded that it was 'not satisfied that the assistance required cannot reasonably be provided by her daughter, Mrs Mohammed'. This was not the criteria it was asked to apply.
>
> It is one thing to ask whether assistance can reasonably be obtained from a relative. It is quite another to ask whether that assistance can reasonably be provided by a relative: see *Issa v MIMA* [2000] FCA 128 at [12]. What a relative is capable of doing and what that person is willing to do are not necessarily the same.

98 [2004] FCA 564 (6 May 2004).

> There is an obvious reason why the subparagraph has the focus it has. Its object is not to effect a form of civil conscription of 'available' relatives. Nor does it require a relative to act selflessly and contrary to that person's own wishes, even if absent any alternative means of assistance that relative might continue to provide assistance for reasons of love, duty etc.

That distinction was identified by Madgwick J in *Issa v MIMA*[99] where his Honour said:

> It occurred to me that the Tribunal member may have misdirected herself by focusing on whether the other Australian relatives and/or welfare services could reasonably make their support available to the applicant, rather than whether she could reasonably obtain it from them. This is not mere semantics. There would be many families in which, if they were minded to, the children could provide a high level of care for a parent, but in which in practice they might not be willing to do so. In such a case the applicant might be quite unable to obtain care and support from their children. The bare language used by the Tribunal member is suggestive that she confused these two concepts.[100]

The distinction was also the subject of examination by Branson J in the matter of *Lin v Minister for Immigration & Multicultural & Indigenous Affairs*.[101] It is instructive in a consideration of how the judiciary approaches cases of Australian residents or citizens with significant need for care. In that case, her Honour recorded that the sponsoring relative:

> ...was paralysed from the chest down after an operation for an aortic aneurysm. He is confined to a wheelchair. Because of his paraplegia, Mr Guo requires substantial care. The Health Services Australia assessment certificate made pursuant to par 1.15AA (1)(b) and subreg 1.15AA(2) records that Mr Guo has a medical condition that satisfies (i)–(iv) of par 1.15AA(1)(b). Mr Guo's impairment rating is 40, which is 10 points above the impairment rating specified by the Gazette Notice. Annexed to the Health Services Australia assessment certificate is a document headed '*Statement of Care Needed*'. The document records that Mr Guo '*needs help with bathing, transfer, turning in bed at night*'. A list of examples of the direct assistance required by Mr Guo because of his medical condition is given. The examples include the following:
>
> | | |
> |---|---|
> | All washing | Preparation of meals |
> | All toileting and bowel care | Motorised wheelchair |
> | Dressing, grooming | Providing medications |
>
> Mrs Lin [Mr Guo's spouse] is primarily responsible for the care of Mr Guo. Mrs Lin is 69 years old. Medical reports indicate that she suffers from a range of medical conditions that include low blood pressure and a history of back strain. The NSW Department of Ageing, Disability and Home Care ('DADHC') provides two hours homecare support in the morning to assist Mr Guo with getting out of bed, and with toileting, washing and grooming and a further half an hour's support assisting him into bed at nights. Mr Guo on occasions spends time in respite care at a nursing home called Ferguson Lodge.

99 [2000] FCA 128 (4 February 2000).
100 [2000] FCA 128 (4 February 2000), [12].
101 [2004] FCA 606 (13 May 2004).

> Mrs Lin is unable to continue to take care of Mr Guo's daily needs such as cleaning, cooking, washing, turning him at night and cleaning him and the bed when his catheter breaks.[102]

The application as a carer was made by Mr Guo's nephew. He had stated that he had no experience in caring for the elderly but wanted to come to Australia to look after his uncle. Statements from Mr Guo's Australian resident wife, daughter, sister-in-law and three nephews were to the effect that they were unable to provide assistance because of illness or work and other family commitments. Mr Guo had access to community welfare services such as respite care or more permanent care in a nursing home, but had claimed that there was no adequate Chinese food in those facilities. The MRT, among other things, was not satisfied that the assistance mentioned in paragraph 1.15AA(b)(iv) cannot be reasonably obtained from welfare, hospital, nursing or community services in Australia.

Her Honour found:

> The Tribunal asked whether Mr Guo's relatives '*cannot reasonably provide some assistance*' rather than whether Mr Guo cannot reasonably obtain assistance from them. I agree with Madgwick J that the distinction is not merely semantic. The failure to make the distinction led the Tribunal to misapprehend the significance of the criterion in the light of the evidence before it. The Tribunal did not consider whether, and if so how, Mr Guo can reasonably obtain assistance from relatives in Australia who are apparently not minded to provide him with assistance.[103]

Nevertheless, the determination did not turn on that failure, as the Tribunal had made a finding in relation to the availability of community assistance. Rather, the court found that the decision-maker had acted outside its jurisdiction by treating Mr Guo's cultural need for Chinese food as an irrelevant consideration. Her Honour reasoned as follows:

> I do not consider that it is to bring an excessively critical eye to the Tribunal's reasons for decision to conclude, as I do, that in considering the possibility of residential nursing home care being available to Mr Guo, the Tribunal proceeded on the basis that Mr Guo's '*preference in terms of remaining with his wife, and in relation to food*' were irrelevant considerations (see [37] of the Tribunal's reasons for decision which is set out in [25] above). It is therefore necessary to determine whether, within the meaning of reg 1.15AA, factors of a kind that might broadly be described as cultural may impact on whether assistance from a particular source or sources may be reasonably obtained.
>
> The certificate issued by Health Services Australia, as required by subreg 1.15AA (2), indicated that Mr Guo needed direct assistance in respect of, amongst other things, the preparation of meals.

102 [2004] FCA 606 (13 May 2004), [8]–[10].
103 [2004] FCA 606 (13 May 2004), [30].

> *'Reasonably'* is a word of broad meaning. *The Oxford English Dictionary* 2nd Edition includes the following meanings:
>
> *'1. According to reason, with good reason, justly, properly . . .*
>
> *3. Sufficiently, suitably, fairly.'*
>
> *The Macquarie Dictionary* 2nd Edition suggests similar meanings.
>
> The Regulations are intended to impact particularly on non-citizens of Australia. In the context which they provide, in the absence of an indication to the contrary, an assessment of what is reasonable in particular circumstances will, in my view, involve, amongst other considerations, consideration of cultural suitability.

The evidence before the Tribunal revealed that the availability of Chinese food was an issue of apparent significance to Mr Guo. In her letter of 11 July 2003 addressed to the Tribunal, Mrs Lin had referred to her husband being sent home from hospital 'so that he can experience once again the warmth of family care the meals he liked'. In the same letter Mrs Lin referred to having 'to prepare all the meals and tea' for her husband herself after the homecare worker has left, and to the applicant knowing Chinese cooking. Mr Guo's evidence to the Tribunal was that he did not contemplate long-term nursing home care because 'the nursing home does not provide Chinese food'. There was also evidence before the Tribunal that suggested that Mr Guo, and to a greater extent Mrs Lin, did not speak English fluently:

> I accept that it was open to the Tribunal to attach weight to, amongst other things, the fact that Mr Guo, to provide respite to his wife, had spent time in nursing homes that did not provide Chinese food and where the staff apparently spoke no Mandarin. It does not necessarily follow, however, that what might be reasonable for a limited period, might not be unreasonable in the longer term. I also accept that notwithstanding Mr Guo's preference for the food of his own culture and his and his wife's apparent lack of fluency in English, the Tribunal may not be satisfied that the assistance that Mr Guo requires cannot reasonably be obtained from a nursing home in Australia.
>
> However, in my view, the Tribunal made an error of law by treating as an irrelevant consideration for the purposes of subreg 1.15AA(1) a consideration raised by the evidence before it, namely the preference of an ill and elderly Chinese person to eat Chinese food. That is, in considering whether the direct assistance in respect of the preparation of meals that Mr Guo required could reasonably be obtained from a source that would not, or might not, be able to provide food that he found acceptable on cultural grounds.[104]

Applicants who are granted permanent residence are issued the visa in the class in which they have been successful, as well as a resident return visa that facilitates re-entry to Australia should they travel abroad. Generally, the return facility expires after five years and is then renewed. Each time the visa-holder enters Australia, he or she can remain permanently. However, permanent residents

104 [2004] FCA 606 (13 May 2004), [33]–[39].

who spend extended periods of time outside Australia may be issued with shorter return visas (see Chapter 9, 'Miscellaneous visas').

5.4.6 Temporary visas for family members of Australian citizens or permanent residents, or eligible New Zealand citizens

In addition to the visas discussed above, there are other classes of visa that applicants with Australian (or eligible New Zealand citizen) relatives may need or want to obtain. These are:

- **Extended Eligibility (Temporary) (class TK)**[105]
- Subclass 445 (Dependent Child)
- **Short Stay Sponsored (Visitor) (class UL)**[106]
- Subclass 459 Sponsored Business Visitor (Short Stay)[107]
- Subclass 679 Sponsored Family Visitor (Short Stay).[108]

These visa applications can be offshore or onshore.

There is an alternative visa for non-New Zealander family members of New Zealand citizen SCV holders, the subclass 461 (New Zealand Citizen Family Relationship (Temporary)) visa.[109] This visa extends to some people who are no longer members of the New Zealand citizen's family unit.[110]

In addition, the Extended Eligibility (Temporary) (class TK) visa class permits dependent children to join their parents where the latter are visa applicants who have been granted provisional or partner visas but whose permanent partner visa (subclasses 100/110 or 801/814) is still undecided and have sponsored the applicant.[111] To do this, the child must complete and lodge form 1002 with a DIAC office (preferably the one at which the visa-holding parents' application is being processed) before the parents' application has been decided. The applicant has the benefit of the same domestic violence provisions that are applicable to the permanent resident partner categories.[112] The visa can be granted offshore or onshore.[113]

Finally, there is the Short Stay Sponsored (Visitor) (class UL),[114] which comprises the subclass 459 Sponsored Business Visitor (Short Stay)[115] and the subclass 679 Sponsored Family Visitor (Short Stay)[116] visas. The subclass 679 visa permits a settled Australian citizen or Australian permanent resident, or a

105 Sch. 1, Item 1211.
106 Sch. 1, Item 1217A.
107 ibid.
108 ibid.
109 Sch. 1, Item 1214BA New Zealand Citizen (Family Relationship) (Temporary) (class UP).
110 Sch. 2, clauses 461.212(3) and (4).
111 Sch. 2, clause 445.211.
112 Sch. 2, clause 445.223.
113 Sch. 2, clause 445.211 and Sch. 1, Item 1211(3).
114 Sch. 1, Item 1217A.
115 ibid.
116 ibid.

government member of parliament or a mayor, to sponsor a self-supporting[117] applicant to visit the applicant's parent, spouse, child, brother or sister for up to 12 months, other than for a purpose related to business or medical treatment.[118] While the law states that the visa can be for 12 months, PAM3 states '[h]owever, it is policy is that the standard period of stay generally be only 3 months'.[119] As a matter of law, decision-makers must follow relevant Ministerial Directions made pursuant to section 499 of the *Migration Act 1958* (Cth).[120] Applicants are subject to assessment for the Schedule 4 'risk factor' condition 4011.[121] The application must be outside Australia at time of grant,[122] and both 'no work' and 'no further stay' conditions will be attached to the visa.[123]

117 Sch. 2, clause 679.212.
118 Sch. 2, clauses 679.211 and 679.214.
119 PAM3: General Guide H, Granting and Evidencing Visitor Visas, s 35.
120 Direction No. 36 of 22 June 2005.
121 Sch. 2, clause 679.228.
122 Sch. 1, Item 1217A(3) and Sch. 2, clause 679.411.
123 Sch. 2, clause 679.611 and Sch. 8, conditions 8101 and 8503.

6

Business and investment visas

6.1 Overview

The migration legislation meets the government's policy aim of strengthening the economy by providing for various temporary and permanent visas that are dependent on the applicant having a successful business or investment history and, for some visas, a willingness to invest and operate in regional areas that are prescribed by Gazette notice.

Permanent visas are divided into two general categories – skilled and business. The skills stream is discussed in the following chapter.

There has been limited litigation in the business/investment area of the migration jurisdiction, and where applicants have failed at the merits level of decision-making it is often because they have failed to meet a threshold criterion that does not require judicial interpretation: for instance, where an applicant cannot demonstrate any responsible role in the operations of a business[1] or where an applicant whose application is dependent on the spouse meeting the relevant criteria is divorced at the relevant time.[2]

Since 1 March 2003,[3] all business skills applicants (with the exception of subclass 132 [Business Talent] applicants) seeking to come to Australia to establish or buy into a business or make a designated investment are required to apply first for a temporary (provisional) visa and subsequently, after a qualifying period of between two and four years in Australia and provided they continue to meet the relevant business/investor criteria, for an equivalent residence visa.

1 Guan, Yihong [2004] MRTA 1946 (26 March 2004).
2 Kieser, Samuel Daniel [2004] MRTA 855 (16 February 2004).
3 The subclass 132 visa is the only exception to the two-stage structure for applying for a permanent business visa.

For visa-holders already in Australia and conducting business, permanent residence can be obtained onshore by being issued a subclass 845 (Established Business in Australia) visa or, for some people, a subclass 846 (State/Territory Sponsored Regional Established Business in Australia) visa.

6.2 Business visa classes and subclasses

In accordance with the structure of the legislation, the classes and subclasses of visa are established in Schedule 1 and the criteria particular to the subclasses are set out in the relevant clause of Schedule 2.[4]

Temporary visa classes and subclasses include:

- **Business Skills (Provisional) (class UR)**[5]
- Subclass 160 (Business Owner (Provisional))[6]
- Subclass 161 (Senior Executive (Provisional))[7]
- Subclass 162 (Investor (Provisional))[8]
- Subclass 163 (State/Territory Sponsored Business Owner (Provisional))[9]
- Subclass 164 (State/Territory Sponsored Senior Executive (Provisional))[10]
- Subclass 165 (State/Territory Sponsored Investor (Provisional)).[11]

The permanent visa classes and subclasses include:

- **Business Skills – Business Talent (Migrant) (class EA)**[12]
- Subclass 132 (Business Talent)[13]
- **Business Skills – Established Business (Residence) (class BH)**[14]
- Subclass 845 (Established Business in Australia)[15]
- Subclass 846 (State/Territory Sponsored Regional Established Business in Australia)[16]
- **Business Skills (Residence) (class DF)**[17]
- Subclass 890 (Business Owner)[18]
- Subclass 891 (Investor)[19]
- Subclass 892 (State/Territory Sponsored Business Owner)[20]
- Subclass 893 (State/Territory Sponsored Investor).[21]

4 For a Table setting out details relevant to those visas, see Lexis Nexis Butterworths *Australian Immigration Law*, Vol. 1, [87], [105A] 'Tables of visa criteria'.
5 Sch. 1, Item 1202A.
6 ibid.
7 ibid.
8 ibid.
9 ibid.
10 ibid.
11 ibid.
12 Sch. 1, Item 1104AA.
13 ibid.
14 Sch. 1, Item 1104A.
15 ibid.
16 ibid.
17 Sch. 1, Item 1104B.
18 ibid.
19 ibid.
20 ibid.
21 ibid.

6.3 Sponsorship

For some visas, the applicant must be sponsored by an 'appropriate state/territory authority'.[22] Those authorities are generally located in dedicated branches of government departments: for instance, the Department of State and Regional Development in New South Wales, the Small Business Development Corporation in Western Australia and the Department of Innovation, Industry and Regional Development in Victoria.

Visas for which state/territory sponsorship is required are Business Skills (Provisional) visa subclasses 163 to 165; Business Skills (Residence) visa subclasses 892, 893 and 846; and Business Skills – Business Talent (Migrant) visa subclass 132.

There is no sponsorship requirement for Business Skills (Provisional) visa subclasses 160 to 162, Business Skills – Established Business (Residence) visa subclass 845 and Business Skills (Residence) visa subclasses 890 and 891.

PAM3 sets out the role that DIAC expects will be fulfilled by state/territory sponsors as follows:

> Under the 2-stage processing arrangements, State and Territory governments play an important role to achieve a better dispersal of business migrants in Australia.
>
> The specific role of State/Territory governments includes:
>
> - promoting business migration to their jurisdiction;
> - assessing requests for sponsorship under the State/Territory sponsored visas;
> - assessing whether a business is of exceptional economic benefit to the State/Territory for the purposes of waiving the age requirement under the State/Territory/ sponsored Business Skills visa subclasses;
> - assessing whether exceptional circumstances apply for the purposes of waiving employee, net business and personal assets and net assets in business requirements under the State/Territory Sponsored Business Owner (Residence) visa subclass at the permanent visa stage;
> - determining the value of business and personal assets sufficient to settle in each State/Territory under the State/Territory Sponsored Business Owner and State/Territory Sponsored Senior Executive visa subclasses;
> - assessing whether sponsorship may still apply in circumstances where applicants are seeking to change the subclass they originally applied for; and
> - in the unsponsored visa categories, receiving notifications from prospective business skills applicants of their business background and intention to engage in business in that state or territory.[23]

Notwithstanding the DIAC policy, a sponsorship decision is made by the relevant state authority, independent of DIAC, and it is that decision itself that becomes one of the criteria for meeting the requirements of business visas that have sponsorship as a condition of the grant. Because the sponsorship decision is

22 As defined in regulation 1.03 and listed in IMMI 10/041, 24 May 2010 – 'Specification of State and Territory departments and authorities for the purposes of the definition of "appropriate regional authority" in regulation 1.03 of the Migration Regulations 1994'.

23 PAM3: Generic Guidelines M – Business Skills Visas 'State/Territory Government Appropriate Regional Authorities' s 6.1.

not made under the migration legislation, it cannot be reviewed by the MRT or appealed to a court under that legislation.

6.4 Spouses

As in other visa applications, an applicant's spouse and other members of the family unit are entitled to the same subclass of visa granted to the applicant, provided they meet the secondary criteria. In business and investment visa subclasses, where there are criteria related to ownership of a business and/or personal assets, the financial interests in the business and the assets of the applicant's spouse or de facto partner are taken into account in combination with the applicant's interests and assets.[24]

6.5 Onshore applications

Applicants can apply for provisional visa subclasses 160–165 while they are physically present in Australia[25] or outside Australia, but they must be outside Australia at the time the visa is granted, as set out in the Schedule 2 'Circumstances Applicable to Grant' subclauses for each visa subclass.[26] That precludes an unsuccessful applicant from having a merits review of the application.[27]

The Established Business (Residence) subclass 845 visa is available to holders of temporary substantive visas[28] who are able to meet the criteria related to business history and success and can pass the assets and business skills points test,[29] as well as meet the general visa requirements. They must be in Australia at the time of the application[30] and the grant.[31]

Apart from the State/Territory Sponsored Regional Established Business in Australia (subclass 846) visa (and subject to the exception referred to below), the sponsored business/investor residence visas are only available to applicants who had previously been granted a provisional visa.[32] For subclasses 891 and 893, the applicant must be the holder of the equivalent provisional visa, while applicants for a subclass 890 (Business Owner) visa can hold any visa of a subclass included in Business Skills (Provisional) (Class UR).[33] There is an exception for applicants for a subclass 892 (State/Territory Sponsored Business Owner) visa

24 For example, see Migration Regulations 1994, Sch. 2, clauses 160.212 and 214. See, further, *Cheung v Minister for Immigration & Multicultural & Indigenous Affairs* [2005] FCAFC 122 (1 July 2005).
25 Migration Regulations 1994, Sch. 1, Item 1202A(3)(b).
26 For example, see Migration Regulations 1994, Sch. 2, clause 160.411(2).
27 *Migration Act 1958* (Cth), s 338.
28 Migration Regulations 1994, Sch. 2, clause 854.211–2.
29 Migration Regulations 1994, Sch. 2, clauses 854.213–7 and 845.222.
30 Migration Regulations 1994, Sch. 1, Item 1104A(3)(b).
31 Migration Regulations 1994, Sch. 2, clause 861.411.
32 Migration Regulations 1994, Sch. 1, Item 1104B(3)(d), (e) and (g).
33 Migration Regulations 1994, Sch. 1, Item 1104B(3)(d).

for holders of a subclass 457 temporary visa[34] whose visa was issued to them as an Independent Executive.[35]

In addition, the Regulations permit the holder of such a subclass 457 visa to apply for a further subclass 457 visa (Temporary Business Entry (Long Stay) visa (Further Application Onshore – 457IE FAO))[36] in order to provide more time in business to meet the eligibility requirements for the Established Business (Residence) visas subclasses 845 and 846 and the State/Territory Sponsored Business Owner (Residence) (subclass 892) visa.

Holders of a Skilled – Independent Regional (Provisional) (Class UX) visa are eligible to apply for the State/Territory Sponsored Business Owner (Residence) (subclass 892) visa, provided they meet the relevant business and residential requirements.[37]

Applications for a subclass 138 visa must be made while the applicant is in Australia, but the applicant must be outside Australia when the visa is granted.

6.6 Documentation

While many of the criteria relevant to various business and investment visas are clear, substantiating that they have been met can be an onerous task, requiring significant amounts of documentation, ranging from complex financial records and contractual agreements to advertising or promotional materials and photographic evidence of business locations or activities. Often, evidence of business or investment activities needs to be demonstrated over two or more fiscal years. The evidentiary burden rests with the applicant and policy requirements regarding the types of evidence DIAC wishes to consider are set out in the relevant PAM for each visa subclass and the generic guidelines for business visas contained in PAM3, as well as in various approved forms. They are summarised in the DIAC publication Booklet 7: *Business Skills Entry*.[38]

6.7 Common criteria and definitions

PAM3 contains an extensive list of definitions and terms, entitled 'Business Skills Legislated and Policy Terms' that are either defined in the legislation or otherwise used in the consideration of business visa applications.[39] It is useful not only for practitioners who might not be accustomed to using business terms, but also for assessing how decision-makers interpret relevant criteria.

34 Migration Regulations 1994, Sch. 1, Item 1104B(3)(f)(ii).
35 Migration Regulations 1994, Sch. 2, clause 457.223(7A).
36 Migration Regulations 1994, Sch. 2, clause 457.223(7A).
37 Migration Regulations 1994, Sch. 2, clauses 892.211–213 and 215–216.
38 Available at DIMIA offices or on its website <www.immi.gov.au/allforms/booklets/books7.html>.
39 PAM3 Generic Guidelines M – Business Skills Visas, following s 50.

Some criteria are relatively straightforward and require little or no explication. For instance:

> 4. All applicants for onshore permanent business visas must show they have been in Australia for a specified period. This is established by an examination of travel documents and the DIMIA movement records that record visa use in and out of Australia.
>
> 5. Each offshore business visa application has a criterion that the applicant has signed a declaration that he/she understands his or her obligations as the holder of the particular subclass. The declaration is included as one of the approved forms that must be lodged with the application.
>
> 6. All unsponsored business visa applicants (except for a subclass 845 visa) must notify the appropriate regional authority of their intention to conduct business within the relevant state.[40]

6.7.1 Age

Unsponsored applicants for provisional visas (subclasses 160–162) must be under 45 years old at the time of application.[41] Sponsored applicants for provisional visas (subclasses 163–165) and business talent (132) applicants must be younger than 45 at the time of application, although this can be waived where the applicant is younger than 55 and proposing to establish a business that the appropriate regional authority has determined is of exceptional economic benefit to the state or territory where the authority is located.[42] Onshore established business subclasses 845 and 846 do not have an upper age limit but applicants must pass the business skills points test, which will be more onerous for older applicants as they receive increasingly fewer points after they turn 45 years old.[43] Applicants for a subclass 138 visa must be aged under 45.

6.7.2 Business skills points test

Applicants for subclass 845 (Established Business in Australia) and 846 (State/Territory Sponsored Regional Established Business in Australia) visas must satisfy the requirements of the points test (see below).

6.7.3 English language skills

Vocational English is a criterion for a number of visas, including unsponsored applicants for provisional visas (subclasses 160–162) and subclasses 121, 138, 139, 880 and 881.

40 See footnote 4.
41 For example, Migration Regulations 1994, Sch. 2, clause 160.215.
42 For example, Migration Regulations 1994, Sch. 2, clause 132.215.
43 Migration Regulations 1994, Sch. 7, Part 2.

Vocational English is defined in regulation 1.15B(4).[44] Onshore established business subclasses 845 and 846 do not have an English language requirement, but applicants must pass the business skills points test, and that will be more onerous for those with limited English, as the scores range from 30 points for better than functional ability in English to zero for no ability in English; however, applicants can score ten points if they are fluent in two or more non-English languages.[45] In regard to assessing language skills, PAM3 advises decision-makers that:

> Officers should note that it is policy that doubts as to English ability, for the purposes of the Business skills points test or for other purposes, be resolved at interview.[46]

6.7.4 Acceptable business activities

All business skills visas have as a Schedule 2 criterion a requirement that the applicant and their spouse or de facto partner 'not have a history of involvement in business activities that are of a nature that is not generally acceptable in Australia'. PAM3 advises decision-makers:

> This criterion should generally not be considered satisfied if the applicant (and/or their spouse or de facto partner) has been involved in business activities or practices that are outside the generally accepted social or cultural norms of most people in Australia; likely to be offensive to large segments of the Australian community; or otherwise likely to give rise to controversy were the applicant to enter Australia as the holder of a Business Skills Class of visa.[47]

6.7.5 Overall successful business career

In relation to provisional, business talent, business owner, senior executive and established business subclasses, PAM3 advises decision-makers:

> Under policy, this criterion generally should not be considered satisfied if:
> - the applicant has been declared bankrupt in the last 5 years; or
> - the applicant is (or has been) actively involved in a business that is (or has been) subject to insolvency, receivership or liquidation; or

44 1.15(B) . . .
(4) A person to whom this subregulation applies has vocational English if:
(a) the person satisfies the Minister that the person has achieved an IELTS test score of at least 5 for each of the 4 test components of speaking, reading, writing and listening in a test conducted:
(i) not more than 12 months before the day on which the application was lodged; or
(ii) during processing of the application; or
(b) the Minister:
(i) determines that it is not reasonably practicable, or not necessary, for the person to be tested using the IELTS test; and
(ii) is satisfied that the person is proficient in English to a standard that is not less than the standard required under paragraph (a).

45 Migration Regulations 1994, Sch. 7, Part 3.

46 PAM3: Sch. 7, s 10.1.

47 PAM3: Generic Guidelines M – Business Skills Visas, s 50.2; examples given are: contravention of government laws (tax evasion, quarantine); criminal convictions related to business activity; not providing 'fair pay' for employment.

- the business has suffered recent trading losses and the business is considered unlikely to be successful in the longer term and this can be attributed to the applicant's role and decision making in the business. (That is, it is not intended that an applicant fail this criterion if the business is likely to be successful in the longer term despite trading losses resulting from external factors such as listed above.)

Officers should take into account:
- the applicant's level of decision making and responsibility in the failed business;
- factors outside the control of the applicant;
- how many times the applicant has experienced bankruptcy or been involved in a failed business; and
- the applicant's history in business since any bankruptcy/failed business.[48]

In making that assessment, PAM3 also warns that external factors should be taken into consideration, including the impact of external economic trends; a fall in property values; a drop in world commodity/raw material prices; changes in taxation/tariff regimes (or similar) adversely affecting the trading position of the business; and whether any recent trading loss incurred by the business was the result of market forces (as described above), other external adverse economic factors or the legitimate movement of assets out of the business, as opposed to poor business acumen and/or poor management decisions by the applicant.[49]

6.7.6 Ownership interest in a qualifying business

In relation to business owner (provisional), investor (provisional), business talent and established business subclasses, the terms 'ownership interest' and 'qualifying business' are defined in the legislation. The length of time that an applicant must demonstrate an ownership interest in a business depends on the particular subclass of visa.[50]

> An 'ownership interest' . . . :
>
> . . . in relation to a business, means an interest in the business as:
> (a) a shareholder in a company that carries on the business; or
> (b) a partner in a partnership that carries on the business; or
> (c) the sole proprietor of the business;
>
> including such an interest held indirectly through one or more interposed companies, partnerships or trusts.[51]

Regulation 1.11A(1) provides that an ownership interest can include a beneficial interest, evidenced by:

> (a) a trust instrument; or
> (b) a contract; or

48 PAM3: Generic Guidelines M – Business Skills Visas, s 53.2.
49 PAM3: Generic Guidelines M – Business Skills Visas, s 53.3.
50 For example, Migration Regulations 1994, Sch. 2, clauses 132.212cf 845.213 cf 892.211(1).
51 *Migration Act 1981* (Cth), s 134(10). See further, *Yu v Minister for Immigration & Multicultural & Indigenous Affairs* [2004] FCA 1477.

(c) any other document capable of being used to enforce the rights of the applicant, or the applicant's spouse or de facto partner, as the case requires, in relation to the asset, eligible investment or ownership interest;

stamped or registered by an appropriate authority under the law of the jurisdiction where the asset, eligible investment or ownership interest is located.[52]

Beneficial interests are only assessed as an ownership interest for the period after they are stamped or registered.[53] DIAC sets out stringent guidelines on the assessment of claimed beneficial interests,[54] including trusts.[55] PAM3 also sets out its own guide for the meaning of 'ownership interest', stating:

> It is also known as owners' equity or owners' interest and may be found in the balance sheet for the business. It is the portion of net assets (i.e. total assets minus total liabilities) that should be distributed to all the owners of the business if the business were to be dissolved. An individual's equity or interest is their individual portion of the total owners' equity of the business. In a business, owners' equity may be called shareholders' equity.[56]

DIAC assesses an applicant's ownership interest through a process of documentation and interview. PAM3 informs:

> There are 2 categories of financial statements:
> - general purposes (required by Corporations Law mainly for investors); and
> - specific purposes (tax, migration, loan application, sale of business, etc).
>
> Specific financial statements are those prepared for particular purposes required by specific stakeholders. DIMIA officers can require visa applicants to submit specific financial statements covering specified criteria under assessment e.g. ownership interest, sources of funds to establish that assets have been lawfully acquired, and in certain circumstances where there are strong doubts about the financial documentation, can also require that the statements be audited.[57]

As well as financial documents, the department may also request items such as title deeds, loan agreements, business testimonials, brochures, flowcharts, organisational structure charts, photographs of the premises and business activities, partnership and franchise agreements and so on.[58]

Financial assessment is also applicable to criteria relating to the net assets of applicants for all business visas except subclass 163 (State/Territory Sponsored Business Owner (Provisional)). Those visas have varying requirements that an applicant and spouse or de factor partner have a minimum level of assets in a qualifying business or qualifying businesses in which the applicant had an ownership interest for a specified period immediately before the application is

52 Migration Regulations 1994, regulation 1.11A(2).
53 Migration Regulations 1994, regulation 1.11A(3).
54 PAM3: Generic Guidelines M, s 36 'Beneficial ownership arrangements'.
55 PAM3: Generic Guidelines M, s 35 'Trusts'.
56 Definitions section PAM3: Generic Guidelines M – Business Skills Visas, following s 57.
57 PAM3: Generic Guidelines M, s 20.2 'Assessing applications'.
58 See DIMIA Booklet 7 *Business Skills Entry*, available at DIMIA offices or on its website <www.immi.gov.au> at pp. 33–35.

made.[59] That criterion can be waived by the appropriate regional authority in exceptional circumstances for applicants for a subclass 892 visa, provided the applicant meets the other two criteria of clause 892.212.[60] A refusal to waive the condition cannot be reviewed, as the relevant authority is a state authority that does not make the decision under the migration legislation.

In addition, each of those visa categories has a requirement (that varies according to the subclass) that the applicant and spouse or de facto partner have a minimum level of personal and business assets.[61] According to PAM3:

> 'Net value' is the sum of the applicant's (and their spouse or de facto partner's assets in the applicant's main business/es; and personal assets i.e. personal assets minus personal liabilities . . . Note that net personal assets can include those shareholdings (if any) that are not included in the calculation of net business assets.[62]

For the purposes of assessing net business assets, DIAC policy is that:

> The net assets of a business is the amount attributable to the owners/shareholders of the business after deducting financial claims upon the business by third parties (i.e. total assets – total liabilities = net assets).[63]
>
> To calculate the net value of an applicant's assets in a business in any given fiscal year, it is necessary to:
>
> - establish the net value of the assets of the business (or owners'/shareholders' equity or funds);
> - calculate the share/portion of those assets attributable to the applicant based on ownership interest and personal investment in the business. To determine the net value, calculate the share of the assets held by the applicant and/or spouse or de factor partner;
> - add the balance of any loans advanced to the business by the applicant (if the directors or major shareholders have made any loans to the company, these should be itemised on the financial statements or in the notes to the accounts); and deduct
> - the balance of any loans the business may have advanced to the applicant; and
> - the value of any other loans the applicant may have taken out to finance their investment in the business not based on personal assets pledged as collateral.[64]

DIAC will require extensive documentation in making the assessment of net assets, although the basic financial document will be the balance sheets for the relevant qualifying periods. In considering balance sheet items, DIAC will ignore real property that is not linked to the operations of the relevant business, goodwill (unless it was an asset purchased at arm's length when the relevant business was purchased), unsecured personal loans by the applicant to the business and loans from non-financial institutions or individuals.[65]

For offshore visas (except investor subclasses), the personal assets of the applicant and spouse or de facto partner must be available for transfer to Australia

59 For example, Migration Regulations 1994, Sch. 2, clause 132.212.
60 Migration Regulations 1994, Sch. 2, clause 892.212(b).
61 For example, Migration Regulations 1994, Sch. 2, clause 132.214.
62 PAM3: Generic Guidelines M, Migration Regulations 1994, s 45 'Net Value'.
63 See further, *Cheung v MRT* [2004] FCA 1725.
64 PAM3: Generic Guidelines M, s 30 'Net Business Assets – Overview'.
65 PAM3: Generic Guidelines M, s 22.

within two years of the date the visa is granted. In subclasses 845 and 846, applicants receive extra points if they have overseas assets available for transfer to Australia within two years of being granted a business visa.[66] In assessing the availability of assets for transfer, DIAC policy is that:

> Nothing requires the applicant to demonstrate the actual transfer of, or an intention to transfer, their (net business and personal) assets to Australia. Officers are limited to considering only whether those assets are 'available for transfer and capable of being transferred' within the prescribed period. It is policy that the applicant satisfies this requirement if (but only if) they satisfy officers that their (net business and personal) assets: can be (not 'will be') readily transferred to Australia (e.g. cash, current bank deposits, stock and share, personal possessions); and/or can be (not 'will be') converted to cash within 2 years and transferred to Australia (e.g. property, business assets, fixed or long term deposits falling due within the prescribed 2 year period). Assets otherwise acceptable for Business Skills visa purposes but held in superannuation/pension schemes, trusts, bonds or long term fixed deposits falling due outside the prescribed 2 year period should not normally be regarded as 'available for transfer and capable of being transferred' unless the applicant can demonstrate that it is possible for them to access those funds in Australia within 2 years of visa grant.

The term 'qualifying business':

> . . . means an enterprise that:
> (a) is operated for the purpose of making profit through the provision of goods, services or goods and services (other than the provision of rental property) to the public; and
> (b) is not operated primarily or substantially for the purpose of speculative or passive investment.[67]

The policy guidelines are:

> . . . a business that does not provide goods and/or services or has been set up for speculative or passive investment does not meet requirements to be a qualifying business.
>
> For example, if the main activity of a business:
> - is holding share portfolios, interest bearing deposits or rental property; or
> - involves currency speculation; or
> - is property speculation (i.e. buying and selling real estate) rather than property development (i.e. building or renovating property);
> - that business is not a qualifying business (and, it follows, cannot be a main business for Business Skills visa purposes).[68]

Applicants for individual and sponsored investor (provisional) visas do not have a mandatory requirement to have an involvement in managing a 'qualifying business' as they have an alternative criterion regarding involvement in managing 'eligible investments'.[69]

66 Pursuant to Migration Regulations 1994, Sch. 7, Part 4.
67 Migration Regulations 1994, regulation 1.03.
68 Definitions section PAM3: Generic Guidelines M – Business Skills Visas, following s 57.
69 Migration Regulations 1994, Sch. 2, clauses 162.212(2)(b) and 165.212(2)(b).

6.7.7 Main business

In relation to business owner, business talent and established business subclasses, the Regulations provide:

> For the purposes of these Regulations and subject to subregulation (2), a business is a main business in relation to an applicant for a visa if:
> (a) the applicant has, or has had, an ownership interest in the business; and
> (b) the applicant maintains, or has maintained, direct and continuous involvement in management of the business from day to day and in making decisions affecting the overall direction and performance of the business; and
> (c) the value of the applicant's ownership interest, or the total value of the ownership interests of the applicant and the applicant's spouse or de facto partner, in the business is or was:
> (i) if the business is operated by a publicly listed company – at least 10% of the total value of the business; or
> (ii) if (A) the business is not operated by a publicly listed company; and (B) the annual turnover of that business is at least AUD$400 000; at least 30% of the total value of the business; or
> (iii) if: (A) the business is not operated by a publicly listed company; and (B) the annual turnover of that business is at least AUD$400 000; at least 51% of the total value of the business; and
> (d) the business is a qualifying business.[70]

An applicant cannot nominate more than two qualifying businesses as main businesses where the latter is a consideration for a particular visa subclass.[71] However, the Federal Court has found that a single 'business' can be comprised of multiple entities, so that a 'main business' can also comprise multiple entities.[72] The tribunal will then consider the ownership structure of each entity to determine whether it meets the definition of 'the business'. Nothing prohibits the tribunal from considering the ownership arrangements of any relevant entity at any time for the purpose of identifying the 'business' forming part of the definition of the 'main business'.[73]

The Full Bench of the Federal Court has considered the meaning of regulation 1.11(1)(c) in *Lobo v Minister for Immigration & Multicultural & Indigenous Affairs*.[74] The applicant had applied for a subclass 845 (Established Business in Australia) visa and needed to demonstrate that she met the requirements of Schedule 2 subclause 845.216:

> In the 12 months immediately preceding the making of the application, the applicant, as the owner of an interest in a main business or main businesses in Australia, maintained direct and continuous involvement in the management of that business or those

70 Migration Regulations 1994, regulation 1.11(1).
71 Migration Regulations 1994, regulation 1.11(2).
72 *Nassif v Minister for Immigration and Multicultural and Indigenous Affairs* [2003] FCA 481 (20 May 2003), [35] per Branson J.
73 *Ibrahim v Minister for Immigration and Citizenship* [2009] FCA 1328 (18 November 2009), [34] per Jagot J.
74 [2003] FCAFC 168 (8 August 2003).

> businesses from day to day and in making decisions that affected the overall direction and performance of that business or those businesses.

Gyles J found, at first instance, that the tribunal had erred in applying a departmental policy to the visa application which was narrower in terms than the relevant criterion that should have applied, but no relief was available because the MRT decision was a privative clause decision for the purposes of section 474 of the Act.[75] The Full Court found:

> It was not disputed that the departmental policy to which the Tribunal adverted was narrower than the criterion for a subclass 845 visa set out in cl 845.216 of the Second Schedule to the Migration Regulations. The criterion requires satisfaction on the part of the Minister that the applicant for the visa as the owner of an interest in a main business '. . . maintained direct and continuous involvement in the management of that business or those businesses from day to day and in making decisions that affected the overall direction and performance of that business or those businesses'. This did not import a requirement that could only be satisfied by demonstrating the exercise of responsibility within the business in terms of decision-making authority, responsibility for employees and/or responsibility for expenditure. There is a variety of ways in which a person might maintain direct and continuous involvement in the management of a business and in making decisions affecting its overall direction and performance.[76]

The Schedule 2 criteria for each of the relevant visa subclasses then have various threshold criteria (depending on the category) in respect of the main business or businesses. They relate to the turnover during a specified period prior to the application,[77] the value of the assets held in the main business by the applicant and spouse or de facto partner,[78] direct involvement in management of the main business[79] or the number of employees over a specified period before the application was made.[80]

For offshore applications for subclasses 132, 160 and 163, the requirement regarding net asset value relates to the applicant and spouse's or de facto partner's combined interests in any 'qualifying business', while only the 'main business' is a reference point for turnover.[81] That differs from onshore applications, where the 'main business' is the reference point for minimum net assets and turnover.[82]

Applicants for subclasses 890 and 892 have a further burden of demonstrating that they have had:

> . . . an ownership interest in 1 or more actively operating main businesses in Australia for at least 2 years immediately before the application is made.[83]

75 [2003] FCAFC 168 (8 August 2003), [5].
76 [2003] FCAFC 168 (8 August 2003), [63].
77 For example, for a subclass 132 (Business Talent) visa, Sch. 2, clause 132.213 provides that 'For at least 2 of the 4 fiscal years immediately before the application is made, the applicant's main business, or the applicant's main businesses together, had an annual turnover of at least AUD$3 000 000.'
78 For example, for a subclass 845 (Established Business in Australia) visa, see Sch. 2, clause 845.215.
79 For example, for a subclass 845 (Established Business in Australia) visa, see Sch. 2, clause 845.216.
80 For subclass 890 and 892 only: Migration Regulations 1994, Sch. 2, clauses 890.214 and 892.212(a).
81 For example, Migration Regulations 1994, Sch. 2, clauses 160.212 cf 160.213.
82 For subclass 890 and 892 only: Migration Regulations 1994, Sch. 2: for example, clauses 892.212(c) and 892.213.
83 Migration Regulations 1994, Sch. 2, clauses 890.211(1) and 892.211(1).

Those applicants must demonstrate that for each 'actively operating main business' they have in Australia:

(a) an Australian Business Number has been obtained; and
(b) all Business Activity Statements required by the Australian Taxation Office (the ATO) for the period mentioned in subclause (1) have been submitted to the ATO and have been included in the application.[84]

6.7.8 Turnover

All business visa categories have criteria related to minimum levels of turnover for specified periods. The levels and qualifying periods can vary from visa to visa, and there is an exception for subclass 892 visas, where the turnover requirement can be waived by the appropriate regional authority in exceptional circumstances.[85] PAM3 defines 'turnover' as:

> Under policy, turnover is to be taken to refer to the revenue generated as a result of the ordinary activities of a main business or a major business.
>
> Revenue consists of the total value received for the sale of goods; fees for services provided; commission revenue; interest earned; capital gains; or government subsidies/bounties.
>
> Turnover is found in the profit and loss statement for the business in any given year. It may also appear as 'revenue' or 'total sales'. Only amounts received and receivable by the enterprise on its own account are considered to be revenue.
>
> Under policy, if (for the purposes of Schedule 7) the business operates as a commission agent only the amount of the service revenue (i.e. as opposed to the sale value) is to be counted towards the turnover of the business.[86]

6.7.9 Genuine and realistic commitment

An applicant for the provisional Business Owner and Senior Executive and the Business Talent visas, subclasses 132, 160, 161, 163 and 164, is required to demonstrate that he or she:

> . . . genuinely has a realistic commitment, after entry to Australia as the holder of a . . . visa:
> (a) either:
>   (i) to establish a qualifying business in Australia; or
>   (ii) to participate in an existing qualifying business in Australia; and
> (b) to maintain a substantial ownership interest in that business; and
> (c) to maintain direct and continuous involvement in management of that business from day to day and in making decisions that affect the overall direction and performance of the business in a manner that benefits Australia economically.

84 Migration Regulations 1994, Sch. 2, clauses 890.211(2) and 892.211(2).
85 Migration Regulations 1994, Sch. 2, clause 892.213(c).
86 Definitions section PAM3: Generic Guidelines M – Business Skills Visas, following ss 57, 29.1.

Sponsored applicants are taken to have demonstrated that commitment by virtue of their sponsorship. Unsponsored applicants are likely to:

> . . . be asked to indicate their business intentions in Australia. Officers should seek broad details of the proposed business activities and assess whether the applicant has an understanding of the Australian business environment in which they would operate. As an applicant may have several business options in mind, officers may wish to assess whether the commitment to follow through one or more of the broad proposals is genuine as well as realistic.[87]

The types of activities and plans PAM3 indicates would benefit the Australian economy are:

> . . . development of links with international markets; creation or maintenance of employment; export of Australian goods or services; substitution of goods or services currently imported to Australia; introduction of new or improved technology; adding to commercial activity and competitiveness within the Australian economy.[88]

6.8 Criteria specific to particular visa subclasses

6.8.1 Investment visas (subclasses 162 and 165)

Applicants for subclasses 162 (Investor (Provisional)) and 165 (State/Territory Sponsored Investor (Provisional)) visas must demonstrate a high level of management skill in relation to the eligible investment or qualifying business activity. That level in management skill is described in PAM3:

> - [. . . as to a qualifying business] they have exercised responsibility over a number of employees;
> - they have been responsible for strategic policy development i.e. that they have had a significant impact and influence over the key elements (such as profits, production activities, (significant) expenditure and major staffing issues) of the business; and
> - their skills are of a sufficient level to allow them to adapt successfully to the Australian business and/or investment management environment.
>
> As to eligible investments . . .] Although a subjective assessment, a high level of management skill in relation to an eligible investment may be demonstrated by the applicant having actively evaluated the performance of their assets and the returns achieved, on the basis of which decisions to buy, sell or retain assets were made.[89]

Applicants in the investor subclasses have an alternative to establishing they have an involvement in managing a 'qualifying business' by establishing an

87 PAM3: Generic Guidelines M – Business Skills Visas, ss 51.1, 51.7.
88 PAM3: Generic Guidelines M – Business Skills Visas, s 51.6.
89 PAM3: Sch. 2, Visa 165, ss 18 and 19.

involvement in managing 'eligible investments' as defined in the interpretation clauses of each of the relevant Schedule 2 parts. Those investments are:

> (a) an ownership interest in a business; or
> (b) a loan to a business; or
> (c) cash on deposit; or
> (d) stocks and bonds; or
> (e) real estate; or
> (f) gold or silver bullion;
>
> that is owned by the person for the purpose of producing a return by way of income or capital gain and is not held for personal use.[90]

PAM3 explains that items of personal wealth are not taken into consideration:

> An eligible investment asset is, among other requirements, limited to being an asset owned 'for the purpose of generating a return by way of income or through capital appreciation'. Returns may take the form of, but are not limited to, interest, royalties, dividends or rental, as well as capital appreciation. It follows that assets held for personal use (for example, the family home . . .) are excluded.
>
> It is apparent that consideration of any eligible investment is limited to its net value. The value of any loans the applicant and/or their spouse or de facto partner have taken out in order to finance the purchase of an eligible investment asset must be deducted from the total value.[91]

The applicant's involvement in managing eligible investments is checked in the same manner that applicants who manage qualifying businesses are checked.[92] Similarly, DIAC will require documentation to establish ownership and management of eligible investments.[93]

Applicants in investor categories are required to make 'designated investments'[94] for specified periods. These are state bonds and are notified by Gazette.[95] Unsponsored applicants must invest $1 500 000 in a designated investment for a period of four years in their, or their de facto partner's name.[96] While there is no legislative requirement that sponsored applicants undertake further activities, it is extremely unlikely that they would be sponsored unless they entered further business arrangements that are satisfactory to the relevant regional authority, as a condition of the sponsorship.

90 Migration Regulations 1994, Sch. 2, clauses 162.111 and 165.111.
91 PAM3: Sch. 2, Visa 162, ss 6.3 – 6.4.
92 See above 6.7.5 'Overall successful business career'.
93 PAM3: Sch. 2, Visa 162, ss 7 and 8.
94 As defined in Migration Regulations 1994, regulation 5.19A.
95 GN 25, 25 June 2005 – Specification for the purposes of regulation 5.19A of the Migration Regulation 1994 of securities in which an investment is a designated investment for the purposes of visa subclasses 131, 162, 165, 844, 891 and 893.
96 Migration Regulations 1994, Sch. 2, clause 162.222.

6.8.2 Established business (residence) visas (subclasses 845 and 846)

Applicants for both these subclasses must pass the business skills points test.[97] However, applicants for the subclass 846 (State/Territory Sponsored Regional Established Business in Australia) visa can still be successful if they do not obtain the requisite score but the relevant regional authority mentioned satisfies the Minister that there are exceptional circumstances that justify the grant of the subclass 846 visa to the applicant.[98] PAM3 explains:

> The 'exceptional circumstances' provision was introduced with effect from 1 November 2000 to provide greater flexibility for regional authorities seeking to sponsor applicants who do not meet the passmark of the REBA points test, but who have established businesses in their jurisdiction that were assessed by the regional authority to be of benefit to the area.[99]

The passmark is gazetted at 105 points[100] and comprises:

- Business attribute Division 1.4 Item 7170, which applies only to the EBA category i.e. visa 845 and which measures the size of the main business/es. The component parts are employee levels and turnover/export levels;
- Business attributes Division 1.5 Items 7180–7181, which apply only to the State/Territory sponsored REBA visa 846 and which measure employee levels;
- Part 2 Age of applicant at time of application, which itemises age groups. It applies to all Business Skills applicants. The policy intention of the points for age is to reflect the applicant's potential contribution to the Australian economy by favouring relative youth (maximum points [30] are allocated to applicants aged 30 to 44);
- Part 3 Language ability of applicant, which itemises language proficiency levels. It applies to all Business Skills main applicants. The policy intention is to reflect the importance of language ability in establishing businesses in Australia, general settlement success and language. The maximum number of language points is where the applicant has better functional English, in which 30 points are allocated;
- Part 4 Net assets of applicant (or applicant and spouse or de facto partner together), which itemises the AUD value of the net assets. It applies to all main Business Skills applicants. The policy intention is to measure the level of personally-owned capital that is available to the applicant and that could be used in establishing a new business in Australia or in participating as an owner or part-owner in an existing business in Australia (note that, under policy, 'the applicant or . . . applicant and applicant's spouse or de

97 Migration Regulations 1994, Sch. 2, clauses 845.222 and 846.222 and Sch. 7.
98 Migration Regulations 1994, Sch. 2, clause 846.222(1B)(b).
99 PAM3: Sch. 2, Visa 846, s 11.2.
100 Notice No. S 238, 27 June 1997 – Points Scores – Business Skills Test.

facto partner together' may be read as meaning the applicant and/or their spouse or de facto partner); and

- Part 5 State/Territory sponsorship, which applies to visa 846 only.[101]

6.8.3 Business Owner (Provisional) subclass 163

An applicant in this class can meet the threshold business skill qualification by demonstrating that:

> [he/she] has, for at least 3 of the 4 fiscal years immediately before the application is made, had an ownership interest in a main business or businesses that had an annual turnover of at least AUD$300 000.[102]

Applicants who are employed as senior managers of a business are not eligible for this visa. According to PAM3, turnover can only be included where the main business is owned for a full fiscal year.[103] It goes on to state:

> This criterion identifies applicants who have had an active involvement in business. By allowing only the main business to be included, turnover is assessed only in relation to business in which the applicant has had a minimum level of ownership and involvement.[104]

6.8.4 Business Skills (Provisional) subclasses 161 (Senior Executive (Provisional)) and 164 (State/Territory Sponsored Senior Executive (Provisional))

Both of these subclasses require that the applicant, for a total of at least two years in the four years immediately before the application is made:

> (a) occupied a position in the 3 highest levels of the management structure of a major business; and
> (b) was responsible for strategic policy development affecting a major component or a wide range of operations of that major business.[105]

For the subclass 161 visa, major business is defined as a business (other than a government business enterprise) the annual turnover of which was at least AUD$50 000 000 for at least two of the four fiscal years immediately before the application is made.[106] In the subclass 164, it is defined as a business (other than a government business enterprise) the annual turnover of which

101 See PAM3: Sch. 7, a 2.
102 Migration Regulations 1994, Sch. 2, clause 163.212.
103 PAM3: Sch. 2, Visa 163, s 8.1.
104 PAM3: Sch. 2, Visa 163, s 8.1.
105 Migration Regulations 1994, Sch. 2, clauses 161.212 and 164.212.
106 Migration Regulations 1994, Sch. 2, clause 161.111.

was at least AUD$10 000 000 in at least two of the four fiscal years immediately before the application is made.[107] Those turnovers provide a context for the level of management skills required by senior executive applicants. PAM3 explains:

> As a general guide only, persons described in the prospectus, annual report and/or other organisational structure chart of a business as: Chief Executive; Group/Chief Manager; General Manager of a division, State or region; Owner/manager; or Senior functional manager are likely to be responsible for 'strategic policy development'. However, this does not mean that they necessarily occupy a position in the 3 highest levels of the management structure.[108]
>
> Policy envisages a person responsible for the aspects of a business prescribed by this provision would also be able to demonstrate several of the following:
>
> (a) a remuneration package in the top 5% of salary earners in the country where the business is operating;
> (b) a direct line of communication to the chief executive and/or board of directors of the business;
> (c) their current range of responsibilities, including management responsibility over other specialist or functional managers;
> (d) affiliations with professional management associations equivalent to a Fellow of the Australian Institute of Management;
> (e) peer and marketplace recognition of their status and reputations (e.g. by recognition of the person in industry publications); or
> (f) that they are highly valued by their organisation (e.g. are they a beneficiary of company options and/or profit-sharing schemes, are they the subject of 'key person' insurance or similar).
>
> This list is not exhaustive. Officers should also consider, for example:
>
> - the method of the applicant's appointment, e.g. were they headhunted;
> - the applicant's contract appointment arrangements; and
> - the applicant's previous experience.[109]
>
> Policy considers that responsibility for 'strategic policy development affecting a major component or a wide range of operations' means responsibility for policy development having a significant impact and influence on the key elements of the overall directions of the business, in areas such as (but not necessarily limited to):
>
> - profits;
> - production activities;
> - (significant) expenditure; and
> - major human resources issues.
>
> It would be expected that such policy development would be carried out:
>
> - if the business operates many small branches (e.g. a large bank), only in the headquarters or general coordinating centre for a country or region; otherwise,
> - only in a headquarters, a regional centre or other general coordinating centre of the business responsible for determining policy.[110]

107 Migration Regulations 1994, Sch. 2, clause 164.111.
108 PAM3: Sch. 2, Visa 161 s 6.3 and PAM3: Sch. 2, Visa 164, s 7.3.
109 PAM3: Sch. 2, Visa 161 s 6.3 and PAM3: Sch. 2, Visa 164, s 7.5.
110 PAM3: Sch. 2, Visa 161 s 6.3 and PAM3: Sch. 2, Visa 164, s 7.6.

6.9 Public interest – health and character requirements

All applicants for skills and business visas, as well as members of their family unit, regardless of whether or not they are secondary applicants, must meet the relevant Schedule 4 health and character requirements, either when a provisional visa is granted or when a permanent visa is granted and, for some criteria, at each of those times.

7

Skills-based visas

7.1 Overview

In addition to business and investment visas considered in the previous chapter, the migration legislation further meets the government's policy aim of strengthening the economy by providing for various temporary and permanent visas that are dependent on the applicant having certain qualifications and/or occupational skills and, for some visas, a willingness to reside and work in regional areas that are prescribed by Gazette notice. The temporary categories are discussed in the following chapter.

There are three sub-categories in the skills stream of permanent visas: general skilled, employer nominations and distinguished talent. A fourth sub-category related to business skills (rather than ownership) was discussed in the previous chapter. In addition, there are two temporary skilled subclasses that are precursors to obtaining permanent residence.

7.2 Visas based on qualifications and/or occupational skills

Visas based on skills have two streams: the independent category and the Australian-sponsored category. Independent migrants have the smallest number of restrictions placed on them. Each has provision for onshore and offshore applications. There are some terms and concepts that are integral to understanding the relevant criteria. These are:

1. **Skilled occupation:** This term is the basic building block of skilled visa applications. It 'means an occupation that is specified by Gazette notice[1] as a skilled occupation for which a number of points specified in the Notice are available'.[2] Visa applicants must nominate a skilled occupation in their application and provide an assessment of that occupation by a relevant assessing authority (see below).
2. **ANZSCO:** The Australian and New Zealand Standard Classification of Occupations replaced the Australian Standard Classification of Occupations (2nd edn, 1997, Australian Bureau of Statistics) with effect from 1 July 2010. It is a dictionary of all occupations in Australia, classified into major groups, sub-major groups, minor groups, unit groups and occupations. A major group may include occupations at several different skill levels and is the broadest level. Sub-major groups are distinguished on the basis of skill level and a broad application of skill specialisation. Minor groups are distinguished from others in the sub-major group on the basis of less broad application of skill specialisation. Unit groups are distinguished on a finer application of skill and occupations on the basis of detailed skill specialisation involving the performance of a common set of tasks. In some cases, several ASCO occupations may correlate to one ANZSCO occupation. In other cases, an ASCO occupation is represented by a larger number of more detailed ANZSCO occupations – for example Registered Nurse was represented by one ASCO code, but is now represented by ten ANZSCO codes, depending on specialisation. All occupations included in skilled visa applications are assessed in light of ANZSCO definitions.
3. **The points test:** On 11 November 2010 the Minister for Immigration and Citizenship announced a new points test that will apply to certain skilled migration applications[3] made on or after 1 July 2011. The new points test will not apply to unfinalised applications lodged prior to 1 July 2011. People who held an eligible student visa on 8 February 2010 still have until the end of 2012 to apply for a Temporary Skilled Graduate visa (subclass 485) under the arrangements in place as at 8 February 2010. Subdivision B of Division 3 of Part 2 of the Act (sections 92 to 96) provides for the application of a 'points' system, under which applicants for relevant visas are given an assessed score based on the prescribed number of points for particular attributes. The prescribed points and the manner of their allocation are provided for in Division 2.6 and Schedule 6B[4] of the Migration Regulations. The score is assessed against the relevant pool

1 IMMI 10/026, 22 June 2010; IMMI 10/079, 3 December 2010.
2 As defined in Regulation 1.15I.
3 Applicable to the following subclasses: 885 – Skilled Independent, 175 – Skilled Independent (Offshore), 886 – Skilled Sponsored, 176 – Skilled Sponsored (Offshore), 487 – Skilled Regional Sponsored, 475 – Skilled – Regional Sponsored.
4 The Sch. 6A points test replaced the Sch. 6 points test for certain skilled migration visa applications made on or after 1 July 1999. Sch. 6 still applies to applications for subclasses 105, 106, 126 and 135 made before that date. Those classes ceased to exist with the July 1999 amendments.

and pass marks. In certain circumstances, attributes of the spouse of an applicant may be taken into account.

Points are allocated for: (i) age qualification; (ii) English language skills; (iii) Australian employment experience; (iv) overseas work experience; (v) educational qualifications, Australian or recognised overseas; (vi) Australian educational qualifications; (vii) other language skills; (viii) partner skills; (ix) sponsorship; (x) professional year; and (xi) designated regional study. Australian-sponsored visa category applicants and independent visa category applicants are assessed against the factors (that is, Schedule 6B, Parts 1–12).[5] Applicants will no longer be awarded points based on their occupations, starting from 1 July 2011, but all applicants must still nominate an occupation on the applicable Skilled Occupation List.

4. **Pool marks and pass marks:** The provision for two levels of points is a statutory means of controlling the flow and level of numbers in points-tested categories. The marks are set from time to time by the Minister by notice in Gazette[6] and may differ from one visa category to the next. Applicants who achieve the pass mark fulfill the points criteria for the purpose of granting a particular visa. Applicants who reach the pool mark but fall short of the pass mark do not fulfill the points criterion for the grant of the particular visa and are put into a reserve list of applicants for up to two years. If the Minister varies the pass mark, those in the pool are assessed against the new pass mark, and if they achieve that mark, they meet the points requirement. It is expected that the pass mark will be set at 65 points, and that there will no longer be a distinction in the pass mark between independent and sponsored visas and permanent and provisional visas.

   As at 1 November 2011, the relevant marks were as follows:

Category	**Current pass mark**	**Current pool mark**
Skilled – Independent	120	100
Skilled – Independent regional (provisional)	100	100
Skilled – Australian sponsored	100	80
Skilled – Independent overseas student[7]	120	120
Skilled – Australian sponsored overseas student	110	110
Skilled – Onshore independent New Zealand citizen	120	120
Skilled – Onshore Australian sponsored New Zealand citizen	110	110

5. **Skilled Occupation List (SOL):** A new SOL came into effect on 1 July 2010.[8] The list is specific to General Skilled Migration, and does not apply to employer-sponsored permanent or temporary visas. The list is based

5 Migration Regulations 1994, regulation 2.26AA.
6 IMMI 10/079, signed 3 December 2010.
7 From 1 April 2005, the pass mark for applications for Skilled – Independent Overseas Student (subclass 880) visas was 120.
8 IMMI 10/26, signed 17 June 2010.

on the ANZSCO occupations and reflects the skills Australia needs. For each occupation, the list shows: the ANZSCO code for the occupation; the relevant assessment authority for the occupation; and the number of points for skill an occupation is awarded for its 'skill' factor under the points test. All the skilled categories require the applicant to nominate a skilled occupation when they apply for their visa. The new list will not apply to: (1) valid applications lodged before 1 July 2010; (2) applicants who on 8 February 2010 held a subclass 485 (skilled graduate) visa, or held a pending 485 visa application, and who apply for a provisional or permanent onshore GSM visa on or before 31 December 2012; and (3) international students who on 8 February 2010 held a subclass 572, 573 or 574 visa and apply for a subclass 485 visa on or before 31 December 2012.

6. **Migration Occupations in Demand List (MODL):** On 8 February 2010 the Minister for Immigration and Citizenship revoked the MODL. There is currently no plan for a new MODL. This is applicable to all GSM applicants except those who on that date held a subclass 485 visa; those who had a pending application and had not yet lodged an application for a provisional or permanent GSM visa and who make an application before 31 December 2012; and those who on that date had a pending GSM visa application. Previously, if an applicant's nominated skilled occupation had been gazetted as a MODL,[9] they were eligible for extra points for skills for the purposes of the skills targeting qualifications of the points test.
7. **Occupations Requiring English (ORE) List:**[10] Listed by Gazette[11] and by reference to ASCO occupations, this list is relevant to skilled Australian-linked and independent classes of visa. If an applicant's nominated occupation is on the ORE list, that applicant must have vocational English.[12] The applicant can submit the evidence of the test results before the decision is taken by the Minister or their delegate.[13] Those applicants must both pass the points test and be assessed against the ORE requirement. Failure on either results in refusal.
8. **National Office of Overseas Skills Recognition (NOOSR):** This is an independent agency that assesses some occupations on the SOL (particularly registrable and licensed occupations) and publishes *Skills Recognition*

9 IMMI 10/025, 24 June 2010.

10 Defined in regulation 1.19 as 'the Minister may publish by notice in the Gazette a list of occupations requiring proficiency in English of at least the standard required for the award of 15 points under Part 3 of Schedule 6'.

11 GN 6, 11 February 1998 – List of occupations requiring English (regulation 1.19).

12 Defined in regulation 1.15B.

13 In *Berenguel v Minister for Immigration and Citizenship* [2010] HCA 8, the High Court interpreted the then requirement in regulation 1.15B in reference to 'vocational English' (which has the same wording as in the current regulation 1.15C in reference to 'competent English'). The court decided the regulation requirement that the requisite test has been conducted 'not more than 2 years before the day on which the application was lodged' should not be construed as the test having to be conducted before the application date, notwithstanding that clause 885.213 is part of the group of clauses headed 'Criteria to be satisfied at the time of application'.

in Australia (used to categorise some occupations) and the *Country Education Profiles*. It assesses overseas qualifications.

10. **Relevant assessing authority:** Occupations nominated by visa applicants in the skills stream are assessed by authorities outside DIAC, known as relevant assessing authorities. Regulation 2.26B provides:
    (1) The Minister may, by an instrument in writing,[14] specify a person or body as the relevant assessing authority for a skilled occupation, and one or more countries, for the purposes of an application for a skills assessment made by a resident of one of those countries.
    (2) The standards against which the skills of a person are assessed by a relevant assessing authority for a skilled occupation must be the standards set by the relevant assessing authority for the skilled occupation.

The Gazette notice mentioned in that regulation sets out the skilled occupation, the assessing authority for that occupation and the number of points that occupation scores for the purposes of the points test. The assessing authorities have internal review procedures but their assessments are not reviewable under the migration legislation.

Some assessing bodies insist upon completion of certain requirements to meet Australian standards to be issued with a suitable skills assessment.[15] The purpose of this is to refuse visas in circumstances where an applicant has minor skills for the occupation he or she nominated but has qualifications or employment experience in a different occupation, for which registration or licensing is required in Australia.[16]

The relevant categories for applicants obtaining permanent residence on the basis of occupational skills are either offshore or onshore.

7.2.1 Offshore

The relevant visa classes are:

- **Skilled – (Migrant) (class VE)**[17]
- Subclass 175 (Skilled – Independent)[18]
- Subclass 176 (Skilled – Sponsored)[19]
- **Skilled (Provisional) (class VF)**[20]
- Subclass 475 (Skilled – Regional Sponsored)[21]
- Subclass 476 (Skilled – Recognised Graduate).[22]

14 IMMI 10/079, 3 December 2010.
15 PAM3: Sch. 6A/Skills, s 32.2.
16 Ibid.
17 Sch. 1, Item 1135.
18 ibid.
19 ibid.
20 Sch. 1, Item 1228.
21 Ibid.
22 Ibid.

Visa subclasses 134 (Skill Matching), 137 (Skilled – State/Territory-nominated Independent), and 138 (Skilled – Australian Sponsored) only apply to the applications made prior to 1 September 2007.[23]

A subclass 175 visa is a permanent visa for people with skills in demand. Applicants are not sponsored and must pass a points test.[24] The applicant must be under 45 years of age[25] and have the skills and qualifications under the SOL, assessed by the relevant authority.[26] There is a threshold requirement that the applicant has been employed in a skilled occupation for at least 12 of the last 24 months,[27] and the applicant is required to have competent English.[28] The applicant cannot change their nominated occupation after making a valid application.[29] The visa is permanent, permitting the holder to travel and enter Australia for five years from the date of grant.[30] The permanent visa allows the holder to remain in Australia indefinitely.[31] Policy states that when a decision maker assesses work experience and other occupation-related criteria, an applicant should not be disadvantaged as a result of the change from ASCO to ANZSCO.[32] This visa is subject to the 'one fails, all fail' requirement: that is, if one person included in the visa application fails to meet some Schedule 1 and Schedule 2 requirement, no one in the application will be granted a visa.[33] The applicant must also meet all the usual public interest critera and be offshore at the time of decision.[34]

The subclass 176 visa has largely the same criteria as above, but is for people who are unable to meet the pass mark of the subclass 175 visa. An applicant must be sponsored by an eligible relative living in Australia or nominated by a participating State or Territory government. The applicant must still pass a points test. The sponsor must have turned 18; be an Australian citizen, Australian permanent resident or an eligible New Zealand citizen; be usually resident in Australia; and be related[35] to the applicant, or the applicant's spouse or de facto partner (if they are also an applicant for the 176 visa).[36] The visa is permanent, permitting the holder to travel and enter Australia for five years from the date of grant.[37]

23 IMMI 10/023, signed 23 June 2010; Sch. 2, clause 138.210.
24 The current pass mark for this visa is 120 points, and the pool mark is 100.
25 Sch. 1, Item 1135(3)(b); PAM3: Sch. 2, Visa 175 – Skilled – Independent, s 7.1.
26 Sch. 2, clause 175.212.
27 Sch. 2, clause 175.211; PAM3: Sch. 2, Visa 175 – Skilled – Independent, s 7.2.
28 As defined in Migration Regulations 1994, regulation 1.15C as and IELTS test score of at least 6 for each of the 4 test components.
29 Ibid 7.3.
30 Sch. 2, clause 175.511.
31 *Migration Act 1958* (Cth), s 30(1).
32 PAM3: Sch. 2, Visa 175 – Skilled – Independent, s 10.4.
33 Ibid., s 4.4.
34 Sch. 2, clauses 175.255 and 175.412.
35 A parent; or a child or stepchild; or a brother or sister, or an adoptive brother or sister, or a stepbrother or stepsister; or an aunt or uncle, or a stepaunt or stepuncle; or a nephew or niece, or an adoptive nephew or niece, or a stepnephew or stepniece.
36 Sch. 2, clause 176.222.
37 Sch. 2, clause 176.511.

The subclass 475 visa is a provisional visa for a period of three years for people who can meet the lower pass mark.[38] An applicant must be sponsored by an eligible relative[39] living in a designated area[40] of Australia or nominated by a participating State or Territory government.[41] After living for two years and working for at least one in a Specified Regional Area,[42] an applicant can apply for a permanent visa. The applicant must be younger than 45[43] and nominate a skilled occupation in which they have been employed for at least 12 months in the period of 24 months ending on the day on which the application was made.[44] The applicant will not need to demonstrate recent skilled employment if they can instead meet the Australian study requirement.[45] The applicant must also show that each degree, diploma or trade qualification used to meet the Australian study requirement was closely related to their nominated occupation, and completed within six months immediately before the visa application was made.[46] When considering the meaning of 'closely related', policy states:

> the critical factor in determining whether the qualification is closely related to the occupation is whether the skill set/s underpinning the qualification/s are complementary and can be used in the nominated occupation, in terms of both subject matter and the level at which those skills were obtained.[47]

The applicant is required to have concessional competent English,[48] meet the relevant public interest criteria and be outside Australia at the time of decision.[49] This visa is also subject to the 'one fails, all fail' requirement.[50]

The subclass 476 visa is an 18 month temporary visa for graduates of recognised overseas educational institutions who have skills in demand in Australia. There is no points test for this visa. A holder of this visa may apply for a permanent visa at any time if they can meet the pass mark of the GSM points test. The applicant must be younger than 45[51] and nominate a skilled occupation,[52] and be nominated by a State or Territory government agency[53] or be sponsored by

38 Sch. 2, clause 475.221.
39 Above, footnote 38. Item 1228(3B) includes a grandparent and first cousin in addition to the above.
40 IMMI 07/060, signed 30 August 2007 – Designated Areas (Item 6701 of Sch. 6).
41 Sch. 2, clause 475.213(2).
42 If the applicant is being sponsored by an eligible relative then the sponsor must be usually resident: anywhere in Victoria, South Australia, Northern Territory, Tasmania, Australian Capital Territory, anywhere in Brisbane and Perth except the metropolitan regions, and in New South Wales – anywhere except Sydney, Newcastle and Wollongong. If the applicant is being sponsored by the State or Territory government, the requirement is Regional Australia/Low population growth metropolitan areas, as set by DIAC: <www.immi.gov.au/skilled/general-skilled-migration/regional-growth.htm>, accessed 15 February 2010.
43 Sch. 1, Item 1228(3)(b)(i).
44 Sch. 2, clause 475.211.
45 Sch. 2, clause 475.211(2)(b); defined in regulation 1.15F.
46 PAM3: Sch. 2, Visa 475, s 12.2.
47 Ibid., s 12.7.
48 Sch. 2, clause 475.214; defined in regulation 1.15E as an IELTS test average band score of at least 6 for the 4 test components; or specified by the Minister in writing (although no score is currently prescribed).
49 Sch. 2, clause 475.412.
50 PAM3: Sch. 2, Visa 475, s 18.3.
51 Sch. 1, Item 1228(3)(b)(i).
52 ibid., 1228(3)(b)(ii).
53 ibid., 1228(3A).

an eligible relative.[54] The applicant must not have previously held a subclass 476 or 485 visa.[55] The applicant must have completed a course 24 months prior to the day on which the application was made, at a specified institution,[56] for the award of a degree or higher in a specified discipline.[57]

7.2.2 Onshore

The relevant visa classes are:

- **Skilled – (Residence) (class VB)**[58]
- Subclass 885 (Skilled – Independent)[59]
- Subclass 886 (Skilled – Sponsored)[60]
- Subclass 887 (Skilled – Regional)[61]
- **Skilled – (Provisional) (class VC)**[62]
- Subclass 485 (Skilled – Graduate)[63]
- Subclass 487 (Skilled – Regional Sponsored).[64]

On 8 February 2010, the Minister for Immigration and Citizenship determined that certain skilled migration visa applications made before 1 September 2007 would be capped and ceased. The cap has now been reached and the applications subject to capping have ceased. This applies to subclasses 880 (Skilled – Independent Overseas Student), 881 (Skilled – Australian-sponsored Overseas Student, 882 (Skilled – Designated Area-sponsored Overseas Student), and 861, 862 and 863 in relation to New Zealand citizens.

The subclass 885 visa allows overseas students who have completed their studies in Australia in the last six months to apply for a permanent visa.[65] There is no sponsorship requirement, but the applicant must pass the points test.[66] The visa is for overseas students or former overseas students; holders of subclass 485 (Skilled – Graduate) or subclass 476 (Skilled – Recognised Graduate) visas;[67] or holders of subclass 471 (Trade Skills Training) visas.[68] The substantive criteria are similar to those required for the offshore subclass 175 (Skilled – Independent) visa, but this visa is only available to eligible overseas students in Australia, who must nominate a 50 or 60-point skilled occupation from the SOL.[69] The qualifications obtained must be closely related to the nominated skill occupation.[70]

54 ibid., 1228(3B).
55 Sch. 2, clause 476.211.
56 IMMI 10/053, signed 21 September 2010.
57 Sch. 2, clause 476.212.
58 Sch. 1, Item 1136.
59 ibid.
60 ibid.
61 ibid.
62 Sch. 1, Item 1229.
63 ibid.
64 ibid.
65 Sch. 2, clause 885.211.
66 Sch. 2, clause 885.221; PAM3: Sch. 2, Visa 885, s 15.
67 Sch. 1, Item 1136(5).
68 Sch. 1, Item 1136(6).
69 Sch. 1, Item 1156(3)(bb)(ii).
70 PAM3: Sch. 2, Visa 885, s 4.

The applicant must be younger than 45[71] and have competent English language skills.[72] The applicant and their family members must satisfy the public interest criteria[73] and the applicant must be in Australia when the visa is granted.[74] This is a permanent visa that allows the applicant, with a secondary applicant, to live as permanent residents in Australia.

Eligible applicants must hold (or have recently held) a specified category of student visa (as a student or student dependant) or a Bridging Visa A or Bridging Visa B pending a subclass 497 (Graduate – Skilled) application.[75] ELICOS, non-award course, AusAID/Defence, Australian government-assisted (including State/Territory governments), foreign government-assisted and multilateral agency-assisted students are not eligible.[76] If the applicant is the holder of a non-student substantive visa or a Bridging Visa A or B, they must have held an eligible student visa within the six months prior to the application.[77]

For subclass 886 visa, applicants must be sponsored by an eligible relative in Australia or nominated by a State or Territory government. The criteria are largely the same as the subclass 885 visa, but with a lower points test. The eligible sponsor must be 18 years of age,[78] and must demonstrate that they are either an Australian citizen, an Australian permanent resident, or an eligible New Zealand citizen.[79] The sponsor must be usually resident in Australia[80] – factors including their physical presence in the country, the length of that residency and their intention to live in the county will be considered.[81] The sponsor must be an eligible relative[82] and be directly related to the main applicant, their spouse or de facto partner.[83] With regard to nomination,[84] a case officer will consider if the nominator is a participating State or Territory government and the applicant's nominated skill occupation appears on the State or Territory shortage list.[85] If these criteria are met, the nomination should be accepted.

To be eligible for the subclass 887 visa the applicant must hold one of the following subclasses of visa: 495 (Skilled – Independent Regional (Provisional)), 496 (Skilled – Designated Area – Sponsored (Provisional)), 475 (Skilled – Regional Sponsored (Provisional)), or 487 (Skilled – Regional Sponsored

71 Sch. 1, Item 1136(4)(b)(ii).
72 Sch. 2, clause 885.213.
73 Sch. 2, clause 885.227.
74 Sch. 2, clause 885.411.
75 Sch. 1, Item 1136(5)(a)(i) and (ii).
76 Sch. 1, Item 1136(4)(ii).
77 ibid.
78 Sch. 2, clause 886.222(3)(a)(i).
79 Sch. 2, clause 886.222(3)(a)(ii).
80 Sch. 2, clause 886.222(3)(a)(iii).
81 PAM2: Sch. 2, Visa 886, s 8.2.
82 Sch. 2, clauses 885.222(3)(a)(iv)(A)–(E).
83 Sch. 2, clause 886.222(3)(a)(iv).
84 Sch. 2, clause 886.222(2)(b).
85 PAM3: Sch. 2, Visa 886, s 7.1.

(Provisional)).[86] The applicant must have lived in a Specified Regional Area for two years[87] and worked full-time in that area for at least one year.[88] The other criteria reflect those above. The periods need not be consecutive[89] and short holidays do not detract from the period of residence.[90] The Specified Regional Area differs according to the condition imposed on the applicant's provisional visa.[91] The 'one fails, all fail' rule applies. The applicant and their family must meet the public interest criteria.[92] This is a permanent visa[93] and the applicant must be in Australia at the time of grant.[94]

The subclass 487 visa is a three-year provisional visa for eligible students and holders of certain visas who can meet the lower pass mark. The applicant must hold one of the qualifying visas[95] and nominate a skilled occupation for which at least 50 points is available on the SOL.[96] Overseas students must have met the Australian Study Requirement[97] in the six months immediately before the application for a 487 visa is made.[98] Where an applicant applies on the basis of holding a subclass 476 (Skilled – Recognised Graduate) or 485 (Skilled – Graduate) visa they must have been granted that visa as the main applicant.[99] Holders of student visa subclasses 570, 571, 575, 576 and 572, 573 and 574 (if study is being undertaken) are ineligible for the subclass 478 visa.[100] Applicants must be sponsored and pass a points test;[101] after living for two years and working for at least one in a Specified Regional Area, they can apply for a permanent visa. The applicant must have concessional competent English[102] and, along with their family, meet the usual public interest criteria.[103] The applicant must be nominated by a State or Territory government,[104] or sponsored by an eligible relative.[105] The skilled related criteria mirror those for the permanent visas discussed above.

Subclass 485 is a temporary visa for overseas students who have obtained a qualification in Australia. The purpose of this visa is to provide an option for those who are unable to meet the points test, so that they can remain in Australia

86 Sch. 1, Item 1136(4), (5), (6) and (7); Sch. 2, clause 887.211.
87 Sch. 2, clause 887.212.
88 Sch. 2, clause 887.213.
89 Sch. 2, clause 11.3.
90 Sch. 2, clause 11.2.
91 PAM2: Sch. 2, Visa 997, s 10.
92 Sch. 2, clause 887.322.
93 Sch. 2, clause 887.551.
94 Sch. 2, clause 887.411.
95 Sch. 1, Item 1229(4), (5), (6) or (7).
96 Sch. 1, Item 1229(4)(b)(ii), 1229(5)(b)(ii), 1229(6)(b)(iii) and 1229(7)(b)(ii).
97 Regulation 1.15F.
98 PAM3: Sch. 2, Visa 487, s 15.1.
99 Sch. 1, Item 1229(5)(b)(i); PAM3: Sch. 2, Visa 487, s 10.1.
100 Sch. 1, Item 1229(4)(a)(ii).
101 Sch. 2, clause 487.222.
102 Sch. 2, clause 487.215.
103 Sch. 2, clause 487.230.
104 Sch. 2, clause 487.225(1).
105 Sch. 2, clause 487.225(3).

for up to 18 months[106] and gain the skills required to submit an application for a permanent or provisional GSM visa. The applicant must hold a qualifying visa[107] and be younger than 45 at the time of application.[108] The applicant must nominate a 50 or 60-point occupation on the SOL.[109] There is no sponsorship or nomination requirement.[110] The applicant must meet the Australian Study Requirement six months before making the application, and each degree used to satisfy this requirement must be closely related to the nominated skilled occupation.[111] The applicant must have competent English[112] and meet the usual public interest criteria.[113]

7.3 Visas based on employer nominations

Employer nominations are divided into two categories: the Employer Nominations Scheme (ENS) and the Regional Sponsored Migration Scheme (RSMS). The latter has less stringent requirements, as an inducement to attract workers to designated areas. The schemes enable Australian employers to recruit skilled and 'highly skilled' workers either from overseas, or from among persons temporarily in Australia, in circumstances where the employer has been unable to fill a vacancy from within the Australian labour market or through their own training efforts.

Both permanent and temporary visas are available through employer nominations. This chapter discusses the requirements for permanent visas. Temporary visas are discussed in the next chapter.

There are two classes of permanent visas: migrant (offshore) and residence (onshore).

- **Employer Nomination (Migrant) (class AN)**[114]
- Subclass 119 (Regional Sponsored Migration Scheme)[115]
- Subclass 121 (Employer Nomination Scheme)[116]
- **Employer Nomination (Residence) (class BW)**[117]
- Subclass 856 (Employer Nomination Scheme)[118]
- Subclass 857 (Regional Sponsored Migration Scheme).[119]

106 Sch. 2, clause 485.511 – the date will be specified by the Minister.
107 Sch. 1, Item 1229(4)(a).
108 Sch. 1, Item 1229(4)(b)(i).
109 ibid.
110 PAM3: Sch. 2, Visa 485, s 1.1.
111 Sch. 2, clause 485.213.
112 Sch. 2, clause 485.215.
113 Sch. 2, clause 485.224.
114 Sch. 1, Item 1114.
115 ibid.
116 ibid.
117 Sch. 1, Item 1114A.
118 ibid.
119 ibid.

7.3.1 The Employer Nomination Scheme (ENS)

The Employer Nomination Scheme (ENS) involves a two-stage process: first, the nomination of the position by the employer and the approval of that nomination by DIAC; and second, the visa application by the employee intending to fill the nominated position. The nomination is subject to the provisions of regulation 5.19 in Part 5 of the Regulations. A successful nomination is defined as an approved appointment.[120] It relates to the position, not to the nominee. The visa requirements are set out in Schedules 1 and 2 of the Regulations.

There are two nomination categories: the ENS and the Regional Sponsored Migration Scheme (RSMS).[121] The latter operates through the requirement that the nomination for the relevant position must be certified by a gazetted Regional Certifying Body.[122]

In addition to using the prescribed form and paying the prescribed fee for a nomination, the requirements for approval of an employer nomination are that: an employer–employee relationship must exist in a business that is operating and located in Australia and there is a vacancy; the employment must be full-time and ongoing – at least for three years, with the possibility of renewal; the employer has an adequate training record or a commitment to training; and there is no suitable Australian citizen or Australian permanent resident worker to fill the position. Australian wages and conditions must apply.[123]

Businesses that are yet to commence operations will need to demonstrate that there is a genuine intention to commence and that the nominated position is important to the future success of the business.[124] The employer–employee relationship is tested by the usual indicators, such as PAYG tax arrangements, employer contributions to superannuation and workcare, the right to hire and fire and so on.[125] In assessing that requirement, DIAC officials will be guided by the ANZSCO dictionary (see above).[126] There are special guidelines related to medical practitioners, academic and scientific research positions, tourist industry positions, chefs and cooks and religious organisations and religious workers.[127]

The training component relates to the employer rather than the employee who fills the nominated position, although the nominee may have a part to play in training. The general consideration relates to having training procedures, programs and/or plans for improving employees' skills in place so as to reduce the need to import skilled labour.[128] The non-availability of an Australian permanent resident or citizen is established by 'testing the labour market'. Unless the

120 Regulation 1.03.
121 Regulation 5.19(2) and (4).
122 IMMI 10/051, 18 November 2010.
123 Regulation 5.19(2)(a)–(f).
124 PAM3: Div. 5.3/reg. 5.19 Approval of nominated positions (Employer Nomination), s 8.2.
125 PAM3: Div. 5.3/reg. 5.19 Approval of nominated positions (Employer Nomination), s 8.1.
126 PAM3: Div. 5.3/reg. 5.19 Approval of nominated positions (Employer Nomination), s 15.
127 PAM3: Div. 5.3/reg. 5.19 Approval of nominated positions (Employer Nomination), ss 21–25.
128 PAM3: Div. 5.3/reg. 5.19 Approval of nominated positions (Employer Nomination), s 12.1 and *Masuoka v Immigration Review Tribunal* (1996) 67 FCR 492, [10].

delegate deciding the nomination application provides a waiver,[129] that testing requires advertising the position during the six months immediately prior to lodging the employer nomination, in appropriate publications or with relevant employment agencies, or providing independent and authoritative advice from recognised professional or industrial bodies.[130] DIAC is wary of advertisements that appear to match the qualifications of a particular person or are not prominently directed at the widest market.[131]

Visa applications can be made onshore – subclass 121 (Employer Nomination Scheme) or offshore – subclass 856 (Employer Nomination Scheme). Onshore applicants are excluded if their last substantive visa was one of those listed in the relevant part of Schedule 2; they must hold a particular subclass of substantive visa to be eligible to apply.[132] The nominee's qualifications and experience need to match the criteria that were applied in approving the nomination.[133]

7.3.2 The Regional Sponsored Migration Scheme (RSMS)

The Regional Sponsored Migration Scheme (RSMS) has a less stringent skill level requirement and period of employment requirement, and no requirement for labour market testing or training.

The RSMS is filtered through prescribed regional certifying bodies (RCBs) that have jurisdiction to assess employment requirements in prescribed areas.[134] All areas of Australia are prescribed except Brisbane, the Gold Coast, Newcastle, Sydney, Wollongong, Melbourne and Perth. Prior to the employer nomination being approved, the relevant RCB must certify that the nominated position is for a genuine vacancy, is for at least two years of full-time employment and cannot be filled locally. Unless the position is approved as an exceptional appointment, the vacancy must be one that requires the occupant to have had training equivalent to an Australian diploma level qualification.[135] The certificate reflects the regulatory requirements for a nominated position in the RSMS.[136]

If the nominee does not have the usual formal qualifications, the nomination may be considered 'exceptional' and approved if the RCB certifies it and, if the occupation being nominated falls within ANZSCO levels 3–4, the position is one that has, for at least two years immediately prior to the nomination being submitted, been filled by the prospective RSMS visa applicant as a subclass

129 Regulation 5.19(2)(f)(ii) and PAM3: Div. 5.3/ reg. 5.19 ss 13.3 and 15.1. The policy guidelines have exceptions (not waivers) for senior academic/scientific research positions, medical practitioners, religious duties and MODL occupations: PAM3: Div. 5.3/reg. 5.19 Approval of nominated positions (Employer Nomination), s 13.3.

130 PAM3: Div. 5.3/reg. 5.19 Approval of nominated positions (Employer Nomination), s 13.

131 PAM3: Div. 5.3/reg. 5.19 Approval of nominated positions (Employer Nomination), s 14.1.

132 Sch. 2, clauses 856.211 and 856.212(4)–(7).

133 Sch. 2, clause 856.213.

134 IMMI 10/051 – Regional Certifying Bodies and Regional Postcodes (paragraph 5.19(4)(e), subregulation 5.19(5), paragraph 2.43(1)(la)), 18 November 2010.

135 As defined in regulation 2.26A(6) (according to policy 'any occupation within ANZSCO skill level 1 and 2 is considered to be a position requiring a diploma or higher qualification – PAM3: Div. 5.3/ reg. 5.19 s 33.1).

136 Regulation 5.19(4).

457 visa-holder, and meets the requirements of regulation 5.19(4).[137] As the nomination is predicated on the relevant RCB certifying the need to fill the position, labour market testing is not a necessity in this category.

Like the ENS, this program has special guidelines related to medical practitioners, academic and scientific research positions, chefs and cooks and religious organisations and religious workers.[138]

Visa applications can be made onshore – subclass 857 (Regional Sponsored Migration Scheme),[139] or offshore – subclass 119 (Regional Sponsored Migration Scheme).[140] Unless there are exceptional circumstances, the applicant must be younger than 45. Applicants for some other classes of permanent skills-based visas are deemed to have applied for a subclass 119 visa,[141] and applicants for Employer Nomination (Residence) (class BW), Skilled – New Zealand Citizen (Residence) (class DB) or Skilled – Independent Overseas Student (Residence) (class DD) visas are deemed to have applied for a subclass 857 visa.[142] As for the ENS visa applicants, there are restrictions on applications according to the subclass of visa that is or was held by the applicant.[143]

The visa can be cancelled if the holder does not commence employment within six months of the grant of the subclass 857 visa or entry to Australia with a subclass 119 visa, or the actual employment ceased before the expiry of two years.[144]

7.4 Labour agreements

The term 'labour agreement' is defined as:

> (a) a formal agreement entered into between the Minister, or the Employment Minister, and
> (b) a person or organisation in Australia;
> under which an employer is authorised to recruit persons to be employed by that employer in Australia.[145]

There are three types of agreement: a 'standard' labour agreement; a Regional Headquarters agreement (RHQ);[146] and an Invest Australia Supported Skills agreement (IASS).[147] RHQ agreements provided streamlined immigration arrangements to organisations that the Minister for Industry, Tourism and Resources determined as being companies managing functions that support an

137 PAM3: Div. 5.3/reg. 5.19, s 33.2.
138 PAM3: Div. 5.3/reg. 5.19, ss 39–47.
139 Sch. 2, clause 857.412.
140 Sch. 2, clause 119.411.
141 Regulation 2.08C Employer Nomination (Migrant) (class AN); Independent (Migrant) (class AT); Skilled – Independent (Migrant) (class BN); Skill Matching (Migrant) (class BR).
142 Regulations 2.08CA and 2.08CB.
143 Sch. 2, clauses 857.211 and 857.212.
144 *Migration Act 1958* (Cth), s 137Q.
145 Regulation 1.03.
146 As defined in regulation 1.16A.
147 As defined in regulation 1.16B.

international operation. They were replaced by the Invest Australia Supported Skills (IASS) program from 1 July 2003. Existing RHQ agreements, however, remain in effect until they expire and are subject to the relevant statutory requirements. PAM3 describes the IASS agreements as follows:

> Invest Australia Supported Skills (IASS) agreements provide streamlined immigration arrangements for organisations that the Minister for Industry, Tourism and Resources has determined as being companies proposing to make a significant and/or strategic investment in Australia, related to 1 of 4 key criteria:
>
> 1 the project will boost Australian industry innovation through increasing research, development and commercialisation capability, the new application of skills and knowledge, technology transfer, and cluster development; or
> 2 the project will provide significant economic benefit to regional Australia taking account of the region's investment needs; or
> 3 the project's estimated investment exceeds $50 million and thus inherently makes a significant contribution to economic growth, employment and/or infrastructure; or
> 4 the company is establishing a regional headquarters or regional operating centre which will support the international operations of the parent company.

The 'labour agreement' definition is relevant in assessing applications for the two permanent resident subclasses listed below and in temporary visa subclasses 418 Educational, 421 Sport, 422 Medical Practitioner and 457 Business (Long Stay). This chapter deals only with the permanent visas, which are as follows:

- **Labour Agreement (Migrant) (class AU)**[148]
- Subclass 120 (Labour Agreement)[149]
- **Labour Agreement (Residence) (class BV)**[150]
- Subclass 855 (Labour Agreement).[151]

Labour agreements are negotiated as a precursor to accessing the migration process, and those negotiations are not caught by migration legislation. PAM3 describes the procedure:

> A labour agreement is a formal arrangement negotiated between an employer or an industry association and the Commonwealth Government, represented by DIMIA and the Department of Employment and Workplace Relations (DEWR). [Their purpose is to] enable Australian employers to recruit a specified number of workers from overseas in response to identified or emerging labour market (or skill) shortages in the Australian labour market. Employees may come to Australia on either a temporary or a permanent basis. An industry body, a company or an umbrella organisation may negotiate for the entry of a number of people to fill positions across a wide range of occupations. Visa applications under a labour agreement receive priority processing. In accordance with the principle of partnership between government and employers, labour agreements should ensure that all relevant stakeholders are included in the negotiations to any

148 Sch. 1, Item 1121.
149 ibid.
150 Sch. 1, Item 1121A.
151 ibid.

> agreement e.g. the State/Territory departments of health on behalf of hospitals where an agreement is proposed for health professionals.
>
> ... employers undertake to nominate each overseas worker whom they wish to recruit to a vacancy under the relevant labour agreement... [and] only DIMIA may decide whether a nomination is in accordance with the relevant labour agreement.[152]

The agreements cover matters such as the period of the agreement, the nature of positions that are the subject of the agreement, including employee salaries and other terms and conditions, the skill levels required and the number of workers required – either temporary or permanent. Once the agreement is made, employers nominate employees to fill specified positions and DIAC assesses whether or not the nomination matches the terms of the agreement and whether or not the nominee matches the specific nomination and passes the criteria for the visa.

As for the ENS, some applicants in other visa subclasses are deemed to have applied for subclass 120 and 885 visas.[153] Applicants need to have skills that match the position set out in the nomination and be younger than 45 unless there are exceptional circumstances.[154] Those applying under an IASS agreement must meet the requirements of the IASS or RHQ agreement – defined in regulations 1.10 and 1.16A respectively.[155] As for onshore ENS and RSMS visa applicants, there are restrictions on onshore labour agreement applications according to the subclass of visa that is or was held by the applicant.[156]

7.5 Distinguished talent

This is a class of visa for people who have outstanding talents in their field and may not otherwise meet the criteria in other visa subclasses, or who have provided specialised assistance to the Australian government in security matters. It is available to applicants both offshore and onshore.[157] Onshore applicants will be refused if they hold or have held certain subclasses of visa.[158] The relevant visas are:

- **Distinguished Talent (Migrant) (class AL)**[159]
- Subclass 124 (Distinguished Talent)[160]
- **Distinguished Talent (Residence) (class BX)**[161]
- Subclass 858 (Distinguished Talent).[162]

152 PAM3: Div. 1.2/reg. 1.03/Labour agreement ss 2–3 and 8.
153 Regulation 2.08C.
154 Sch. 2, clauses 120.211 and 855.213.
155 Sch. 2, clauses 120.211(4)(b) and 855.213(3)(b).
156 Sch. 2, clauses 855.211 and 855.212.
157 Sch. 2, clauses 858.411 and 124.411.
158 Sch. 2, clause 858.211.
159 Sch. 1, Item 1112.
160 ibid.
161 Sch. 1, Item 1113.
162 ibid.

Both offshore and onshore applicants must meet the same substantive criteria. If the applicant is a minor, there is provision to include a parent and the members of that parent's family unit in their application.[163] All applicants must be nominated by an Australian permanent resident or citizen, or an eligible New Zealand citizen who has a national reputation in the applicant's area of distinction.[164] The applicant must demonstrate that he or she:

(a) has an internationally recognised record of exceptional and outstanding achievement in one of the following areas:
  (i) a profession;
  (ii) a sport;
  (iii) the arts; or
  (iv) academia and research, and that he or she:
(b) is still prominent in the area; and
(c) would be an asset to the Australian community; and
(d) would have no difficulty in obtaining employment, or in becoming established independently, in Australia in the area.[165]

Applicants applying on the grounds of providing security assistance are, in effect, recommended either by the Minister responsible for an intelligence agency or by a security agency within the meaning of the *Australian Security Intelligence Organisation Act 1979* (Cth) or the Director-General of Security.[166]

PAM3 gives guidance on the level of talent that is required to meet the criteria for subclass 124:

> Claims of an 'excellent' level of performance at a job, particularly where the benefits of such a performance may only be realised locally, would not be regarded as 'exceptional'; a single achievement by the applicant, particularly where that appears to be the only significant achievement, would not be regarded as 'exceptional'. Achievement in an occupation, profession or activity, at a level less than an international (or national, if comparable) recognition would not generally be regarded as exceptional achievement.
>
> [The applicant] should contribute to the betterment of the community economically, socially or culturally (i.e. depending on the applicant's intended field of activity), for example by introducing and transferring new skills or significantly raising local sporting or artistic standards . . .
>
> . . . the applicant's achievements must be at an international (or national, if comparable) level irrespective of the extent of relevant local talent within Australia.
>
> Achievement in a sport or the arts, at a level less than an international (or national, if comparable) recognition would not generally be regarded as exceptional achievement. In ascertaining the international standing of the applicant, officers should give consideration to the comparative standard of that art or sport in the applicant's country. For example, an applicant rated 20 nationally, in a sport where thousands

163 Regulation 1.12(6) and (7).
164 Sch. 2, clauses 124.211(2)(d) and 858.212(2)(e).
165 Sch. 2, clauses 124.221(a)–(d) and 858.212(2)(a)–(d). In *Wolseley v MIMA* [2006] FMCA 1149, it was held that the applicant does not need to be of exceptional benefit to the Australian community as a whole, as was indicated in the relevant PAM3 at the time.
166 Sch. 2, clauses 124.211(4) and 858.212(4).

> of people are in contention, would be expected to have an exceptional record of achievement.[167]

Applicants for permanent residence in the skills categories, if their application is unsuccessful or is put into a queue as a consequence of capping the number of visas, might succeed in obtaining a temporary visa. These categories are discussed in the next chapter.

167 PAM3: Sch. 2, Visa 124, s 2.

8

Temporary visas

8.1 Overview

The migration legislation provides a range of visas for temporary workers and business people, and working holiday-makers and students, as well as visas for tourists and people visiting friends and relations. In addition, some temporary visas are issued for special purposes.

8.2 Temporary workers

Temporary workers and business people can be employer-sponsored or independent. They range from working holiday-makers to those with a need for long-term, but not permanent, residence.

8.2.1 Working Holiday (Temporary) (class TZ)[1]

- Subclass 417 (Working Holiday)[2]

The subclass 417 visa aims to allow young people who are holders of passports issued by specified countries[3] to holiday in Australia and supplement their funds through incidental work. The application procedures are relatively simple and

1 Sch. 1, Item 1225.
2 ibid.
3 IMMI 09/008, 22 April 2009 'Class of Persons (Subparagraph 1225(3)(b)(i)' (Belgium, Canada, Denmark, Finland, France, Italy, Norway, Sweden, The Netherlands, The Republic of Ireland, The United Kingdom, Estonia, Germany, Japan, Malta, Hong Kong, The Republic of Cyprus, Korea and Taiwan).

brief, and in many countries can be done on the internet.[4] Applicants cannot have held a previous working holiday visa, must have turned 18 but not turned 31, must not be accompanied by any dependent children during their stay, and must demonstrate the intention to have a working holiday (that is, not dedicated to either work or residence) and that they have sufficient funds for that purpose.[5] PAM3 advises that 'generally, AUD$5000 [in addition to funds for a return airfare] ... may be regarded as sufficient to cover the costs of the initial 3 month stage of the 12 month working holiday for an applicant'.[6] There is no provision for members of the family unit, so spouses or de facto partners must make their own applications.

There are restrictions on AusAID students or recipients, although these can be waived in some circumstances.[7] The work and study capacity of successful visa applicants is restricted by Schedule 8 conditions[8] being attached to the visas.[9] Working holiday-makers may, in some circumstances, apply for visitor or temporary work visas if they meet the requirements that are relevant to those visas.

The Regulations make provision for a subclass of 'Work and Holiday' (subclass 462) visa, but its issue is contingent on particular countries (that have entered relevant arrangements with the Australian government) being prescribed by Gazette; in the absence of any relevant gazettal, the visa is unavailable.

8.2.2 Electronic Travel Authority (class UD)[10]

- Subclass 956 (Electronic Travel Authority (Business Entrant – Long Validity))[11]
- Subclass 976 (Electronic Travel Authority (Visitor))[12]
- Subclass 977 (Electronic Travel Authority (Business Entrant – Short Validity))[13]

The government has streamlined temporary entry for business applicants from certain countries the government views as having a 'high volume/low risk' trading relationship with Australia. Applications can be made offshore or onshore (including in immigration clearance – that is, at entry control points).[14] The applications are computerised and visas are issued electronically (without physical

4 Applicants from countries listed in IMMI 09/008 (see preceding footnote) can apply on the internet or by submitting paper forms.
5 Sch. 2, clauses 417.211.
6 PAM3: Sch. 2, Visa 417 s 19.2.
7 Sch. 2, clause 417.221(6)–(7).
8 Sch. 8, Condition 8108 – The holder must not be employed in Australia by any one employer for more than three months, without the prior permission in writing of the Secretary. Condition 8201 – While in Australia the holder must not engage, for more than three months, in any studies or training.
9 Sch. 2, clause 417.612.
10 Sch. 1, Item 1208A.
11 ibid.
12 ibid.
13 ibid.
14 Sch. 1, Item 1208A(3)(a) and regulation 2.07AB 'Applications for Electronic Travel Authority visas'.

visa labels) by an extensive range of travel agents, airlines or overseas posts.[15] Applicants must hold an 'ETA eligible passport'[16] issued by prescribed countries.[17] The subclass 956 provides for multiple travel, three months stay on each visit and a validity for travel for the life of the passport.[18] The 'Short Validity' version (subclass 977) specifies the number of entries to Australia (for up to three months) the applicant may make within a maximum of 12 months (shorter if the visa expires beforehand).[19] Provided the applicant holds a relevant passport, they meet the substantive requirement of the visa by stating an intention to visit Australia temporarily for the purpose of business.[20]

8.2.3 Temporary Business Entry (class UC)[21]

- Subclass 456 (Business (Short Stay))[22]
- Subclass 457 (Business (Long Stay))[23]

Applications for this class of visa are taken to be valid if the applicant is the holder of a valid passport issued by a designated APEC economy[24] or is one of certain permanent residents of Hong Kong who have applied for an APEC Business Travel Card.

The subclass 456 Business (Short Stay) visa is for genuine business visitors seeking a short-term (up to three months) entry to Australia for business purposes. The purpose of the applicant's visit must be consistent with their personal attributes and business background and generally relate to their existing business activities (whether in or outside Australia). There should also be a demonstrated need for the applicant to be in Australia for business purposes.[25] PAM3 describes business purposes as: the applicant's existing business activities and/or occupation overseas; any existing business activities in Australia; or exploring business opportunities in Australia ... Conference attendance or training purposes [are] acceptable if relevant to the applicant's occupation and business activities.[26]

The subclass 457 Business (Long Stay) visa is primarily intended to provide streamlined entry arrangements for businesses needing to recruit staff from overseas on a temporary basis (up to four years). It also provides for the temporary stay of independent executives (holders of the subclass 457IE visa) who wish to

15 IMMI 09/059 'Approval of Agents for Electronic Travel Authority Applications (Regulations 1208A(3)(bb)(ii) and (bc)(ii).
16 As defined in Regulation 1.11B.
17 GN 5, 4 February 2004 – Specification of ETA-eligible passports.
18 Sch. 2, clause 956.511(b).
19 Sch. 2, clause 977.511(b).
20 PAM3: Sch. 2 – Electronic Travel Authorities (ETAs), s 14.3.
21 Sch. 1, Item 1223A.
22 ibid.
23 ibid.
24 As defined in regulation 1.03 and specified in GN IMMI 08/096 – Designated APEC economy (Brunei Darussalam, Canada, Chile, The Hong Kong Special Administrative Region of the People's Republic of China, Republic of Indonesia, Japan, The Republic of Korea, Malaysia, Mexico, Papua New Guinea, People's Republic of China, Peru, The Republic of the Philippines, Singapore, Taiwan, Thailand, the United States of America, Vietnam).
25 Sch. 2, clause 456.211(a).
26 PAM3: Sch. 2, Visa 456, s 26.1.

maintain ownership of an existing business in Australia conducted by them as a principal, for entry of business representatives aiming to establish a system for the sale of services, and for the special category of people accorded certain privileges and immunities under specified legislation.

Applicants must meet the requirements of one of the following subclauses of Schedule 2, clause 457.223: (2) labour agreements (LAs); (4) standard business sponsorship; (7A) independent executives (further application onshore); (8) service sellers; or (9) persons accorded certain privileges and immunities.[27]

Independent executives (visa 457IE holders) in Australia can apply for a further 457IE (FAO)[28] or for permanent residence if they meet the criteria for a subclass 845 (Established Business in Australia), 846 (State/Territory-sponsored Regional Established Business in Australia) or 892 (State/Territory-sponsored Business Owner (Residence)) visa.[29]

Applicants for a further 457IE (FAO) must have been conducting the relevant business as a principal for 15 months or the application will be ruled invalid and the applicant will fail a substantive Schedule 2 criterion.[30]

'Service sellers' are persons who are representatives of suppliers of services located outside Australia who propose to represent the supplier in Australia. They must plan to negotiate, or enter into agreements, for the sale of services, but not be involved in the actual supply or sale of the services.[31]

Persons accorded certain privileges and immunities are persons to whom privileges and immunities will be accorded under the *International Organisations (Privileges and Immunities) Act 1963* (Cth) or the *Overseas Missions (Privileges and Immunities) Act 1995* (Cth) and whose application the Foreign Minister has recommended in writing to the Minister should be granted.[32]

Applicants for the Australian business and overseas business categories both require a sponsorship from the relevant business. The sponsorship is an approval of the business for the purpose of employing workers.[33] A single sponsorship can be for one or more employees.

From 14 September 2009 a new legislative framework in relation to sponsors and nominators came into effect. The nomination must identify the primary visa-holder or the applicant who will work in the nominated occupation.[34] An approved sponsor is defined under section 5(1) of the *Migration Act 1981* (Cth) as an approved person or a person who is party to a labour agreement. Under the Regulations, the person must, as part of the nomination:[35]

27 Sch. 2, clause 457.223(1)–(10).
28 Sch. 1, Item 1223A(3)(ad). A spouse who held a 457 visa can, if they meet other criteria, become the principal applicant for a 457IE (FAO) visa: Sch. 1, Item 1223A(3)(ae).
29 See Chapter 5.
30 Sch. 1, Item 1223A(3)(ad) or Item 1223A(3)(ae) and Sch. 2, clause 457.223(7A)(b)(i).
31 Sch. 2, clause 457.223(8)(a) and (b).
32 Sch. 2, clause 457.223(9).
33 In *Moller v MIMA* [2007] FMCA 168, it was stated that the employer must be a legal entity distinct from the applicant in order to be legally capable of incurring the separate obligations. Thus an applicant cannot establish an unincorporated business in Australia and then use this to sponsor themselves.
34 Regulation 2.72(5).
35 Regulations 2.72(5), 2.72(8) and 2.73(4)(a).

- provide identification of the person who will work in the nominated occupation (that is, 'the nominee'); and
- specify the 6-digit ANZSCO code and/or the name of the occupation.

Standard business sponsors must certify that:[36]

- the qualifications and experience of the nominee are commensurate with the qualifications and experience described in the relevant occupation dictionary or legislative instrument; and
- the tasks or duties of the nominated occupation will include a significant majority of the tasks or duties described in the relevant occupation dictionary or legislative instrument; and
- if the sponsor is an 'overseas business':
  - the nominated occupation is a position in the business or
  - the nominated occupation is an occupation which is exempt from this requirement and
- if the sponsor is an Australian business:
  - the nominated occupation is a position in the business or
  - the nominated occupation is a position in an 'associated entity' of the business or
  - the nominated occupation is an occupation which is exempt from this requirement.

Parties to a labour agreement must provide, as part of the nomination, that:

- the tasks or duties of the position will include a significant majority of the tasks or duties of the nominated occupation listed in the occupation dictionary, or the nominated occupation specified in the labour agreement, and
- the qualifications and experience of the nominee are commensurate with the qualifications and experience specified for the occupation in the labour agreement.[37]

The requirements for nominations under labour agreements, RHQ agreements and IASS agreements are the same as for permanent residence applications and are set out in Chapter 6.

Once the employer's sponsorship and nominations have been approved, the nominated employee can make a visa application. In practice, they are often all lodged at the same time. Onshore applicants must hold, or have held, one of the visas set out in Schedule 2, clause 457.211. In the four categories that require nominations, they must be the person nominated for the position, have the skills and experience for the position, and be remunerated at the minimum salary level or above and in accordance with the salary specified in the nomination form or (for regional applicants) specified by an award or legislation.[38]

36 Regulation 2.73(4)(b).
37 Regulations 2.73(4)(c) and 2.72(11)(b).
38 See the relevant parts of Sch. 2, clause 457.223(2)–(10).

All subclass 457 visas (except for Independent Executives) are issued with the Schedule 8 condition 8107 attached.[39] That condition effectively precludes holders from changing employers or working in a position or occupation inconsistent with the position or occupation in relation to which the visa was granted. If the holder ceases to work for the particular employer or in the particular position, he/she must lodge a fresh visa application and the new employer must lodge a fresh sponsorship and nomination related to the position to be filled and the visa applicant nominated to that position.

8.2.4 Short Stay Sponsored (Visitor) (class UL)[40]

- Subclass 459 Sponsored Business Visitor (Short Stay)[41]
- Subclass 679 Sponsored Family Visitor [42]

The subclass 459 visa is similar to the subclass 456 visa (see above), with the added requirements that it can only be obtained offshore[43] and the applicant must be sponsored by an Australian citizen or permanent resident or eligible New Zealand citizen who is a Commonwealth or state member of parliament or a mayor of a municipality, or by a Commonwealth, State or Territory government agency or instrumentality.[44] PAM3 advises: 'The 459 visa critera largely mirror those for the Business (Short Stay) 456 visa, other than the visa requirements that applicants be sponsored and the capacity to request a security bond.'[45]

8.2.5 Medical Practitioner (Temporary) (class UE)[46]

- Subclass 422 (Medical Practitioner)[47]

This visa will no longer be available for new applicants from 1 July 2010. Those who currently hold this visa will remain on that visa until: the end of the validity period of their visa; or they change their employer sponsor; or they are granted a new visa under another subclass. New applicants will have to apply under the subclass 457 – Business (Long Stay) visa program.

8.2.6 Work and Holiday (Temporary) (class US)[48]

The purpose of this visa is to enable young people[49] to holiday and work in Australia to improve cultural understanding. This visa can only be accessed

39 Sch. 2, clause 457.611.
40 Sch. 1, Item 1217A.
41 ibid.
42 ibid.
43 Sch. 1, Items 1217A(3)(a) and (b).
44 Sch. 2, clause 459.214.
45 PAM3: Generic Guidelines H, Sch. 2, Visa 459, s 29.1.
46 Sch. 1, Item 1214AA.
47 ibid.
48 Sch 1, Item 1224A.
49 Regulation 462.212: The applicant must be between the ages of 18 and 30 (inclusive).

once.[50] The application must be made from outside Australia. This is only available to citizens of countries with which Australia has reciprocal work and holiday arrangements.[51] The decision-maker must take into account the MOU with each such country,[52] and will be guided by a program cap.[53] Currently this visa is only available to applicants from the Islamic Republic of Iran, the Kingdom of Thailand, Chile, the Republic of Turkey, the United States of America, Malaysia, Indonesia and Bangladesh.[54] The visa remains in effect for 12 months after grant[55] and conditions 8547 and 8548 are imposed.[56]

8.2.7 Domestic Worker (Temporary) (class TG)[57]

- Subclass 426 (Domestic Worker (Temporary) – Diplomatic or Consular)[58]
- Subclass 427 (Domestic Worker (Temporary) – Executive)[59]

Subclass 426 is for adult domestic workers employed in a private capacity by diplomatic and consular representatives posted to Australia,[60] taking into consideration international bilateral relations and the Vienna Conventions on diplomatic and consular status.[61] People employed directly by the overseas mission (rather than privately) are eligible for subclass 996 diplomatic (temporary) visas (these will not be covered in this book). Applications are made offshore unless an onshore applicant already holds or has held a subclass 426 visa,[62] and must have the support of the Foreign Minister.[63] The visa is granted subject to Schedule 8 work restriction conditions 8110[64] and 8107, confining holders to the position for which the visa was granted.[65]

Despite the usual policy concerns about labour market testing, subclass 427 visas allow the entry of domestic workers for certain executives who hold a visa subclass 457 (or subclasses 412 (Independent Executive) and 413 (Executive) visas),[66] a concession recognising the representational and entertainment responsibilities of such holders while working in Australia.[67] Applications can be made offshore and onshore by specified visa-holders.[68] Applicants must be sponsored, either indirectly through their employer's sponsor

50 PAM3: Sch. 2, Visa 462 – Work and Holiday, s 1.
51 Regulation 462.216.
52 Ibid; PAM3: Sch. 2, Visa 462 – Work and Holiday, s 15.
53 PAM3: Sch. 2, Visa 462 – Work and Holiday, s 15.
54 IMMI 10/050, Arrangements for Work and Holiday Visa Applications, signed 15 December 2010.
55 Regulation 462.512.
56 Regulation 462.611.
57 Sch. 1, Item 1207.
58 ibid.
59 ibid.
60 Sch. 2, clause 426.222(b).
61 As set out in the DFAT publication *Manual of Consular Instructions*.
62 Sch. 1, Item 1207(3) and Sch. 2, clause 426.211.
63 Sch. 2, clause 426.223.
64 8110 The holder: (a) must not engage in work in Australia except in the household of the employer in relation to whom the visa was granted; and (b) except with the permission in writing of the Foreign Minister, must not remain in Australia after the permanent departure of that employer.
65 See 4.3, Restrictions on visa applications.
66 Sch. 2, clause 427.222(b).
67 PAM3: Sch. 2, Visa 427, s 1.2.
68 Sch. 1, Item 1207(3) and Sch. 2, clause 427.211.

or directly by the employer.[69] Sponsors must meet certain financial and employment obligations;[70] while labour market testing might be requested, it is not a requirement if there are compelling circumstances, established through the employer's representations.[71] Visas are granted for the period of the employer's stay up to a maximum of two years, with the total subject to another two-year extension, but are not to exceed four years,[72] and have work restrictions equivalent to those of subclass 426 visa-holders (see above).[73]

8.3 Cultural/Social (Temporary) (class TE)[74]

- Subclass 411 (Exchange)[75]
- Subclass 416 (Special Program)[76]
- Subclass 420 (Entertainment)[77]
- Subclass 421 (Sport)[78]
- Subclass 423 (Media and Film Staff)[79]
- Subclass 428 (Religious Worker)[80]

These subclasses of visa are available offshore and onshore. As a threshold requirement, onshore applicants must be holders (or former holders) of the limited subclasses of substantive visas specified in the part of Schedule 2[81] – relating to the particular subclass – and AusAID students must have support from the responsible Minister, although that requirement can be waived.

Exchange visa (411) is for the entry of skilled people under exchange arrangements giving Australian residents reciprocal opportunities to work with overseas organisations.[82] The visa is issued with Schedule 8 condition 8107.[83]

Special program visa (416) is for applicants undertaking an organised working visit to Australia to participate in a youth exchange program, or for people who have been nominated by a community-based non-commercial organisation in Australia to take part in a seasonal program of activity that has the object of cultural enrichment or community benefits.[84] The exchange and cultural/community programs must be approved by the DIAC Secretary.[85]

69 Sch. 2, clauses 427.223 and 427.224.
70 Sch. 2, clauses 427.224, 427.225 and 427.227.
71 Sch. 2, clause 427.225(a) and PAM3: Sch. 2, Visa 427, s 10.2.
72 PAM3: Sch. 2, Visa 427, s 18.1.
73 Sch. 2, clause 427.611.
74 Sch. 1, Item 1205.
75 ibid.
76 ibid.
77 ibid.
78 ibid.
79 ibid.
80 ibid.
81 Sch 2, clauses 411.211, 416.211, 420.211, 423.211 and 428.211.
82 Sch. 2, clause 411.222; PAM3: Sch. 2, Visa 411, s 1.1.
83 See 4.3, Restrictions on visa applications.
84 Sch. 2, clause 416.222.
85 Listed at the end of the PAM3 'Special Program – Visa 416'.

Special programs are intended to promote opportunities for persons to experience other cultures and enhance international relations and to broaden their experience and knowledge by participating in certain youth exchange schemes or community-based non-commercial programs. The types of programs approved are typically operated by educational, religious and cultural groups; student visas are appropriate if the purpose of the visit to Australia is primarily to study. Similarly, a temporary business visa is more appropriate if the primary purpose of the visit is business. If offshore applicants do not apply for the appropriate visa, they may be invited to make application for a more suitable visa if it appears that such an application would be successful.[86]

Primary applicants must establish that they have adequate means of support, subject to work rights.[87] PAM3 states:

> ... for accommodation, food, household services/maintenance, clothing/footwear and transport, a single person spent approximately AUD$485 per week. This translates to about AUD$25 220 a year (subject to increases for a partner, first child and any additional children).[88]

Entertainment visa (420) is for applicants involved in the entertainment industry, including both commercial and non-commercial performers for film, television, opera, ballet and circuses, other entertainers, and support personnel and non-performing production/technical personnel for productions to be shown in, or concerts or recordings to be performed in, Australia.[89] PAM3 states that the purpose of the visa is to:

> Enhance general cultural standards, facilitate the Australian community's access to a wide range of social and cultural events and activities and take into account the need to protect the employment of Australian residents in the entertainment industry. It is not intended for the following persons:
>
> - Musicians, conductors or musical directors under employment contracts ... these applicants [should] first see Stream 3 – Performing in Production not related to film or television, of ANZSCO.
> - Persons involved in the production of documentaries or commercials exclusively for overseas use ... should be assessed against visa 423 Media and Film Staff criteria.
> - Media staff based in Australia as employees of overseas news organisations should be assessed against visa 423 Media and Film Staff criteria.
> - Media staff covering a specific event or events for overseas news media should apply, and be assessed against criteria, for a Business (Short Stay) visa 456, eVisitor (Business) or Business ETA.
> - Members of amateur performance groups (such as a choir or youth ensemble similar, perhaps, to the Australian Youth Orchestra) – provided tourism is the main purpose of the visit i.e. performances will be incidental – may apply, and be considered against criteria for, a Tourist Visitor visa (subclass 676).

86 Regulation 2.11.
87 Sch. 2, clause 416.322.
88 PAM3 'Special Program – Visa 416', s 12.15.
89 Sch. 2, clause 420.222; PAM3: Sch. 2, Visa 420, s 1.1.

- Persons attending promotional activities (for example, actors in Australia for a red carpet premiere, a rock band for a promotional tour but no performances, an author promoting a book with a public reading where a fee is paid) may be eligible for a Business (Short Stay) visa 456, eVisitor (Business) or Business ETA.[90]

It is a threshold requirement that the application be accompanied by a completed sponsorship form (1379),[91] and the sponsor will be expected to provide a performance contract that will permit decision-makers to assess the nature of the performances and the itinerary, the sponsor's intention to employ their nominee in accordance with Australian legislation and awards, and any requirements for support staff.[92] Performers and entertainers[93] must also provide a certificate given by the Arts Minister, confirming that relevant Australian content criteria have been met, Australian workers have been provided opportunity to participate and certain foreign or private investment levels have been provided.[94]

Sport visa (421) provides for the temporary entry of sportspersons. The categories covered are: individuals or sporting groups and their support staff taking part in specific sports events or contests (Stream 1); players, coaches and instructors joining Australian sports clubs, teams or similar organisations (Stream 2), participants undertaking a structured sports training program in Australia (Stream 3), and judges and adjudicators (Stream 4).[95] DIAC will require evidence from relevant sporting bodies to assess the level of the sports activity and the reputation of sportspeople.[96]

Sports instructors must demonstrate that they enter under a labour agreement or that no Australian worker is available for the position.[97] Sponsors are required to adequately remunerate successful visa applicants, to accept responsibility for all financial obligations to the Commonwealth incurred by the visa-holder arising out of the visa-holder's stay in Australia, for the visa-holder's compliance with all relevant legislation and awards in relation to any employment entered into by the visa-holder and, unless DIAC decides otherwise, for the visa-holder's compliance with their visa conditions.[98]

The visa is issued with Schedule 8 condition 8107, confining holders to the position for which the visa was granted.[99] While no period for the visa is specified, policy is that where there is a sponsor, the visa should be granted to have effect for

90 PAM3: Sch. 2, Visa 420, ss 1.2–1.3.
91 Sch. 1, Item 1205(3)(c).
92 PAM3: Sch. 2, Visa 420, s 9.1 and Sch. 2, clauses 420.222(2)(a) or 420.222(3)(a).
93 PAM3: Sch. 2. Visa 420. It defines 'performer' as 'any person who performs or appears on stage or screen or before a microphone or audience as part of a theatre, film, television or radio production or presentation, audio or video recording, concert or other form of entertainment': s 6.2.
94 Sch. 2, clauses 420.222(2)(c) and (3)(c).
95 PAM3: Sch. 2, Visa 421, s 1.1.
96 PAM3: Sch. 2, Visa 421, s 3; see also specific criteria under Stream 1–4: ss 6–19.
97 See 'labour market requirements' as defined in regulation 1.11.
98 Regulation 1.20(2)(b).
99 See 4.3, Restrictions on visa applications.

two years or the period of stay agreed to by DIAC, having regard to the proposed period of stay as indicated in the sponsorship, nomination or letter of support (as applicable), whichever is the earlier.[100]

Media and film staff (423) visas are intended for persons seeking a temporary stay as professional media staff of overseas news organisations (print, radio, TV or film media) assigned to Australia as accredited representatives of that organisation, and television or film crew, including actors, production and support staff and still-photographers, involved in the production of documentaries or commercials for use overseas.[101]

Applicants for this subclass are to be differentiated from applicants in subclass 420 (for entertainers). Applicants staying for more than three months must be sponsored, except for offshore applicants entering under a country-to-country agreement.[102] The sponsorship obligations are the same as for sponsors in the subclass 423 visa, above.

Religious worker (428) visas are primarily for applicants who are sponsored by a religious organisation in Australia to undertake work in Australia that directly serves the religious objectives of the organisation.[103] The purpose is to help the sponsor access specific religious skills not readily available within the Australian community.[104] Visa applications made prior to 14 September 2009 are assessed against the sponsorship provisions in place at that time.[105] Since 14 September 2009 there has been a three-stage process: (1) a sponsorship by the inviting organisation; (2) a nomination stage; and (3) a visa application stage.[106] There is no legislative requirement that the applicant already be qualified and/or experienced, and it is policy to approve applications from trainees, provided the sponsor has an agreement with DIAC and has provided a clear structure for the proposed training, the objectives and expected outcomes of the training program, the prerequisites to undertaking a training position on the part of the sponsored visa applicant, the length and number of hours of the training program and the way in which the training is to be delivered, and by whom.[107]

The visa is not for applicants employed by religious institutions in other capacities, such as building, fundraising or providing domestic services. Such applicants may be eligible for other temporary visas that are more appropriate for the work they are to perform.

Sponsors must be a 'religious institution'. That term is defined under Regulation 1.03 as a body:

(a) the activities of which reflect that it is a body instituted for the promotion of a religious object; and

100 PAM3: Generic Guidelines F – Temporary Residence Visas, s 14.4.
101 PAM3: Sch. 2, Visa 423, s 1.1.
102 Sch. 2, clause 423.223
103 Sch. 2, clause 428.222.
104 PAM3: Sch. 2, Visa 428, s 1.
105 Regulation 1.20AA.
106 PAM3: Sch. 2, Visa 428, ss 1.1 and 1.2.
107 PAM3: Sch. 2, Visa 428, ss 4.2 and 5.1.

(b) the beliefs and practices of the members of which constitute a religion due to those members:
   i. believing in a supernatural being, thing or principle; and
   ii. and accepting the canons of conduct that give effect to that belief, but that do not offend against the ordinary laws; and

(c) that meets the requirement of section 50.50 of the *Income Tax Assessment Act 1997*; and

(d) the income of which is exempt from income tax under section 50.1 of that Act.[108]

Under clause 428.222, to be eligible for the grant of a visa 428 an applicant is required to be the subject of an approved nomination at the time of decision. The sponsorship obligations are the same as for sponsors in the subclass 423 visa, above, and the visa is issued with Schedule 8 condition 8107, confining holders to the position for which the visa was granted.[109]

8.4 Educational (Temporary) (class TH)[110]

- Subclass 406 (Government Agreement)[111]
- Subclass 415 (Foreign Government Agency)[112]
- Subclass 419 (Visiting Academic)[113]
- Subclass 442 (Occupational Trainee)[114]

The government agreement (406) visa provides for the entry to Australia of people who meet the terms and conditions of certain bilateral agreements between the Commonwealth or a State/Territory government and the government of another country.[115] It also provides for those who direct the operations of the British Council; the Alliance Française; the Goethe Institute; or the Italian Cultural Institute.[116] There is no nomination requirement, but the applicant must be able to show they have the support of the relevant parties to the agreement.[117] Condition 8107 will be imposed.[118]

Foreign government agency (415) visas are granted to representatives of foreign governments (or foreign government agencies, as described below) who are not entitled to a subclass 995 diplomatic (temporary) visa solely because the Department of Foreign Affairs and Trade (DFAT) has declined to accredit them, as well as to certain foreign language teachers who are to be employed in

108 PAM3: Sch. 2, Visa 428, s 3.2.
109 See 4.3, Restrictions on visa applications.
110 Sch. 1, Item 1208.
111 ibid.
112 ibid.
113 ibid.
114 ibid.
115 PAM3: Sch. 2, Visa 406, s 1.1.
116 PAM3: Sch. 2, clause 406.222.
117 PAM3: Sch. 2, clause 406.222.
118 Sch. 2, clause 406.611.

Australia by their government or government agency.[119] All applicants must be sponsored by a foreign government agency[120] or, for onshore applicants staying longer than three months, by the intended employer.[121] Since 14 September 2009 there has been a new two-stage sponsorship in force.[122] The first stage involves the inviting foreign government agency applying to be approved, and being approved, as a foreign government agency sponsor; the second is the visa application stage.[123] Applications made prior to 14 September 2009 will be assessed against the provisions in force at that date.[124] Applications can be made offshore or onshore[125] and the visa is granted for the period covered by the invitation and with Schedule 8 condition 8107, confining holders to the position for which the visa was granted.[126]

The visiting academic (419) visa is for academics or researchers in tertiary or research institutions in overseas countries whose primary purpose of stay is to observe or participate in research projects at the invitation of an Australian tertiary institution or research organisation,[127] and who will not receive any form of payment from the inviting institution, other than an allowance towards living expenses.[128] It suits academics on sabbatical leave, but is not suitable for academics who are remunerated by an institution in Australia. Since 14 September 2009 there has been a three-stage sponsorship program in force.[129] The first step is a sponsorship stage: the inviting Australian tertiary or research institution must apply to be, and be approved as, a sponsor; the second step is the nomination stage; and the third step is the application stage.[130] Applications can be made offshore or onshore[131] and the visa is granted with Schedule 8 condition 8107, confining holders to the position for which the visa was granted.[132]

An occupational trainee (442) visa is issued to an occupational trainee[133] for workplace-based training that will give the applicant additional or enhanced skills that the applicant will be able to utilise in the applicant's employment after leaving Australia and without adversely affecting the occupational opportunities available to Australian citizens or permanent residents.[134] There is a three-stage application process: the organisation or government agency in

119 Sch. 2, clause 415.222.
120 Sch. 2, clause 415.223 and regulation 1.03 (defining 'foreign government agency').
121 Sch. 2, clause 415.229(c).
122 PAM3: Sch. 2, Visa 415, s 1.5.
123 ibid.
124 PAM3: Sch. 2, Visa 415, s 1.4.
125 Sch. 1, Item 1208(3) and Sch. 2, clauses 415.4 and 415.211.
126 See 4.3, Restrictions on visa applications.
127 Sch. 2, clause 419.222.
128 Sch. 2, clauses 419.224 and 419.611 and Sch. 8 condition 8103.
129 PAM3: Sch. 2, Visa 419, s 1.3.
130 ibid.
131 Sch. 1, Item 1208(3) and Sch. 2, clauses 419.4 and 419.211.
132 See above, *Restrictions on changing positions or employer*.
133 Defined in Regulation 1.03 as holders of the subclass 442 visa.
134 Sch. 2, clause 442.223.

Australia applies for approval as an occupational trainee sponsor; an organisation or government agency in Australia which has approval (or has lodged an application for approval) as an occupational trainee sponsor submits a nomination for occupational training; and then the primary sponsored person identified in the nomination at stage two lodges a visa application.[135] Applications can be made offshore or onshore,[136] and the visa is granted with Schedule 8 work restriction condition 8102.[137]

8.5 Student visas

There are some often-used terms and acronyms that are common in student visa applications.[138] These include:

19. *CRICOS:* Commonwealth Register of Institutions and Courses for Overseas Students;
20. *CoE:* Confirmation of Enrolment;
21. *eCoE:* electronic Confirmation of Enrolment;
22. *DEEWR:* Department of Education, Employment and Workplace Relations;
23. *IELTS:* International English Language Testing System;
24. *ELICOS:* English Language Intensive Course for Overseas Students;
25. *OSP:* Overseas Student Program;
26. *PRISMS:* The Provider Registration and International Student Management System of DEEWR.

Special provisions for student visas are set out in Division 1.8 of the Migration Regulations 1994.[139] Those provisions were established in response to a view that student visa-holders abused the visa system to work or otherwise reside in Australia. They provide a framework for student visas, with the detail being in various Gazette notices, as well as Schedules 2 and 5A. The regulations create seven subclasses of student visa related to seven education sectors. Applicants must be overseas students who hold eligible passports,[140] and the types of courses related to each visa subclass (except 576 AusAID or Defence Sector) are specified by Gazette.[141] They range from short-term English language courses to postgraduate university degrees, as indicated in the following Schedule 1 visa class:

135 Sch. 2, clause 442.222; PAM3: Sch. 2, Visa 442, s 1.2.
136 Sch. 1, Item 1208(3) and Sch. 2, clause 442.4.
137 8102 'The holder must not engage in work in Australia (other than in relation to the holder's course of study or training)'.
138 See PAM3: Generic Guidelines G – Student Visas 'OSP Legislated and Policy Terms'.
139 See regulations 1.40–1.44.
140 GN 39, 1 October 2003 – Specification of passports for the purposes of paragraphs 1.40(1)(a) and (b).
141 Regulation 1.40A and GN 25, 29 June 2005 – Specification of types of courses for the purposes of regulation 1.40A.

8.5.1 Student (Temporary) (class TU)[142]

- Subclass 570 Independent ELICOS Sector[143]
- Subclass 571 Schools Sector[144]
- Subclass 572 Vocational Education and Training Sector[145]
- Subclass 573 Higher Education Sector[146]
- Subclass 574 Postgraduate Research Sector[147]
- Subclass 575 Non-Award Sector[148]
- Subclass 576 AusAID or Defence Sector[149]
- Subclass 580 Student Guardian[150]

Under the *Education Services for Overseas Students (ESOS) Act 2000* (Cth), only education providers[151] registered on CRICOS are permitted to offer education or training services to overseas students. Registration can be suspended under the ESOS Act if the Minister is satisfied that too many students from that provider are entering or remaining in Australia 'for purposes not contemplated by their visas'.[152]

A student visa application is an application to study within a particular education sector in Australia. If an application is to study for more than one course (for instance, an ELICOS course followed by a university course), one of the courses (the second course, which is contingent on the first) is designated the principal course.[153] That designation has ramifications, as Schedule 2 criteria for individual student subclasses are based on the assessment level applicable to the principal course (see below). The applicant must enrol with the particular education provider and supply the certificate of enrolment[154] as a Schedule 2 criterion of the particular visa subclass.

The grant of a student visa is determined by the applicant's assessment level.[155] The assessment levels are based on risk profiles of the country of the applicant and are a statistically based assessment of the applicant's propensity to abide by the conditions of their student visa. The levels of risk range from 5 (extremely high) to 1 (low).[156] The levels are used to determine the evidence

142 Item 1222.
143 ibid.
144 ibid.
145 ibid.
146 ibid.
147 ibid.
148 ibid.
149 ibid.
150 ibid.
151 As defined in regulation 1.03.
152 ESOS Act Part 6 Division 2 (s 97–s 103).
153 Regulation 1.40(2) and (3).
154 Defined in regulation 1.03.
155 Defined in regulation 1.03 'assessment level, in relation to a Subclass 570, 571, 572, 573, 574, 575 or 576 visa, means the level of assessment (being level 1, 2, 3, 4 or 5) specified under Division 1.8 for a kind of eligible passport, within the meaning of regulation 1.40, and for an education sector'.
156 Regulation 1.41 and PAM3: Div. 1.8 'Special provisions for student visas', s 37.

that a particular applicant must provide to establish that he or she is a genuine student. A Gazette notice specifies an assessment level that matches the applicant's eligible passport to each subclass of student visa the passport-holder applies for.[157] For instance, for a subclass 573 higher education sector visa, the holder of a passport from Iceland has an assessment level of 1, while the holder of an Indian passport has a level of 4. There are currently no countries specified at level 5.

The evidentiary requirements for each assessment level are set out in Schedule 5A. The Schedule is divided into visa subclasses, with each subclass having discrete evidentiary requirements for each assessment level, related to English language proficiency, financial capacity, educational qualifications and some other matters, depending on the visa category, such as the length of the course, its connection with the applicant's employment and the applicant's age. Financial capacity is calculated against Item 5A104 of Schedule 5A: 'Meaning of living costs and school costs'.

For subclasses 570–576, applications can be made both offshore and onshore, although onshore applications are restricted to holders or former holders of specified visas and applicants in assessment levels 3–5 need to establish compelling reasons for being granted a further student visa. Some student visa applications can be electronically lodged by applicants from gazetted assessment level 1 countries.[158]

Student visas are subject to conditions, including that the student meets course requirements, maintains health insurance and does not change course provider,[159] as well as to work restrictions. Initially all student visas are issued with Schedule 8 condition 8101 (no work), but once the course has commenced there is a relatively simple means of re-applying for the same subclass of visa with condition 8105, which limits employment to 20 hours per week during course time.

Student Guardian (580) is not strictly a student visa, as it is issued to allow, in limited circumstances, for a student guardian to provide appropriate care and welfare arrangements for a minor student (and some who are 18 or older).[160] The guardian must be nominated by the student,[161] provide for his/her own support and is subject to several restrictions,[162] including a no work condition, limited study, and the residential restriction of Schedule condition 8537, which provides that while the nominating student is in Australia, the student guardian must reside in Australia, and while in Australia, the

157 IMMI 10/003, 26 March 2010 – Student Visa Assessment Levels (Regulation 1.41).
158 Sch. 1, Item 1222(1) and Item 1222(1)(aa)(ii); IMMI 10/008 – Class or Persons (Sub Item 1222(1)).
159 Sch. 8, conditions 8202, 8505 and 8206.
160 Sch. 2, clauses 580.222 and 580.223.
161 Sch. 2, clause 580.226.
162 Sch. 2, clause 580.611.

student guardian must stay with the nominating student and provide appropriate arrangements for the student's accommodation, support and general welfare.

8.6 Other temporary visas[163]

8.6.1 Subclass 410 (Retirement) (class TQ)[164]

Applicants who are over 55 years old,[165] wish to spend some retirement years in Australia, have no dependants (other than a spouse or de facto partner)[166] and are able to be self-supporting in Australia without cost to Australia's social and welfare services, may be eligible for a subclass 410 retirement visa. The applicant and spouse or de facto partner (if any) must both demonstrate that they have made adequate arrangements in Australia for health insurance.[167] It is policy that this health criterion generally cannot be satisfied unless the applicant produces evidence of comprehensive health insurance (covering hospital and medical costs) with an Australian insurer (including Medicare if the applicant is eligible).[168] The application can be made offshore or onshore.[169]

163 It is important to note that from 1 November 2005, the following temporary visa subclasses were abolished:

- 424 (Public Lecturer);
- 425 (Family Relationship);
- 430 (Supported Dependant);
- 432 (Expatriate (Temporary)); and
- 446 (Confirmatory (Temporary)).
  Applicants who previously were eligible for these visas can still apply for other visas which have have similar eligibility and stay criteria and conditions. These are set out by DIAC, at <www.immi.gov.au/legislation/amendments/lc01112005_9.htm>, as follows:
- Subclass 424 (Public Lecturer)
  The Cultural/Social (Temporary) (class TE) visa retains the six other visa subclasses. Applicants may therefore continue to be eligible for this visa class, and in addition may be eligible for the subclass 456 (Business (Short Stay)) visa or the subclass 457 (Business (Long Stay)) visa.
- Subclass 425 (Family Relationship)
  Applicants may now be eligible for the Tourist visa or the subclass 679 (Sponsored Family Visitor) visa.
- Subclass 430 (Supported Dependant)
  Applicants who intend to stay in Australia for a short time without work rights may be eligible for tourist and visitor visas. Alternatively, applicants who require work rights may be eligible for temporary residence visas. For example, skilled persons may be eligible for a temporary business visa. Applicants requiring a longer stay in Australia may be eligible for a spouse visa.
- Subclass 432 (Expatriate (Temporary))
  Applicants who intend to stay in Australia for less than three months may be eligible for tourist visas. Children of school age may be eligible for a student visa in order to attend school.
- Subclass 446 (Confirmatory (Temporary))
  This visa is no longer necessary as overseas applicants can be granted the visa for which they originally applied.

164 Item 1217.
165 Sch. 2, clause 410.221(2).
166 Sch. 2, clauses 410.221(3) and (4).
167 Sch. 2, clauses 410.221(8) and 410.321(3).
168 PAM3: Sch. 2, Visa 410, ss 7.3 and 7.4.
169 Sch. 1, Item 1217(3) and Sch. 2, clause 410.211.

8.6.2 Medical Treatment (Visitor) (class UB)[170]

- Subclass 675 Medical Treatment (Short Stay)[171]
- Subclass 685 Medical Treatment (Long Stay)[172]

The subclass 675 visa is for applicants who wish to visit or stay in Australia for no more than three months in order to undertake medical treatment (including consultation) (other than that related to surrogate motherhood), or to receive an organ transplant or donate an organ or to accompany an organ recipient or donor, or as a Western Province Papua New Guinean citizen medically evacuated to Queensland.[173] In the latter case, the applicant must be approved by the Queensland Department of Health for medical evacuation to a hospital in Queensland. In each of the other cases, the Minister must be satisfied that arrangements have been concluded to carry out the planned treatment. Applicants are ineligible for Medicare, even if they are from countries that have reciprocal health arrangements with Australia (among other reasons, because they have pre-existing conditions) and must make all medical and hospital payments in advance of the visa being granted.[174] If the treatment is to be provided in a public hospital, public clinic or other public medical facility, written approval from that facility and from the relevant State/Territory health authority is necessary. Such written approval is required in order to establish that no Australian resident would be disadvantaged in obtaining medical treatment or consultation.[175]

The subclass 685 visa makes similar provisions for people who wish or need to stay longer than three months. In addition, it provides certain onshore unsuccessful visa applicants who are unfit to leave Australia with permanent visas. Those people must be in Australia, be at least 50 years old and have applied for a permanent visa and satisfied all criteria except the Schedule 4 Public Interest Health criterion 4005 and, consequently, been refused that permanent visa.[176]

170 Sch. 1, Item 1214A.
171 ibid.
172 ibid.
173 Sch. 2, clause 675.212.
174 Sch. 2, clause 675.221(2)(f)–(h).
175 ibid.
176 Sch. 2, clause 685.212(6).

9

Miscellaneous visas

9.1 Citizenship

One of the most important and defining aspects of sovereignty is that a state can establish its own criteria regarding citizenship of the nation. Citizenship is the strongest connection that a person can have with Australia. Citizens have an unrestricted right to live and work in Australia and to travel in and out of the country without restriction. The presence and activities of citizens are not controlled by the Department of Immigration and Citizenship – it only has the authority to administer rules in relation to non-citizens. Thus, citizenship is not central to the topic of this book. However, for the sake of completeness we provide a brief overview of the topic.

As a general principle, permanent residents share the same rights and duties as citizens. However, there are some rights and duties that are unique to citizens. These include the right to an Australian passport, the right to stand for public office and for election for parliament, to serve in Australia's defence force and claim diplomatic protection while overseas, and to serve on juries. Only citizens can enrol on the electoral register to vote at Commonwealth, state and local elections.

Citizenship is governed by the *Australian Citizenship Act 2007* (Cth), which commenced on 1 July 2007.[1] Citizenship can be obtained in several ways. The most common are via birth,[2] descent (that is, on the basis of citizenship of

1 This supersedes the *Australian Citizenship Act 1948* (Cth) and makes a number of changes to the grant of citizenship, including removing the age and time limitations for registration of citizenship by descent; extending the residence requirement in order to be eligible for citizenship and changes to the rules relating to resuming and revoking citizenship.
2 *Australian Citizenship Act 2007* (Cth), s 12.

one's parents)[3] or adoption.[4] Permanent residents are also eligible to apply for citizenship after being present in Australia for a defined period of time.[5]

The residence requirement for permanent residence was recently doubled from two to four years. This was part of a suite of controversial changes to citizenship laws. In addition to the extended residency requirement, applicants must now have a basic knowledge of the English language and an adequate knowledge of the responsibilities and privileges of Australian citizenship.[6] This requires them to pass a citizenship knowledge test.

The rationale for the increased residence requirement is set out below:

> Australian citizenship is a privilege not a right. The former Parliamentary Secretary to the Minister for Immigration and Multicultural Affairs, the Hon Andrew Robb AO MP, stated that the Government is focused on ensuring that citizenship applicants have spent a reasonable period of time living in Australia so that they are familiar with the Australian way of life, and appreciate the commitment that they are required to make to become citizens.
>
> The new requirements also recognise the changes in the migration programme over the years which have resulted in an increasing number of people spending significant periods of time in Australia as temporary residents prior to becoming permanent residents.
>
> **Are the new residence requirements similar to those in other countries?**
>
> Yes. The United Kingdom requires five (5) years lawful residence with no more than 450 days absence during that time. The United States requires five (5) years permanent residence with absences of up to six (6) months each year. Canada requires three (3) years of permanent residence.[7]

Citizenship, once obtained, is not irrevocable. There are a number of ways in which Australian citizenship can be lost. For example, it can be lost where a person renounces his or her Australian citizenship;[8] serves in the armed forces of a country at war with Australia;[9] is a child of a person who loses citizenship;[10] or acquired citizenship fraudulently and it would be contrary to the public interest for the person to continue to be an Australian citizen.[11] People who have lost their citizenship may be eligible to resume their citizenship pursuant to Part 2, Subdivision C of the *Migration Act 1958* (Cth). There are a number of circumstances in which a person can regain his or her citizenship. These include where the person ceased to be a citizen because they renounced their citizenship in order to acquire or retain the nationality of another country or to avoid suffering significant hardship or detriment.[12]

3 *Australian Citizenship Act 2007* (Cth), s 15A.
4 *Australian Citizenship Act 2007* (Cth), s 13.
5 *Australian Citizenship Act 2007* (Cth), s 22.
6 *Australian Citizenship Act 2007* (Cth), s 21.
7 <www.citizenship.gov.au/law-and-policy/legislation/changesResidenceRequirementsQA.htm>.
8 *Australian Citizenship Act 2007* (Cth), s 33.
9 *Australian Citizenship Act 2007* (Cth), s 35.
10 *Australian Citizenship Act 2007* (Cth), s 36.
11 *Australian Citizenship Act 2007* (Cth), s 34.
12 *Australian Citizenship Act 2007* (Cth), ss 29, 33.

9.2 Absorbed person visa

Absorption is a concept that arose from cases addressing the immigration and emigration power of section 51(xxvii) of the Australian Constitution. The High Court found that at some point certain persons were absorbed into the Australian community and ceased to be 'immigrants' for the purpose of the *Migration Act 1958* (Cth). Parliament resolved this issue by shifting the constitutional basis of the Act to the 'naturalisation and aliens' power contained in section 51(xix) of the Constitution. The shift took effect on 2 April 1984 by way of the *Migration Amendment Act 1983* (Cth). The *Migration Act 1958* (Cth) from then on referred to 'non-citizens' rather than 'immigrants', thereby removing the issue of 'absorption'. This was because the only way non-citizens cease to be non-citizens is by acquiring Australian citizenship. As a matter of policy, it was considered that persons who, prior to 2 April 1984, had become absorbed should not become unlawful if they remained continuously in Australia.[13]

Prior to 1 September 1994, the effect of the absorption doctrine was that a number of absorbed persons were lawfully in Australia as permanent residents but were not the holders of entry permits. By the operation of section 34 of the *Migration Act 1958* (Cth) (from 1 September 1994), those people hold a permanent visa. Whether or not a person was 'absorbed' prior to 2 April 1984 is a question of fact that is determined by consideration of various issues that have been established through case law, including whether or not the person: married (and/or had a longstanding stable relationship with) an Australian citizen or Australian permanent resident; established a permanent home; had children born and educated in Australia; obtained and retained remunerative employment; purchased property and acquired significant assets; made efforts to become part of the community (learning to speak English/making inquiries about citizenship); and abided by the law.

A further consideration is the length of the person's residence in Australia and whether or not any departure from Australia was only for a temporary purpose, such as an overseas visit or to study (and the person returned before 2 April 1984). If they arrived after 2 April 1979, they will not be considered as an absorbed person.[14]

The 'absorbed person visa' is a visa to remain in, but not to re-enter, Australia. If an absorbed person wishes to depart Australia he or she will have the same entitlement to a resident return visa as any other permanent visa-holder.

This visa category was considered by the Federal Court in *Johnson v Minister for Immigration & Multicultural & Indigenous Affairs*,[15] and expressly approved of by the full court in *Moore v Minister for Immigration and Citizenship* (2007) 161 FCR 236 at [49] to [56], and by Branson J in *Charlie v Minister for Immigration*

13 PAM3: Migration Act – Act-based visas – Absorbed person visas.

14 *Harry Tjandra aka Jimmy Yek v Minister for Immigration and Ethnic Affairs* (FC, unreported, 23 July 1996, per Lindgren J).

15 *(No. 3)* [2004] FCA 137 (25 February 2004).

and Citizenship (2008) 171 FCR 44 at [31] and [32]. The applicant was a New Zealand citizen who came to Australia at the age of six with his family in 1981. The Federal Court held that the applicant had become an absorbed person by 1984, and made a number of observations regarding the operation of this visa category. French J stated:

> 59. I accept the affidavit evidence tendered on behalf of Mr Johnson Snr [the applicant's father] in so far as it relates to the absorption question as at April 1984. On the basis of that evidence, I make the following findings:
>
> 1. Mr Johnson Snr first came to Australia in October 1980 and decided that he intended to make it his home.
> 2. He secured employment almost immediately.
> 3. He brought his two eldest sons to Australia in February 1981 so they could begin their education at high school.
> 4. The rest of the Johnson family, including Silas Johnson, came to Australia with their mother in June 1981.
> 5. From June 1981, Silas Johnson's parents have continued to reside in Australia treating it as their permanent home.
> 6. Mr Johnson Snr and his wife between them, participated in, and contributed to, sporting activities in their local community from the outset and prior to April 1984.
> 7. The family lived in rented accommodation.
> 8. Between 1981 and 1984 none of the family members returned to New Zealand.
> 9. Mr Johnson Snr and his wife were at all times law abiding citizens and did not get into any trouble with the law.
> 10. Silas Johnson remained at all material times up to April 1984, part of the Johnson family unit.
>
> 60. The judgment about membership of the Australian community with respect to the Johnsons must be made as at April 1984. It is not, however, irrelevant to consider the family's subsequent history to the extent that it may inform an assessment of their pre-existing degree of commitment to, and membership of, the Australian community. So far as the parents are concerned their subsequent history supports rather than undermines a finding that they had achieved membership of the Australian community in 1984.
>
> 61. In my opinion, all the relevant indicators, other than time elapsed since the move to Australia, point strongly to the proposition that the Johnson family had become part of the Australian community as at 2 April 1984. Absent any statutory constraint upon the speed with which absorption may occur, there is no bright line for judging the minimum time that must elapse before a person ceases to be an immigrant for constitutional purposes. The lapse of time is not of itself necessarily a condition of membership of the Australian community but may constitute part of the evidence that such membership has been achieved. In my opinion, in this case, although the time since entry was probably at or close to the lower bound of the time necessary to move beyond immigrant status in the constitutional sense, the evidence taken as a whole indicates that as a matter of substance the Johnsons had become members of the Australian community at the relevant time. That being so, in my opinion, Silas Johnson had ceased to be an immigrant as at 2 April 1984. He was in Australia at that date and did not leave Australia between that date and 1 September 1994. He was therefore, in

my opinion, deemed to have been granted an absorbed person's visa on 1 September 1994.

62. That being so, the Minister's decision to purportedly cancel a special category visa held by him was effected by jurisdictional error on the principles already discussed. The application must therefore succeed.

9.3 Tourists

Tourist visas permit visitors to come to Australia to visit their friends or family, to travel, or otherwise remain as a visitor. The simplest tourist visa is the Schedule 2 subclass 976 Electronic Travel Authority (Visitor) visa.

Applications for the 976 Electronic Travel Authority (Visitor) visa can be made offshore or onshore (including in immigration clearance – that is, at entry control points).[16] The applications are computerised and visas are issued electronically (without physical visa labels) by an extensive range of travel agents, airlines or overseas posts.[17] Applicants must hold an 'ETA eligible passport'[18] issued by prescribed countries.[19] The subclass 976 (Visitor) visa provides for multiple travel, with a three-month stay on each visit and a validity for travel of up to 12 months (depending on passport validity). The applicant must state an intention to visit Australia temporarily for the purpose of tourism.[20]

Prior to 1 July 2005, there were two classes of tourist visas: class TR and class TN. The latter visa has now been abolished and the tourist visa process has been streamlined, so that there is now only one type of visa: class TR, which has one subclass: 676. The Tourist Class TR visa (subclass 676) permits holders to remain in Australia for up to 12 months, but the visa is normally only granted for either three or six months.

The central requirements are that the applicant's intention to visit Australia is genuine;[21] that the applicant seeks to visit Australia for the purpose of visiting an Australian citizen or an Australian permanent resident who is a relative, or for a purpose other than a purpose related to business or medical treatment;[22] that the applicant has adequate funds, or access to adequate funds, for the visit;[23] or that compelling reasons exist for the grant of the visa.[24]

16 Sch. 1, Item 1208A(3)(bb)(ii) and (bc)(ii) and Migration Regulations 1994, regulation 2.07AB 'Applications for Electronic Travel Authority visas'.
17 IMMI 06/059 25 August 2006 – 'Approval of Agents for Electronic Travel Authority Applications (Regulations 1208A(3)(bb)(ii) and (bc)(ii)'.
18 As defined in regulation 1.11B.
19 GN 5, 4 February 2004 – Specification of ETA-eligible passports.
20 Sch. 2 clause 976.222.
21 Sch. 2, clause 676.211.
22 Sch. 2, clause 676.212.
23 Sch. 2, clause 676.213.
24 Sch. 2, clause 676.221(3)(f).

Applications can be made offshore and onshore, although only current (or former) holders of certain substantive visas are eligible for onshore applications.

Applicants with ETA eligible passports can lodge their applications via the internet.

9.3.1 Sponsored Family Visitor (class UL)

This visa is designed for a visitor of an Australian citizen or permanent resident who is a parent, spouse, de facto partner, child, brother or sister of the applicant; or for a purpose other than medical or business-related.[25] The applicant must be sponsored by a settled Australian citizen or settled permanent resident.[26] The period of visa will be no more than 12 months.[27] The decision-maker has the discretion to impose a security bond and condition 8531 (mandatory no further stay).[28] This visa is useful for families where DIAC may think the visa-holder will try to remain in Australia.

9.4 Bridging visas

Bridging visas are a means of ensuring that non-Australian permanent residents or citizens (or eligible New Zealand citizens) remain lawful in order to avoid detention and removal.[29] A bridging visa can only be granted to an eligible non-citizen who satisfies the criteria for a bridging visa prescribed under section 73 of the *Migration Act 1958* (Cth).[30] They are for applicants whose visas have ceased and who are waiting for a decision on an application for a substantive visa, or non-citizens making arrangements to leave Australia, or non-citizens who do not have a visa but whom it is not necessary to keep in immigration detention. The basic principles are:

- A bridging visa provides the holder with lawful status. However, the holding of a bridging visa is not taken to be the holding of a visa for the purposes of satisfying the criteria for grant of a visa of another class.
- Generally a valid application for a substantive visa in Australia is also a valid application for a bridging visa. Bridging visas can only be granted to those applicants who have made a valid application for a substantive visa of a kind which can be granted if the applicant is in Australia. The bridging visa application is intended to be decided immediately, before the substantive visa application. For example, an applicant for the subclass 572 Student visa will be automatically granted a subclass 010 Bridging visa A.

25 Regulation 679.211.
26 Regulation 679.214.
27 Regulation 679.511.
28 Regulation 679.611.
29 See Chapter 3.1.1 Entry, stay and departure.
30 *Migration Act 1958* (Cth), s 73.

- Only one bridging visa is held per substantive visa application.
- One class of bridging visa permits the holder to travel to and enter Australia. To be eligible for a visa of this class, generally an applicant must have held a substantive visa at the time they made their application for a further substantive visa and have substantial reasons for travel.
- Classes are structured according to: the status of the non-citizen at the time of application for a further substantive visa, that is lawful or unlawful; and/or whether an unlawful non-citizen was detected by departmental compliance action.
- Once a non-citizen is detained, they are generally eligible for only limited classes of bridging visa (unless they have been subsequently granted a substantive visa).
- Permission to work given with a bridging visa generally depends on the permission to work held at the time of application for the substantive visa (with certain exceptions – see part 8 below). Bridging visa holders with work restrictions may apply for and be granted another bridging visa of the same class without work restrictions in certain circumstances (see part 8 below).
- A bridging visa comes into effect when a substantive visa ceases (if one is held) or when granted (if no substantive visa is held). If a substantive visa is cancelled, the bridging visa ceases.
- A bridging visa provides lawful status to an applicant during processing of their substantive visa application until the visa is granted or until twenty-eight days after notification of the final decision on the application (that is, the first decision made on the application or, if merits review has been sought, the decision when all avenues of merits review have been exhausted).
- Applicants seeking judicial review generally can be granted the same class of bridging visa as that granted in connection with their substantive visa application if they apply to the Federal Court within the statutory time limits.
- If a person has more than one substantive visa application under consideration, they will hold more than one bridging visa. Only one bridging visa is in effect at any time. The bridging visa in effect is the one that is most beneficial to the applicant (see regulation 2.21).
- Bridging visas which permit the holder to remain in Australia (but not travel and enter) cease when the holder leaves Australia, regardless of whether the holder has another visa which permits return to Australia (section 82(8)). A replacement bridging visa of the same class can be granted on application where the bridging visa would not have ceased if the holder had remained in Australia.[31]

A central concept in bridging visas is the definition of 'eligible non-citizen':[32] a non-citizen who has been immigration cleared, is in a prescribed class of persons,[33] or is determined by the Minister to be an eligible non-citizen. There is a distinction between an eligible non-citizen and a lawful non-citizen, which is defined as 'a non-citizen in the migration zone who holds a visa that is in effect'.[34]

31 PAM3: Sch. 2, Bridging Visas – Visa application & related procedures.
32 As defined in *Migration Act 1958* (Cth), s 72.
33 Classes of persons are prescribed in regulation 2.20.
34 *Migration Act 1958* (Cth), s 13(1).

The available types of bridging visa classes and subclasses are:

	Schedule 1 class	Schedule 2 subclass
Item 1301.	Bridging A (Class WA)	010 (Bridging A)
Item 1302.	Bridging B (Class WB)	020 (Bridging B)
Item 1303.	Bridging C (Class WC)	030 (Bridging C)
Item 1304.	Bridging D (Class WD)	040 (Bridging (Prospective Applicant))
		041 (Bridging (Non-applicant))
Item 1305.	Bridging E (Class WE)	050 (Bridging (General))
		051 (Bridging (Protection Visa Applicant))
Item 1306.	Bridging F (Class WF)	060 (Bridging F)
Item 1307.	Bridging R (Class WR)	070 (Bridging R)

With a few exceptions,[35] when a non-citizen who is in Australia (but not in immigration clearance) makes a valid application for a substantive visa of a kind which can be granted if the applicant is in Australia, the relevant substantive visa application forms include an application for a bridging A, C or E visa.

Bridging A is granted to eligible non-citizens lawfully in Australia and not in immigration detention, who hold a substantive visa or a bridging A or B visa, and apply for another substantive visa or, within the legislated timelines, for merits or judicial review of a refused visa application.[36]

Bridging B is granted to certain applicants who hold a bridging A or B visa and need to travel overseas during the processing of a substantive visa application until it is finally determined, or during judicial review proceedings.[37] It is not available to holders of subclass 785 (Temporary Protection) visas,[38] as these are granted specifically without a re-entry facility as part of the policy to deter undocumented arrivals in Australia.[39]

Bridging C is granted to eligible non-citizens who do not hold a substantive visa, are not in detention, have not been granted a bridging visa by compliance and have made a valid application for a substantive visa; or to applicants who apply within the specified time for judicial review of a decision to refuse a visa and held a bridging C visa during the processing of the application which is subject to judicial review.[40]

There are two subclasses of bridging D visas: subclass 040 is for applicants who are immigration cleared, or eligible non-citizens, but are unlawful non-citizens (or will become unlawful within three days of the application) and have attempted to make a substantive visa application but need more time; and subclass 041 is for applicants who are unlawful and unable or unwilling to make

35 See regulation 2.07A.
36 Sch. 1, Item 1301(3); Sch. 2, clause 010.21. The visa ceases when a substantive visa is granted, not when the individual is notified of the grant: *Hossain v MIMIA* [2007] FMCA 35. For other judicial consideration regarding aspects of this visa, see *SZCCZ v MIMA* [2006] FMCA 506; *Sayed v MIMA* [2006] FMCA 936.
37 Sch. 1, Item 1302(3); Sch. 2, clause 020.21.
38 Sch. 1, Item 1302(3)(bb).
39 For judicial consideration regarding aspects of this visa, see *SZCCZ v MIMA* [2006] FMCA 506.
40 Sch. 1, Item 1303(3); Sch. 2, clause 030.21.

a substantive visa application, and compliance staff are not available to assist them.[41]

If a non-citizen (who is not in detention) sends DIAC an application for a substantive visa which is found not to be valid, an application is taken to be made for a bridging D visa[42] unless the reason the application is invalid is because of the operation of section 48 or section 48A of the Act[43] or the substantive visa application is for a class UQ (Graduate – Skilled (Temporary)) visa, a class DD (Skilled – Independent Overseas Student (Residence)) visa or a class DE (Skilled – Australian-sponsored Overseas Student (Residence)) visa.

There are two subclasses of bridging E visas. Subclass 050 is for people who are unlawful[44] and detected or detained by compliance; or unlawful non-citizens in criminal detention; or non-citizens who have made a valid substantive visa application and hold or last held a bridging E visa; or for bridging D (subclass 041) visa-holders.[45] It is suitable for unlawful non-citizens wishing to make arrangements to leave Australia or awaiting review of a decision and are not entitled to any other visa.

Subclass 051 is for certain unauthorised arrivals who have applied for a protection visa and are eligible non-citizens who are under 18 or over 75 years old, or have special health requirements or have an Australian spouse or are a member of the family unit of an Australian citizen.[46]

In order to secure a bridging R (Removal Pending visa) visa, the applicant must be in immigration detention[47] and it is not reasonably practical to remove the applicant. The visa expires when removal of the visa-holder is reasonably practicable.[48]

9.5 Resident return

It is a common provision of the grant of permanent residence visas that the visa permits the holder to travel to and enter Australia for a period of five years from the time of the grant. That is, the holder can remain permanently in Australia, but if they wish to depart and re-enter, they need permission for the re-entry. Therefore, after the initial five years lapse, they require another visa that will permit the re-entry.

Resident return visas (RRV) facilitate the re-entry into Australia of non-citizen permanent residents and aim to ensure that only those people who have a genuine

41 Sch. 1, Item 1304(3); Sch. 2, clauses 040.21 and 041.21.
42 Regulation 2.22.
43 See 4.3, Restrictions on Visa Applications.
44 But 'not an eligible non-citizen of the kind set out in subregulations 2.20(7), (8), (9), (10) or (11)': Sch. 2, clause 050.211(2).
45 Sch. 1, Item 1305(3); Sch. 2, clause 050.21.
46 Regulation 2.20(7), (8), (9), (10) and (11): Prescribed classes of eligible non-citizens.
47 Sch. 2, clause 070.411.
48 Sch. 2, clause 070.511.

commitment to residing in Australia, or who are contributing to Australia's well-being, retain the right to return to Australia and remain permanently. To meet the second purpose, the period of time granted for successive RRVs depends on how much time the holder of the permanent resident visa has resided in Australia. The relevant visas are:

- **Return (Residence) (class BB): Sch. 1, Item 1128**
- Sch. 2 subclasses: 155 (Five Year Resident Return); 157 (Three Month Resident Return)
- **Resident Return (Temporary) (class TP): Sch. 1, Item 1216**
- Sch. 2 subclass: 159 (Provisional Resident Return).

Applications for subclasses 155 and 157 can be made offshore or onshore and via the internet. Within Australia, an application for a return (residence) (class BB) visa can be made on a prescribed form, by letter, or orally at a DIAC office.[49] An applicant does not have to be a permanent resident (that is, hold a permanent visa) at the time of application, provided that he or she has held a permanent visa in the past and their most recently held permanent visa was not cancelled. Applicants must first establish that they are, or were, permanent residents entitled to the particular visa. Evidence of a permanent visa is normally a visa label in a passport; if the passport is not available, DIAC can check whether a person holds or held a permanent visa by checking its movement database. Where an applicant overseas has applied for an RRV and cannot satisfy the criteria for grant because they cannot prove their permanent residence, the decision-maker can refuse the application for a return (residence) (class BB) visa and invite the applicant to apply for the resident return (temporary) (class TP) visa.[50]

For the five-year visa, generally the applicant must demonstrate that he/she was lawfully present in Australia, as a permanent resident, for a period of, or periods that total, not less than two years in the period of five years immediately before the application for the visa.[51] Exceptions can be made where the applicant has been absent for longer periods and can demonstrate substantial business, cultural, employment or personal ties with Australia and has not been absent from Australia for five years or more, unless there are compelling reasons[52] or the applicant is a member of the family unit of a person who has met or meets the foregoing requirements.[53] Successful applicants are granted a further five-year return visa, but members of the family unit of a person who already holds a subclass 155 visa are granted the same period as the holder of that visa.[54]

If applicants are not able to meet the requirements for a subclass 155 visa, they may meet those for the 157 visa. The general requirement is that the applicant was lawfully present in Australia for a period of, or periods that total, not less than

49 Sch. 1, Item 1128(1) and (3).
50 PAM3: Sch. 2, RRV – Resident Return Visas and Regulation 2.11(2A)(3).
51 Sch. 2, clause 155.212(2).
52 Sch. 2, clauses 155.212(3)(a) and (b) and 155.212(3A).
53 Sch. 2, clause 155.212(4).
54 Sch. 2, clause 155.511.

one day but less than two years in the period of five years immediately before the application for the visa and either has compelling and compassionate reasons for departing Australia or, if outside Australia, had compelling and compassionate reasons for his or her last departure from Australia.[55] The department does not require the applicant to demonstrate compelling and compassionate reasons for their entire absence from Australia, but the compelling reasons must exist from the date that the applicant's absence from Australia reaches five years, until the date of application.[56]

Compelling and compassionate reasons include, but are not limited to:

- severe illness or death of an overseas family member
- the applicant or the applicant's accompanying family members have had acute medical conditions requiring treatment and preventing travel
- the applicant has been involved in legal proceedings such as sale of property, custody, or contractual obligations and the timing was beyond the applicant's control or
- the applicant has been caught up in a natural disaster, political uprising or other similar event beyond their control.[57]

If the application is being made offshore, the applicant must also demonstrate that he/she has not been absent from Australia for a continuous period of more than three months immediately before making the application for the visa, unless the Minister is satisfied that there are compelling and compassionate reasons for the absence.[58] Successful applicants are granted a permanent visa permitting the holder to travel to and enter Australia for a period of three months from the date of grant.[59] That is, they can remain permanently in Australia but if they depart, must return before the expiry of three months from the date the visa was granted. If they remain for two years, they will become eligible for the class 155 visa.

The subclass 159 (Provisional Resident Return) visa is only available for offshore applicants.[60] It is for an applicant who claims, but is unable to prove, that immediately before going overseas he or she was an Australian permanent resident or an Australian citizen who was usually resident in Australia and, if the claim was proved, would satisfy the criteria for the grant of a subclass 155 or 157 visa. The applicant also needs to demonstrate urgent and compelling reasons for travelling to Australia before proving the claim.[61] If successful, the grant is for a temporary visa permitting the holder to travel to and enter Australia once only within three months of grant and to remain in Australia for three months.[62] During that three months, the applicant must satisfy the requirements for either of subclasses 155 or 157.

55 Sch. 2, clause 157.212(2)(b) and (3).
56 PAM3: Sch. 2, Visa 157, s 10.3.
57 PAM3: Sch. 2, Visa 157, 10.4; PAM3 Sch. 2, Visa 157, s 13.
58 Sch. 2, clause 157.213.
59 Sch. 2, clause 157.511.
60 Sch. 1, Item 1216(3)(a) and Sch. 2, clause 159.411.
61 Sch. 2, clauses 159.211–159.213.
62 Sch. 2, clause 159.611.

9.6 Other Australia-based visas

Some visas which do not fall into the three main visa streams are issued to applicants who have established certain connections with Australia. These are in the special eligibility, New Zealand citizens[63] and permanent residents of Norfolk Island visa classes.[64]

9.6.1 Special eligibility

- Special Eligibility (class CB)

From 1 November 2005, the former resident/close ties visas (subclasses 832 and 151) were merged into one class and one subclass. The amended subclass 151 visa incorporates the same criteria as the subclass 832 visa and the earlier subclass 151 visa. The new subclass 151 (Former Resident) visa is available for both onshore and offshore applicants.

The visa is intended for people (including certain unlawful non-citizens) who have spent their formative years in Australia, but who did not take out citizenship, and people who completed service with the Australian Armed Forces prior to 19 January 1981. Thus, the visa relates to two different types of applicants: defence force personnel and long residence applicants.

In relation to long resident applicants, it is necessary to establish that they have:

(a) spent the greater part of their life before the age of eighteen in the migration zone as an Australian permanent resident; and
(b) did not at any time acquire Australian citizenship; and
(c) have maintained business, cultural or personal ties with Australia; and
(d) have not turned forty-five years of age at the time of application.[65]

9.6.2 Confirmatory (Residence) visa 808

- Confirmatory (Residence) (class AK): Sch. 1, Item 1111
- Sch. 2 subclass 808 (Confirmatory)

The subclass 808 visa provides for a permanent visa to be granted to people who have entered Australia on a 'conditional' basis as applicants who are eligible for a permanent visa subject to their satisfying criteria which they were then unable to satisfy before entry. The applicant must:

- hold a resident return (temporary) visa subclass 159 because they applied outside Australia for a return (residence) visa, were unable to prove then their claim to be an Australian permanent resident but can now prove that claim; or

63 See section 4.6, Special classes of person, in this book.
64 Not discussed in this book.
65 Sch. 2, clause 151.22.

- hold an emergency (temporary) visa subclass 302, have travelled to Australia before satisfying all criteria for an offshore visa (as described in PAM3: 'Generic guidelines B – non-humanitarian migration (offshore and onshore)' and can now satisfy those criteria; or
- hold a border (temporary) visa subclass 773 and can now satisfy the decision maker that they would have been eligible for a return (residence) visa when the border (temporary) visa was granted; or
- hold a transitional (temporary) visa on the basis of having held, under the Migration (1993) Regulations, a Class 301 Australian requirement visa or entry permit, and can now satisfy outstanding requirements.[66]

For holders of the subclass 302 visa, all members of the family unit of the applicant must satisfy the public interest criteria applicable to them,[67] on the 'one fails, all fail' principle. Successful applicants are granted a permanent visa.[68]

The subclass 303 visa is for certain persons in Australia who hold a visa 303 emergency (temporary visa applicant).

9.7 Emergency visas

These visas are to facilitate entry to Australia for applicants for other classes of visa who have some outstanding criteria to meet, and for whom there are urgent and compelling reasons to travel to Australia and no reason to anticipate that they will not be met in Australia. PAM3 points out that 'it is not intended that persons be invited to apply for a visa 302 where the primary reason is the applicant's convenience', such as complying with travel arrangements already made.[69]

- **Emergency (Temporary) (class TI)**
- Sch. 1, Item 1209(1): Form 1003
- Sch. 2 subclasses: 302 (Emergency (Permanent Visa Applicant)); 303 (Emergency (Temporary Visa Applicant))

The subclass 302 visa is intended mainly to facilitate the travel to Australia of persons who have applied for a migrant (that is, an offshore application for permanent residence) visa (other than visas 300, 309 or 310) and for whom there are one or more public interest criteria yet to be assessed in respect of any family unit member; or an assurance of support has been requested but not yet received and/or approved; or an AOS bond is required but has not yet been paid; but there is an urgent and compelling need for the applicant(s) to travel to

66 Sch. 2, clause 808.211(a)–(d).
67 Sch. 2, clause 808.212.
68 Sch. 2, clauses 808.511 and 808.512.
69 PAM3: Sch. 2, Visa 302, s 5.2.

Australia; and there is no reason to believe that the remaining criteria will not be satisfied after the applicant's entry to Australia.[70]

Onshore applicants need to demonstrate that it is not possible to satisfy the remaining criteria before the visa that he or she holds ceases.[71]

For applications made outside Australia, a 302 visa is granted on the understanding that the holder(s) will subsequently apply in Australia for a confirmatory (residence) 808 visa (see below). In that respect, after the holder of a 302 visa enters Australia, the remaining criteria become criteria (to be satisfied at time of application) for the grant of a confirmatory (residence) 808 visa.[72]

For the class 303 visa, the applicant must be an applicant for one of the prescribed temporary or provisional visas and have satisfied all the criteria for the grant of that visa other than public interest criteria or criteria that can be satisfied only after the applicant has entered Australia.[73] The applicant must make a written request to the Minister with a statement of the applicant's urgent and compelling reasons for travelling to Australia before the remaining criteria have been satisfied, and the Minister must be satisfied that there are urgent and compelling reasons and that the applicant is reasonably likely to satisfy the remaining criteria after arrival in Australia.[74] Onshore applicants need to demonstrate that it is not possible to satisfy the remaining criteria before the visa that he or she holds ceases.[75]

9.8 Other special visa categories

The *Migration Act 1958* (Cth) provides for some other special categories of visa. These are:

- **Special Purpose visa:** taken, by the operation of law, to be granted to visiting dignitaries, seamen, members of foreign military forces, airline crews, some transit passengers and some traditional Indonesian fishermen.[76] The visas include family and staff travelling with the primary recipient, but they are not for uninvited or unexpected arrivals.
- **Criminal Justice visa:** issued to people facing criminal charges or acting as a witness at a criminal trial. The *Migration Act 1958* (Cth) authorises the issuing of criminal justice entry visas, criminal justice stay visas and temporary criminal justice stay certificates by Commonwealth and State authorities.[77] The States are responsible for issuing those visas for the

70 Sch. 2, clauses 302.21 and 302.22; PAM3: Sch. 2, Visa 302, s 1.1.
71 Sch. 2, clause 303.226(a).
72 PAM3: Sch. 2, Visa 302, s 1.1.
73 Sch. 2, clause 303.212.
74 Sch. 2, clauses 303.221 and 303.224.
75 Sch. 2, clause 303.226(a).
76 *Migration Act 1958* (Cth), s 33.
77 *Migration Act 1958* (Cth), s 38 and Division 4.

administration of criminal justice in the States, and the Commonwealth for areas over which the Commonwealth has jurisdiction.[78]

- **Enforcement visa:** issued to suspected illegal fisherman for the purposes of detaining them and bringing them into Australia. It is valid until the holder is released or escapes from detention.[79]

78 That is, (i) the *Extradition Act 1988*; or (ia) the *International War Crimes Tribunals Act 1995*; or (ib) the *International Criminal Court Act 2002*; or (ii) the *Mutual Assistance in Criminal Matters Act 1987*; or (iii) the administration of criminal justice in relation to an offence against a law of the Commonwealth.
79 *Migration Act 1958* (Cth), s 38A and Division 4A.

10

Common visa requirements

10.1 Overview

Many visa applicants require a sponsor or nominator, and for many visas, there is a requirement for an assurance of support and/or a social security bond. Nearly all visas have requirements related to members of the family unit of the primary applicant, called 'secondary criteria' in Schedule 2, even though, in some cases, those 'secondary' people are not included in the visa application. Like all people who have already made a visa application in Australia, they may be refused a second opportunity to make an application. Those matters are canvassed in Chapter 4.

Most visas have application charges, and several of the permanent visas require those payments to be made in two instalments. The second instalment might include a health charge or payment for English language classes. Those payments are set out in the relevant visa class in Schedule 1.

Criteria related to the health and character of visa applicants are included in all the prescribed Schedule 2 visas and are commonly known as the public interest criteria (PIC). Failure to meet those criteria will usually result in an application being refused, notwithstanding that the applicant may have met the signature criterion (for instance, establishes a genuine marriage in an application for a spouse visa). An exception is for protection visa applicants (onshore refugee applications), who do not have to 'pass' the health test, but still have to be assessed.[1] That concession does not extend to offshore refugee/humaniatarian applicants.

1 Sch. 2, clauses 866.223–866.224B.

10.2 Health

The applicant and all members of the family unit, regardless of whether or not they are included in the visa application, must meet health requirements in nearly all applications for permanent visas. Only family members who are included in temporary visa applications need to meet health requirements.[2] The term 'health criterion' is defined as:

> . . . in relation to a visa, . . . a prescribed criterion for the visa that:
> (a) relates to the applicant for the visa, or the members of the family unit of that applicant (within the meaning of the regulations); and
> (b) deals with:
> (i) a prescribed disease; or
> (ii) a prescribed kind of disease; or
> (iii) a prescribed physical or mental condition; or
> (iv) a prescribed kind of physical or mental condition; or
> (v) a prescribed kind of examination; or
> (vi) a prescribed kind of treatment;[3]

Regulation 2.25A obliges the Minister to seek, and accept as correct, the opinion of a medical officer of the Commonwealth (MOC) in determining whether or not a visa applicant meets the health criteria set out in Schedule 4.[4] There is an exception where the application is for a permanent visa and it is made from a country that is a country specified by legislative instrument for the purposes of this paragraph and there is no information known to immigration (either through the application or otherwise) to the effect that the person may not meet those requirements. Those countries are generally Western European and some Asian trading partners of Australia.[5]

Basically, health assessment relates to public safety, cost and access to care and treatment for Australian permanent residents and citizens. The policy requirements for examination are set out in PAM3:

> Under policy, all applicants to whom Schedule 4 health criteria apply (except ETA and eVisitor applicants) are required to do one or more of the following, as detailed elsewhere in this document, to demonstrate [that] they meet the health requirement:
> - obtain a medical certificate from their doctor
> - have a medical examination
> - in certain cases, have a human immunodeficiency virus (HIV) test, hepatitis B test and/or C test or other specific test
> - have a chest x-ray (radiological) examination, if 11 years or older
> - have a medical examination instead of a chest x-ray, if under 11 years (or a chest x-ray, if appropriate on clinical grounds) or
> - have other tests as may be requested by a MOC.

2 See Sch. 2, Criteria for particular visa subclasses.
3 *Migration Act 1958* (Cth), s 5(1).
4 Items 4005(a), 4005(b), 4005(c), 4006A(1)(a), 4006A(1)(b), 4006A(1)(c), 4007(1)(a), 4007(1)(b) or 4007(1)(c).
5 IMMI 08/013 – Specification of countries (Regulation 2.25A(1)(b)).

> In all cases (where the various Schedule 4 criteria are imposed on the relevant visa subclass) the health requirement continues to apply – there are simply differences under policy, depending on the factors listed above, in how the applicant is required to demonstrate that they meet the health criteria. For example, for most visitors, a personal declaration on the application form is accepted as evidence that a person has met the health criteria, whereas permanent visa applicants need to undertake a chest x-ray, a full medical examination and an HIV test.[6]
>
> ... As a general rule, applicants who are required to undergo health examinations under policy should be asked to do so at an early stage of visa processing to minimise the possibility of unresolved health matters delaying a decision on their application.[7]

The Schedule 4 health criteria match the definition (above), though the only prescribed disease is tuberculosis.[8] Otherwise, the criteria are that an applicant should not have a disease or condition that is, or may result in the applicant being, a threat to public health in Australia or a danger to the Australian community, or a disease or condition that, during the person's proposed period of stay in Australia, would be likely to result in a significant cost to the Australian community in the areas of health care or community services or prejudice the access of an Australian citizen or permanent resident to health care or community services.

The primary difference between the Schedule 4 health criteria and the health-related Public Interest Criteria (PIC) is that PIC 4005 prescribes the 'standard' health requirement, while both PIC 4006A and 4007 prescribe the standard health requirement but also provide for a 'health waiver'. While the decision-maker cannot go behind the MOC's medical opinion as being 'correct', it is the decision-maker's responsibility to determine whether or not the waiver applies. The relevant principles are established in *Bui v MIMA*,[9] where French, North and Merkel JJ found:

> [46] Item 4007(2) specifies the conditions under which the power to waive the requirements of par 4007(1)(c) may be exercised. They are that the Minister is satisfied that the granting of the visa would be unlikely to result in:
> (i) Undue cost to the Australian community; or
> (ii) Undue prejudice to the access to health or community services of an Australian citizen or permanent resident.
>
> There are obviously broad judgments to be made in determining what amounts to 'undue cost' and 'undue prejudice'. Reading together the criteria in Item 4007(1)(c)(i) and the criterion for waiver in 4007(2)(b)(i) it is apparent that the occasion for the exercise of the waiver will only arise where it is already established that the cost to Australia, if the visa is granted, is likely to be 'significant'. The Minister will therefore need to be satisfied that a likely 'significant' cost will nevertheless not be 'undue'. In the

6 PAM3: Sch. 4/4005, s 7.2.
7 PAM3: Sch. 4/4005, s 45.
8 Regulation 5.16.
9 [1999] FCA 118.

former determination he or she is evidently to be bound by the opinion of a Medical Officer of the Commonwealth.

> [47] The evaluative judgment whether the cost to the Australian community or prejudice to others, if the visa is granted, is 'undue' may import consideration of compassionate or other circumstances. It may be to Australia's benefit in moral or other terms to admit a person even though it could be anticipated that such a person will make some significant call upon health and community services. There may be circumstances of a 'compelling' character, not included in the 'compassionate' category that mandate such an outcome. But over and above the consideration of the likelihood that cost or prejudice will be 'undue' there is the discretionary element of the ministerial waiver. And within that discretion compassionate circumstances or the more widely expressed 'compelling circumstances' may properly have a part to play.

The matter was considered by the MRT in *N01/04446*.[10] In that case, the applicant was diagnosed as HIV-positive and the MOC found that the likely cost to the Australian community, including the health and medical systems, was $250 000. Member Duignan noted that the MOC did not believe there would be any prejudice to access to health services for Australian citizens arising from the visa applicant's condition. The Member canvassed the requirements of Schedule 4, Item 4007, together with the policy guidelines in PAM3, 'About the PIC 4007 Health Waiver', and found that the cost for the Australian community would be 'substantial' but not 'undue' after taking into consideration the personal qualities and resourcefulness of both the applicant and his nominator, as well as the consequences of the visa being refused.

The proper test by which an MOC assesses the matters referred to in PIC 4005(c) is set out by Siopis J in *Robinson v Minister for Immigration and Multicultural and Indigenous Affairs* (with Addendum dated 18 November 2005).[11] At issue was the MOC's opinion that the appellant's son's 'mild' Down's Syndrome would be likely to result in a significant cost to the Australian community. The court held that such opinions had to be made on a case-by-case basis by reference to the actual disease or condition suffered by the applicant, as opposed to a generalised assessment of the applicant's condition. In rejecting the submissions that a generalised assessment was permissible, the court noted:

> 57. If, as the first respondent contends, the RMOC [Review Medical Officer of the Commonwealth] need make the assessment called for under Public Interest Criterion 4005(c) only by reference to a person suffering from the disease or condition generally, it seems that such an assessment could be made in the abstract. For example, an assessment could be made in the abstract as to whether a person with a typical form of Down's Syndrome would be likely to require health care or be eligible for income or community support services, and whether provision of that care or those services would be likely to result in significant cost to the Australian community. Thus, on the basis of such abstract assessments, it would have been open to Parliament to have identified in the Regulations a number of specific diseases or conditions which, if suffered by any person in the typical form, would preclude that person from satisfying Public Interest

10 [2004] MRTA 1772 (29 March 2004).
11 [2005] FCA 1626 (10 November 2005).

Criterion 4005(c); and to have provided that a person who is not 'free from' that specific disease or condition fails the health requirement. The fact that Parliament has not done so, except in the case of tuberculosis (par 4005(a)), supports the construction contended for by the applicant, namely, that Parliament intended the assessment made under Public Interest Criterion 4005(c) to be made on a case by case basis by reference to the form or level of the disease or condition actually suffered by the applicant. Further, the applicant's contention is also supported by the contrast between the use of the words 'free from' in par 4005(a) – which import the notion that the applicant be free from the disease or condition in any form – and the qualifications imposed in Public Interest Criterion 4005(c)(i) and (ii) on the words 'disease or condition' in Public Interest Criterion 4005(c).

10.3 Character

Section 501(1) of the *Migration Act 1958* (Cth) provides that the Minister may refuse or cancel a visa if he/she is not satisfied that the visa applicant or holder passes the character test.[12] That requirement is included in most visa subclasses as a requirement to meet Schedule 4 PIC 4001, but even where it is absent (as in an ETA), the Minister still has the power under section 501 to refuse a visa. As with the health criteria, family members of applicants for permanent visas must pass the character test, regardless of inclusion in the visa application. Decisions to refuse or cancel a visa on the grounds of character must abide by the code of procedure set out in Subdivision AB of Division 3 of the *Migration Act 1958* (Cth), particularly the requirement to provide adverse information for comment by the applicant.[13]

The decision to refuse or cancel a visa on character grounds is discretionary and review of an adverse decision rests first with the Administrative Review Tribunal.[14] Applicants do not pass the character test if they have a substantial criminal record, have associated with suspected criminals, have a record of past or present criminal conduct, or would be likely to engage in various types of criminal or anti-social behaviour that would be a threat to the Australian community. In addition, 'Ministerial Direction No. 21: Visa refusal and cancellation under section 501'[15] sets out other considerations that must be taken into account in assessing character for the purposes of section 501. Among other things, it mentions continual debt evasion or avoiding family maintenance payments, contempt or disregard for the law or human rights and providing misleading information to DIAC. On the other hand, the ministerial direction requires decision-makers to take into account countervailing factors before deciding to refuse or cancel a visa, such as recent good behaviour, the likelihood of recidivism, the best interests of Australian children or hardship for other family members.

12 As defined in s 501(6).
13 *Migration Act 1958* (Cth), ss 52–64, particularly s 57.
14 See *Migration Act 1958* (Cth), s 501(6) and (7).
15 Made pursuant to *Migration Act 1958* (Cth), s 499.

10.4 Exclusion periods and re-entry bans

Former visa-holders who overstayed, or had their visas cancelled, or were removed or deported from Australia are penalised by being subject to exclusion for specified periods.[16] These are commonly called re-entry bans. Schedule 5 provides for such bans. Those deported for criminal or security breaches are permanently banned.[17] Those who were 'removed' (that is, did not leave voluntarily but were not deported) and their dependants, and dependants of a deportee, cannot make an application for a temporary or permanent visa for 12 months after removal unless there are compelling or compassionate circumstances to justify such a grant.[18]

There is a three-year ban for people whose visa has been cancelled for various breaches of visa condition, or providing false information, but it only applies to applications for temporary visas (excluding temporary or provisional visas that lead to the grant of permanent residence). In cases where a visa has been cancelled for the above reasons, that ban can be waived in compelling or compassionate circumstances.[19] There is also a three-year re-entry ban on applicants who overstayed their visa by more than 28 days. This applies to making applications for a limited range of temporary visas (again, excluding temporary or provisional visas that lead to the grant of permanent residence).[20]

Applicants who owe money to the Commonwealth (such as to the Department of Social Security, the Department of Justice or the Australian Taxation Office) cannot be granted a visa until they have made satisfactory repayment arrangements.[21] Applicants who have been held in immigration detention are also likely to have a debt to the Commonwealth that must be discharged or subject to an arrangement before they will be granted a visa. Such debts are not a re-entry ban, but are a condition of the grant of a visa. They can be paid in instalments or waived in certain circumstances.[22]

10.5 Visa conditions

Schedule 8 criteria impose various conditions on visas, relating to work, study, reporting to DIAC, health insurance, period of stay, and the capacity to apply for further visas. Criterion 8101 imposes a no work condition that is included in all tourist visas. It is common for students to have their visas cancelled because they work more than 20 hours per week – this is the amount that is usually

16 Sch. 4, Items 4013 and 4015 and Sch. 5.
17 Sch. 5, Item 5001.
18 Sch. 5, Item 5002.
19 Sch. 4, Item 4013.
20 Sch. 4, Item 4014.
21 Sch. 4, Item 4004.
22 PAM3: Sch. 4/4004 – Debts to the Commonwealth, s 5.

prescribed.[23] One of the more common conditions is the 'no further stay' criterion 8503, imposed to deter visa-holders from staying longer than they state they will stay. It is frequently litigated because it can be waived, and applicants seek to extend their stay in Australia for a variety of reasons. The judicial decisions are useful in interpreting criterion 8503, because they address the meaning of the phrase 'compelling and compassionate', which arises in several contexts of the migration legislation.

In the case of *Terera v Minister for Immigration and Multicultural and Indigenous Affairs*,[24] a five-year-old child from Zimbabwe applied to visit her mother in Australia. Her visitor visa was endorsed with condition 8503 'no further stay'. Her mother was about to remarry and applied for the condition to be waived so that her child could obtain permanent residence to stay with her. One of the reasons the waiver application was refused was that the marriage was foreseeable. Sub-regulation 2.05(4) sets out the circumstances in which the Minister may waive conditions of the kind referred to in par 41(2)(A) of the Act and provides:

> (a) since the person was granted the visa that was subject to the [8503] condition, compelling and compassionate circumstances have developed:
> (i) over which the person had no control; and
> (ii) that resulted in a major change to the person's circumstances.

Kenny J, having noted that 'It is inherently unlikely that the then five-year-old applicant "fully understood" the significance of the imposition of condition 8503' when the original visa was issued in Harare, went on to find that:

> [23] There is, moreover, nothing in reg 2.05(4)(a) that would make the 'foreseeability' of any major change in an applicant's circumstances a disqualifying factor. As the decisions in *Schaap v MIMA* (2000) 63 ALD 65 ('*Schaap*') [2000] FCA 1408 and *Naidu v MIMA* [2000] FCA 951 ('*Naidu*') indicate, earlier versions of the Procedures Advice Manual (which may provide a decision-maker with some guidance) referred to a notion of foreseeability. This led the decision-makers in those cases into error. Although the version of the Manual that was current at the time of the decision under review now contained no such reference, the delegate in the present case also relied on the fact that the applicant's marriage was 'foreseeable' (by her) as a factor telling against the waiver of the condition. This consideration is no less irrelevant in this case than in *Schaap* and *Naidu*. Regulation 2.05(4)(a) contains no criterion of foreseeability: see *Minister for Aboriginal Affairs v Peko-Wallsend Limited* (1986) 162 CLR 24 at 39. If compelling and compassionate circumstances had developed since 28 December 2001, resulting in a major change in the applicant's circumstances outside his control, then it would be immaterial that the circumstances were in any sense 'foreseeable' by him or anyone else.
>
> [24] In the circumstances, the delegate's failure to address the question arising under reg 2.05(4)(a) constitutes jurisdictional error and may well have affected the outcome of the decision under review, notwithstanding the fact that there was only a little over

23 Sch. 8, Item 8105.
24 [2003] FCA 1570.

a fortnight between the grant of the visa, subject to condition 8503, in Harare and the application for waiver of the condition in Melbourne.

[25] In *Thongpraphai v MIMA* [2000] FCA 1590 at [21], O'Loughlin J held that the words 'compelling and compassionate' in reg 2.05(4)(a) 'call for the occurrence of an event or events that are far-reaching and most heavily persuasive'. In a general sense, this is probably correct, although, for my part, I prefer not to put any exegetical gloss, by way of explanation, on the plain words of reg 2.05(4)(a). When a visa-holder requests the Minister, or Ministerial delegate, to waive a 'no further stay' condition imposed on his or her visa, then the question for the decision-maker will be whether, in the particular case, compelling and compassionate circumstances have developed since the visa was granted, over which the visa-holder has no control and resulting in a major change to his or her circumstances. Whether the decision-maker finds that these circumstances exist will depend entirely upon the facts of the case under consideration, particularly the circumstances of the individual visa-holder.

[26] This is well illustrated by the decision by *Nguyen v MIMA* (2001) 109 FCR 169 ('*Nguyen*'). In *Nguyen*, the applicant entered Australia from Vietnam on 2 June 2000 on a business visa subject to condition 8503. The following month he married an Australian citizen and, six days later, applied for a spouse visa. His claim that the condition was invalid was treated by the Minister's delegate as a request for waiver, and the request was refused. Dealing with the visa-holder's contention that his marriage entitled him to the waiver of the condition, Marshall J said at 173 that '[t]he fact of a marriage to an Australia citizen without more . . . can rarely if ever constitute an event which is a compelling or compassionate circumstance'. The case presently before the Court is, however, entirely different from the situation in *Nguyen* and cannot be dealt with in this straightforward manner.

More recently, Gray J in *El Ess v Minister for Immigration & Multicultural & Indigenous Affairs*[25] expounded:

[52] It is not easy to see why Parliament adopted the form of condition described in s 41(2)(a) of the Migration Act and then adapted it by s 46 for the purpose of invalidating an application. On its face, the condition says nothing about the making of an application. It only prohibits the holder of a visa subject to the condition being granted a visa (other than a protection visa) after entering Australia and while remaining in Australia. Nothing in the terms of the condition would prevent the making of an application. Nor would it prevent an application made from being successful, provided that the holder of the earlier visa left Australia before a decision was made to grant the visa the subject of the application made while in Australia. It is not at all uncommon for people to be placed by the Migration Regulations in the position of having to leave Australia in order to enable a decision to be made to grant them further visas. If the intention of legislating in the terms of s 41(2)(a) was to prevent the making of a further application, it is surprising that Parliament did not cast the provision in those terms. The only possible explanation is that whoever drafted the provision wished to draft it in terms that would bring home to the holder of a visa subject to the condition that he or she would not be entitled to a further visa. Even if that were the case, there would have been nothing to prevent the drafting of a condition with two limbs, one being the inability to make a further application and the other being the inability to be granted

25 [2004] FCA 1038.

a further visa. The end achieved by the combination of s 41(2)(a) and s 46(1)(e), now s 46(1A), has been achieved by very indirect means.

[53] This analysis is of some importance in relation to condition 8503 when it is imposed as an exercise of a discretion pursuant to s 41(3). On its face, condition 8503 would not prevent the making of a further application for a visa by the holder of a visa containing the condition, while the visa holder was in Australia. If it were possible to make an application for a further visa, and if the Minister's delegate considering that application were satisfied that the person applying met the criteria laid down in the Migration Regulations for the further visa, s 65 of the Migration Act would oblige the delegate to grant the visa. The visa could not be refused on the ground that a condition disentitling the person applying for it to a further visa was present in a visa already held by that person. If applied merely in its terms, therefore, condition 8503 would be ineffective to achieve any goal. Only if the criteria for a further visa included a specific criterion that the person applying for it did not already hold a visa subject to a condition in the form of condition 8503 would the condition have any effect at all.

[54] A legislative instrument should not be read to be ineffective if there is reasonably open a construction that would save it. Plainly, condition 8503 is intended to be effective to disentitle a person holding a visa subject to that condition from obtaining any further visa while the person remains in Australia. It would only be effective to do so if s 46(1)(e), now s 46(1A), were to be construed as applying to that condition. In other words, only if condition 8503, when inserted as an exercise of a discretion pursuant to s 41(3), can be regarded as 'a condition described in paragraph 41(2)(a)' would such a condition be effective. Since it is conceded on behalf of the applicants that Parliament has authorised the imposition of a condition in that form as a matter of discretion, pursuant to s 41(3), and not merely as a matter of automatic imposition, it is unlikely that Parliament intended the condition inserted as a matter of discretion to be ineffective.

[55] A purposive approach to the construction of the phrase 'a condition described in paragraph 41(2)(a)' therefore leads to the conclusion that the phrase includes such a condition when imposed as an exercise of discretion, pursuant to s 41(3), as well as when imposed directly by a provision in the Migration Regulations, pursuant to s 41(2)(a) itself.

11

Compliance: Unlawful non-citizens, removal and deportation

11.1 Unlawful non-citizens: an overview

A person in Australia who is not a citizen and does not have a current visa is an unlawful non-citizen.[1] This is contrasted with a lawful non-citizen, which is defined as a person in the migration zone who holds a visa that is in effect.[2] It is not an offence to become an unlawful non-citizen, but such people face mandatory detention,[3] removal from Australia[4] and the costs of enforcement action.[5]

In 2004–05, 18 341 unlawful non-citizens were located, compared with 20 003 in 2003–04 (following a doubling over the previous three years). This includes those located through compliance fieldwork (9062) and those who voluntarily approached DIMIA at their own initiative or at departmental request (9279).[6]

The department's fact sheet 86 states:

> the department uses a wide range of sources to locate unlawful non-citizens and people breaching their visa conditions. These include referrals from employers, educational institutions, departmental investigations, community information, police and other government agencies.

Three government departments – Immigration and Citizenship, Centrelink and the Australian Taxation Office – work together in areas of the cash economy to

1 *Migration Act 1958* (Cth), s 14.
2 *Migration Act 1958* (Cth), s 13.
3 *Migration Act 1958* (Cth), s 189.
4 *Migration Act 1958* (Cth), s 198.
5 *Migration Act 1958* (Cth), ss 204–207, 210, 212–224.
6 www.immi.gov.au/media/publications/compliance/managing-the-border/pdf/mtb-chapter7.pdf.

locate non-citizens who are employed illegally, or claiming welfare payments and benefits to which they are not entitled.[7]

The principal focus of this book is the manner in which non-citizens can immigrate to Australia: that is, how they become lawful non-citizens. However, for considerations of completeness in this chapter we briefly consider issues relating to unlawful non-citizens.

11.2 Becoming unlawful

11.2.1 Overstayers

There are several different ways in which a person can become an unlawful non-citizen. The most common is where a person overstays his or her visa. A person becomes an unlawful non-citizen immediately upon expiry of his or her visa.[8] 'Overstayers' account for the vast majority of unlawful non-citizens. At 30 June 2004, it was estimated that there were fewer than 51 000 overstayers, a reduction from 59 800 the previous year. The groups of people who most commonly overstay are tourists (43 629), students (3100) and temporary residents (1760). There were also 1760 overstayers who had held other categories of visas. The vast majority of overstayers had been in Australia less than one year (17 per cent) or more than ten years (30 per cent). The overall overstay rate for the period of 1 July 2003 to 30 June 2004 was 0.41 per cent, that is, 16 128 overstayers out of 3 944 443 arrivals. The nine nationalities from which overstayers most commonly came were China (2616); Indonesia (1909); South Korea (1195); United Kingdom (1018); Fiji (859); Malaysia (800); Thailand (759); Hong Kong (648); and the Philippines (567).[9] By 30 June 2006, the number of overstayers had reduced to 46 000.[10] The DIAC Annual Report 2009–2010 estimated that the number of people who had overstayed their visas and were in Australia at 30 June 2010 was about 53 900.[11]

11.2.2 Entry without authority

The second category of unlawful non-citizens are people who arrive in mainland Australia without authority to enter the country.[12] People who arrive in Australia unlawfully – that is, those who do not obtain 'immigration clearance' – become unlawful as soon as they enter the migration zone.[13] People are classified as arriving unlawfully in Australia if they arrive with no travel documentation or

7 www.immi.gov.au/media/fact-sheets/86overstayers-and-other-unlawful-non-citizens.htm.
8 *Migration Act 1958* (Cth), s 82(7).
9 DIMIA, *Fact Sheet 86. Overstayers and People in Breach of Visa Conditions* (23 September 2004).
10 www.immi.gov.au/about/reports/annual/2005–06/DIMA_AR/overview/Overview_3.html.
11 www.immi.gov.au/about/reports/annual/2009–10/html/outcome-4/program4–1.htm.
12 See *Migration Act 1958* (Cth), ss 172(4), 173 and 177.
13 *Migration Act 1958* (Cth), s 15.

present with invalid travel documentation (for example, a fraudulent passport or visa). Australia has seen ebbs and flows of undocumented arriavals, particularly by boat. In 2001–02 there were 1193 people who arrived in Australia without travel documentation or with improper travel documentation or were not believed to be *bona fide* travellers. By comparison, the number of unlawful arrivals who are stowaways is much smaller. In 2000–01 the figure was 29.[14] In more recent times, since the federal Labor government abandoned the 'Pacific Solution' implemented by the preceding government, there has been a substantial increase in the number of arrivals by boat. In 2009 the figure was 61 boats and 2849 people (including crew). As of 20 September 2010, the figure stood at 96 boats and 4822 people.[15]

This group of people is placed in immigration detention – this is mandatory – while their reasons for being in Australia are investigated. Thus, if unlawful arrivals apply for protection they will remain in reception and processing centres until their application is finalised. People who arrive by boat at an excised area[16] without authority, or are intercepted at sea and brought to Australia, are detained and transferred to Christmas Island. These unauthorised arrivals undergo an assessment process, to establish if they have a legitimate reason for staying in Australia. This process includes: assessing identity (many people dispose of all personal papers en route to Australia); assessing whether the person is raising claims which may engage Australia's protection obligations (ostensibly an assessment of their refugee status); and obtaining formal police clearances from countries of first asylum in which they have resided for at least 12 months (to confirm that they are of good character).[17]

Any unauthorised arrival who is found not to raise claims which, *prima facie*, may engage Australia's protection obligations has a right to judicial review.[18] Ultimately, if they do not engage Australia's protection obligations they are subject to removal from Australia under the provisions of the *Migration Act 1958* (Cth) and are removed as soon as is practicable.[19]

11.2.3 Cancellation of visas

Visas, once granted, are never final and DIAC retains the right to cancel them. The third way in which a person becomes an unlawful non-citizen is where his or her visa is cancelled because he or she failed the character test[20] or has breached a visa condition (unless the person holds another visa that is in effect).[21]

14 DIMIA, Fact Sheet 74, *Unathorised Arrivals by Air and Sea* (October 2002).
15 www.aph.gov.au/library/pubs/bn/sp/boatarrivals.htm.
16 *Migration Act 1958* (Cth), s 5.
17 www.immi.gov.au/media/fact-sheets/75processing-unlawful-boat-arrivals.htm.
18 *Plaintiff M61/2010E v Commonwealth of Australia*; *Plaintiff M69 of 2010 v Commonwealth of Australia* [2010] HCA 41; 11 November 2010
19 www.immi.gov.au/media/fact-sheets/75processing-unlawful-boat-arrivals.htm.
20 *Migration Act 1958* (Cth), s 501.
21 *Migration Act 1958* (Cth), s 15.

There are a number of grounds upon which visas can be cancelled. Most often they are cancelled where a visa condition is breached or a prescribed requirement is not satisfied. The effect of cancellation is that the person becomes an unlawful non-citizen. The power to cancel visas is normally discretionary and normally subject to review by the Migration Review Tribunal (MRT), unless the cancellation is made by the Minister personally on character grounds.

DIAC has power to detain a visa-holder for 'questioning detention' where it reasonably suspects that a visa could be cancelled because incorrect information was provided, because visa conditions were breached, because a business skills visa-holder failed to establish the business or participate in management, or on character grounds.[22] This power can only be used where the visa-holder will not co-operate. The maximum period of detention is four hours.[23]

Visas are generally not cancelled automatically (unless the person is overseas, in which case the department can cancel a visa without notice).[24] The visa-holder will receive a 'notice of intention to cancel' informing him or her of the reasons for the cancellation.[25] This provides the visa-holder with an opportunity to respond to the allegation and state why the visa should not be cancelled.

We now briefly consider the main grounds upon which visas can be cancelled.

11.2.3.1 Cancellation because of inaccurate information

The department has wide-ranging powers to cancel visas that were issued on the basis of incorrect information or bogus documentation.[26] Cancellation can occur whether the misinformation was provided deliberately, innocently or inadvertently.[27] The duty to provide accurate information extends to notifying the department of circumstances that have changed between when the application is lodged and the person arrives in Australia. After a visa is granted people remain under an obligation to inform the department of any errors or misinformation provided in the application.[28]

11.2.3.2 General cancellation power

Sections 116 to 118 of the *Migration Act 1958* (Cth) also confer general cancellation power on DIAC in relation to *temporary* visas. Section 116 provides:

> (1) Subject to subsections (2) and (3), the Minister may cancel a visa if he or she is satisfied that:
> (a) any circumstances which permitted the grant of the visa no longer exist; or
> (b) its holder has not complied with a condition of the visa; or

22 *Migration Act 1958* (Cth), s 192.
23 *Migration Act 1958* (Cth), s 192.
24 *Migration Act 1958* (Cth), ss 118A–127.
25 See the statutory code of procedure: *Migration Act 1958* (Cth), ss 52–64.
26 *Migration Act 1958* (Cth), ss 97–115, esp s 109.
27 *Migration Act 1958* (Cth), s 100. However, the onus is on the department to show that the information is incorrect: *Tarasovski* (1993) 45 FCR 570.
28 *Migration Act 1958* (Cth), ss 104, 105.

(c) another person required to comply with a condition of the visa has not complied with that condition; or
(d) if its holder has not entered Australia or has so entered but has not been immigration cleared – it would be liable to be cancelled under Subdivision C (incorrect information given by holder) if its holder had so entered and been immigration cleared; or
(e) the presence of its holder in Australia is, or would be, a risk to the health, safety or good order of the Australian community; or
(f) the visa should not have been granted because the application for it or its grant was in contravention of this Act or of another law of the Commonwealth; or
(fa) in the case of a student visa:
   (i) its holder is not, or is likely not to be, a genuine student; or
   (ii) its holder has engaged, is engaging, or is likely to engage, while in Australia, in conduct (including omissions) not contemplated by the visa; or
(g) a prescribed ground for cancelling a visa applies to the holder . . .

(2) The Minister is not to cancel a visa if there exist prescribed circumstances in which a visa is not to be cancelled.
(3) If the Minister may cancel a visa under subsection (1), the Minister must do so if there exist prescribed circumstances in which a visa must be cancelled.

Section 117 prescribes when a visa can be cancelled:

(1) Subject to subsection (2), a visa held by a non-citizen may be cancelled under section 116:
   (a) before the non-citizen enters Australia; or
   (b) when the non-citizen is in immigration clearance (see section 172); or
   (c) when the non-citizen leaves Australia; or
   (d) while the non-citizen is in the migration zone.
(2) A permanent visa cannot be cancelled under section 116 if the holder of the visa:
   (a) is in the migration zone; and
   (b) was immigration cleared on last entering Australia.

11.2.3.3 Cancellation of business visa

Section 134 creates a cancellation power that is specific to business visas (other than an established business in Australia visa, an investment-linked visa or a family member's visa). This power can be exercised where the visa-holder:

(1) . . .
   (a) has not obtained a substantial ownership interest in an eligible business in Australia; or
   (b) is not utilising his or her skills in actively participating at a senior level in the day-to-day management of that business; or
   (c) does not intend to continue to:
      (i) hold a substantial ownership interest in; and
      (ii) utilise his or her skills in actively participating at a senior level in the day-to-day management of; an eligible business in Australia.
(2) The Minister must not cancel a business visa under subsection (1) if the Minister is satisfied that its holder:

(a) has made a genuine effort to obtain a substantial ownership interest in an eligible business in Australia; and
(b) has made a genuine effort to utilise his or her skills in actively participating at a senior level in the day-to-day management of that business; and
(c) intends to continue to make such genuine efforts.

The specific power to cancel business visas does not prevent the more general cancellation powers being invoked in relation to business visas.

11.2.3.4 (Automatic) cancellation of student visas

A registered education provider must send a notice to a non-citizen who breaches a condition of the non-citizen's visa relating to attendance or satisfactory academic performance. The visa-holder must then attend a DIAC office within 28 days to explain the breach. Failure to do so results in automatic cancellation of the student visa.[29] If the visa is cancelled in this way, the visa-holder can apply to the Minister for revocation of the cancellation.

The Minister can revoke the cancellation if:

- the person did not in fact breach the relevant visa condition or conditions; or
- the breach was due to exceptional circumstances beyond the non-citizen's control; or
- the Minister is satisfied of any other matter prescribed in the regulations.[30]

However, a cancellation cannot be revoked on the ground that the non-citizen was unaware of the notice or of the effect of the cancellation.

It should be noted that even where a person does not write to the Minister seeking revocation, the Minister may, on his or her own initiative, revoke the cancellation if the Minister thinks that it is in the public interest to do so.

11.2.3.5 Cancellation on the basis of bad character

A visa can be cancelled if the visa-holder does not pass the 'character test' set out in section 501(6) of the *Migration Act 1958* (Cth). The onus is on the visa-holder to satisfy DIAC that he or she satisfies this test. Section 501(6) states:

(6) For the purposes of this section, a person does not pass the character test if:
(a) the person has a substantial criminal record (as defined by subsection (7)); or
(b) the person has or has had an association with someone else, or with a group or organisation, whom the Minister reasonably suspects has been or is involved in criminal conduct; or
(c) having regard to either or both of the following:
(i) the person's past and present criminal conduct;
(ii) the person's past and present general conduct; the person is not of good character; or
(d) in the event the person were allowed to enter or to remain in Australia, there is a significant risk that the person would:

29 *Migration Act 1958* (Cth), ss 137J–137P.
30 Migration Act 1958 (Cth), s 137L.

(i) engage in criminal conduct in Australia; or
(ii) harass, molest, intimidate or stalk another person in Australia; or
(iii) vilify a segment of the Australian community; or
(iv) incite discord in the Australian community or in a segment of that community; or
(v) represent a danger to the Australian community or to a segment of that community, whether by way of being liable to become involved in activities that are disruptive to, or in violence threatening harm to, that community or segment, or in any other way.

Otherwise, the person passes the character test.

Pursuant to section 501(7), a person will have a substantial criminal record if:

(a) the person has been sentenced to death; or
(b) the person has been sentenced to imprisonment for life; or
(c) the person has been sentenced to a term of imprisonment of 12 months or more; or
(d) the person has been sentenced to 2 or more terms of imprisonment (whether on one or more occasions), where the total of those terms is 2 years or more; or
(e) the person has been acquitted of an offence on the grounds of unsoundness of mind or insanity, and as a result the person has been detained in a facility or institution.

The decision to cancel a visa pursuant to this power can be made by DIAC or the Minister. Where it is made by the Minister the decision is not reviewable by a tribunal, but it is still open to judicial review. Where the decision is made by the department it is reviewable by the Administrative Appeals Tribunal (AAT).

The power to cancel a visa on this basis is obviously very wide-ranging, and accordingly there is considerable scope for inconsistency and abuse in the decision-making process. A Ministerial Direction has been issued which provides further guidance regarding the test, setting out the matters to be taken into consideration in exercising the discretion to cancel a visa on character grounds.[31] Where a visa is cancelled on character grounds, any visa (except a protection visa) is cancelled. In addition to this, any other visa application, apart from a protection visa, is deemed to be refused.

In addition to the above cancellation powers, there are other cancellation powers that apply for certain classes of visas. These cancellation powers relate to: regional sponsored employment visas;[32] criminal justice visas;[33] and temporary safe haven visas.[34]

31 *Migration Act 1958* (Cth), ss 137J–137P; see Ministerial Direction No. 21. The scope and background to this cancellation power was considered by the Full Federal Court in *Minister for Immigration & Multicultural & Indigenous Affairs v Godley* [2005] FCAFC 10 and the reasoning was approved of in *Mujedenovski v Minister for Immigration & Citizenship* [2009] FCAFC 149, 45, where the court held that the principle for determining an appeal in the context of s 501(6) was set out by the Full Federal Court in Godley (No. 2).

32 *Migration Act 1958* (Cth), ss 137Q–137T.

33 *Migration Act 1958* (Cth), ss 162–164.

34 *Migration Act 1958* (Cth), s 500A.

11.3 Options for unlawful non-citizens

Unlawful non-citizens have three broad options. First, they can elect to stay in Australia unlawfully. However, if they are detected by migration officials,[35] they face a number of penalties and sanctions, which are discussed below. In addition, during their time in Australia they are not entitled to welfare payments, a tax file number or Medicare, and they cannot study.

Second, unlawful non-citizens can seek to voluntarily leave the country. Where the unlawful non-citizen can show that acceptable arrangements have been made to depart Australia (for example, they have purchased their ticket out of the country) they will, on application, be granted a bridging visa E,[36] which gives them temporary lawful status until their departure. If they do not have this visa, they will still be permitted to leave Australia, provided that they are not wanted in relation to legal proceedings.

Third, unlawful non-citizens can seek to become lawful non-citizens by obtaining a valid visa. Where a visa has been cancelled pursuant to one of the above cancellation powers, the former visa-holder can apply for only a limited class of visas while they are still in Australia. Regulation 2.12, which is made pursuant to section 48 of the Act, states:

> (1) For section 48 of the Act (which limits further applications by a person whose visa has been cancelled, or whose application for a visa has been refused) the following classes of visas are prescribed:
> (a) Partner (Temporary) (Class UK);
> (b) Partner (Residence) (Class BS);
> (c) Protection (Class XA);
> (ca) subject to subregulation (3), Medical Treatment (Visitor) (Class UB);
> (d) Territorial Asylum (Residence) (Class BE);
> (e) Border (Temporary) (Class TA);
> (f) Special Category (Temporary) (Class TY);
> (g) Bridging A (Class WA);
> (h) Bridging B (Class WB);
> (i) Bridging C (Class WC);
> (j) Bridging D (Class WD);
> (k) Bridging E (Class WE);
> (l) Resolution of Status (Temporary) (Class UH);
> (m) Resolution of Status (Residence) (Class BL);
> (ma) Bridging F (Class WF);
> (mb) Bridging R (Class WR);
> (n) Child (Residence) (Class BT);
>
> (3) Paragraph (1)(ca) applies to a person if and only if he or she meets the requirements of subclause 685.212(6) or (7) of Schedule 2.
>
> (4) For section 48 of the Act the following classes of visas are prescribed if, and only if, the person has received an invitation under regulation 2.11 to apply for a visa of that class:

35 *Migration Act 1958* (Cth), s 5(1).
36 See Chapter 9.

(a) a Skilled – Independent Overseas Student (Residence) (Class DD) visa;
(b) a Skilled – Australian-sponsored Overseas Student (Residence) (Class DE) visa;
(c) a Skilled – Independent Regional (Provisional) (Class UX) visa;
(d) a Skilled – Independent (Migrant) (Class BN) visa;
(e) a Skill Matching (Migrant) (Class BR) visa;
(f) a Skilled – Australian-sponsored (Migrant) (Class BQ) visa;
(g) a Skilled – New Zealand Citizen (Residence) (Class DB) visa.

Applications by unlawful non-citizens are also subject to the restrictions contained in Schedule 3 of the Regulations.

People who have had their visas cancelled can lodge an application from overseas for either a temporary or a permanent visa. However, it is often difficult to obtain another visa once a person has breached a condition of a visa, because they could have difficulty meeting the 'genuine intention' requirements attached to many visa categories, and applicants for temporary visas face re-entry bans.[37]

Detainees have strict time limits for applying for another visa. *Migration Act 1958* (Cth) section 195 provides that the person must apply within two working days of being detained or within five working days where the detainee has informed an officer in writing of his or her intention to apply for another visa. Detainees who do not apply for a visa within this time may not apply for any visa other than a bridging visa or a protection visa.[38]

Where a person has not been immigration cleared, the only substantive visa that he or she can apply for is a protection visa. The people who most commonly fit into this category are asylum-seekers who arrive by boat.

11.4 Consequences of being unlawful: removal and deportation

DIAC has wide-ranging powers in relation to unlawful non-citizens. These include the right of arrest, detention and deportation, and of placing restrictions on re-entry.

The *Migration Act 1958* (Cth) states that unlawful non-citizens must be detained.[39] They must be held on detention (in either an immigration detention centre or prison) until a visa is granted or the person is removed or deported.[40] In some cases a visa can be granted almost immediately. Unlawful non-citizens are liable to pay the costs of their detention.[41] In some circumstances the liability will be waived. These circumstances include where the person is granted refugee status and where extenuating circumstances exist.[42]

37 See Chapter 10, section 10.4, 'Exclusion periods/re-entry bans'.
38 *Migration Act 1958* (Cth), s 195.
39 *Migration Act 1958* (Cth), ss 189, 190.
40 *Migration Act 1958* (Cth), s 195.
41 *Migration Act 1958* (Cth), ss 207, 210, 212–224.
42 See *Audit Act 1901* (Cth).

Removal and deportation from Australia have different meanings. While they both involve expelling a person from Australia, the reasons for the expulsion are fundamentally different. Deportation involves expelling a non-citizen essentially for security reasons. Deportation can occur where a person has been a permanent resident in Australia for less than ten years and is sentenced to imprisonment for at least 12 months;[43] or is a threat to national security.[44] Deportation can also occur where a person has been convicted of certain serious offences, such as treason and sabotage.[45] In relation to the latter ground, deportation can occur even where the person has been a permanent resident for more than ten years.

Removal occurs when DIAC locates an unlawful non-citizen and arranges for his or her departure from Australia. The *Migration Act 1958* (Cth) requires immigration officers to remove unlawful non-citizens as soon as reasonably practicable in certain circumstances. These circumstances are listed in section 198 of the *Migration Act 1958* (Cth). In essence, the obligation to remove unlawful non-citizens crystallises where the detainee asks to be removed, or has exhausted all avenues for obtaining a visa and all avenues of review.[46]

People who are deported or removed from Australia are normally returned to their county of citizenship unless they request to go to another country. They are liable for the costs of the travel. Where they do not have the funds to cover the travel costs, the sum is paid by the government and becomes a debt owed to the government by the person who is removed or deported.[47] People who are removed from Australia cannot apply for a visa for 12 months, unless compelling circumstances exist. People who are unlawful for more than 28 days and then leave Australia (with a bridging E visa or no visa) cannot apply for a temporary visa for three years unless there are compelling circumstances. People who are deported cannot return to Australia.[48]

11.5 Offences that can be committed by unlawful non-citizens

There are a number of offences that can be committed by an unlawful non-citizen.[49] These include working contrary to a visa condition prohibiting work

43 *Migration Act 1958* (Cth), s 201. This power is discretionary, not mandatory. Thus, not all people who have been sentenced to imprisonment for 12 months or longer will be deported. This process is assessed on a case-by-case basis. To this end, Ministerial Direction No. 9 provides that relevant considerations include the Australian community's expectation to be protected from harm, the best interests of children of the potential deportee, hardship that the potential deportee and others would suffer, the risk of re-offending and the nature and seriousness of the crime.
44 *Migration Act 1958* (Cth), s 202.
45 *Migration Act 1958* (Cth), s 203.
46 *Migration Act 1958* (Cth), s 198.
47 See Chapter 10, section 10.4, 'Exclusion periods/re-entry bans'.
48 ibid.
49 *Migration Act 1958* (Cth), ss 228A–236.

(whether paid or unpaid), refusing to answer questions asked by an officer where the person is a detainee, and presenting false documents in connection with entry or stay in Australia. There are also offences prohibiting people from assisting, concealing or harbouring unlawful non-citizens, and offences that specifically deal with people who smuggle unlawful non-citizens into Australia.

12

History of the Refugees Convention and definitional framework

12.1 History of the Convention

We commence our discussion of refugee law by providing a brief overview of the instruments underpinning refugee law in Australia. This provides insight into the development of the legal definition of a 'refugee' and the objectives of the parties involved in framing the definition. This potentially plays an important role in understanding the nature and scope of refugee law.

International refugee law is principally governed by the 1951 Convention Relating to the Status of Refugees as modified by the 1967 Protocol Relating to the Status of Refugees[1] (hereafter together referred to as the Convention). The Convention provides a definition of a refugee and confers a number of rights and protections onto persons falling within this definition.

The origins of the Convention can be traced back to the early 20th century. Prior to this time, customary international law imposed an obligation on states to protect their own nationals only. This obligation did not extend to individuals from other nations who found themselves within the borders of a state. States had the discretion to accept immigrants whom they perceived would contribute to the economy or society in a positive way, and to expel refugees under the assumption that the right to do so was inherent in a state's sovereign powers.[2]

During the inter-war years of 1919–39, numerous violent conflicts and political problems in Europe and the Middle East led to the displacement of large numbers of people.[3] This exodus clashed with the desire of individual states

1 See *MIMA v Savvin* [2000] FCA 478 (12 April 2000) per Katz J, [124].
2 T. Musgrave, 'Refugees', in S. Blay, R. Piotrowicz & B.M. Tsamenyi (eds), *Public International Law: An Australian Perspective* (Melbourne, Oxford University Press [OUP], 1997) p. 301.
3 ibid.

to control immigration and led the international community to respond to the refugee issue. The League of Nations did so[4] by formulating agreements to provide for refugee protection. Such agreements related to *specific* refugee situations and were thus *ad hoc* in nature. Moreover, they contained a group or category approach, where the sufficient and necessary conditions to achieve refugee status were that someone was (a) outside his or her country of origin and (b) without the protection of the government of that state.[5] There was neither a general definition of refugee status, nor any standardised measure of international protection for refugees during this period.[6]

When masses of people were uprooted during and after World War II, it was perceived that the refugee problem was not a temporary one, and that an instrument with a broader approach would more effectively address emerging refugee crises. Thus, the 1951 Convention Relating to the Status of Refugees was adopted by a special United Nations Conference[7] on 28 July 1951, and entered into force on 21 April 1954. It was drafted between 1948 and 1951 by a combination of United Nations organs, *ad hoc* committees and a conference of plenipotentiaries, at which 26 states were represented.[8] These negotiations (the *travaux preparatoires*) are recorded in various forms,[9] and provide some insight into the deliberations and intentions of the framers. The fact that so many parties and interest groups contributed to the drafting necessarily reduced the prospect that the definition would be based on a coherent overarching theory.

Unlike earlier instruments, the 1951 Convention purported to provide a *general* definition of who was to be considered a refugee. Essentially, a refugee was defined as a person who feared being subjected to serious harm for five enumerated reasons if he or she returned to his or her country of origin.[10] The 1951 Convention also provided a guarantee of non-refoulement, whereby refugees could not be returned to their country of origin if doing so would subject them to persecution.[11]

4 UNHCR, *The State Of The World's Refugees 2000: Fifty Years of Humanitarian Action* (Geneva & New York, OUP, 2000), p. 15.
5 G. Goodwin-Gill, *The Refugee in International Law* (2nd edn) (Oxford, OUP, 1996), p. 4.
6 Musgrave, 'Refugees', p. 302.
7 Goodwin-Gill, *The Refugee in International Law*, p. 4.
8 J. Hathaway, *The Law of Refugee Status* (Toronto, Butterworths, 1991), p. 6. For a history of the process leading to the drafting of the Convention, see P. Weis, *The Refugee Convention, 1951: The Travaux Preparatoires Analysed* (Cambridge, Grotius Publications, 1995). Note that the earlier international agreements entered into on behalf of refugees are referred to in article 1A(1) of the Convention.
9 See, for example, Weis, *The Refugee Convention, 1951*.
10 Article 1A(2). In 1969, the Organisation for African Unity (OAU) adopted a Convention on Refugee Problems in Africa which adopts a broader refugee definition. The OAU defines as a refugee 'every person who, owing to external aggression, occupation, foreign domination or events seriously disturbing public order in either part or the whole of his country of origin or nationality, is compelled to leave his place of habitual residence in order to seek refuge in another place outside his country of origin or nationality'. In 1984 Latin American countries adopted the 'Cartagena Declaration' which incorporates a similar refugee definition: www.unhcr.ch/refworld/refworld/legal/instrume/asylum/ref_afre.htm. Unlike the definition in the Convention, neither of these is of universal application. Hence for the purpose of this paper, we focus on the definition in the Refugee Convention.
11 Article 33.

Despite its universal overtones, the 1951 Convention was limited by the fact that it protected mainly Europeans fleeing after World War II.[12] Furthermore, the definition of a refugee set out in Article 1A(2) of the 1951 Convention defined refugees only in terms of those who had a well-founded fear of being persecuted 'as a result of events occurring before 1 January 1951'. These restrictions were removed and the definition was expanded by the 1967 Protocol relating to the Status of Refugees.[13] Accession to the 1967 Protocol enabled states to apply the substantive provisions of the Convention to refugees as defined by the Convention, but without the temporal and geographic limitations. Hence, the Convention now applies to all persons who are refugees because of events occurring at *any time*. Denmark was the first state to ratify the 1951 Convention (in 1952) and since then, over 140 states have acceded to the Convention.[14]

The normative overtone of the Convention glosses over the fact that it was developed and entered into mainly to assist European refugees, and to serve Western political and economic needs.[15] This is a point emphasised by Hathaway:

> The two main characteristics of the Convention refugee definition are its strategic conceptualisation and its Eurocentric focus. The strategic dimension of the definition comes from successful efforts of Western States to give priority in protection matters to persons whose flight was motivated by pro-Western political values. As anxious as the Soviets had been to exclude political emigres from the scope of the Convention for fear of exposing their weak flank, so the more numerous and more powerful Western states were preoccupied to maximise the international visibility of that migration. In the result, it was agreed to restrict the scope of protection in much the same way as had been done in the post-World War II refugee instruments: only persons who feared 'persecution' because of their civil or political status would fall within the international protection mandate. This apparently neutral formulation facilitated the condemnation of Soviet bloc politics through international law in two ways. First, the persecution standard was a known quantity, having already been employed to embrace Soviet bloc dissidents in the immediate post-war years. Second, the precise formulation of the persecution standard meant that refugee law could not readily be turned to the political advantage of the Soviet bloc. The refugee definition was carefully phrased to include only persons who have been disenfranchised by their state on the basis of race, religion, nationality, membership of a particular social group, or political opinion, matters in regard to which eastern bloc practice has historically been problematic. Western vulnerability in the area of respect for human rights, in contrast, centers more on the guarantee of socio-economic human rights than on respect for civil and political rights. Unlike the victims of civil and political oppression, however, persons denied even such basic rights as food, health care or education are excluded from the international refugee regime (unless that deprivation stems from civil or political status). By mandating protection for those whose (Western inspired) socio-economic rights are at risk, the Convention adopted an incomplete and politically partisan human rights rationale... In addition to their desire for the refugee Convention to serve

12 Goodwin-Gill, *The Refugee in International Law*, p. 19. Note that the definition included an optional geographical limitation that permitted States, on ratification, to limit their obligations to refugees from 'events occurring within Europe' prior to the critical date – article 1B.
13 Hathaway, *The Law of Refugee Status*, p. 10.
14 DIMIA, *Interpreting the Refugees Convention – An Australian Contribution* (Canberra, DIMIA, 2002), p. 1.
15 Hathaway, *The Law of Refugee Status*, p. 6.

> strategic political objectives, the majority of the States that drafted the Convention sought to create a rights regime conducive to the redistribution of the post-war refugee burden from European shoulders.[16]

Thus the history of the Convention reflects the fact that the plight of displaced or 'needy' people was subordinated to the needs and wants of the state parties who drafted the Convention, and that refugees were defined by reference to the interests of nation states preoccupied with Cold War politics.[17] It has been noted by Hathaway that: 'it remains tragically true that international human rights law – the intended means of permitting the world community to respond to wrongs committed by a country within its own territory – has not been permitted to evolve to a state of genuine efficacy'.[18]

In these circumstances, it is not surprising that some are starting to question the relevance of the Convention in today's world.

In 1998, the Austrian President of the European Union (EU) suggested replacing the Convention with an EU asylum law 'which meets today's requirements rather than those of a geopolitically outdated situation'. In the same year, the General Secretary of Germany's Liberal Party called, in effect, for default from the Convention on the grounds that it was 'an invitation to abuse and to unrestricted and unregulated migration'. In April 2002 the United Kingdom's Home Secretary, Jack Straw, criticised the Convention as 'too broad for conditions in the twenty-first century', and as 'no longer an adequate guide to policy in the age of mass air travel and economic migration'. Conservative Party leader William Hague described the asylum system as 'near collapse in today's utterly different world'.[19]

In light of such criticism, the manner in which the Convention is interpreted is particularly important. In the last chapter of this book, we revisit this issue and suggest an alternative, more principled definition of a refugee.

At this point it is important to note that for the purposes of the Convention, a refugee is defined, pursuant to Article 1A(2), as any person who:

> . . . owing to well-founded fear of being persecuted for reasons of race, religion, nationality, membership of a particular social group or political opinion, is outside the country of his nationality and is unable, or owing to such fear, is unwilling to avail himself of the protection of that country; or who, not having a nationality and being outside the country of his former habitual residence as a result of such events, is unable or, owing to such fear, is unwilling to return to it.
>
> In the case of a person who has more than one nationality, the term 'the country of his nationality' shall mean each of the countries of which he is a national, and a person shall not be deemed to be lacking the protection of the country of his nationality if, without any valid reason based on well-founded fear, he has not availed himself of the protection of one of the countries of which he is a national.

16 Hathaway, *The Law of Refugee Status*, pp. 7–8 [footnotes omitted].
17 ibid., pp. 232–33.
18 ibid., p. v.
19 Millbank, *The Problem with the 1951 Refugee Convention* (Canberra, Social Policy Group Research Paper No. 5, Department of the Parliamentary Libaray, 2000).

At the level of international law this definition has remained (effectively)[20] unchanged. However, there has been a considerable amount of uncertainty at the domestic level concerning the precise meaning that should be given to important aspects of the definition, such as 'particular social group' and 'persecution'.

If a person meets the definition of a refugee set out in Article 1A(2), a range of rights and protections pursuant to the Convention, the most important of which is non-refoulement or 'non-return' to the state from which she or he has fled, are conferred onto that person. Chapter 13 of this book outlines the protections provided to refugees under Australian law.[21]

Prior to discussing the manner in which Australia discharges its obligations under the Convention, we first provide an overview of the definitional framework regarding the definition of a refugee.

12.2 The four elements

In *Minister for Immigration and Ethnic Affairs v Guo*,[22] the High Court noted that the Convention definition of 'refugee' has four main elements:

(1) The applicant must be outside his or her country of nationality;
(2) The applicant must fear 'persecution';
(3) The applicant must fear such persecution 'for reasons of race, religion, nationality, membership of a particular social group or political opinion'; and
(4) The applicant must have a 'well-founded' fear of persecution for one of the Convention reasons.

Elements 2, 3 and 4 are considered at length in the following chapters. Prior to examining these elements we briefly discuss one aspect of the framework of the definition of a refugee.

12.3 Protection not a key element: It is external, not internal

Despite earlier case law to the contrary[23] in *MIMA v Respondents S152/2003*[24] the High Court unanimously held that the term 'protection' in Article 1A(2) refers to diplomatic or consular protection extended by a country to its nationals outside the borders of that country. In their joint judgment, Gleeson CJ, Hayne and Heydon JJ stated:

20 The only change is pursuant to the Protocol of 1967, which made no substantive changes to the definition. It merely removed a temporal and geographic limitation – see above.
21 Article 3 confers a right to not be discriminated against, Article 4 covers freedom of religion, Article 16 provides for free access to the courts, Article 21 provides a right to housing, Article 22 provides a right to access to education. See also Articles 21, 23, 26 and 32.
22 [1997] HCA 22 (13 June 1997).
23 See *MIMA v Kandasamy* [2000] FCA (10 February 2000), [31].
24 [2004] HCA 18 (21 April 2004).

> As explained in Khawar... we accept that the term 'protection' there refers to the diplomatic or consular protection extended abroad by a country to its nationals. In the present case, the first respondent must show that he is unable or, owing to his fear of persecution in Ukraine, unwilling to avail himself of the diplomatic or consular protection extended abroad by the state of Ukraine to its nationals. Availing himself of that protection might result in his being returned to Ukraine. Where diplomatic or consular protection is available, a person such as the first respondent must show, not merely that he is unwilling to avail himself of such protection, but that his unwillingness is owing to his fear of persecution. He must justify, not merely assert, his unwillingness. As the Supreme Court of Canada put it in *Canada (Attorney General) v Ward*... a claimant's unreasonable refusal to seek the protection of his home authorities would not satisfy the requirements of Art 1A(2).[25] [Footnotes omitted.]

As such, the word 'protection' is not one of the constituent elements of the definition of a refugee. Nevertheless, the court in *S152/2003* approved the view of the majority of the House of Lords in *Horvath v Secretary of State for the Home Department*,[26] that where the persecutor is a non-state agent, internal protection of the state is relevant to several integral elements of the definition of a refugee:

> ... whether the relevant conduct constitutes persecution; whether the fear is well-founded; and whether the person is unable or, owing to their fear, unwilling to avail himself or herself of the protection of their state because the state provides insufficient protection for discriminatory reasons.[27]

The relevance of protection to these other elements is considered in the following chapters.

25 [2004] HCA 18 (21 April 2004), [19]. In relation to external protection, circumstances where a person is *unable* to avail him or herself of such protection include where the country of origin does not have representation in the receiving country, or the person is denied a passport or loses his or her rationality. A person is unwilling to avail him or herself of protection where he or she refuses to accept the protection of their country or origin.
26 [2001] 1 AC 489 at 495.
27 [2001] 1 AC 489, [21] and [23].

13

Refugee and humanitarian visas: The statutory structure

13.1 Overview

Australia became a signatory to the 1951 United Nations Convention Relating to the Status of Refugees (the Convention) in 1954 and to the 1967 Protocol in 1973. It thereby assumed certain obligations under the Convention, the principal one being to grant asylum to people who fall within the definition of a refugee as set out in Article 1A(2). The process or manner in which asylum is granted is not expressly stipulated in the Convention. It is governed by the *Migration Act 1958* (Cth).

The *Migration Act 1958* (Cth) provides for visas to be issued on refugee and humanitarian grounds to applicants under the government's humanitarian program. That program is made up of onshore protection for those people already in Australia, whether or not they arrived with temporary visas or without a visa at all, and resettlement in Australia for people in humanitarian need overseas (including those who are classified as refugees by the UN High Commissioner for Refugees (UNHCR) and recommended for resettlement). Previously, both the onshore and offshore visa categories included both permanent and temporary residence visas. Now temporary visas have been abolished.[1]

The government has capped the number of humanitarian visa places at 13 750 – a ceiling which has remained relatively steady over the past few years. The Annual Report of DIAC for the 2009–10 year sets out the manner in which these humanitarian and refugee visas were allocated. In total, 13 770 visas were granted under the humanitarian program.

1 See *Migration Act 1958* (Cth), s 30.

The number of offshore refugee visas was 6003. There were 3233 offshore visas granted under the special humanitarian program. There were 4515 onshore protection visas, with an additional 19 other humanitarian visas.

In relation to offshore visas, the main areas of origin were the Asia-Pacific (39 per cent); Middle East and South-West Asia (32 per cent) and Africa (29 per cent), with the main countries being Burma (1959), Iraq (1688), Bhutan (1144) and Afghanistan (951). The onshore grants were mainly to arrivals from Afghanistan (1514); Sri Lanka (505); China (492); Iraq (321); and Iran (282).

In the 2009–10 year, 8749 people were placed into immigration detention; this is double the number of previous years. Of these people 81 per cent were unauthorised arrivals – with about three-quarters of these arriving by boat and the balance by plane. The others were people who had overstayed or otherwise breached their visa conditions. At 30 June 2010 there were 4077 people in immigration detention. This is a fourfold increase from the previous year and is mainly attributable to the large increase in boat arrivals during the year.

The principal visa classes and their corresponding subclasses areas are:[2]

- **Onshore visas: Protection (class XA):**[3]
- Subclass 866 (Protection)[4]
- Subclass 851 (Resolution of Status)[5]
- **Offshore visas:**[6] Refugee and Humanitarian (class XB):[7]
- Subclass 200 (Refugee)[8]
- Subclass 201 (In-country Special Humanitarian)[9]
- Subclass 202 (Global Special Humanitarian)[10]
- Subclass 203 (Emergency Rescue)[11]
- Subclass 204 (Woman at Risk)[12]
- Subclass 451 (Secondary Movement Relocation (Temporary)).[13]

13.2 Onshore applications

The central issue in determining an onshore application for a protection visa (subclass 866) is whether Australia owes protection obligations to the applicant

2 See Migration Regulations 1994, regulations 1.06(a), 1.07 and 2.02.
3 Sch. 1, Item 1401.
4 Sch. 1, Item 1401(4).
5 See Sch. 1, Item 1227A.
6 See Sch. 1, Item 1402(3) and Sch. 2, clauses 200.411, 201.411, 202.411, 203.411, 204.411, 447.411 and 451.411.
7 Sch. 1, Item 1402.
8 Sch. 1, Item 1402(4).
9 ibid.
10 ibid.
11 ibid.
12 ibid.
13 ibid.

under the Convention.[14] Consequently, onshore applicants for a protection visa must demonstrate that they meet the definition of refugee set out in Article 1A(2) of the Convention.[15] In turn, that definition must be interpreted with reference to sections 91R and 91S of the *Migration Act 1958* (Cth). Section 91R concerns the meaning of 'persecution' and includes the stipulation that persecution involves 'serious harm'. It goes on to provide examples of serious harm, such as threats to a person's life or liberty. Section 91S requires decision-makers to disregard membership of a particular social group that consists of the applicant's family in certain circumstances. These provisions are discussed further in Chapters 14 and 15.

Applicants who fall within the definition in Article 1A(2) of the Convention will not be recognised as refugees if their refugee status is found to have ceased under Article 1C(1) to (6), or if they are excluded under Articles 1D to 1F of the Convention.[16] Furthermore, sections 36(2) to (6) of the *Migration Act 1958* (Cth) exclude those applicants who have a right to enter and reside in another country, provided they do not face persecution in that country. In essence, Australia will only afford protection to those protection visa applicants who are defined as refugees pursuant to Article 1A(2) of the Convention and who do not have 'effective protection' in a 'safe third country'.[17]

Recognition as a refugee for the purposes of engaging Australia's protection obligations includes the accompanying spouse and dependants of a successful primary applicant.[18] Unlike the definition of 'dependant' for family members in the family stream of visas, in which the issue rests on demonstrating financial dependence, the definition in most of the humanitarian stream of visas is extended to take in those who are also dependent for psychological and physical support.[19]

There is an exception to the requirement to meet the refugee definition for the purposes of a successful protection visa application, where the Minister for Immigration exercises the non-compellable discretion provided under section 417 of the Act to replace a negative decision of the Refugee Review Tribunal (RRT) with a more favourable decision.[20] However, a successful applicant under section 417 will not necessarily be issued a protection visa; he or she can be issued another class of visa of the Minister's choosing.

Asylum-seekers who have not been immigration cleared and who therefore cannot meet one of the threshold requirements for a subclass 866 (Protection) visa may apply for a subclass 785 (Temporary Protection) visa, provided they have not arrived in a part of Australia that has been excised from the 'migration

14 *Migration Act 1958* (Cth), s 36(2); Sch. 2, Item 866.211.
15 See 12.1 above.
16 Discussed in Chapter 17.
17 See Chapter 17.
18 *Migration Act 1958* (Cth), s 36(2)(b). Sch. 2, Item 866.211.
19 Regulation 1.05(2).
20 See MSI 386 Guidelines on Ministerial Powers Under Sections 345, 351, 391, 417, 454 and 501J of the *Migration Act 1958* (Cth).

zone'. Those who arrive at an 'excised offshore place'[21] are defined as 'offshore entry persons'[22] and are denied the right to make a valid application for any visa (including a protection visa) by the operation of section 46A of the Act. That legislative package is the framework for what was colloquially named the 'Pacific Solution', as it resulted in people caught by that legislation being removed to detention centres in some Pacific Islands, where they did not have access to Australia's refugee determination system. The Pacific Solution has now been abandoned, and although the legislative regime regarding undocumented arrivals remains in place, the current Australian government has introduced policy guidelines that permit undocumented arrivals to be detained while they have their claims for protection assessed. As an issue of policy, the Minister for Immigration has stated that, pursuant to section 46A(2) of the *Migration Act 1958* (Cth) he will consent to an application for a protection visa by offshore entry persons who have been assessed as refugees and who meet health and character requirements.[23]

The High Court has recently considered the lawfulness of the current government's policy for processing undocumented arrivals by boat, who are known as irregular maritime arrivals. In the case of *Plaintiff M61/2010E v Commonwealth of Australia and Plaintiff M69 of 2010 v Commonwealth of Australia* [2010] HCA 41, 11 November 2010, the court found that the Minister could process refugee assessments and that the government could retain independent reviewers who are not officers of the Commonwealth, but it concluded that DIAC assessors and independent reviewers are bound by law to make the protection assessment in

21 Defined in *Migration Act 1958* (Cth), s 5 as:
(a) the Territory of Christmas Island;
(b) the Territory of Ashmore and Cartier Islands;
(c) the Territory of Cocos (Keeling) Islands;
(d) any other external Territory that is prescribed by the regulations for the purposes of this paragraph;
(e) any island that forms part of a State or Territory and is prescribed for the purposes of this paragraph;
(f) an Australian sea installation;
(g) an Australian resources installation.
The excised areas prescribed by the Regulations are:
5.15C (1) For paragraph (d) of the definition of *excised offshore place* in subsection 5(1) of the Act, the Coral Sea Islands Territory is prescribed.
(2) For paragraph (e) of the definition of *excised offshore place* in subsection 5(1) of the Act, the following islands are prescribed:
(a) all islands that:
(i) form part of Queensland; and
(ii) are north of latitude 21° south;
(b) all islands that:
(i) form part of Western Australia; and
(ii) are north of latitude 23° south;
(c) all islands that:
(i) form part of the Northern Territory; and
(ii) are north of latitude 16° south.

22 *Migration Act 1958* (Cth), s 5.

23 46A (1) An application for a visa is not a valid application if it is made by an offshore entry person who:
(a) is in Australia; and
(b) is an unlawful non-citizen.
(2) If the Minister thinks that it is in the public interest to do so, the Minister may, by written notice given to an offshore entry person, determine that subsection (1) does not apply to an application by the person for a visa of a class specified in the determination.

accordance with the *Migration Act 1958* (Cth) and judicial precedents. Otherwise, the Minister could not be properly informed as to who was or wasn't a refugee when requested to exercise his discretion under section 46A(2). To deal with the assessment otherwise is an error of law.

The court also found that the officials involved in the assessment process must observe the requirements of procedural fairness. Notwithstanding those decisions, the court also confirmed that the non-compellable aspect of exercising discretion under section 46A, contained in subsection (7), is valid, and that the discretion is personal to the Minister and is not compellable.[24]

13.3 Offshore applications

The Refugee and Humanitarian (class XB) visas have attracted scant public interest compared with the public interest in onshore protection visa issues in Australia in recent years. Yet, of the 13 770 visas granted under DIAC's humanitarian program during the 2009–10 financial year, 9236 were granted offshore.[25]

Applications for one of the subclasses of Refugee and Humanitarian visas are subject to criteria that can place greater emphasis on government policy than on the circumstances of an individual applicant.

This is most apparent in the requirement common to all subclasses within the Refugee and Humanitarian (class XB) visa: that a visa will not be granted if it results in the number of visas of that subclass, or of a class including that subclass, exceeding a predetermined maximum number for a particular financial year.[26] This has become a significant issue for offshore applicants since the increase in the number grants of protection visas to boat people and of 'split family' Global Humanitarian (subclass 202) visas to the immediate families of those successful claimants, because the quota of visas for the humanitarian program is largely filled by those applications.

The humanitarian program has three main components:

- **Refugee:** for people who meet the UN Convention definition of a refugee and have been identified in conjunction with UNHCR as in need of resettlement;
- **Special Humanitarian Program (SHP):** for those who have suffered discrimination amounting to gross violation of human rights, displacement or hardship, and who have strong support from an Australian citizen or resident or a community group in Australia; and

24 *Plaintiff M61/2010E v Commonwealth of Australia and Plaintiff M69 of 2010 v Commonwealth of Australia* [2010] HCA 41, at [70].

25 DIMA Annual Report 2009–10, Outcome 2: www.immi.gov.au/about/reports/annual/2009-10/html/outcome-2/departmental2-1-1.htm.

26 *Migration Act 1958* (Cth), ss 85, 86 and Sch. 2, clauses 200.225, 201.225, 202.226, 203.225, 204.225, 447.224 and 451.224.

- **Onshore Protection Visas:** for those assessed as refugees and granted protection visas in Australia.

The effects of government policy are most apparent on Refugee and Humanitarian (class XB) visas, which constitute the greatest proportion of visas granted in this area.

The following criteria must also be satisfied in order for an applicant to be granted one of the Refugee and Humanitarian (class XB) visa subclasses:

Subclass 200 (Refugee) visa

An applicant must face persecution in his or her home country and be living outside that country; or the applicant must be an immediate family member of a person who has held a subclass 200 (Refugee) visa, who is an Australian citizen or permanent resident, and who has 'proposed' the applicant's entry to Australia.[27]

Subclass 201 (In-country Special Humanitarian) visa

An applicant must face persecution in his or her home country and be living inside that country; or the applicant must be an immediate family member of a person who has held a subclass 201 (In-country Special Humanitarian) visa, who is an Australian citizen or permanent resident, and who has 'proposed' the applicant's entry to Australia.[28]

Subclass 202 (Global Special Humanitarian) visa

An applicant must face 'substantial discrimination, amounting to gross violation of human rights' in his or her home country and be living outside that country; or the applicant must be an immediate family member of a person who has held a subclass 201 visa/subclass 866 visa/special assistance visa, who is an Australian citizen or permanent resident, and who has proposed the applicant's entry to Australia.[29]

The type of discrimination envisaged in this visa subclass includes, but is not limited to:

- arbitrary interference with the applicant's privacy, family, home or correspondence;
- deprivation of all means of earning a livelihood, denial of work commensurate with training and qualifications and/or payment of unreasonably low wages;
- relegation to substandard dwellings;
- exclusion from the right to education;
- enforced social and civil inactivity;
- removal of citizenship rights;
- denial of a passport;
- constant surveillance or pressure to become an informer.[30]

This visa subclass is the only one for which it is mandatory that the applicant have an Australian proposer (sponsor). The sponsor can be an Australian citizen or permanent

27 *Migration Act 1958* (Cth), clause 200.211.
28 *Migration Act 1958* (Cth), clause 201.211.
29 ibid., clause 202.211.
30 PAM3: Sch. 2, Visa 202, Generic Guidelines D – The offshore humanitarian program, s 13.2.

resident or an eligible New Zealand citizen, or 'a body operating in Australia'.[31] Such bodies include recognised community, ethnic and religious organisations. Policy considerations suggest that DIMIA will give preference to applicants who have registered with the UNHCR.[32]

Subclass 203 (Emergency Rescue) visa

An applicant must face persecution in his or her home country, whether or not the applicant is living in that country; or the applicant must be an immediate family member of a person who has held a subclass 203 (Emergency Rescue) visa, who is an Australian citizen or permanent resident, and who has 'proposed' the applicant's entry to Australia.[33]

In addition, at the time of the decision, the Minister must be satisfied that 'there are urgent and compelling reasons for the applicant to travel to Australia'.[34] DIAC interprets this provision to mean 'that applicants must be in unique circumstances threatening life or freedom that can only be avoided by travelling to Australia for resettlement purposes'.[35]

Except for Central America, these applications usually come to notice through referral from the UNHCR Resettlement Section in Geneva.[36] It is not necessary for the grant of a subclass 203 (Emergency Rescue) visa that an applicant have a 'connection' with Australia,[37] however there is no reason why people who know of a person in imminent danger should not bring it to the attention of DIMIA. In such cases, it would be helpful to have the support of an organisation such as Amnesty International or another refugee support group.

Subclass 204 (Woman at Risk) visa

An applicant must be a female who faces persecution in her home country, or is registered with the UNHCR as a person 'of concern'; who is not living in that country; and who 'does not have the protection of a male relative and is in danger of victimisation, harassment or serious abuse because of her sex'.[38] Alternatively, an applicant must be an immediate family member of a person who has held a subclass 204 (Woman at Risk) visa, who is an Australian citizen or permanent resident, and who has 'proposed' the applicant's entry to Australia.[39]

An applicant for a subclass 200 (Refugee) visa, a subclass 202 (Global Special Humanitarian) visa, or a subclass 204 (Woman at Risk) visa must not have resided for a continuous period of seven days in a country where he or she could have obtained effective protection since leaving his or her home country.[40]

31 Sch. 2, clause 202.225.
32 PAM3: Sch. 2, Visa 202, s 1.3.
33 Sch. 2, clause 203.211.
34 ibid., clause 203.224.
35 PAM3: Sch. 2, Visa 203, s 2, clause 203.22.
36 PAM3: Sch. 2, Visa 203.
37 Sch. 2, clauses 203.211(1)(a) and 203.224.
38 Sch. 2, clauses 204.211(1)(a) and 204.222.
39 Sch. 2, clause 204.211.
40 Sch. 2, clauses 200.212, 202.212 and 204.213. These provisions also allow for the Minister to exercise discretion to waive this requirement if he/she is satisfied that it is in the public interest to do so.

13.4 General provisions

The RRT conducts merits reviews of applications for Protection (class XA) visas. It does not have any jurisdiction over offshore applications. The Federal Magistrates Court and the Federal Court have jurisdiction to review RRT decisions. The High Court also has jurisdiction to review RRT decisions and has, in addition, the jurisdiction to issue prerogative writs. Applicants can also seek judicial review of decisions that are made abroad.

13.4.1 Health

For onshore applicants, each person included in the application must have undergone a medical examination carried out by a specified medical practitioner.[41] Other health requirements include, with exceptions, that the applicant has undergone X-ray examination by an Australian radiologist;[42] that a relevant medical practitioner has considered the results of any tests of the medical examination and the radiological report;[43] and that, if a relevant medical practitioner or medical officer of the Commonwealth (MOC) considers that the applicant has a disease or condition that is, or may be, a threat to public health in Australia or a danger to the Australian community, arrangements have been made to place the applicant under professional supervision to undergo necessary treatment.[44] It is not a requirement that the applicants 'pass' any medical test.

Offshore applicants and members of their family unit also must meet health requirements, but the relevant part of Schedule 2 for each of the offshore permanent visa categories has a provision to the effect that applicants must satisfy public interest criterion 4007 [the health test] 'unless the Minister is satisfied that it would be unreasonable to require the person to undergo assessment in relation to that criterion'. PAM3 then states:

> As 'unreasonable' does not have a legislated definition, officers must give it its usual dictionary meaning, but bear in mind that policy intends that this provision be used sparingly. To do otherwise may give rise to an expectation of subsequent visa entitlement.[45]

Public Interest Criterion (PIC) 4007(1)(c)(ii)(A) provides for a failure to meet the health requirement on the basis that the visa applicant has a condition that would be likely to require health care or provision of community services that would result in a significant cost to the Australian community. However, there is provision for a waiver in PIC 4007(2) in circumstances where the Minister is satisfied that the granting of the visa would be unlikely to result in either undue cost to the Australian community or undue prejudice to the access to health care or community services of an Australian citizen or permanent resident.

41 Sch. 2, clauses 785.224 and 866.223.
42 Sch. 2, clauses 785.225 and 866.224.
43 Sch. 2, clauses 785.225A(a) and 866.224A(a).
44 Sch. 2, clauses 785.225A(b) and 785.225B; and 866.224A(b) and 866.224B.
45 PAM3: Sch. 4/4005 'The health requirement', s 71.2.

13.4.2 Public interest character requirements

For both onshore and offshore refugee and humanitarian visas, the applicant must satisfy the PIC in 4001, 4002 and 4003 of Part 1 of Schedule 4 to the Regulations. PIC 4001 specifies that the applicant and family members must satisfy the Minister that the applicant passes the character test;[46] or satisfy the Minister, after appropriate inquiries, that there is nothing to indicate that the applicant would fail to satisfy the Minister that he or she would pass the character test; or the Minister has decided to grant a visa to the applicant despite reasonably suspecting that the applicant would not pass the character test; or the Minister has decided to grant a visa to the applicant despite not being satisfied that the applicant passes the character test.

PIC 4002 requires that the applicant has been assessed by competent Australian authorities as, either directly or indirectly, not being a risk to national security.

Offshore applicants and onshore applicants who have made visa applications on or after 1 November 2000 also must satisfy PIC 4003, which requires that the applicant not be a person whose presence in Australia is, or would be, prejudicial to relations between Australia and a foreign country; or may be directly or indirectly associated with the proliferation of weapons of mass destruction, as determined by the Foreign Minister or his delegate.

In addition, offshore applicants must satisfy PIC 4004, relating to debts to the Commonwealth.

13.4.3 National interest

The Protection (subclass 866) visa has a requirement that the Minister is satisfied that the grant of the visa is in the national interest.[47] The term 'national interest' is not defined in the legislation and where it does appear, is a matter that is determined to the Minister's satisfaction. Some guidance might be found in policies about terrorism and criminal deportation, and in most cases, it is likely that an applicant whose stay in Australia would not be in the national interest would fail the character requirements. Offshore visa grants are contingent on a requirement to the effect that permanent settlement in Australia would not be contrary to the interests of Australia. For the latter, PAM3 provides further guidance:

> Unless there is reason to think otherwise, officers may consider this criterion satisfied without further enquiry. They may seek the views of the Head of Mission and Humanitarian Entry Section, Refugee and Humanitarian Division, DIMA CO if the case gives rise to concern that there may be adverse impact on bilateral relations.[48]

46 As defined in *Migration Act 1958* (Cth), s 501(6).
47 Sch. 2, clause 866.226.
48 See, for instance, Sch. 2, clause 200.224(b).

14

Convention grounds

14.1 Overview of grounds

Article 1A(2) of the Refugee Convention defines a refugee in terms of the reasons why a person fears being persecuted. A refugee must have a well-founded fear of being persecuted 'for reasons of race, religion, nationality, membership of a particular social group, or political opinion'. After referring to Article 1 of the Convention, Gummow J explained in *Applicant A v MIEA*:

> . . . [w]hilst as a matter of ordinary usage, a refugee might be one whose flight has been from invasion, earthquake, flood, famine or pestilence, the definition is not concerned with such persons. Accordingly, care is needed in resolving any apparent obscurity in the text of the definition by seeing the definition as reflecting, in a broad sense, humanitarian concerns for displaced persons.[1]

Kirby J commented in the same case that the drafters of the Convention would not have included 'categories of persecution' in Article 1A(2) had they intended refugees to be defined as people who feared persecution for *any* reason.[2]

In *MIMA v Ibrahim*, the High Court considered the meaning of 'persecution' in the context of the civil war that had been occurring in Somalia since 1991.[3] In his discussion of the scope and purpose of the Convention,[4] Gummow J cited observations made by Professor Hathaway on the restricted definition of 'refugee' contained in the Convention:

1 [1997] HCA 4 (24 February 1997).
2 [1997] HCA 4 (24 February 1997).
3 *MIMA v Ibrahim* [2000] HCA 55 (26 October 2000).
4 *MIMA v Ibrahim* [2000] HCA 55 (26 October 2000), [139].

> This phraseology was clearly adequate to comprise the traditional preoccupations of racial and religious minorities and would moreover bolster the condemnation of Soviet bloc politics through international law in two ways. First, the persecution standard was a known quantity, having already been employed to embrace Soviet bloc dissidents under the [International Refugee Organization] regime. It was understood that the concept of 'fear of persecution' was sufficiently open-ended to allow the West to continue to admit ideological dissidents to international protection. Moreover, the new Refugee Convention added significantly to the scope for ideologically influenced interpretations by allowing each contracting state to make its own eligibility determinations. Thus, for example, the United States and others have routinely assumed that all persons in Communist states are by definition in fear of persecution.
>
> Second, the precise formulation of the persecution standard meant that refugee law could not readily be turned to the political advantage of the Soviet bloc. The refugee definition embraces only persons who have been disfranchised by their state on the basis of race, religion, nationality, membership of a particular social group, or political opinion, areas where East Bloc practice has historically been problematic . . . By mandating protection for those whose civil and political rights are jeopardized, without at the same time protecting persons whose socioeconomic rights are at risk, the Convention continued the lopsided and politically biased human rights rationale for refugee law of the immediate post-war years.
>
> In sum, the first main feature of modern international refugee law is its rejection of comprehensive humanitarian or human rights-based assistance in favour of a more narrowly conceived focus.[5]

And Hathaway's view on the effect of the Protocol on that definition:

> Although a Protocol was adopted in 1967 which updated the Convention by removing the temporal and geographical limitations, the Protocol failed to review the substantive content of the definitions it embraced. Specifically, even after the 'universalization' effected by the 1967 Protocol, only persons whose migration is prompted by a fear of persecution in relation to civil and political rights come within the scope of Convention-based refugee protection. This means that most Third World refugees remain de facto excluded, as their flight is more often prompted by natural disaster, war, or broadly based political and economic turmoil than by 'persecution', at least as that term is understood in the European context.[6]

Section 91R(1)(a) of the *Migration Act 1958* (Cth) provides that Article 1A(2) of the Convention does not apply in relation to persecution for one or more of the reasons set out in that Article unless 'that reason is the essential and significant reason, or those reasons are the essential and significant reasons, for the persecution'.

The Commonwealth government inserted section 91R into the *Migration Act 1958* (Cth)[7] in response to a 'trend' by Australian courts to interpret 'persecution' more widely than the government considered acceptable.[8] Indeed, Senator

5 J.C. Hathaway, 'A Reconsideration of the Underlying Premise of Refugee Law', (1990) 31 *Harvard International Law Journal* 129 at 149–50 [citations omitted].
6 ibid., at 162 [citations omitted].
7 *Migration Legislation Amendment Act (No. 6) 2001* (Cth).
8 Revised Explanatory Memorandum, Migration Legislation Amendment Bill (No. 6) 2001 (Cth), paragraph 19.

Robert Hill stated during the second reading speech for the Migration Legislation Amendment Bill (No. 6) 2001:

> The legislation will also provide that to invoke protection the convention reason must be the essential and significant reason for the persecution.
>
> The convention was not designed to protect people who fear persecution for personal reasons that have little or nothing to do with the convention – for example because they have failed to pay their family's debts.[9]

14.2 Race

The drafters of the Convention did not specifically define 'race', but the historical context indicates that the drafters' intent was to include those Jewish victims of Nazism who had been persecuted because of their ethnicity, whether or not they practised their religion. According to Hathaway, this historical rationale is important because it legitimises the attribution of a broad social meaning to the term 'race', a meaning which includes all persons of identifiable ethnicity.[10] Grahl-Madsen has observed that the term 'race' within the Convention includes not only persons at risk by reason of their membership in a particular scientific category of race, but also other groups, such as gypsies, whose physical or cultural distinctiveness has caused them to suffer social prejudice.[11]

The UNHCR *Handbook on the Procedures and Criteria for Determining Refugee Status* suggests that the term should be interpreted broadly:

> Race, in the present connection, has to be understood in its widest sense to include all kinds of ethnic groups that are referred to as 'races' in common usage. Frequently it will also entail membership of a specific group of common descent forming a minority within a larger population. Discrimination for reasons of race has found world-wide condemnation as one of the most striking violations of human rights. Racial discrimination, therefore, represents an important element in determining the existence of persecution . . . The mere fact of belonging to a certain racial group will not normally be enough to substantiate a claim for refugee status. There may, however, be situations where, due to particular circumstances affecting the group, such membership will be a sufficient ground to fear persecution.[12]

A similarly broad view of race was taken by the Federal Court in *Calado v MIMA*, where Tamberlin J observed:[13]

> When considering the meaning of the expression 'race' in a case such as the present, it is appropriate to take into account the 'popular' understanding of the term which accords

9 Commonwealth, *Second Reading Speech*, Senate, 24 September 2001, 27603 (Minister for the Environment and Heritage).
10 Hathaway, *The Law of Refugee Status*, p. 141.
11 A. Grahl-Madsen, *The Status of Refugees in International Law* (Leyden, A.W. Sijthoff, 1966), pp. 217–18.
12 UNHCR, *Handbook on Procedures and Criteria for Determining Refugee Status* (Geneva, UNHCR, 1992), paragraphs 68–70. This publication does not have an authoritative status at the domestic law level. However, the High Court of Australia has indicated that it does serve as a practical guide for those making refugee determinations: *Chan v MIEA* [1989] HCA 62 (9 December 1989), [20].
13 [1997] FCA 1490 (19 December 1997).

> importance to physical appearance, skin colour and ethnic origin. There can be no single test for the meaning of the expression 'race' but the term connotes considerations such as whether the individuals or the group regard themselves and are regarded by others in the community as having a particular historical identity in terms of colour, and national or ethnic origins. Another consideration is whether the characteristics of members of the group are those with which a person is born and which he or she cannot change. These questions are discussed by Brennan J in *Commonwealth v Tasmania* (1983) 158 CLR 1 at 243–244. At the latter page his Honour said:
>
>> 'As the people of a group identify themselves and are identified by others as a race by reference to their common history, religion, spiritual beliefs or culture as well as by reference to their biological origins and physical similarities, an indication is given of the scope and purpose of the power granted by par (xxvi). The kinds of benefits that laws might properly confer upon people as members of a race are benefits which tend to protect or foster their common intangible heritage or their common sense of identity. Their genetic inheritance is fixed at birth; the historic, religious, spiritual and cultural heritage are acquired and are susceptible to influences for which a law may provide. The advancement of the people of any race in any of these aspects of their group life falls within the power.'
>
> In that case his Honour was concerned with the meaning of the expression 'race' in the Australian Constitution, which in section 51(xxvi) confers power on the Commonwealth Parliament to make special laws for the people of any race. Of course, in interpreting the conferral of a constitutional power it is appropriate that the term should be given a liberal and practical interpretation. In our view, a similar approach should be taken in considering the Convention in the present case. In the course of his discussion of 'race', Brennan J referred to UNESCO studies on race and racial discrimination which indicate the difficulties of giving any precise definition to the term. The native language of individuals, in our view, is clearly an important part of the cultural heritage and group identification of that person. In the present case it is evident that the appropriate language for consideration of the persecution question is the native language spoken by the Bakongo.

Apart from the decision of *Calado*, the issue of race has not been the subject of considered judicial interpretation by Australian courts. There are two reasons for this. The first is that given the overlapping nature of the Convention grounds it is rare, where race is an issue, that an applicant cannot squarely place his or her claim within one of the other grounds, such as political opinion or particular social group. Thus the occasion has not arisen where judicial consideration of the scope of the term 'race' has been of practical importance.

Second (and related to the first reason) is that the term 'race' has been given a broad meaning, so it is often not difficult for applicants to base their claim on this ground. However, to the extent that there is a convergence of views regarding the parameters of the term, the following points emerge:

- Race typically focuses on immutable aspects of a person's biological makeup,[14] which normally find expression in their physical attributes, such as skin colour, complexion and facial features (such as eye shape);

14 See *Mandla v Dowell Lee* [1983] 1 QB 1.

- Race does not only include immutable traits. It also includes people who have a common descent. The common descent is often referable to other attributes that constitute a Convention ground, such as nationality or religion.
- Race also extends to people who share cultural or spiritual traits – or a language – which in the eyes of the group and others distinguish them from the rest of the community. Thus, similarities forged on the basis of important shared practices can constitute a race.

14.3 Nationality

The term 'nationality' was first introduced as a ground for persecution in the Constitution of the International Refugee Organisation in 1946, and was thereafter carried into the Convention definition as one of the grounds for persecution.[15] In *Applicant A v MIEA*,[16] Gummow J described the background to its introduction:

> The international instruments identified in par (1) of s A of the Convention attempted to deal with particular hardships consequent upon the collapse of the Russian and Ottoman Empires, and the advent of the Bolshevik and later the National Socialist regimes. These regimes took measures to render stateless sections of their citizenry, including persons abroad. The process became known as 'Denationalisation'. Nationals whilst abroad were treated by customary international law as remaining under the supremacy of their home state and in various municipal legal systems matters of personal status were governed by the law of nationality. The stateless refugee thus was left in particularly difficult circumstances . . .
>
> Refugees might suffer hardships in their country of refuge even without loss of their nationality of origin. They might have been denied in fact if not law (as the 1938 Convention postulated) the protection of the law of their country of nationality or be unwilling for good reason to avail themselves of that protection. The international instruments identified above were designed to protect these and stateless individuals until a new nationality had been acquired, and to do so by providing a substitute at least as to some aspects of civil status. Group rather than individual characteristics determined membership of the class of refugees.[17]

The UNHCR *Handbook on the Procedures and Criteria for Determining Refugee Status* favours a broad interpretation of the term:

> The term 'nationality' in this context is not to be understood only as citizenship. It refers also to membership of an ethnic or linguistic group and may occasionally overlap with the term 'race'. Persecution for reasons of nationality may consist of adverse attitudes and measures directed against a national (ethnic, linguistic) minority and in certain circumstances the fact of belonging to such a minority may in itself give rise to a well-founded fear of persecution . . . The co-existence within the boundaries of a State of two or more (ethnic, linguistic) groups may create situations of conflict

15 T. Musgrave, 'Refugees', in S. Blay, R. Piotrowicz & B.M. Tsamenyi (eds), *Public International Law: An Australian Perspective* (Melbourne & New York, OUP, 1997), pp. 301, 308.
16 [1997] HCA 4 (24 February 1997).
17 [1997] HCA 4 (24 February 1997).

> and also situations of persecution or danger of persecution. It may not always be easy to distinguish between persecution for reasons of nationality and persecution for reason of political opinion when a conflict between national groups is combined with political movements, particularly where a political movement is identified with a specific 'nationality'... Whereas in most cases persecution for reason of nationality is feared by persons belonging to a national minority, there have been many cases where a person belonging to a majority group may fear persecution by a dominant minority.[18]

As is noted in the discussion regarding race, this ground often overlaps with the 'race' ground. In *Calado v MIMA* Tamberlin J observed:[19]

> The references in the definition of 'refugee' to race, religion, nationality and social groups are not discrete, independent categories, but rather they overlap. In some circumstances persons of the same race may also form an independent social community or have the same nationality. A common language may be a feature of such communities or groups. As Hathaway points out in *The Law of Refugee Status*, 1991 at pp. 144–145:
>
>> 'In addition to notions of formal nationality, it is generally suggested that nationality encompasses linguistic groups and other culturally defined collectivities, thus overlapping to a significant extent with the concept of race. Because many such groups share a sense of political community distinct from that of the nation state, their claims to refugee protection may reasonably be determined on the basis of nationality as well as on race.'

From the above, it is evident that as with race, the nationality ground is poorly defined. This lack of precision is explicable for the same reason as in the case of race: it is rarely a practical issue in litigation, and decision-makers assume that it does not matter whether an applicant frames his or her application on the ground of nationality or an overlapping Convention ground where either of them will suffice. The lack of controversy regarding the race and nationality grounds has resulted in a level of academic disinterest regarding the precise meanings of both terms.

Germov and Motta suggest that race refers to immutable aspects of a person such as their physical characteristics, whereas nationality should be preserved for the description of ethnic and cultural groups with a common or shared identity, perhaps through shared ancestry, but often because of commonalities of cultural practices and language. In support of this view, they note that the terms 'national origin' (akin to citizenship) and 'nationality' are not identical and refer to the situation of Kurds, who live in territory encompassed by the states of Iran, Iraq and Turkey. They assert that even though Kurds do not have a nation, it is best to regard the matters that unite them as equating with 'nationality'.[20]

This issue has not been subject to considered analysis by an Australian court and hence there is considerable scope for debate concerning the meaning of the two terms. We suggest that although little of practical importance is likely to turn

18 UNHCR, *Handbook on Procedures and Criteria for Determining Refugee Status*, paragraphs 74–76.
19 (1997) FCA 1490 (19 December 1997).
20 R. Germov and F. Motta, *Refugee Law in Australia* (Melbourne, OUP, 2003), pp. 251–61.

on the scope of the terms, the view proposed by Germov and Motta should be rejected. The term 'nationality' should be interpreted consistent with its natural meaning: referring to the nation state to which a person belongs. A person can, of course, in some cases have more than one nationality. It strains the language, in our view, to assert that the nationality of a person can be described by reference to a region which is not, and never has been, recognised as a nation state. To this end, the Kurdish experience in fact supports this view. The commonalities forging the Kurds are a historical and loose blood relationship, shared cultural practices, and language. It is not the fact that they come from a territorial region that sets them apart from other people.

In some circumstances, it is desirable to stretch or alter the natural meaning of a term in order that the law can operate in a more favourable fashion. However, this is not the situation in relation to this part of the Convention. If our approach is adopted, the residual meaning that Germov and Motta would attribute to the word 'nationality' is removed and fully transported to the term 'race', where it more naturally sits. In addition, the interpretation we are proposing sits more comfortably with the judicial authority that exists regarding the definition of 'race', limited though it is.[21]

14.4 Religion

Religion has long been a major reason for persecution,[22] and the content of the right to freedom of thought, conscience and religion continues to be a subject in many human rights inquiries.[23] Despite the fact that the meaning of 'religion' has been explored by Australian courts, the term has not been precisely defined. Nevertheless, it is clear that a religion is defined by its form – not its substance.[24] Thus, whether or not an ideology or movement refers to itself as a religion is not the critical issue. Rather, the nature of the beliefs held by its adherents is the main focus of any inquiry.

In *Wang v MIMA*,[25] Merkel J stated that there are two central aspects of religion for the purpose of the Convention: 'the first is as a manifestation or practice of personal faith or doctrine, and the second is the manifestation or practice of that faith or doctrine in a like-minded community.'[26]

21 To this end we note that nationality has also been interpreted broadly: see *Macabenta v Minister for Immigration & Multicultural Affairs* [1998] 1643 FCA (18 December 1998).
22 Musgrave, 'Refugees', p. 301.
23 See, for example, Implementation of the Declaration on the Elimination of all Forms of Intolerance and of Discrimination Based on Religion or Belief. Reports of the Special Rapporteur of the Commission of Human Rights on Religions and Intolerance: UN Doc. E/CN.4/1993/62 (6 Jan 1993).
24 The definitions which have been advanced by the High Court of Australia are at best only partial and instructive, as opposed to definitive: see, for example, *Church of New Faith v The Commissioner of Pay Roll Tax (Victoria)* [1983] HCA 40. For Federal Court discussion, see *Wang v MIMA* (2000) FCA 1599 (10 December 2000).
25 [2000] FCA 1599 (10 November 2000).
26 [2000] FCA 1599 (10 November 2000), [81].

Because religion encompasses both beliefs that one may choose to hold and behaviour that stems from those beliefs, religion as a Convention ground can be seen to include two dimensions.[27] The first is the protection of persons who are at risk of being persecuted because they are identified as adherents of a particular religion; the second is the protection of those who are at risk of persecution because they engage in religious activities consistent with their religious convictions.[28]

Persecution based on religion usually involves prohibitions or restrictions against practising a religion and the imposition, or at least threat, of punishment for breaching the ban or restriction.[29] In *Applicant NABD/2002 v MIMA*,[30] the High Court considered the case of an Iranian asylum-seeker who had converted from Islam to Christianity. The RRT had refused his protection visa application on the basis that he practised his faith in a 'low profile' manner, whereas, generally, it was those Christians who actively proselytised who faced persecution in Iran. At issue was whether the tribunal had imposed a requirement on the applicant to practise his religion discreetly in Iran in order to avoid persecution. A majority of the court[31] found that the tribunal had not imposed such a requirement,[32] and that it had correctly distinguished between Christians who practised their religion discreetly and Christians who proselytised or practised Christianity aggressively in Iran in assessing the applicant's risk of being persecuted in that country.[33]

In addition, persecution for religion also includes the infliction of serious harm because the applicant does not belong to a certain religion or does not participate in activities or practices prescribed by tenets of a religion, or where the applicant commits an act which offends the religious convictions of others.[34] In the latter case, it is clear that the driving force for the persecution is religion. There is no

27 Grahl-Madsen, *The Status of Refugees in International Law*, p. 218; Goodwin-Gill, *The Refugee in International Law*, pp. 27–28; Hathaway, *The Law of Refugee Status*, p. 146.

28 Hathaway, *The Law of Refugee Status*, p. 147. Note that the second proposition, regarding religious behaviour, is limited by the International Covenant of Civil and Political Rights, which states that religious freedom is 'subject only to such limitations as are prescribed by law and are necessary to protect public safety, order, health, or morals or the fundamental rights and freedoms of others'. This limitation has been interpreted broadly in some instances and restrictively in others.

29 The UNHCR *Handbook on Procedures and Criteria for Determining Refugee Status* states at paragraph 71–73: 'The Universal Declaration of Human Rights and the Human Rights Covenant proclaim the right to freedom of thought, conscience and religion, which rights include the freedom of a person to change his religion and his freedom to manifest it in public or private, in teaching, practice, worship and observance . . . Persecution for 'reasons of religion' may assume various forms, e.g. prohibition of membership of a religious community, or worship in private or public, of religious instruction, or serious measures of discrimination imposed upon persons because they practise their religion or belong to a particular religious community . . . Mere membership of a particular religious community will normally not be enough to substantiate a claim to refugee status. There may, however, be special circumstances where mere membership can be a sufficient ground.'

30 [2005] HCA 29 (26 May 2005).

31 Gleeson, CJ and Hayne and Heydon JJ.

32 Cf *Appellant S395/2002 v MIMA* [2003] HCA 71 (9 December 2003).

33 See the judgment of Gleeson CJ, [8]–[10] and the joint judgment of Hayne and Heydon JJ, [166]. See also *MIMA v VWBA* [2005] FCAFC 175 (26 August 2005) (Sundberg, Marshall and North JJ), [15] where the Full Federal Court approved the RRT's reasoning that an 'ordinary' and 'private' Falun Gong practitioner would not be 'restricted' in practising the Falun Gong religion in China to the extent that such a restriction would constitute persecution.

34 *Prashar v MIMA* [2001] FCA 57; *Cameirao v MIMA* [2000] FCA 1319.

meaningful difference between whether it is the religion of the persecutor, or of the person being persecuted, that is the catalyst for the serious harm:

> The Convention speaks of a 'well-founded fear of being persecuted for reasons of... religion...' In my opinion, if persons are persecuted because they do not hold religious beliefs, that is as much persecution for reasons of religion as if somebody were persecuting them for holding a positive religious belief. The Convention protects people in relation to the subject matter of religious belief. It does not protect believers and leave non-believers to the wolves.[35]

The fact that a law has a religious origin and imposes punishment on those who do not obey the law does not necessarily entail that it is persecutory. This is so even where there is a gross disproportion between the offence and the penalty. Thus, a person who is sentenced to death for adultery under a law of general application could not (as a general rule) claim persecution on the basis of religion.[36] By way of example, the issue of whether the enforcement of a law of general application could constitute persecution for religious reasons was considered in the Full Federal Court case of *Lama v MIMA*.[37] The applicant was a Buddhist and a national of Nepal who claimed to face persecution in the form of the enforcement of Nepalese criminal law against him (and in the form of community violence) because he had killed a cow. The Full Court agreed that a law motivated by a desire to preserve or promote Hindu religious values was not, by itself, sufficient to establish that the applicant had a well-founded fear of being persecuted for religious reasons; and that it was 'well open' on the evidence before the tribunal to find that the law against bovicide in Nepal was not enforced in a discriminatory or selective manner.[38]

Further, as we discuss in more detail in Chapter 15, it is not the case that states are not permitted to impose any restrictions on religious practices. Restrictions are permitted where the law has a legitimate objective and is appropriate and adapted to meeting that objective. However, the mere fact that a law is of general application does not mean that it is not persecutory. In *Wang v MIMA*,[39] the Full Court of the Federal Court found that the RRT had been wrong to find that the applicant did not have a well-founded fear of being persecuted for religious reasons in the People's Republic of China. The RRT accepted that the applicant genuinely intended to practise as a Protestant Christian at an unregistered church if he returned to China, and that he would be persecuted if he did so. The RRT accepted the applicant's evidence that he could not worship faithfully in a registered Protestant Christian church, yet found that he would not be deprived of religious freedom if he practised in a registered or official church subject to

35 *Prashar v MIMA* [2001] FCA 57 (7 February 2001), [19].
36 For example, see *MIMA v Darboy* [1998] FCA 931; *MMM v MIMA* (1998) 170 ALR 1 and [1998] FCA 1664; *Z v MIMA* [1998] FCA 1578.
37 [1999] FCA 1620.
38 [1999] FCA 1620, [13–14]. For further discussion regarding the notion of a law of general enforcement, see Chapter 15.
39 [2000] FCA 1599 (10 November 2000).

some state controls. In relation to the question of whether the enforcement of laws of general application can constitute persecution, Merkel J explained:

> While, generally, punishment for breach of a criminal law of general application will not constitute persecution for a Convention reason, the proposition contended for by the Minister that prosecution under generally applicable laws cannot amount to persecution for a Convention reason is erroneous. Before such a conclusion can be reached in a particular case the circumstances of the individual concerned must be considered. That consideration will usually occur in the context of an inquiry into the nature of the law, the motives behind the law, whether the law is selectively or discriminatorily enforced or impacts differently on different people. Further, where the punishment is disproportionately severe, that can result in the enforcement of the law in that case being persecutory for a Convention reason: see *Namitabar v Canada (Minister of Employment & Immigration)* (1994) 2 Can.F.C. 42 and *Fathi-Rad v Canada (Secretary of State)* (1994) 77 F.T.R. 41.[40]

The following general observations emerge from the discussion of religion as a Convention ground:

- The term 'religion' has not been exhaustively defined. However, it is clear that the courts have interpreted the term broadly.
- Religion requires a belief that is at least partially dependent upon faith. Thus, if the tenets held by an individual are all rationally verifiable, those tenets do not form the foundation for a religion.
- There is no limitation regarding the core tenets of the faith. That is, there is no restriction on the objects of the faith.
- Whether or not a belief or practice constitutes a religion is determined by objective criteria. The views of adherents concerning whether or not the practice is a religion are important but not decisive of this issue.
- A system of ideas or beliefs, in order to constitute a religion, normally requires adherents to follow particular forms of conduct. However, the fact that an individual does not diligently follow the code of conduct does not mean that he or she does not belong to the religion. The code of conduct normally involves some degree of communal activity, normally prayer, but this is not necessarily the case.
- Persecution based on religion usually involves prohibitions or restrictions against practising a religion and the imposition, or at least threat, of punishment for breaching the ban or restriction. To constitute persecution, the restriction must constitute a meaningful fetter on the individual practising his or her religion. Thus, a law restricting a person's right to proselytise may amount to persecution where this is one of the practices expected or condoned by the religion.[41]
- Persecution for religion also includes the infliction of serious harm because the applicant does not belong to a certain religion, does not participate in

40 [2000] FCA 1599 (10 November 2000), [63].
41 See further, *Thalary v MIEA* [1997] FCA 201 (4 April 1997), where the court noted: 'there is some basis for the applicant's claim that the tribunal erred in law in concluding that the practice of proselytising is not relevant to her right to practise her religion'.

activities or practices prescribed by tenets of the religion, or where the applicant commits an act which offends the religious convictions of others.

- The fact that a law has a religious foundation and imposes punishment on those who do not obey the law does not necessarily entail that it is persecutory. As a general rule, a religion-based law of general application is not persecutory as long as it is not enforced in a discriminatory manner for a Convention reason.

14.5 Political opinion

Dissenting political opinion is the most documented form of persecution.[42] As with the other Convention grounds, the meaning and scope of 'political opinion' is unclear. The Convention's drafters noted that in addition to 'diplomats thrown out of office' and persons 'whose political party had been outlawed', even 'individuals who fled from revolutions' ought to be encompassed by this ground.[43] That is, protection on the basis of political opinion was to be extended not only to those with identifiable political affiliations or roles, but also to other persons at risk from political forces within their home community.[44]

So what is the meaning of 'political opinion'? A useful starting point for examining its meaning is the discussion in the UNHCR's *Handbook on Procedures and Criteria for Determining Refugee Status*, excerpts of which have been cited with approval by Australian courts. For example, in *Tharmalingan v MIEA*, Lindgren J noted:

> In *Welivita v Minister for Immigration and Ethnic Affairs*, 18 November 1996, I set out (at 24–25), with approval, the following paragraphs from the Handbook on Procedures and Criteria for Determining Refugee Status under the 1951 Convention and the 1967 Protocol Relating to the Status of Refugees (Geneva, January 1992):
>
> 84. Where a person is subject to prosecution or punishment for a political offence, a distinction may have to be drawn according to whether the prosecution is for political opinion or for politically-motivated acts. If the prosecution pertains to a punishable act committed out of political motives, and if the anticipated punishment is in conformity with the general law of the country concerned, fear of such prosecution will not in itself make the applicant a refugee.
>
> 85. Whether a political offender can also be considered a refugee will depend upon various other factors. Prosecution for an offence may, depending upon the circumstances, be a pretext for punishing the offender for his political opinions or the expression thereof. Again, there may be reason to believe that a political offender would be exposed to excessive or arbitrary punishment for the alleged offence. Such excessive or arbitrary punishment will amount to persecution.
>
> 86. In determining whether a political offender can be considered a refugee, regard should also be had to the following elements: personality of the applicant, his political opinion, the motive behind the act, the nature of the act committed, the

42 M. Falcon, 'Gender Based Persecution', (2002) 21 *Refugee Survey Quarterly* 133.
43 UN Doc. E/AC.7/SR.172, August 12, 1950, at 18–23, and UN Doc. E/AC.7/SR.173, 12 August 1950, at 5.
44 Hathaway, 'A Reconsideration of the Underlying Premise of Refugee Law', p. 149.

> nature of the prosecution and its motives; finally, also, the nature of the law on which the prosecution is based. These elements may go to show that the person concerned has a fear of persecution and not merely a fear of prosecution and punishment – within the law – for an act committed by him.[45]

We now examine some of the main issues which have emerged in relation to this ground.

14.5.1 Political opinion generally interpreted broadly

The Convention's drafters adopted a liberal view of the notion of persecution based on 'political opinion'.[46] Goodwin-Gill stated that the expression 'political opinion':

> Should be understood in the broad sense to incorporate, within substantive limitations now developing generally in the field of human rights, any opinion on any matter in which the machinery of State, government and policy may be engaged.[47]

The view that 'political opinion' should be interpreted broadly is reflected in Australian case law. The relevant authorities and principles are summarised in the following passage by Hill J from *Applicant N403 of 2000 v MIMA*:

> The Court has not embarked upon an attempt to define, in a comprehensive way, precisely what political opinion may be. In *MIMA v Y* (unreported, FCA, 15 May 1998), Davies J said that in the context of the Convention, an opinion could be a political opinion:
>
>> 'If it were such as to indicate that its holder, the claimant for refugee status, held views which were contrary to the interests of the State, including the authorities of the State. A person may be regarded as an enemy of the State by virtue of holding and propounding views which are contrary to the views of the State or its Government, or which are antithetic to the Government and the instruments which enforce the power of the State, such as the Armed Forces, Security Forces, and Police Forces, or which express opposition to matters such as the structure of the State or the territory occupied by it and like matters.'
>
> His Honour's views were approved by a Full Court of this Court in *V v Minister for Immigration and Ethnic Affairs* (1999) 92 FCR 355, subject, perhaps, to the implicit suggestion in them that the view had to be one that had actually been publicly expressed. Wilcox J said at para 16:
>
>> 'As I understand Davies J, as a matter of law it is enough that a person holds (or is believed to hold) views antithetic to instruments of government and is persecuted for that reason. It is not necessary that the person be a member of a political party or other public organisation or that the person's opposition to the instruments of government be a matter of public knowledge. Of course, the higher the person's

45 [1998] 537 FCA (19 May 1998).
46 Hathaway, *The Law of Refugee Status*, p. 149. Hathaway contends that most of the contemporary Canadian jurisprudence reflects this historical conceptualisation.
47 Goodwin-Gill, *The Refugee in International Law*, p. 50. This quote was referred to in the Canadian case of *Canada (Attorney-General) v Ward* [1993] 2 SCR 689 and in the Australian case *Saliba v MIMA* (1998) 89 FCR 38 [49]; [1998] 1461 FCA.

political profile, the easier it may be to persuade a tribunal of fact that the person has been persecuted on account of political opinion, rather than for some other reason; but that is a matter going to proof of the facts, not a matter of law.'

In the same case I said at para 33:

> 'It is not necessary in this case to attempt a comprehensive definition of what constitutes "political opinion" within the meaning of the Convention. It clearly is not limited to party politics in the sense that expression is understood in a parliamentary democracy. It is probably narrower than the usage of the word in connection with the science of politics, where it may extend to almost every aspect of society. It suffices here to say that [it is] the holding of an opinion inconsistent with that held by the government of a country explicitly by reference to views contained in a political platform or implicitly by acts . . . With respect, I agree with the view expressed by Davies J in *Minister for Immigration and Ethnic Affairs v Y* . . . that views antithetical to instrumentalities of government such as the Armed Forces, security institutions and the police can constitute political opinions for the purposes of the Convention. Whether they do so will depend upon the facts of the particular case.'[48]

14.5.2 Political opinion must be known or imputed by the persecutor

It is axiomatic that persons claiming refugee status on the basis of political opinion believe that persons targeting them for that reason have at least imputed to them an opposing or inconsistent political opinion. In *NAEU v MIMA*,[49] Madgwick J stated:

> In my opinion, it is not sufficient, as submitted by counsel for the appellant, that the appellant need only establish that there was a fear of harm and a Convention reason (in this case, his political opinion) for that harm to qualify for protection under the Convention. The appellant was also required to establish that his persecutors had actual or imputed knowledge of his political opinion and would exact punishment at least partly because of that political opinion. In *Minister for Immigration & Ethnic Affairs v Guo* (1997) 191 CLR 559, a case involving a fear of persecution because of the respondent's membership to a particular social group of Chinese citizens who opposed the government's 'one child policy', the following comments were made by Brennan CJ, Dawson, Toohey, Gaudron, McHugh and Gummow JJ (at 570–71):
>
> > 'An applicant for refugee status who has established a fear of persecution must also show that the persecution which he or she fears is for one of the reasons enumerated in Art 1A(2) of the Convention. The first respondents claimed before the Tribunal that they feared persecution in the form of punishment for contravening the PRC government's "one child policy" and for their illegal departures and that such persecution would be inflicted for the Convention reason of "political opinion" and/or "membership of a particular social group".'
>
> For the purposes of the Convention, a political opinion need not be an opinion that is actually held by the refugee. It is sufficient for those purposes that such an opinion is imputed to him or her **by** the persecutor. In *Chan* Gaudron J said:

48 [2000] FCA 1088 (23 August 2000), [21]–[22].
49 [2002] FCAFC 259 (24 October 2003).

> 'persecution may as equally be constituted by the infliction of harm on the basis of perceived political belief as of actual belief.'

In the same case, McHugh J said that:

> 'It is irrelevant that the appellant may not have held the opinions attributed to him. What matters is that the authorities identified [Mr Chan] with those opinions and, in consequence, restricted his liberty for a long and indeterminate period.'[50]

Thus an imputed political opinion will suffice to invoke this ground. This often has more to do with perceptions than reality. In most cases there will be no direct evidence regarding the perceptions of the persecutors, given that they invariably do not give evidence in relation to refugee matters. Accordingly, it is often difficult for decision-makers to assess the validity of claims based on imputed political opinion. Nevertheless, in these circumstances decision-makers can assess 'independent evidence', such as whether there are instances of such persecution described in human rights reports concerning an applicant's home country; and may well pay particular attention to the detail, consistency and plausibility of an applicant's evidence in support of a protection visa application. It will often be the case that, unless the applicant adduces evidence that his or her persecutors have communicated to him or her that they believe he or she has a particular political opinion, such a claim will be rejected. Evidence from the applicant that his or her persecutors communicated to a friend or family member that he or she was being targeted for political reasons will often be unpersuasive. Thus, in the context of imputed political claims, an applicant's response to the question '*How* do you know that you are being targeted?' can be of great significance.

If the political opinion is not known by the authorities at the time a person flees his or her country, yet could be known by the authorities in the reasonably foreseeable future, it is possible that an applicant will be found to be a refugee.[51]

14.5.3 Political opinion need not be expressed

Political opinions need not necessarily be expressed. The Convention refers to 'political opinion', not 'political activity or involvement'. Hence an applicant does not need to have *acted* upon his or her beliefs prior to departure from the country of origin.[52] As noted in the Canadian decision of *Juan Alejandro Araya Heredio*:

> The Convention speaks not of political activities but of political opinions. Opinions are often, but not necessarily, expressed in action, and history has taught us that some political regimes . . . persist in pursuing some of their nationals simply because the latter supported a former regime or collaborated with it, or simply because they oppose or, owing to their former loyalties, constitute a challenge to the authority now in power.[53]

50 [2002] FCAFC 259 (24 October 2003), [14].
51 See Chapter 16.
52 Hathaway, 'A Reconsideration of the Underlying Premise of Refugee Law', p. 149.
53 Immigration Appeal Board Decision 76–1127, 6 January 1977. Cited in Hathaway, ibid. This principle has been endorsed in Australian cases: see *V v MIMA* [1999] FCA 428 (14 April 1994).

There are various reasons for which a refugee applicant may not express his or her political opinion. For example, it may have been practically impossible to express a dissenting political opinion while in the home state.[54] Alternatively, a person may not have held the opinion at the time of departure.

14.5.4 What if the applicant can avoid coming to the notice of authorities?

Human rights instruments such as the Universal Declaration of Human Rights enshrine the right of all people to freedom of political expression and opinion.[55] Do the provisions for political rights in such instruments render it inappropriate for a decision-maker to downgrade the risk that an applicant will be persecuted for reasons of political opinion on the basis that the applicant could avoid detection, and hence persecution, by keeping a low profile or 'keeping quiet'? After all, if the right to a political opinion is a core human right,[56] then arguably a person should be free to fully express it. Nevertheless, it seems that freedom to hold or express a political opinion is not a freedom that has been respected or fully appreciated in some refugee status decisions.[57] For example, in the Canadian case of *Marina Galvis de Cardona*,[58] the Immigration Appeal Board dismissed the claim of a Colombian student, noting that her participation in a peaceful protest march was an 'imprudent action taken knowingly and deliberately'. Similarly, in *Mauricio Esteban Lemoine Guajardo v Minister of Employment and Immigration*,[59] the Canadian Federal Court of Appeal suggested that voluntary self-identification as a Socialist would in some sense undercut the case of the Chilean applicant. Hathaway has argued that this reasoning is at odds with the human rights context in which refugee law was established, and is inexplicably unsympathetic to persons who demonstrate the courage to challenge the conformism of authoritarian states. Others have argued along the same lines as Hathaway, including Grahl-Madsen, who noted:

> In view of the fact that the first paragraph of the Preamble to the Refugee Convention contains a direct reference to the Universal Declaration and the principle which thereby has been affirmed, 'that human beings shall enjoy fundamental rights and freedoms without discrimination', it seems reasonable to infer that a person may justly fear persecution 'for reason of political opinion' in the sense of the Refugee Convention if he is threatened with measures of a persecutory nature because of his exercise of or his insistence on certain of the 'rights' laid down in the Universal Declaration.[60]

54 Hathaway, 'A Reconsideration of the Underlying Premise of Refugee Law', p. 149.
55 Adapted and proclaimed by General Assembly resolution 217A(III) on 10 December 1948.
56 As asserted by Hathaway, 'A Reconsideration of the Underlying Premise of Refugee Law', p. 150.
57 For example, the Canadian case of *Wai Che Lee*, Immigration Appeal Board Decision V87–6512X, 21 December 1987.
58 Immigration Appeal Board Decision 77–1120, 2 August 1979, cited in Hathaway, *The Law of Refugee Status*.
59 Federal Court of Appeal Decision A-6243–30, 2 April 1981, at 2, cited in Hathaway, *The Law of Refugee Status*, p. 151.
60 Grahl-Madsen, *The Status of Refugees in International Law*, p. 227.

As one of us has previously noted, it is contradictory to claim both that one has a right and that disadvantages can flow from its exercise.[61] This follows from fundamental aspects of the nature of rights. Having an advantage is obviously not sufficient to have a right, but it is a necessary aspect of a right. It follows that it is inconsistent to assert that a right does not involve an advantage. The High Court has in other contexts accepted this point. In the case of *Petty and Maiden v The Queen*, which concerned the scope of the pre-trial right of silence, it was stated:

> *An incident* of that *right* of silence is that *no adverse inference can be drawn* against an accused person by reason of his or her failure to answer questions or provide information. To draw such an adverse inference would *be to erode the right of silence or to render it valueless*.[62] [Emphasis added.]

A decision-maker's refusal to accept that an asylum-seeker has an unqualified right to express his or her political opinion may be explained by an underlying ambivalence by the decision-maker about the proposition that a person's capacity to express his or her political view is in fact a 'right', as opposed to, say, a privilege. Moreover, it is perhaps explained by the fact that no right is absolute. All rights at some point yield to the weight of other interests, particularly the common good. As is noted in Chapter 18, the nature, scope, and existence of rights are much in dispute. And merely labelling something a right is hardly probative of that fact.[63] At the same time, the approach taken in relation to political rights in the above cases suggests that the concept of personal responsibility cannot be totally ignored.[64]

In the recent High Court case of *Appellant S395/2002 v MIMA*,[65] Gleeson CJ observed:

> [P]ersecution does not cease to be persecution for the purpose of the Convention because those persecuted can eliminate the harm by taking avoiding action within the country of nationality. The Convention would give no protection from persecution for reasons of religion or political opinion if it was a condition of protection that the person affected must take steps – reasonable or otherwise – to avoid offending the wishes of the persecutors. Nor would it give protection to membership of many a 'particular social group' if it were a condition of protection that its members hide their membership or modify some attribute or characteristic of the group to avoid persecution. Similarly, it would often fail to give protection to people who are persecuted for reasons of race or nationality if it was a condition of protection that they should take steps to conceal their race or nationality.[66]

This observation was made in the context of a homosexual who could have avoided persecution by being discreet in relation to his sexual orientation and

61 See M. Bagaric, 'The Diminishing Right of Silence', (1997) 19 *Sydney Law Review* 266.
62 [1991] HCA 35, [2] per Mason CJ, Deane, Toohey and McHugh JJ.
63 Bagaric, 'The Diminishing Right of Silence', 266.
64 See, further, Chapter 15.
65 [2003] HCA 71.
66 [2003] HCA 71, [40]. See also Gummow and Hayne JJ, [80].

behaviour. A potential point of difference between such a case and a case involving 'discretion' in relation to political opinion is that one's sexual orientation is a far more defining aspect of one's personhood and is thus more difficult to suppress than one's political sentiment. The High Court is yet to decide a case where a political asylum-seeker has been refused refugee status on the basis that he or she can act to avoid political persecution in his or her home country by keeping a low profile.

14.5.5 Forms of political opinion

In *Applicant A v MIEA*, Gummow J stated that: 'Political opinions . . . may be diverse, imprecise, and even idiosyncratic.'[67] However, there are limits to the sort of behaviour that can be tolerated on the basis of the right to express one's political opinion. In *Applicant A*, McHugh J noted:

> Punishment for expressing ordinary political opinions or being a member of a political association or trade union is prima facie persecution for a Convention reason. Nevertheless, governments cannot be expected to tolerate political opinion or conduct that calls for their violent overthrow. Punishment for expressing such opinions is unlikely to amount to persecution. Nevertheless, even in these cases, punishment of the holders of the opinions may amount to persecution. It will certainly do so when the government in question is so repressive that, by the standards of the civilised world, it has so little legitimacy that its overthrow even by violent means is justified. One who fled from the regime of Hitler or Pol Pot could not be denied the status of refugee even if his or her only claim to that status relied on a fear or persecution for advocating the violent overthrow of that regime.[68]

Thus it is important to note that the 'political opinion' ground is not so open-ended that every action that potentially has a political dimension can enliven it. The case of *Ye Hong* involved an applicant who was opposed to the 'one-child policy' of the Chinese government. Tamberlin J stated:

> In the present case I have considerable doubt as to whether expressions of strong objection to the one-child policy can be properly described as an expression of 'a political opinion'. It is not an expression of a political view or position in the sense of an opinion promoted by a political group or party wishing to displace or oppose the present government. The objection in the present case has the character of a personal viewpoint on what is essentially a matter of conscience as to the controversial way in which the government seeks to implement its birth control program. While the strongly held objection on the part of the applicant is, in a sense, in opposition to 'a policy' of the government, the opposition is really based upon personal, humanitarian and compassionate grounds. It is essentially a disagreement on the means adopted by the government to achieve what is considered by the government to be a desirable end to alleviate problems such as starvation, illiteracy and illness arising from overpopulation.[69]

67 [1997] HCA 4 (24 February 1997).
68 [1997] HCA 4 (24 February 1997).
69 *Ye Hong v MIMA* [1998] FCA 1356 (2 October 1998).

It can be argued that disobedience or non-observance of any law involves a political statement or opinion. However, not every act of civil disobedience evinces, or will be imputed to evince, an adverse sentiment regarding the rulers of the country or a display of political opposition. An action that violates the law of a state will constitute an expression of political opinion only where by its nature it strikes (or is perceived to strike) at a central tenet of the government's ideology. A self-serving refusal or inability to abide by a law is often just that, and lacks the political connotation to enliven this ground.

14.6 Particular social group

14.6.1 Formal test

The 'particular social group' ground is the most nebulous Convention ground. The leading authority on the definition of 'particular social group' is *Applicant A v MIEA*.[70] In order to constitute a particular social group, there must be a collection of persons who share a certain characteristic or element that unites them and enables them to be set apart from society at large. Not only must such persons exhibit some common element; the element must unite them, making those who share it a cognisable group within their society. Dawson J, in *Applicant A*, stated:

> The adjoining of 'social' to 'group' suggests that the collection of persons must be of a social character, that is to say, the collection must be cognisable as a group in society such that its members share something which unites them and sets them apart from society at large. The word 'particular' in the definition merely indicates that there must be an identifiable social group such that a group can be pointed to as a particular social group. *A particular social group, therefore, is a collection of persons who share a certain characteristic or element which unites them and enables them to be set apart from society at large*. That is to say, not only must such persons exhibit some common element; the element must unite them, making those who share it a cognisable group within their society.[71]

McHugh J, in the same case, stated:

> The use of [the term 'membership'] in conjunction with 'particular social group' connotes persons who are defined as a distinct social group by reason of some *characteristic, attribute, activity, belief, interest or goal* that unites them. If the group is perceived by people in the relevant country as a particular social group, it will usually but not always be the case that they are members of such a group. Without some form of internal linking or unity of characteristics, attributes, activities, beliefs, interests or goals, however, it is unlikely that a collection of individuals will or can be perceived as being a particular social group. Those indiscriminately killed or robbed by guerillas, for example, are not a particular social group. [Emphasis added.][72]

70 [1997] HCA 4 (24 February 1997).
71 [1997] HCA 4 (24 February 1997).
72 [1997] HCA 4 (24 February 1997).

The meaning of the expression 'particular social group' was most considered by the High Court in *Applicant S*.[73] In a joint judgment, Gleeson CJ, Gummow and Kirby JJ summarised the steps involved in determining whether a group falls within the Convention definition of particular social group as follows:

- First, the group must be identifiable by a characteristic or attribute common to all members of the group.
- Second, the characteristic or attribute common to all members of the group *cannot be the shared fear of persecution*. This matter was also discussed by Dawson J in *Applicant A v MIMA*:

> 'There is more than a hint of circularity in the view that a number of persons may be held to fear persecution by reason of membership of a particular social group where what is said to unite those persons into a particular social group is their common fear of persecution. A group thus defined does not have anything in common save fear of persecution, and allowing such a group to constitute a particular social group for the purposes of the Convention "completely reverses the statutory definition of Convention refugee in issue (wherein persecution must be driven by one of the enumerated grounds and not vice versa)". That approach would ignore what Burchett J in *Ram v Minister for Immigration* called the "common thread" which links the expressions "persecuted", "for reasons of", and "membership of a particular social group", namely: a motivation which is implicit in the very idea of persecution, is expressed in the phrase "for reasons of", and fastens upon the victim's membership of a particular social group. He is persecuted because he belongs to that group.'[74]

- Third, the possession of that characteristic or attribute *must distinguish the group from society at large*.

McHugh J's summary of the issue in *Applicant S*[75] is in similar terms:

> To qualify as a particular social group, it is enough that objectively there is an identifiable group of persons with a social presence in a country, set apart from other members of that society, and united by a common characteristic, attribute, activity, belief, interest, goal, aim or principle.

It is important to note that it is not necessary that persecutors actually perceive the group as constituting a particular social group. It is enough that the persecutor or persecutors single out an individual for being a member of a class whose members possess a 'uniting' feature or attribute, and the persons in that class are cognisable objectively as a particular social group. Furthermore, the joint judgment by Gleeson CJ, Gummow and Kirby JJ in *Applicant S* makes it clear that there is no requirement of recognition or perception by the relevant society that the collection of individuals comprises a particular social group.[76] Nonetheless, their Honours also make it clear that perceptions held by the community may amount to evidence that a social group is a cognisable group within the community.[77]

73 [2004] HCA 25 (27 May 2004).
74 *Applicant A v MIMA* [1997] HCA 4 (24 February 1997).
75 [2004] HCA 25 (27 May 2004).
76 [2004] HCA 25 (27 May 2004), [27].
77 [2004] HCA 25 (27 May 2004).

The importance of the role of perceptions by the community of particular social groups is discussed by Burchett J in *Ram v MIEA*:

> A social group may be identified, in a particular case, by the perceptions of its persecutors rather than by the reality. The words 'persecuted for reasons of' look to their motives and attitudes, and a victim may be persecuted for reasons of race or social group, to which they think he belongs, even if in truth they are mistaken. Hitler's ghastly views about race, for instance, led to persons being classified as Jewish who had appropriately regarded themselves as German; the perception of the authorities was then the important reality which determined their fate.[78]

While this will ordinarily be a sufficient condition to constitute a particular social group, it is not a necessary or essential condition. A particular social group may exist although it is not recognised or perceived as such by the society in which it exists. Communities may deny the existence of particular social groups because the common attribute shared by its members offends religious or cultural beliefs held by a majority of the community. Or, as explained by McHugh J in *Applicant S*, the society may perceive its members as aberrant individuals without, however, perceiving these individuals as constituting a particular social group.[79] Nevertheless, those living outside that society may easily recognise the individuals concerned as comprising a particular social group. As McHugh J pointed out in *Applicant S*, such cases are likely to be rare.

To the extent that such cases do exist, cultural, social, religious and legal norms pointing to the existence of a particular social group may be ascertained objectively. For example, 'country information' gathered by international bodies and nations other than an applicant's country of nationality may contain opinions held by those bodies or the governments of those nations. From such information it is possible to draw conclusions as to whether a group is cognisable within the community.

14.6.2 Difficulties in practical application of the test[80]

14.6.2.1 Infinite number of personal traits

The formal test for particular social group has been clearly articulated by the High Court. However, many of the terms used in the test are, necessarily, imprecise, and the factual exercise involved in the process of identifying a particular social group is often complex. More particularly, applying the test is difficult for several other reasons. The first relates to the formless and indistinct nature of the central concept in the definition: a group. There are an infinite number of traits by which a person or a group may be described and there are an infinite number of groups to which each person belongs. These descriptions can themselves be broken down into any number of sub-groups. Thus, people can be described by their intrinsic

78 No. SG 17 of 1995 FED No. 433/95 Immigration (1995) 130 ALR 314 [11].
79 HCA 25 (27 May 2004), [68].
80 The discussion below relating to particular social groups is derived from RRT reference: V03/16412 (6 July 2004).

traits, such as their gender, IQ score, (natural) hair colour or height. People can also be described by their social antecedents, such as the school they attended, their marital status, the football team they support and their occupation. They can also be described by reference to considerations such as their past behaviour, including criminal history. There is, of course, some overlap between these sub-groups. Given the complexity of the human condition, there is no objectively correct method of identifying the relevant characteristics of a person for the purpose of designating which group/s they belong to.

The exercise is made all the more complex by the fact that there is no objectively correct universal methodology for describing groups of people as perceived in a society. Thus, using the facts from *MIMA v Khawar*,[81] a group to which a person belongs can be described as: (i) women; (ii) women living in country X; (iii) women living in a certain region in country X; (iv) poor married women in country X; (v) married women in country X with no children; (vi) married women living in a household without a male blood relation; or (vii) married women living in a household which did not include a male blood relation to whom the women might look to for protection against violence by other members of the household. The list obviously does not end there. It could be married women living in a house that is more than 100 metres from the nearest police station or married women who live in a household without a telephone. There is literally no end to the number of different group classifications that can be articulated in relation to each person.[82]

14.6.2.2 Group description is context sensitive

Moreover, in defining groups there is no objectively correct level of generality regarding the description that is employed. This stems from the meaning of a group, as simply being a number of persons or things that have some common feature and hence are related in some way. Broad groups include descriptions such as women or human beings; a narrow group, for example, consists of people present in a certain household at a given time. Ultimately, the level of generality that is employed is always context sensitive – it depends on the purpose for which the group classification is being made. People wishing to sell football jumpers would be best to identify the group as supporters of the teams whose jumpers they are selling; people wishing to predict the result of the next election would be best placed to identify the group as all eligible voters; police wishing to find the culprit of a crime would be best placed to identify the relevant group as people who were at the location of the crime at the time it happened; a bartender wishing to know who to serve next should look to the group of people standing

81 [2002] HCA 14 (11 April 2002).
82 See *Secretary of State for the Home Department v K: Fornah v Secretary of State for the Home Department* [2006] UKHL 46 (18 October 2006), in which the appellant (Fornah) claimed to fear being persecuted in Sierre Leone because she would be subjected to female genital mutilation if she returned there. In particular, see comments in relation to the definition of the 'relevant particular social group' per Lord Bingham, [27]–[31]; Lord Hope of Craighead, [54]–[57]; Lord Roger of Earlsferry, [80]; and Baroness Hale of Richmond, [113].

at the bar. Thus group selection is always influenced by the purpose behind the selection of the group and in this way some degree of objectivity is brought into the process of group identification.

However, given the inherently broad nature of the cognisable social group test there is no firm point of reference against which group size and structure can be defined. There are no human traits that are necessarily ruled in or excluded on the basis of the current test. Not surprisingly, then, refugee applicants often, without any hint of logical incongruity, define themselves as belonging to a myriad of particular social groups.

14.6.2.3 Persecution and group selection

In the context of refugee law, one obvious method by which group classification could have been constrained and circumscribed is by focusing on the concept of persecution. Thus it could be asserted that a particular social group is one whose members are persecuted. However, as noted above, the High Court has decisively rejected this approach. An approach that adopts fear of persecution as the touchstone of defining a particular social group would, apparently, be inconsistent with the definition of a refugee in the Convention that prescribes that a person must be persecuted *by reason of* membership of a particular social group. It has been held that the fact of persecution cannot also define the group.

Nevertheless, the fact that a group is persecuted can provide evidence that the group is in fact a genuine particular social group. However, as a general rule, in order for the group to be a particular social group it must be identifiable as a group before the onset of the persecution. Alternatively, if persecution defines the group, it will normally take a considerable period of time before it is recognisable as a distinct social group. This then invites consideration of how else a group can be identified in practice. It is necessary to undertake this exercise to avoid charges being made that decision-makers engage in 'toss of the coin' justice.

14.6.2.4 The history of drafting the Convention is not a useful guide to identifying a particular social group

The process of obtaining practical guidance concerning the meaning of a particular social group is not assisted by the history surrounding the inclusion of 'particular social group' as a Convention ground. The Convention debates reveal that there is no relevant history to the concept. There is no rational explanation for the inclusion of the phrase. It is 'a throw-away line', included at the request of the Swedish representative at the Conference of Plenipotentiaries held at Geneva 2–25 July 1951, who noted that, in addition to the Convention grounds, there were still people who feared persecution because of their membership of a 'particular social group'.[83] Thus it seems that this Convention ground was added in recognition of the finite and distinct protection offered by the other Convention grounds. Considering these circumstances, it is not surprising that courts

83 A. Helton, 'Persecution on Account of Membership of a Particular Social Group as a Basis for Refugee Status', (1983) 15 *Columbia Law Review* 39.

around the world have failed to settle on a consistent interpretation of the phrase that is capable of providing meaningful guidance to refugee status decision-makers.

14.6.2.5 In principle guidance can be sought from the humanitarian underpinning of the Convention

While nothing of substance can be gleaned from the history of the drafting of the Convention to shed light on the meaning of 'particular social group', some guidance can be obtained from the overall purpose of the Convention.

As is noted in Chapter 18, at its broadest, the purpose of the Convention is to enable blameless people who fear serious harm in one nation to gain protection in another nation. The Convention thus has a humanitarian purpose. Refugee law is one of the few areas of international law where the needs of the individual trump the needs of sovereign states.

However, the protection offered by the Convention is limited in nature. To this end, the two main touchstones are the concept of persecution and the Convention grounds. As a matter of principle, as is discussed in Chapter 18, it is a curious aspect of the definition of a refugee in Article 1A(2) of the Convention that people who fear being killed or tortured in their state of origin through no fault of their own will only be granted asylum if their fear relates to one of the five stipulated grounds. This undercuts the humanitarian underpinning of the Convention. People are no less dead if they are shot because of a domestic feud or a civil war than if they are shot for supporting the 'wrong' political party.

In this manner, as a matter of principle, the Convention grounds are arbitrary and hence potentially operate in a discriminatory fashion against people who fear serious harm for non-Convention reasons. There is no relevant (logical or normative) basis for giving preferential treatment to a person who is persecuted because of his or her political or religious beliefs as opposed to, say, his or her economic, social or sporting convictions. The level of pain is the same, and the conduct is equally egregious – directly harming an innocent person is always repugnant. To this end, it is especially unsatisfactory that an individual's eligibility for refugee status should be contingent upon such a 'fine' consideration as whether there are a sufficient number of other similarly placed people being mistreated. When it comes to being eligible for compassion, there does not seem to be anything special about belonging to a (particular social) group. If anything, the converse is often true – (social) isolation can of itself be a cause of distress.

The explanation for this curious state of affairs is that the grounds were not selected by reference to some overarching normative theory, but merely because they aligned with the strategic interests and political realities of the Western world at the time the Convention was drafted and settled. As is noted in Chapters 12 and 18, the Convention was entered into largely to assist European refugees, and to serve Western political and economic needs.

14.6.2.6 A humanitarian approach supports an expansive definition of 'particular social group'

A commitment to eradicating or at least reducing the arbitrary nature of the assistance offered by the Convention and remaining true to the overarching underpinning of refugee law would require an expansive interpretation of the Convention grounds. To this end, the ground that has the greatest inclusive scope is 'particular social group'. This is because the phrase does not have a settled linguistic meaning and, consistent with the little background that there is in relation to its history, it is apparent that it was inserted to cover cases where people were persecuted for reasons not covered by the other grounds. It has even been suggested that 'particular social group' should be extended to include not only women, but also men, that is, the whole human species.

It is unlikely that a court in any jurisdiction would expressly come to this conclusion. However, it may well be the case that it is possible for this result to be achieved indirectly. In Australia and the United Kingdom[84] it has been held that women in some countries constitute a particular social group. A group can be formed by the fact that its members either share a trait or lack a trait. Thus, a group can be defined by exclusion on the basis that its members lack a certain trait or quality. It arguably follows that men too can constitute a particular social group, by a process of exclusion from the group constituted by women.

14.6.2.7 Gaining insight into application by looking at previous paradigm examples of limited utility

In order to provide guidance regarding how to recognise a particular social group, certain 'paradigm' examples have been cited by the courts. These include Jews in Nazi Germany;[85] men, women and children who were guillotined during the French Revolution because they belonged to a class seen as 'dangerous to the emerging democratic state';[86] people who had a capacity to influence public opinion (such as teachers and doctors) in Cambodia under Pol Pot; homosexuals; and Kulaks (affluent Russian peasants) who were persecuted by Stalin.[87] However, it is not clear that these examples actually provide practical guidance. All these groups were in fact persecuted; and it is a relatively straightforward matter – after the fact – to identify them as a particular social group. The examples raise the question of whether Kulaks in Russia and doctors and teachers in Cambodia, and so on, belonged to particular social groups before a change in government policy determined that such groups should be persecuted. If the answer is yes, then what is it exactly about such groups that marked them out as particular social groups?

84 See *MIMA v Khawar* [2002] HCA 14 and the House of Lords decision *in Islam (A.P.) v Secretary of State for the Home Department, Regina v Immigration Appeal Tribunal and Another Ex Parte Shah (A.P.)* (Conjoined Appeals, 25 March 1999).
85 See *Applicant A v MIEA* [1997] HCA 4 (24 February 1997).
86 See *Ram v MIEA* SG 17 of 1995 FED No. 433/95 Immigration (1995) 130 ALR 314.
87 *Applicant A v MIEA* [1997] HCA 4 (24 February 1997).

14.6.2.8 Matters that assist in identifying a particular social group

There is no clear answer to this. In the normal scheme of events it is atypical for societies (or outsiders looking into a society) to view a single trait (or even a collection of traits) as so defining of an individual that it sets that individual apart from the rest of the community. People-grouping is rarely as wide-ranging or decisive as that. As noted above, all individuals are classified into certain groups for one purpose or another. However, it is rare that any trait is so telling as to set individuals apart for more than a limited purpose. An individual can belong to the groups known as married men, men with children, people with houses, people who are left-handed, people who support the Collingwood Football Club, people who do not eat meat, people who do not own a television set, wealthy people, dog owners, non-public transport users and so on, but these are all generally transient descriptions which are typically employed by others who have a strategic purpose in isolating certain distinctive traits.

14.6.2.9 Nonchalance and dispassion do not lead to differentiation

Thus there are very few traits that are so distinctive as to mark a person (and hence a group) as being different for all or at least many purposes as far as a society is concerned. To this end, as noted above, it is important to emphasise that, to come within the scope of the Convention, the trait or traits in question must indeed distinguish that person in the eyes of the society in question (as opposed to only a small section of the society) or outsiders looking into that society. This follows from the term 'social' and the emphasis by the High Court on perceptions of society regarding the classification of the group. In order to identify the sorts of traits that are capable of being viewed in this light, it is necessary to identify the matters that the collective psyche of the society in question regards as being defining of an individual's disposition, i.e. what sort of things or people are either most (or at least highly) reviled or valued in a society.

We use the terms 'value' or 'revile' because as a general rule a community will not resolve to set apart others unless it is *moved* to do so. Nonchalance and dispassion do not lead to differentiation. History tells us that the differences by which people are marked out generally relate to the matters by which people personally define themselves; they are the things that people most strongly and commonly define themselves by. Typically, the most powerful defining traits are ethnicity, nationality and religion. This is clear from the number of wars fought even in recent history over these issues. These traits are of course already separately demarcated in the definition of a refugee.

Whether or not other traits are so important to cause a person (or group of people) to be marked out by the rest of the community will depend on the customs or collective psyche of the state in question. The relative nature of this inquiry makes it difficult to provide accurate and consistent answers to particular social group claims. Many societies have their own peculiar or unique cultural values and beliefs and are moved by different things. What is cardinal in one society can be irrelevant in another. Extra-marital sex by females is one example;

devotion to religion is another. In many circumstances, to make anything more than an approximate guess concerning whether a trait or combination of traits constitutes a particular social group requires the decision-maker to have a thorough understanding of the value and belief system of the culture in question, which is often far removed from the cultural norms that they have experienced. This deep level of understanding will often not reside in people not ingrained in that culture. Thus considerable weight should often be placed on an applicant's evidence regarding the particular social groups that exist in his or her country of origin. It is only a person with a thorough appreciation of Australian culture, for example, who could understand that elite sportspeople and television personalities (due to the privileges often bestowed on them) and Aborigines (on the basis of statistical evidence regarding how poorly they fare on most indicia of flourishing, including life expectancy, education and income levels and imprisonment rates) are probably particular social groups, while homosexuals probably are not (the level of tolerance and acceptance towards homosexuals means that they are no longer demarcated for any relevant purpose).

Country information reports, whether from government agencies or non-government organisations, while relevant, are normally less informative in relation to particular social group claims than about other issues relating to refugee status. This is because these reports are principally concerned with identifying people in a community who are persecuted. They rarely provide further insights into whether the group was set apart prior to the persecution.

14.6.3 How to spot a particular social group, applying the existing law – a summary

As a general rule, the following points emerge from the above discussion:

- There are an infinite number of traits by which people can be described.
- Each personal trait can potentially qualify a person for membership of a particular social group.
- There is no objectively correct method for classifying people into groups.
- Group classification is context sensitive. It depends on the reason for which the classification is made.
- Most group classifications of people are undertaken for strategic reasons (for example, marketing drives where it is advisable to target people with certain traits, such as 'being under forty years of age' or 'a football fan'), and to that end do not operate to set apart people in that group from the rest of society for any meaningful purpose.
- As a general rule, there are few human traits that societies regard as being so cardinal that they result in a different disposition towards people with that trait.
- To the extent that a trait sets apart an individual, the trait normally relates to matters that are regarded as being important to the society in

question. Common examples include ethnicity, nationality and religion. Sexual orientation is another example.

- It is always a question of fact whether there are other traits that a society regards as being so defining of a person that they could result in the formation of a particular social group. In many societies, there will be no such traits (apart from perhaps the traits that are already separately demarcated in the Convention definition of a refugee) and hence there will be no particular social groups in that society.
- The fact that a group is persecuted is some evidence that it constitutes a particular social group; however, this is never decisive. Over time, though, an act of persecution may identify or in some cases even create a particular social group. In most cases the defining characteristic that distinguishes a group from the rest of society must pre-exist the persecution.[88]
- There is no limit to the number of people who can belong to a particular social group. However, as a general rule people do not distinguish other people on the basis of fine or subtle traits. Societies normally make crude generalisations when marking people out as being different. People are persecuted for their religion or ethnicity, for example. It is for this reason that McHugh J noted that if a definition of a group has to be hedged with qualifications to relate it to an alleged persecution act, the proper conclusion may be that the reason for the persecution was not membership of the group but the conduct of the individual.[89]
- The characteristics uniting the group need not be immutable or intrinsic. The group can be constituted by actions that have been performed by its members. However, where the group consists of people who have performed a particular action, as a causal reality, it is often the case that it is the action (or the application of a legal rule or cultural practice) that places members of the group at risk – not the fact that they belong to a particular social group.
- The perceptions of the society in question are important to the issue of whether or not people with a unifying trait constitute a particular social group. However, while this is an important consideration, it is not decisive. A particular social group may exist although it is not recognised or perceived as such by the society in which it exists. In some cases, those living outside the society in question may recognise the individuals concerned as comprising a particular social group.

14.6.4 Examples of particular social group claims

There is a myriad of different social group claims that have been considered by the courts in Australia. It is often not helpful to attach considerable weight to examples drawn from other cases, given the context sensitive nature of the

88 See also *Aliparo v MIMA* [1999] FCA 79 (12 February 1999).
89 See especially *Applicant A* [1997] HCA 4 (24 February 1997).

inquiry at hand. However, for illustrative purposes it is useful to set out some of the decided instances. A list of social group claims that have been accepted and rejected in various jurisdictions is set out by Kirby J in *Applicant A v MIEA*:

> The following categories have been **upheld** as particular social groups:
> - members of the nobility of a former Eastern European kingdom; . . .
> - farmers in areas of military operations in El Salvador;
> - a former funeral director and his wife engaged in the private sector in pre-communist Poland; . . .
> - homosexual and bisexual men and women in countries where their sexual conduct, even with adults and in private, is illegal; . . .
> - young males who have evaded or deserted from compulsory military service in countries engaged in active military operations condemned by the international community;
> - members of stigmatised professional groups and trade unions;
> - soldiers of the army of the former regime in South Vietnam; . . . and
> - Freemasons escaping from Cuba.
>
> On the other hand, claims that have been **rejected** [include]:
> - the 'capitalist class' in a former East European country;
> - an Indian woman who had married out of her caste;
> - members of a recreational club;
> - a person accused of corruption in Ghana; . . .
> - a member of the wealthy Sikh community returning to the Punjab with money which would be subject to the risk of robbery and extortion; . . . and
> - a stepson of a Colombian storekeeper whose shop was blown up by a drugs cartel when he refused to trade for them.[90] [References omitted, formatting undertaken.]

Recently, in *Minister for Immigration and Citizenship v SZNWC* [2010] FCAFC 157 the Full Federal Court upheld an RRT finding that 'Bangladeshi ship deserters' constituted a particular social group.

14.6.5 Statutory change to family as a particular social group

In relation to some countries, the family unit has been recognised as a particular social group. *Migration Act 1958* (Cth) section 91S amends the law where the social group relied upon is membership of a family. The effect of this section is that a person who is at risk of harm because he or she is a relative of a person who is targeted for a non-Convention reason is not a refugee.

Section 91S of the Act (which was inserted by the *Migration Legislation Amendment Act (No 6) 2001* (Cth)), provides:

> For the purposes of the application of this Act and the regulations to a particular person (the first person), in determining whether the first person has a well-founded fear of

90 *Applicant A v Minister for Immigration and Ethnic Affairs* [1997] HCA 4 (24 February 1997). In this case, the High Court rejected the claim that people in China who are opposed to China's one child policy constitute a particular social group. For further particular social group examples, see Germov and Motta, *Refugee Law in Australia*, p. 298–300.

being persecuted for the reason of membership of a particular social group that consists of the first person's family:

(a) disregard any fear of persecution, or any persecution, that any other member or former member (whether alive or dead) of the family has ever experienced, where the reason for the fear or persecution is not a reason mentioned in Article 1A(2) of the Refugees Convention as amended by the Refugees Protocol; and

(b) disregard any fear of persecution, or any persecution, that:
    (i) the first person has ever experienced; or
    (ii) any other member or former member (whether alive or dead) of the family has ever experienced;

where it is reasonable to conclude that the fear or persecution would not exist if it were assumed that the fear or persecution mentioned in paragraph (a) had never existed.

Thus the effect of section 91S is that in determining whether a person has a well-founded fear of persecution for reason of membership of a particular social group that consists of the person's family, the matters set out in section 91S are to be disregarded.

The revised Explanatory Memorandum in relation to section 91S provides the background to the section:

Section 91S Membership of a particular social group

30. This item inserts [a] new section 91S into the Act which deals with 'membership of a particular social group'. This proposed provision addresses a recent court finding that a relative of a person facing persecution for a non-Refugees Convention reason, such as pursuit by criminal elements for repayment of debts, is themselves facing persecution for the Convention ground of membership of a particular social group when the attentions of the agents of persecution turn to them, for example for repayments of the debts. This type of situation falls outside the range of grounds for persecution covered in the Refugees Convention.

31. New section 91S provides that certain matters must be disregarded in determining whether a particular person ('the first person') has a well-founded fear of persecution for the reason of membership of a particular social group that consists of the person's family.

32. The matters that must be disregarded are:

- any fear of persecution or any persecution that any other family member (whether alive or dead) has ever experienced where that fear or persecution is not for a reason mentioned in Article 1A(2) of the Refugees Convention; and
- any fear of persecution or any persecution that the first person has ever experienced or any other family member (whether alive or dead) has ever experienced where it is reasonable to conclude that the fear or persecution would not exist if it were assumed that the fear of persecution mentioned in the above point had never existed.

33. The above provisions do not prevent a family, per se, being a particular social group for the purpose of establishing a Convention reason for persecution. However, they prevent the family being used as a vehicle to bring with[in] the scope of the Convention persecution motivated for non-Convention reasons.

In the second reading speech the Minister explained section 91S as follows:

> The legislation will also provide that to invoke protection the Convention reason must be the essential and significant reason for the persecution. The Convention was not designed to protect people who fear persecution for personal reasons that have little or nothing to do with the Convention – for example, because they have failed to pay their family's debts.
>
> Yet a recent Federal Court case provides for this very scenario.
>
> The legislation will also prevent people from using elaborate constructs to claim that they are being persecution [sic] as a member of a family and thus under the Convention ground of a particular social group when there is no Convention-related reason for the persecution.
>
> *This will remove a potential avenue for criminal families to claim protection on the basis of gang wars* – not those that the government would see as warranting international protection.[91] [Emphasis added.]

This interpretation has been endorsed by the majority High Court judgment in *STCB v MIMA*,[92] where the appellant had claimed to fear persecution in Albania as a result of a 'blood feud' involving his family. Because his grandfather had murdered a member of another family in Albania in the 1940s, the applicant feared that the victim's family would harm him to avenge their family member's murder. In relation to his claim to fear persecution for reasons of his membership of his own family, the majority stated:

> Applying s 91S(a), it is clear that the grandfather had a fear of persecution for a reason other than those mentioned in Art 1A(2) of the Convention – revenge for murder. Section 91S(a) requires that fear of persecution to be disregarded. Section 91S(b)(i) requires the appellant's fear of persecution to be disregarded, for it is reasonable to conclude that that fear would not exist if the grandfather's fear had never existed. And s 91S(b)(ii) requires that the brother's and the father's fear of persecution be disregarded, for it is reasonable to conclude that neither of those fears would exist either if the grandfather's fear had never existed. The result of disregarding the fears of persecution of the grandfather, the appellant, the father and the brother is that the appellant is to be treated as not having a well-founded fear of persecution for the reason of membership of a particular social group that consists of the appellant's family.[93]

In other words, where an applicant has a fear due to a threat directed at his or her family, the *operating* cause for this threat must be identified. It is only in circumstances where the operating cause of the threat to the family is Convention-related that a member of the family may legitimately claim to be a refugee.

Thus, section 91S deals with a causation issue that has arisen in the interpretation of the Convention. It provides that where a family member fears persecution because of his or her membership of a family and the reason for the threat to that family is not Convention-related, the *effective cause* of that fear is not the person's membership of the family unit; rather, the (substantive) *cause* is the

91 House of Representatives, 28 August 2000, Hansard, at 3422.
92 [2006] HCA 61 (14 December 2006) per Gleeson CJ, Gummow, Callinan and Heydon JJ.
93 [2006] HCA 61 (14 December 2006), [24].

reason for the threat. If the harm threatened is for a Convention reason, then section 91S has no operation and the person may be eligible for refugee status on the basis of the threat to the family, but where the underlying reason for the threatened harm is not Convention-related, section 91S operates to exclude such claims.

15

Persecution

15.1 Overview of persecution

As noted in Chapter 11, in order to qualify for refugee status, the harm feared by a claimant must constitute 'persecution'. This renders the notion of 'persecution' central to the concept of a refugee.

The term 'persecution' derives from the Latin *persequi*, which means 'to follow with hostile intent, or pursue'.[1] The Convention drafters deliberately did not define the term 'persecution' with any degree of exactness, to ensure that the concept could be applied to new situations.[2] To judge if a person has suffered, or is at risk of suffering, persecution under the Convention, the severity of the harm and the importance of the right affected are measured on quantitative and qualitative levels. Although the level of severity of harm must generally be high, it may vary depending on the importance of the relevant human right.[3] As is noted by the UNHCR, 'there is no universally accepted definition of "persecution", and various attempts to formulate such a definition have met with little success'.[4] Thus states have a wide discretion in interpreting the term. This has resulted in numerous irreconcilable decisions regarding its meaning. Goodwin-Gill has commented in relation to the concept of persecution that 'practice reveals no coherent or consistent jurisprudence'.[5]

1 J-Y. Carlier et al. (eds), *Who Is a Refugee?* (The Hague, Kluwer Law International, 1997), p. 702.
2 S. Kneebone: www.law.monash.edu.au/castancentre/submissions/migration6.html.
3 Carlier et al., *Who Is a Refugee?*, p. 707.
4 UNHCR *Handbook on Procedures and Criteria for Determining Refugee Status*.
5 Goodwin-Gill, *The Refugee in International Law*, p. 67. For some common themes in interpretation, see R. Bacon and K. Booth, 'The Intersection of Refugee Law and Gender: Private Harm and Public Responsibility', (2000) 23 *UNSW Law Journal* 135, pp. 143–45. For an examination of the position in the United States and also a discussion of the merits of a clear definition of persecution see S. Pirie, 'The Need for a Codified Definition of Persecution in US Refugee Law', (1986) 39 *Stanford Law Review* 187.

Although 'persecution' is not defined in the Convention, there is a large amount of case law on its meaning. This is discussed in sections 15.3 and 15.4 below. Prior to examining the principles that have emerged from case law and their relevance, we first provide an overview of the relevant legislative principles.

15.2 Overview of relevant statutory principles

Under Australian law, the term 'persecution' in Article 1A(2) is now qualified by section 91R of the *Migration Act 1958* (Cth). Section 91R(1) states that for the purposes of the Act, Article 1A(2) does not apply in relation to persecution for one or more of the Convention reasons unless:

- that reason is the *essential and significant* reason, or those reasons are the essential and significant reasons, for the persecution;
- the persecution involves *serious harm* to the person; and
- the persecution involves *systematic and discriminatory* conduct.

As is discussed below, the main change to the pre-existing meaning of 'persecution' lies in the serious harm requirement. The 'essential and significant reason' and 'systematic and discriminatory conduct' requirements are merely a statutory endorsement of the existing legal standards. We examine each of these elements in turn, starting with the concept of serious harm.

15.3 Serious harm

15.3.1 Overview of legislation

'Serious harm' is the threshold of harm that must be reached before an individual is entitled to the protection of another state. It is the degree of suffering which a person must endure before the effective concern of other nations is sufficiently touched to admit that person into the community as a refugee.

Subsection 91R(2) sets out a number of examples that constitute serious harm:

(a) a threat to the person's *life* or *liberty*;[6]
(b) significant *physical harassment* of the person;
(c) significant *physical ill-treatment* of the person;
(d) significant *economic hardship* that threatens the person's capacity to subsist;
(e) denial of access to basic services, where the denial threatens the person's capacity to subsist;
(f) denial of capacity to earn a *livelihood* of any kind, where the denial threatens the person's capacity to subsist. [Emphasis added.]

6 In *VBAO v MIMA* [2006] HCA 60 (14 December 2006), Gleeson CJ and Kirby J (in a joint judgment) and Gummow J held that the word 'threat' in s 91R(2)(a) refers to the likelihood that a person's life or liberty will be harmed, as distinct from a communication or declaration of an intention to harm.

The above approach to serious harm was adopted in response to concerns caused by court decisions that lowered the threshold of harm that sufficed to qualify as persecution.[7] As noted by Marshall J in *MIMA v VBAO of 2002*:

> The Explanatory Memorandum to the Migration Legislation Amendment Bill (No. 6) 2001 . . . stated at [19] by way of introducing the new section 91R, that: 'claims of persecution have been determined by Australian courts to fall within the scope of the Refugees Convention even though the harm feared fell well short of the level of harm accepted by the parties to the Convention to constitute persecution'.[8]

15.3.2 Case law prior to statutory changes

The case law relating to the meaning of 'serious harm' prior to the changes is well summarised in the following extract from the Full Federal Court decision of *Minister for Immigration & Multicultural & Indigenous Affairs v Kord*:[9]

> We commence with the decision of the High Court in *Chan Yee Kin v Minister for Immigration and Ethnic Affairs* (1989–1990) 169 CLR 379. A particular passage in the judgment of Mason CJ is of considerable importance for reasons which will emerge at a later stage. The passage (at 388) is as follows:
>
>> The Convention and the Protocol do not define the words 'being persecuted'. . . . The delegate was no doubt right in thinking that some forms of selective or discriminatory treatment by a State of its citizens do not amount to persecution. When the Convention makes provision for the recognition of the refugee status of a person who is, owing to a well-founded fear of being persecuted for a Convention reason, unwilling to return to the country of his nationality, the Convention necessarily contemplates that there is a real chance that the applicant will suffer some serious punishment or penalty or some significant detriment or disadvantage if he returns. Obviously harm or the threat of harm as part of a course of selective harassment of a person, whether individually or as a member of a group subjected to such harassment by reason of membership of the group, amounts to persecution if done for a Convention reason. The denial of fundamental rights or freedoms otherwise enjoyed by nationals of the country concerned may constitute such harm, although I would not wish to express an opinion on the question whether any deprivation of a freedom traditionally guaranteed in a democratic society would constitute persecution if undertaken for a Convention reason.
>
> Dawson J (at 396–7) said: . . .
>
>> 'Persecution' is not defined in the Convention, although Arts 31 and 33 refer to those whose life or freedom may be threatened. Indeed, there is general acceptance that a threat to life or freedom for a Convention reason amounts to persecution . . . Some would confine persecution to a threat to life or freedom, whereas others would extend it to other measures in disregard of human dignity . . . It is unnecessary for present purposes to enter the controversy whether any and, if so, what actions other than a threat to life or freedom would amount to persecution.

7 S. Haddad, 'Qualifying the Convention Definition of Refugee', in *Immigration Review* (Sydney, Butterworths, 2002).
8 [2004] FCA 1495 (19 November 2005), [20].
9 [2002] FCA 334 (28 March 2002), [15]–[31].

McHugh J said at 429–31: . . .

> Moreover, to constitute 'persecution' the harm threatened need not be that of loss of life or liberty. Other forms of harm short of interference with life or liberty may constitute 'persecution' for the purposes of the Convention and Protocol. Measures 'in disregard' of human dignity may, in appropriate cases, constitute persecution . . . The Federal Court of Appeal of Canada rejected the proposition that persecution required deprivation of liberty. It was correct in doing so, for persecution on account of race, religion and political opinion has historically taken many forms of social, political and economic discrimination. Hence, the denial of access to employment, to the professions and to education or the imposition of restrictions on the freedoms traditionally guaranteed in a democratic society such as freedom of speech, assembly, worship or movement may constitute persecution if imposed for a Convention reason . . .

In *Applicant A v Minister for Immigration and Ethnic Affairs* (1996–97) 190 CLR 225 at 232, Brennan CJ observed that:

> When a person has a well-founded fear of persecution, the enjoyment by that person of his or her fundamental rights and freedoms is denied . . .

McHugh J said at 258–9:

> Persecution for a Convention reason may take an infinite variety of forms, from death or torture to the deprivation of opportunities to compete on equal terms with other members of the relevant society . . .

Gummow J said at 284:

> In ordinary usage, the primary meaning of 'persecution' is:
>
> 'The action of persecuting or pursuing with enmity and malignity; the infliction of death, torture or penalties for adherence to a religious belief or an opinion as such, with a view to the repression or extirpation of it; the fact of being persecuted; an instance of this' . . .

In *Minister for Immigration and Ethnic Affairs v Guo* (1997) 191 CLR 559 at 570, the majority (Brennan CJ, Dawson, Toohey, Gaudron, McHugh and Gummow JJ) said:

> In *Chan*, Mason CJ referred to persecution as requiring 'some serious punishment or penalty or some significant detriment or disadvantage'. One other statement of his Honour in that case is also relevant to this appeal. His Honour said:
>
> 'Discrimination which involves interrogation, detention or exile to a place remote from one's place of residence under penalty of imprisonment for escape or for return to one's place of residence amounts prima facie to persecution unless the actions are so explained that they bear another character.'

In the same case, Dawson J said that:

> . . . there is general acceptance that a threat to life or freedom for a Convention reason amounts to persecution . . . Some would confine persecution to a threat to life or freedom, whereas others would extend it to other measures in disregard of human dignity.

In *Chan*, McHugh J said that 'persecution was selective harassment and that in appropriate cases it could include single acts of oppression and measures "in disregard" of human dignity' . . .

> Finally we turn to the decision of the High Court in *MIMA v Ibrahim* (2000) 204 CLR 1. In that case the majority disposed of the matter upon the basis that the applicant had fled his country for fear of the consequences of disorder and internecine warfare rather than for fear of persecution for a Convention reason. However, Gaudron and McHugh JJ (who were in the minority) also addressed the meaning of 'persecution'. Their Honours' views do not seem to have been inconsistent with the views of the majority and appear to be consistent with earlier decisions . . .

McHugh J said (at [55]–[65]):

> [55] Persecution involves discrimination that results in harm to an individual, but not all discrimination amounts to persecution. With the express or tacit approval of the government, for example, some employers may refuse to employ persons on grounds of race, religion or nationality. But discriminatory though such conduct may be, it may not amount to persecution. Other employment may be readily available. The Convention protects persons from persecution, not discrimination. Nor does the infliction of harm for a Convention reason always involve persecution. Much will depend on the form and extent of the harm. Torture, beatings or unjustifiable imprisonment, if carried out for a Convention reason, will invariably constitute persecution for the purpose of the Convention. But the infliction of many forms of economic harm and the interference with many civil rights may not reach the standard of persecution. Similarly, while persecution always involves the notion of selective harassment or pursuit, selective harassment or pursuit may not be so intensive, repetitive or prolonged that it can be described as persecution . . .
>
> [60] All these statements are descriptive rather than definitive of what constitutes persecution for the purpose of the Convention. In particular, they do not attempt to define when the infliction or threat of harm passes beyond harassment, discrimination or tortious or unlawful conduct and becomes persecution for Convention purposes. A passage in my judgment in [Chan] suggests that a person is persecuted within the meaning of the Convention whenever the harm or threat of harm 'can be seen as part of a course of systematic conduct directed for a Convention reason against that person as an individual or as a member of a class'. Read literally, this statement goes too far. It would cover many forms of selective harassment or discrimination that fall short of persecution for the purpose of the Convention. Moreover, it does not go far enough, if it were to be read as implying that there can be no persecution unless systematic conduct is established.
>
> [61] Given the objects of the Convention, the harm or threat of harm will ordinarily be persecution only when it is done for a Convention reason and when it is so oppressive or recurrent that a person cannot be expected to tolerate it . . .
>
> [62] Dr Hathaway in his book *The Law of Refugee Status* thought that the Canadian Immigration Appeal Board had 'succinctly stated the core of the test' of persecution when it said that '[t]he criteri[on] to establish persecution is harassment, harassment that is so constant and unrelenting that the victims feel deprived of all hope of recourse, short of flight, from government by oppression' . . .
>
> [64] The emphasis on the tolerability of the applicant's situation gives effect to the principal rationale for the Convention. It was persecution on grounds such as race,

> religion, nationality and political opinion that led to the involuntary migration of large numbers of persons before and after the Second World War and which brought about the Convention. The Convention should be interpreted against that background. Given that background, the parties to the Convention should be understood as agreeing to give refuge to a person when, but only when, he or she 'is outside the country of his [or her] nationality and is unable or, owing to such [well-founded] fear, is unwilling to avail himself [or herself] of the protection of that country'.
>
> [65] Framing an exhaustive definition of persecution for the purpose of the Convention is probably impossible. Ordinarily, however, given the rationale of the Convention, persecution for that purpose is:
>
> - unjustifiable and discriminatory conduct directed at an individual or group for a Convention reason
> - which constitutes an interference with the basic human rights or dignity of that person or the persons in the group
> - which the country of nationality authorizes or does not stop, and
> - which is so oppressive or likely to be repeated or maintained that the person threatened cannot be expected to tolerate it, so that flight from, or refusal to return to, that country is the understandable choice of the individual concerned. [References omitted, italics added.]

Although the courts have not exhaustively defined the serious harm component of 'persecution', an analysis of the cases draws attention to two themes. First, the concept of persecution is connected with notions of human rights and dignity. Second, persecution can include the deprivation of interests that do not come close to threatening subsistence. For example, it has been held that discrimination in the form of restrictions on employment and educational opportunities constituted persecution.[10] To meet the persecution requirement, it was not necessary for the applicant to be denied the opportunity of *any* employment; merely being denied the opportunity to work in his or her chosen field was sufficient.[11]

On any measure the courts adopted a broad view of the level of harm that can amount to persecution – it has certainly not been the case that only persons enduring unbearable or even considerable levels of suffering have been found to have suffered persecution.[12]

15.3.3 Likely meaning to be given to 'serious harm': An examination of statute in light of case law

15.3.3.1 Ample scope of divergent judicial interpretations of 'serious harm'

As noted above, section 91R(2) was enacted in response to concerns created by court judgments that significantly lowered the threshold concerning the types of harm that would enable a person to qualify for refugee status. As indicated by

10 See also *Thalary v MIEA* [1997] 201 FLA (4 April 1997); *Gunaseelan v MIMA* [1997] 434 FLA (9 May 1997).
11 See, for example, *Ahmadi v MIMA* [2001] FCA 1070 (8 August). See also K. Walker, 'Sexuality and Refugee Status in Australia', (2000) 12 *International Journal of Refugee Law* 175, 193–194.
12 Some decisions are taking a more narrow view: for example, see *MIMIA v UBAQ of 2002* [2004] FLA 1945.

the Explanatory Memorandum, in order to be entitled to Convention protection it is not enough for a person to show that he or she would suffer discrimination or disadvantage in their home country, or in comparison to the opportunities or treatment they could expect in Australia.

Nevertheless, under the new legislation there remains ample scope for judicial interpretation, creativity and ultimately expansion of the types of harm that constitute serious harm. In fact, the legislature has left it open to the judiciary to tenably interpret 'serious harm' in effectively the same manner as it did prior to the changes. The argument that would lead to such an approach is not difficult to make out. The courts could simply invoke the oft-used maxims of statutory interpretation that (i) the definition employed by the legislature is inclusive, not exhaustive,[13] and (ii) important rights should not be removed unless there is a clear statutory intention to do so.[14] Moreover, the Explanatory Memorandum indicates that even mental harm can constitute serious harm. Judges could also justify an expansive interpretation by invoking the notion that the section should be interpreted consistent with the humanitarian objectives of the Convention.[15]

As is generally the case with statutory interpretation, there are contrary maxims that can be invoked that will lead to a more restrictive interpretation of 'serious harm'. In this case, there is the *ejusdem generis* rule.[16] It is evident from the list of examples of harm set out in section 91R that the types of harms referred to are those affecting the most basic of rights. That is, the list of interests relates to matters that impact on subsistence as opposed to those that adversely impact on flourishing. The rights to life, liberty, and the protection of one's physical integrity are the most basic rights. Other interests (such as economic hardship) are also recognised, but only to the extent that they threaten the subsistence of the person. Accordingly, all the other nominated harms are derivative from the right to life. Hence it can be argued that the courts should not find that a form of mistreatment constitutes serious harm unless it interferes with one's subsistence. In addition, a more narrow definition of 'serious harm' is favoured by the maxim that statutory provisions are assumed to have some effect.[17] In these circumstances, it would be inappropriate to simply apply pre-existing case law.

It may also be argued that Article 31(1) of the Vienna Convention on the Law of Treaties is relevant to the interpretation of serious harm. It provides:

> A treaty shall be interpreted in good faith in accordance with the ordinary meaning to be given to the terms of the treaty in their context and in the light of its objects and purpose.

13 See, for example, *Sheritt Gordon Mines Ltd v FCT* (1976) 10 ALR 441, 455.
14 *Plaintiff S157/2002 v Commonwealth of Australia* [2003] HCA 2 (4 September 2002).
15 For an argument in favour of an expansive interpretation of 'persecution' see P. Matthew, 'Conformity or Persecution: China's One Child Policy and Refugee Status', (2000) 23 *UNSW Law Journal* 103.
16 For example, see *Canwan Coals Pty Ltd v FCT* (1974) 4 ALR 223.
17 *Commonwealth v Baume* (1905) HCA 11 (10 April 1905); *Maddalozzo v Maddick* (1992) 84 NTR 27.

Article 31(4) provides that 'a special meaning shall be given to a term if it is established that the parties so intended'.

In terms of the significance of Article 31 in domestic law, the High Court has held that it forms the basis for treaty interpretation unless the legislature has expressed an intention to the contrary. In *Applicant A v MIEA*, Dawson J said:

> Deciding that question [the interpretation of the Refugees Convention] involves the construction of a domestic statute which incorporates a definition found in an international treaty. Such a provision, whether it is a definition or otherwise, should ordinarily be construed in accordance with the meaning to be attributed to the treaty provision in international law. By transposing the provision of the treaty, the legislature discloses the *prima facie intention that it have the same meaning in the statute as it does in the treaty*. Absent a contrary intention, and there is none in this case, such a statutory provision is to be construed according to the method applicable to the construction of the corresponding words in the treaty... The general rule of interpretation of treaty provisions appears in article 31 of the Vienna Convention on the Law of Treaties (the Vienna Convention)
>
> ... Under that rule, the starting point must be the text of the treaty. Of course, the text of the treaty is often couched in fairly general terms due to differences in language and legal conceptions among those to whom it is to be addressed and as part of an attempt to reach agreement among diverse nations. Accordingly, technical principles of common law construction are to be disregarded in construing the text. Article 31 plainly precludes the adoption of a literal construction which would defeat the object or purpose of the treaty and would be inconsistent with the context in which the words being construed appear. To say as much is, perhaps, to state no more than the accepted canon of construction that an instrument is to be construed as a whole and that words are not to be divorced from their context or construed in a manner which would defeat the character of the instrument.[18]

In a similar vein, Brennan CJ stated:

> In interpreting a treaty, it is erroneous to adopt a rigid priority in the application of interpretative rules. The political processes by which a treaty is negotiated to a conclusion preclude such an approach. Rather, for the reasons given by McHugh J, it is necessary to adopt an holistic but ordered approach. The holistic approach to interpretation may require a consideration of both the text and the object and purpose of the treaty in order to ascertain its true meaning. Although the text of a treaty may itself reveal its object and purpose or at least assist in ascertaining its object and purpose, assistance may also be obtained from extrinsic sources. The form in which a treaty is drafted, the subject to which it relates, the mischief that it addresses, the history of its negotiation and comparison with earlier or amending instruments relating to the same subject may warrant consideration in arriving at the true interpretation of its text.[19]

In essence, the principal guide to the interpretation of international treaties, including the Refugees Convention, is the text of the document. However, this is to be complemented by reference to the objects and purposes of the treaty.

18 [1997] HCA 4 (24 February 1997). Murphy J in *Commonwealth v Tasmania* stated that the relevant international convention (in that case the UNESCO Convention for the Protection of the World Cultural and National Heritage) should be interpreted in a manner that gives 'primacy to the ordinary meaning of its terms in their context and in light of its objects and purpose' (1983) 158 CLR 1, 177.
19 (1997) 190 CLR 225, 231.

Militating against the importance of the text and purpose of the treaty is the fact that domestic law (including principles of statutory interpretation) prevails over international law documents. This means that the legislature is free to depart from general principles of treaty interpretation and to change the meaning of a treaty when it imports the treaty into domestic law.

The principal domestic law governing statutory interpretation is the *Acts Interpretation Act 1901* (Cth). Pursuant to sections 15AA and 15AB, the text of a statute is paramount and the objects and purpose of a statute are only to be considered where the text is ambiguous. Thus the meaning of 'serious harm' should principally be derived from the terms of the statute. However, as is noted by Dawson J above, unless a contrary intention appears in the statute, it should be given the same meaning as in a treaty. This, effectively, takes the interpretive issue full circle: whether or not the phrase 'serious harm' is meant to change the meaning of 'persecution' in the Convention depends on the weight given to the statutory maxims discussed above. The main point to emerge from this discussion of the 'principles' of statutory interpretation is that in light of this expansive range of interpretive tools (neither being more logically persuasive or legally imperative than the other) there is obviously ample scope for the courts to interpret 'serious harm' in the manner they deem most appropriate.[20]

15.3.3.2 Towards a narrow meaning of 'serious harm'

Human rights lawyers and advocates will no doubt urge the courts to adopt a liberal interpretation of 'serious harm'. Hathaway and other commentators assert that in order for the Convention to remain relevant today, 'persecution' must be interpreted broadly.[21] According to the Committee on Population and Refugees in the Council of Europe:

> The concept of persecution should be interpreted and applied liberally and also adapted to the changed circumstances which may differ considerably from those existing when the Convention was originally adopted . . . [A]ccount should be taken of the relation between refugee status and the denial of human rights as laid down in different international instruments.[22]

Such an approach would give the courts greater power to grant asylum to people from states where people flourish to a lesser degree than in Australia. This reflexive approach is arguably short-sighted, failing to recognise the practical realities of dealing with mass population movements and the dichotomy between refugee and migration law.

Given the preparedness of the courts to expand the notion of serious harm, it is not surprising that refugees and economic migrants are often confused in the eyes

20 For a general discussion regarding the open-textured principles of statutory interpretation, see D.C. Pearce and R.S. Geddes, *Statutory Interpretation in Australia* (Sydney, Butterworths, 1996).

21 Hathaway, *The Law of Refugee Status*, p. 104.

22 Cited in remarks by J. Thomas in A. Woods (ed.), 'Refugees: A New Dimension in International Human Rights', (1976) 70 ASILP 58, at 69.

of the community. This can lead to unfortunate results. As High Commissioner Ruud Lubbers stated to the UN Commission on Human Rights in March 2001:

> Today, refugees and economic migrants – along with the criminal element – have become seriously confused – even assimilated – in the public mind. Extremist politicians have been quick to exploit public fears – stereotyping refugees as economically motivated, a burden to public health and a social threat.[23]

15.3.3.3 Refugee realities – no appetite for uninvited arrivals

Those arguing in favour of an expanded definition of 'serious harm' fail to appreciate a paradox that emerges as a result of judicial expansion of the concept of serious harm. On first glance, courts and other legal bodies appear to be assisting the 'refugee cause' by expanding the type of harm that qualifies for assistance. A broad approach to the meaning of 'serious harm' expands the pool of candidates who may qualify for refugee status. However, this is unlikely to result in a greater number of refugees being accepted.

Nations have limited sympathy for those in need. As is detailed in Chapter 18, the refugee system worldwide is buckling under the strain of the constant tide of asylum-seekers. The appetite for these asylum-seekers is finite and a small one at that. As noted by Niraj Nathwani, 'refugee law is in crisis precisely because altruism has reached its limits . . . We need to face the fact of donor fatigue.'[24]

Given that the world's collective sympathy for refugees is unlikely to grow in the years to come, the decision of who qualifies for asylum is critical – in effect each person who is accorded refugee status potentially deprives another more needy person of asylum.[25] Any proposed change to the definition or interpretation of 'refugee' should be approached in a manner that is consistent not only with the Convention's founders' goal to safeguard important human rights, but also with their concern to respect state sovereignty, which is what enables states to control migration flows.[26]

At what height the hurdle for 'serious harm' is set remains unclear. As noted above, the principal determinant in this regard is the willingness of sovereign states to accept newcomers. The greater the preparedness, the lower the height to which the bar should be raised. However, the desire to help comes in limited doses. Given this, it is important to properly target those who require assistance. An expansive approach to the definition of 'serious harm' would lead to people who are at risk of being tortured or killed fighting for refugee places against people who 'struggle' to secure university places or who cannot fully express their political opinion.

23 As cited by J. Fitzpatrick, in 'The Refugee Convention at 50', in US Committee for Refugees, *World Refugee Survey 2001* (New York, 2002), pp. 22, 23.
24 N. Nathwani, 'The Purpose of Asylum', (2000) 12 *International Journal of Refugee Law*, 354, 356.
25 See Part 3 of Chapter 12, concerning the Australian government setting maximum number of visas to be granted for various visa classes.
26 See further the comments by the former Australian Minister for Immigration, Philip Ruddock, in the foreword to *Interpreting the Refugees Convention – an Australian Contribution* (Canberra, DIAC, 2002). See also this report at 80.

Thus assistance should be limited to people whose lives are in peril or who have a real fear that their physical integrity (including their life) or liberty will be violated. This, effectively, means that the principal right that is being protected is the right to life. We do not think it is controversial to claim that the right to life is the most important of all rights. Logically, the right to life is the most basic and fundamental of all human rights – non-observance of it would render all other human rights devoid of meaning.[27] Every society has some prohibition against taking life,[28] and 'the intentional taking of human life is . . . the offence which society condemns most strongly'.[29] This approach means that denial of job opportunities or welfare should not constitute serious harm unless it will impair the capacity of a person to subsist.

15.3.3.4 The flourishing versus subsistence dichotomy

Refugee law represents an acceptance by the international community that the rights of the individual should in some cases override the economic and material interests of a state. Expanding the concept of a refugee to a point where refugee status is extended to people who are simply failing to flourish, as opposed to those whose existence is imperilled, loses sight of the small level of compassion that nations have for foreigners, and makes the lot of those whose survival is threatened even more precarious. An enlightened approach to the interpretation of 'serious harm' is likely to lead to the courts significantly elevating the level of harm that is necessary to satisfy the definition of 'serious harm'. Deprivations of welfare, employment and education rights, while undesirable, are significantly less damaging than a threat to one's subsistence. The flourishing/subsistence dichotomy is a doctrine that courts may invoke in the future to draw the line between genuine refugees and economic refugees.

15.4 Other elements of persecution: The nexus between the grounds and the serious harm

15.4.1 Overview of nexus

As noted above, persecution has a number of elements. In order to constitute persecution, it is not sufficient that an individual is at risk of serious harm. There must also be a nexus between the serious harm and one of the Convention grounds. This nexus has several different elements. The conduct must be systematic and discriminatory conduct. Persecution also implies an element of motivation. Further, as we saw in Chapter 14, while the persecution feared need not be solely

27 See, further, M. Nowak, *UN Covenant on Civil and Political Rights: CCPR Commentary* (Kehl am Rhein, N.P. Engel, 1993), p. 104; S. Joseph, 'The Right to Life', in D. Harris and S. Joseph (eds), *The International Covenant on Civil and Political Rights and United Kingdom Law* (Oxford, Clarendon Press, 1995), p. 155.
28 P. Singer, *Practical Ethics* (2nd edn) (Cambridge, Cambridge University Press, 1993), p. 85.
29 House of Lords, *Report of the Select Committee on Medical Ethics* (1994) vol. 1, 13. For further discussion regarding the foundation and scope of the right to life, see K. Amarasekara and M. Bagaric, *Euthanasia, Morality and Law* (New York, Peters Lang Publishing, 2002), ch 5.

attributable to a Convention reason, persecution for multiple motivations will not satisfy the relevant test unless a Convention reason or reasons constitute at least the essential and significant motivation for the persecution feared. We now examine the elements of the nexus more closely.

15.4.2 Nexus elements of discrimination, systematic conduct, motivation and causation

The elements that we discuss first are discrimination, motivation and systematic conduct.

15.4.2.1 Discrimination

The concept of discrimination is an aspect of persecution. In *Applicant A v MIEA*, McHugh J stated:

> When the definition of refugee is read as a whole, it is plain that it is directed to the protection of individuals who have been or who are likely to be the victims of intentional discrimination of a particular kind. The discrimination must constitute a form of persecution, and it must be discrimination that occurs because the person concerned has a particular race, religion, nationality, political opinion or membership of a particular social group. Discrimination – even discrimination amounting to persecution – that is aimed at a person as an individual and not for a Convention reason is not within the Convention definition of refugee, no matter how terrible its impact on that person happens to be. The Convention is primarily concerned to protect those racial, religious, national, political and social groups who are singled out and persecuted by or with the tacit acceptance of the government of the country from which they have fled or to which they are unwilling to return. Persecution by private individuals or groups does not by itself fall within the definition of refugee unless the State either encourages or is or appears to be powerless to prevent that private persecution. The object of the Convention is to provide refuge for those groups who, having lost the *de jure* or *de facto* protection of their governments, are unwilling to return to the countries of their nationality . . . Persecution for a Convention reason may take an infinite variety of forms from death or torture to the deprivation of opportunities to compete on equal terms with other members of the relevant society. Whether or not conduct constitutes persecution in the Convention sense does not depend on the nature of the conduct. It depends on whether it discriminates against a person because of race, religion, nationality, political opinion or membership of a social group. Ordinarily, the persecution will be manifested by a series of discriminatory acts directed at members of a race, religion, nationality or particular social group or at those who hold certain political opinions in a way that shows that, as a class, they are being selectively harassed. In some cases, however, the applicant may be the only person who is subjected to discriminatory conduct. Nevertheless, as long as the discrimination constitutes persecution and is inflicted for a Convention reason, the person will qualify as a refugee.[30]

30 HCA 4 (24 February 1997).

15.4.2.2 Element of motivation

The discriminatory element of persecution involves an element of motivation on the part of those who persecute. Gummow J in *Applicant A v MIEA* stated:

> I agree with the following formulation by Burchett J in giving the judgment of the Full Federal Court in *Ram v Minister for Immigation:* Persecution involves the infliction of harm, but it implies something more: an element of an attitude on the part of those who persecute which leads to the infliction of harm, or an element of motivation (however twisted) for the infliction of harm. People are persecuted for something perceived about them or attributed to them by their persecutors. Not every isolated act of harm to a person is an act of persecution.[31]

Although persecution requires an element of motivation, it does not require an attitude of antipathy. In their joint judgment in *Applicant S v MIMA*, Gleeson CJ, Gummow and Kirby JJ stated:

> Persecution can proceed from reasons other than 'enmity' and 'malignity' . . . From the perspective of those responsible for discriminatory treatment, the persecution might in fact be motivated by an intention to confer a benefit.[32]

Thus the element of motivation has been interpreted very broadly. It amounts to the requirement that there is a connection between the grounds and the conduct.

15.4.2.3 Systematic conduct

The courts have emphasised that persecution also requires systematic targeting for a Convention reason. This is reinforced by section 91R of the *Migration Act 1958* (Cth), which, as noted above, expressly provides that persecution involves conduct that is systematic as well as discriminatory.

The relevant case law regarding the requirement of systematic conduct is summarised by Kenny J in *Roguinski v MIMA*:[33]

> The High Court discussed [the meaning of 'persecution'] in *Chan Yee Kin v Minister for Immigration and Ethnic Affairs* (1989) 169 CLR 379: see at 388–389 per Mason CJ; 399–400 per Dawson J; 416 per Gaudron J; 429–431 per McHugh J. At 429–430, McHugh J said:
>
>> The notion of persecution involves selective harassment. It is not necessary, however, that the conduct complained of should be directed against a person as an individual. He or she may be 'persecuted' because he or she is a member of a group which is the subject of systematic harassment . . . Nor is it a necessary element of 'persecution' that the individual should be the victim of a series of acts. A single act of oppression may suffice. As long as the person is threatened with harm and that harm can be seen as part of a course of systematic conduct directed for a Convention reason against that person as an individual or as a member of a class, he or she is 'being persecuted' for the purposes of the Convention. The threat need not be the product of any policy of the government of the person's country of nationality. It may be enough, depending on the circumstances, that the government has failed or

31 HCA 4 (24 February 1997).
32 [2004] HCA 25 (27 May 2004), [38].
33 *Roguinski v MIMA* [2001] FCA 1327 (17 September 2001), [24]–[25].

> is unable to protect the person in question from persecution . . . Moreover, to constitute 'persecution' the harm threatened need not be that of loss of life or liberty. Other forms of harm short of interference with life or liberty may constitute 'persecution' for the purposes of the Convention and Protocol. Measures 'in disregard' of human dignity may, in appropriate cases, constitute persecution. [Citations omitted.]

McHugh J elaborated on the meaning of the term 'systematic conduct' in *MIMA v Ibrahim*:

> It is an error to suggest that the use of the expression 'systematic conduct' in either *Murugasu* or *Chan* was intended to require, as a matter of law, that an applicant had to fear organised or methodical conduct, akin to the atrocities committed by the Nazis in the Second World War. Selective harassment, which discriminates against a person for a Convention reason, is inherent in the notion of persecution. Unsystematic or random acts are non-selective. It is therefore not a prerequisite to obtaining refugee status that a person fears being persecuted on a number of occasions or 'must show a series of coordinated acts directed at him or her which can be said to be not isolated but systematic'. . . The fear of a single act of harm done for a Convention reason will satisfy the Convention definition of persecution . . . if it is so oppressive that the individual cannot be expected to tolerate it so that refusal to return to the country of the applicant's nationality is the understandable choice of that person.[34] [Citations omitted.]

Thus the expression 'systematic conduct' is interpreted broadly. It does not necessarily refer to a series of acts, but can refer to 'non-random' acts or a single act of harm. Given this interpretation, it is doubtful whether anything is added to the concept of discrimination as elaborated upon above. Indeed, the term 'systematic' is effectively employed synonymously with the concept of discrimination.[35]

15.4.2.4 Causation

In addition to the above requirements, the phrase 'for reason of' expressly imports a causal connection between the Convention ground and the persecution feared by an asylum-seeker. Philosophically, the notion of causation is a complex one. The courts in other contexts have struggled, with little success, to develop a coherent and exhaustive test of causation. Refugee law is no exception to this. While the courts have at times focused on the meaning of this phrase, they have not provided useful guidance on the issue other than to note that a bare causal connection is not sufficient.[36]

The absence of a test for causation is expressly noted by Kirby J in *Chen Shi Hai v MIMA*:

> Causation bedevils the law in many of its aspects . . . The phrase in the Convention 'for reasons of' obviously imports certain notions of causation. There must be some relevant causal link between the postulated ground (membership of a 'particular social group') and the entitling condition ('well-founded fear of being persecuted'). The one

34 [2000] HCA 55, [99].
35 Germov and Motta, *Refugee Law in Australia*, p. 202.
36 *Jahazi v Minister for Immigration and Ethnic Affairs* (1995) 133 ALR 437.

must provide the reason for the other... Coincidence in time and circumstance will not alone be sufficient. The membership of a particular social group must precede the persecution and not solely be the result of it... Such membership is not a general 'catch-all' which obviates the necessity for all of the other specified Convention grounds. Obviously, however, persecution may later give an element of common identity and even cohesiveness to a 'particular social group', especially if they decide to resist the persecution, to seek solace in mutual support or to seek redress. But the 'group' is not a club or necessarily cohesive and identified to the public or to all persons affected by the same persecution. In some circumstances, self-identification with a 'group' could be extremely dangerous or even fatal for the persecuted.

The meaning of any statutory notion of causation depends upon the precise context in which the issue is presented... Providing that meaning will usually involve the decision-maker in introducing considerations of policy which cannot be reduced to a strictly logical deduction from word... Thus, in the field of torts law, the matter cannot be expressed as a simple formula. The 'but for' test, which was formerly much favoured by the common law, needs to be tempered by 'the infusion of policy considerations'... In the context of the expression 'for reasons of' in the Convention, it is neither practicable nor desirable to attempt to formulate 'rules' or 'principles' which can be substituted for the Convention language.

In the end it is necessary for the decision-maker to return to the broad expression of the Convention, avoiding the siren song of those who would offer suggested verbal equivalents. The decision-maker must evaluate the postulated connexion between the asserted fear of persecution and the ground suggested to give rise to that fear. The decision-maker must keep in mind the broad policy of the Convention and the inescapable fact that he or she is obliged to perform a task of classification. Quite simply, many acts lend themselves to ready assignment to different 'reasons'. Human conduct is rarely, if ever, uni-dimensional. In the present context this point was made neatly by Lord Hoffmann in his speech in *R v Immigration Appeal Tribunal; Ex parte Shah* by reference to some vivid contemporary illustrations:

> Suppose oneself in Germany in 1935. There is discrimination against Jews in general, but not all Jews are persecuted. Those who conform to the discriminatory laws, wear yellow stars out of doors and so forth can go about their ordinary business. But those who contravene the racial laws are persecuted. Are they being persecuted on grounds of race? In my opinion, they plainly are. It is therefore a fallacy to say that because not all members of a class are being persecuted, it follows that persecution of a few cannot be on grounds of membership of that class. Or to come nearer to the facts of the present case, suppose that the Nazi government in those early days did not actively organise violence against Jews, but pursued a policy of not giving any protection to Jews subjected to violence by neighbours. A Jewish shopkeeper is attacked by a gang organised by an Aryan competitor who smash his shop, beat him up and threaten to do it again if he remains in business. The competitor and his gang are motivated by business rivalry and a desire to settle old personal scores, but they would not have done what they did unless they knew that the authorities would allow them to act with impunity. And the ground upon which they enjoyed impunity was that the victim was a Jew. Is he being persecuted on grounds of race? Again, in my opinion, he is. An essential element in the persecution, the failure of the authorities to provide protection, is based upon race. It is true that one answer to the question 'Why was he attacked?' would be 'because a competitor wanted to drive him out of business'. But another answer, and in my view the right answer

> in the context of the Convention, would be 'he was attacked by a competitor who knew that he would receive no protection because he was a Jew'.[37]

As noted above, the causation test is supplemented by section 91R(1)(a) of the *Migration Act 1958* (Cth). The harm feared need not be *solely* attributable to a Convention reason. However, under section 91R(1)(a), where the harm feared is attributable to a number of motivations, it will be insufficient that a Convention ground or grounds constitute a minor or non-central motivation. To fall within Article 1A(2), a Convention ground or grounds must constitute at least the essential and significant reason or reasons for the persecution.

15.4.3 Prosecution and persecution distinction

15.4.3.1 States have unlimited power to prosecute citizens

There is an uneasy tension between the notion of persecution and prosecution. A basal aspect of state sovereignty is that states can pass laws of any nature, subject to the constitution of the state (which in any event can always be changed – with varying degrees of procedural difficulty). Thus in the Australian context it is widely agreed that a law prescribing that blue-eyed babies must be killed would be a valid exercise of law-making power.[38]

Given the breadth of law-making power it is permissible for nation states to pass laws restricting matters such as political and religious freedoms and imposing punishment on those who flout such laws. Laws aimed at limiting such freedoms do not necessarily constitute persecution – no matter how severe the sanction. This stems from the fact that no right is absolute and there is no such thing as a universal maximum limit on the severity of punishment for breaching a law – no matter how trivial the law may appear to be. Moreover, all nations have laws that to varying degrees curtail one's freedom to express one's political opinion or participate in political activities or act in accordance with one's religious convictions. This was a point expressly noted in *MIMA v Darboy*,[39] where the Federal Court referred to the following passage from the High Court's judgment in *Church of New Faith v The Commissioner of Pay-Roll Tax (Victoria)*:

> The freedom to act in accordance with one's religious beliefs is not as inviolate as the freedom to believe, for general laws to preserve and protect society are not defeated by a plea of religious obligation to breach them . . . Conduct in which a person engages in giving effect to his faith in the supernatural is religious, but it is excluded from the area of legal immunity marked out by the concept of religion if it offends against the ordinary laws, i.e. if it offends against laws which do not discriminate against religion generally

37 [2000] HCA 19 (13 April 2000) [67]–[69].
38 A.V. Dicey, *Introduction to the study of the Law of the Constitution* (1st edn, 1885), [80]. See also *British Rail Board v Pickin* [1974] AC 765, where the House of Lords stated that 'in the courts there may be argument as to the correct interpretation of the enactment; there must be none as to whether it should be on the statute books at all . . . The courts have no power to declare enacted law to be invalid.'
39 (1998) 931 FCA (6 August 1998).

> or against particular religions or against conduct of a kind which is characteristic only of a religion.[40]

Thus, in Australia, for instance, it is impermissible to express one's political allegiance by posting billboards in public places (without prior approval) or shouting one's political opinion at all hours; people convicted of certain offences are ineligible to run for political office; and Muslim males are prevented from having more than one wife at the same time. There are also a large number of laws that disproportionately adversely affect minority groups. A good recent example is the 'three strikes law' in the Northern Territory, which resulted in the incarceration of large numbers of Indigenous Australians for relatively minor offences.[41] The 'three strikes' laws in the United States have a similar effect on African-Americans.[42]

In principle, such laws are not different in nature from a law that, for example, imposes the death penalty on people who participate in political demonstrations. On its face, there is no question that such a law is a valid exercise of law-making power. Human rights advocates would obviously find the law offensive. However, probably no less offensive is the California 'three strikes' law that mandated a 25-year prison term for a person convicted of stealing a slice of pizza.[43] As noted earlier, the validity of a law mandating the death penalty for political protesters stems from the fact that there is no universal right to participate in political activities; nor is there a requirement that the severity of the sanction must correlate with the seriousness of the wrongdoing.

The capacity for states to criminalise any sort of behaviour, and the absence of any limits regarding the severity of sanctions that can be imposed for breaches of the criminal law, highlights the uncomfortable tension between persecution and prosecution. On the one hand, refugee status is meant to be accorded to individuals who are at risk of being unfairly harmed. On the other, a cardinal aspect of national sovereignty is that states are free to prosecute their citizens for whatever behaviour they deem blameworthy and in any manner they see fit.

The prosecution and persecution dilemma has occupied courts and academic commentators for several decades. A number of different tests have been advocated to demarcate the difference between prosecution and persecution. As a general rule, refugee status is only accorded where a person fears persecution, not prosecution. However, as is discussed below, it is often difficult to separate the two concepts. The general rule that prosecution claims do not meet the Convention definition of a refugee is noted in the UNHCR *Handbook on Procedures and Criteria for Determining Refugee Status*, which states:

40 *Church of New Faith v The Commissioner of Pay-Roll Tax (Victoria)* (1982–1983) 154 CLR 120, 135–136.

41 Pursuant to this legislative scheme, adults faced a mandatory 14 days imprisonment for a first property offence, 90 days for a second offence and 12 months where the offender had two or more prior property offences. The laws are now repealed: *Sentencing Amendment Act (No. 3) 2001* (NT).

42 See M. Bagaric, *Punishment and Sentencing: A Rational Approach* (London, Cavendish Publishing, 2001), Ch. 8.

43 See L. Stolzenberg and S.J. D'Alessio, 'Three Strikes and You're Out: The Impact of California's New Mandatory Sentencing Law on Serious Crime Rates', (1997) 43 *Crime and Delinquency* 457.

> Persecution must be distinguished from punishment for a common law offence. Persons fleeing from prosecution or punishment for such an offence are not normally refugees. It should be recalled that a refugee is a victim – or potential victim – of injustice, not a fugitive from justice.[44]

Hathaway makes a similar point with respect to refugee claims based on prosecution:

> Such claims are outside the scope of the Convention because the risk faced by the claimant is only the potential criminal liability of every citizen, and is therefore not linked to a form of civil or political status enumerated in the definition.[45]

15.4.3.2 Overlaps and tension: Prosecution and persecution

As noted by Plender, while persecution and prosecution are not coterminous, neither are they mutually exclusive.[46] Overlap between them is possible because a government with persecutory intent can use the criminal law as a means of persecuting people.[47] Generally, there is little difficulty distinguishing between prosecution and persecution where the effective trigger on the *face* of a criminal proscription is Convention-related. Thus, laws imposing punishment on people of a particular race for engaging in freedoms (such as opening a business) that are available to the rest of the community, or which make it an offence to engage in political dialogue or prohibit displays of religious observance are often persecutory.[48]

However, in many cases persecution is more subtle. Possible examples are laws that impose prison terms upon people who engage in political advertising only on election day, or open up their business on a religious holiday. In such cases, as is discussed below, detailed analysis of the laws and their enforcement is necessary to determine whether they are persecutory. Unfortunately, given the uncertainty of the legal principles that distinguish between persecution and prosecution, it is often difficult to find a clear answer in such cases.

Refugee claims based on fear of prosecution have inconsistent outcomes as decision-makers struggle to distinguish between criminal and political actions. Where a claim is premised on the commission of a political offence, it is essential that decision-makers understand the context in which the offence took place. Deficiencies in much of the case law are summed up best by Aleinikoff's pointed observation that 'playing the "prosecution not persecution" card is a conclusory conversation stopper: it substitutes a slogan for analysis'.[49]

44 Paragraph 56.
45 Hathaway, *The Law of Refugee Status*, p. 169.
46 R. Plender, 'Admission of Refugees', (1977) 15 *San Diego Law Review* 45, 54.
47 Goodwin-Gill, *The Refugee in International Law*, p. 10.
48 However, as is discussed below, this is not necessarily the case.
49 See www.refugee.org.nz/ChapterOne.htm#N-7.

Existing case law suggests that three factors are normally considered when making a decision:

(i) whether the law in question is a law of *general application*;
(ii) if it is a law of general application, whether it is *applied and/or enforced* in a discriminatory way; and
(iii) if the law targets only certain people or groups, whether the law has a *legitimate* objective and is *appropriate and adapted* to achieving the objective (this we term the 'legitimate purpose and appropriate and adapted' test).[50]

Application of these considerations often leads to inconsistent or unjust outcomes. We now discuss these considerations in greater detail.

15.4.3.3 What is a law of general application?

It is sometimes unclear whether or not a law is of general application. Courts have stated that determining this depends upon identifying those members of the population to whom the law applies.[51]

15.4.3.4 General laws not persecutory

In *Applicant A*, McHugh J stated that 'the enforcement of a generally applicable law (criminal or otherwise) does not ordinarily constitute persecution'.[52] Moreover, laws of general application do not amount to 'persecution' under the Convention simply because an accepting country may disagree with those laws.

In *Chen Shi Hai v MIMA* it was noted:

> Laws or policies which target or apply only to a particular section of the population are not properly described as laws or policies of general application. Certainly, laws which target or impact adversely upon a particular class or group – for example, 'black children' as distinct from children generally – cannot properly be described in that way. Further and notwithstanding what was said by Dawson J in *Applicant A*, the fact that laws are of general application is more directly relevant to the question of persecution than to the question [of] whether a person is a member of a particular social group. In *Applicant A*, McHugh J pointed out that '[w]hether or not conduct constitutes persecution in the Convention sense does not depend on the nature of the conduct [but] . . . on whether it discriminates against a person because of race, religion, nationality, political opinion or membership of a social group' . . . In that context, his Honour also pointed out that 'enforcement of a generally applicable criminal law does not ordinarily constitute persecution' . . . That is because enforcement of a law of that kind does not ordinarily constitute discrimination . . . To say that, ordinarily, a law of

50 Similar principles apply in the United States. It has been noted that the 'fact that an applicant has been subjected to criminal prosecution can support an asylum claim' where the punishment is imposed without judicial process. See *Blanco-Lopez v INS*, 858 F.2 d 531 (9th Cir. 1988) (when a government harms or punishes someone without undertaking formal prosecutorial measures, it engages in persecution, not legitimate prosecution); where the punishment is excessive in the context of the accepted norms of civilised society, violates internationally accepted norms, or is disproportionate to the crime alleged, see *Ramirez-Rivas v INS*, 899 F.2 d 864 (9th Cir. 1990) (even punishment of persons who are actually guilty of criminal acts amounts to persecution if the punishment is excessive and arbitrary [extrajudicial]); or the punishment is a pretext, actually imposed not for the alleged crime, but to punish the individual because of race, religion, nationality, membership in a particular social group, or political opinion: INS Law Manual, *supra*, at 23. See also *Hernandez-Montiel v INS*, 225 F.3 d 1084 (9th Cir. 2000).

51 See *Weheliye v MIMA* [2001] FCA 1222 (31 August 2001), [50].

52 [1997] HCA 4 (24 February 1997).

> general application is not discriminatory is not to deny that general laws, which are apparently non-discriminatory, may impact differently on different people and, thus, operate discriminatorily. Nor is it to overlook the possibility that selective enforcement of a law of general application may result in discrimination. As a general rule, however, a law of general application is not discriminatory . . . And *Applicant A* held that, merely because some people disagree with a law of that kind and fear the consequences of their failure to abide by that law, they do not, on that account, constitute a social group for the purposes of the Convention.[53]

While selective enforcement of a law of general application may constitute persecution, grossly disproportionate punishment does not normally constitute persecution. In *Lama v MIMA*[54] it was noted that:

> There is no selective harassment to be found in the punishment imposed by the . . . authorities, even though viewed through Australian eyes the punishment may appear grossly disproportionate to the crime. The question to be addressed is not whether the law is inappropriate or inconsistent with Australian policy but rather whether the operation of the law gives rise to selective harassment for a Convention reason.

Thus the doctrine of 'law of general application' has been invoked by the courts as a guide, rather than a definitive test, to distinguish between prosecution and persecution. If a law is expressed generally, it may be necessary to look beyond that law to see whether the law itself is in reality discriminatory in its intent or whether it has a discriminatory impact on members of a group recognised under the Convention.

It is unclear whether the law of general application test focuses solely on the form of the law (in which case the selective enforcement test – see below – is not part of the test) or whether it focuses on the practical effect of the law – in which case the next consideration discussed below is in reality part of this test. However, for reasons that we now discuss, this issue is probably a moot one.

At this point, it is instructive to note that the relevance of the notion of a law of general application has been disputed by some commentators. Germov and Motta, in the context of noting the inadequacy of the law of general application standard, state:

> The difficulty stems from the simple characterisation of . . . laws as being of general application. In a sense all laws discriminate, namely against those who commit acts contrary to their stated purposes. Thus all criminal laws are so characterised. But these too 'discriminate', as they only apply to those who transgress their terms. Up until such time as a person breaches a criminal law, the law does not operate against them – and hence such laws never operate against a vast portion of the population who are not in the habit of committing crimes. But this does not mean that merely because the law is said to apply universally within a state . . . such a law cannot be discriminatory . . . This creates somewhat of a conundrum – to merely characterise a law as being of general application requires a lack of inquiry on the part of the decision-maker, and, in a sense, an acceptance of a value judgment that the law is neutral in its intention. But this

53 *Chen Shi Hai v MIMA* [2000] HCA 19 (13 April 2000), [21].
54 *Lama v MIMA* [1999] FCA 918 (8 July 1999), [30].

> represents a gloss on what may be the true purpose of such a law. In this regard, perhaps the only way to reconcile this conundrum in terms of the requirements of the Convention is to assess whether the law in fact serves a legitimate purpose: that is, does it target an already existing particular social group or target persons for other Convention reasons, or does it create the group against whom it simultaneously inflicts harm and in this sense is legitimately a law of general application that therefore falls outside the Convention . . . This analysis might appear like the ultimate form of cultural imperialism – the imposition of Western European standards on all countries regardless of culture, religion etc, however if human rights standards are to possess any efficacy there must be a bottom line concerning the rights that are considered as protected and which should be respected by all nations.[55]

15.4.3.5 Selective enforcement of a law of general application

As noted above, selective enforcement of a law of general application can constitute persecution. This matter is clarified by Gleeson CJ, Gummow and Kirby JJ in *Applicant S v Minister for Immigration and Multicultural Affairs*:

> Further, what was said in *Israelian does not establish a rule that the implementation of laws of general application can never amount to persecution*. It could scarcely be so given the history of the Nuremberg Laws against the Jews enacted by Nazi Germany which preceded, and help to explain, the purposes of the Refugees Convention. Rather, the Court majority determined that, on the facts of that case, it had been open to the Tribunal to conclude that the implementation by Armenia of its laws of general application was not capable of resulting in discriminatory treatment. *A law of general application is capable of being implemented or enforced in a discriminatory manner*.[56] [Emphasis added.]

Thus selective prosecutions, or the imposition of punishments greater than they would otherwise have been, for a Convention reason, would make enforcement by a country of one of its prohibitory criminal laws of general application persecution for a Convention reason.

The concept of discrimination is elaborated below. However, for present purposes it is relevant to note that the above two tests are no more than an application of principles that are normally regarded as being part of the concept of discrimination. A law can discriminate in two ways: directly or indirectly. The adoption of the law of general application test as a formal standard is in reality no more than a statement of the fact that laws that are neutral on their face do not normally constitute persecution. In this sense, 'neutral on its face' means that, according to the relevant criteria stipulated by the Convention definition, the law is non-offensive. A law is neutral on its face in this regard if it does not select one of the Convention grounds as being the trigger for the additional burden. Thus, a law of general application is simply one that in form does not subject people to the risk of serious harm for a Convention reason. In the language of discrimination law, it is a law that does not constitute direct discrimination. Selective enforcement of a law of general application equates to the concept of indirect or substantive

55 Germov and Motta, *Refugee Law in Australia*, p. 240.
56 [2004] HCA 25 (27 May 2004), [42]–[44].

discrimination. The test of whether the law is applied and/or enforced in a discriminatory manner means no more than that laws which are neutral on their face can nevertheless result in persecution if in substance they target people for a Convention reason or disproportionately impact[57] on people for a Convention reason.

15.4.3.6 The 'legitimate objective and appropriate and adapted' test

In some circumstances, a law that appears to discriminate (either on its face or as a result of the manner in which it is enforced) for a Convention reason does not constitute persecution. This is so where the law and its enforcement have a legitimate objective and the means chosen to achieve the objective are appropriate and adapted to achieve that objective. Gleeson CJ, Gummow and Kirby JJ, in *Applicant S v Minister for Immigration and Multicultural Affairs*, stated:

> The criteria for the determination of whether a law or policy that results in discriminatory treatment actually amounts to persecution were articulated by McHugh J in *Applicant A*. His Honour said that the question of whether the discriminatory treatment of persons of a particular race, religion, nationality or political persuasion or who are members of a particular social group constitutes persecution for that reason ultimately depends on whether that treatment is 'appropriate and adapted to achieving some legitimate object of the country [concerned]'. These criteria were accepted in the joint judgment of Gleeson CJ, Gaudron, Gummow and Hayne JJ in *Chen*. As a matter of law to be applied in Australia, they are to be taken as settled. This is what underlay the Court's decision in *Israelian*. Namely, that enforcement of the law of general application in that particular case was appropriate and adapted to achieving a legitimate national objective. [References omitted, emphasis added.][58]

More insight into when a law is appropriate and adapted to achieving a legitimate objective is provided by McHugh J in *Applicant A*:

> Conduct will not constitute persecution . . . if it is appropriate and adapted to achieving some legitimate object of the country of the refugee. A legitimate object will ordinarily be an object whose pursuit is required in order to protect or promote the general welfare of the State and its citizens. The enforcement of a generally applicable criminal law does not ordinarily constitute persecution. Nor is the enforcement of laws designed to protect the general welfare of the State ordinarily persecutory *even though the laws may place additional burdens on the members of a particular race, religion or nationality or social group*. Thus, a law providing for the detention of the members of a particular race engaged in a civil war may not amount to persecution even though that law affects only members of that race.[59] [Emphasis added.]

However, laws or actions stemming from considerations such as state security concerns do not provide an automatic exception to the Convention. As Germov and Motta note, 'such acts do not excuse examination as to whether they serve

57 The premise that disproportionate impact of a law can constitute persecution is examined below.
58 [2004] HCA 25 (27 May 2004), [42]–[44].
59 *Applicant A v MIEA* [1997] HCA 4 (24 February 1997).

merely as a pretext for targeting individuals or groups for harm for a Convention reason'.[60]

In *Applicant A*, McHugh J further stated:

> [W]here a racial, religious, national group or the holder of a particular political opinion is the subject of sanctions that do not apply generally in the State, it is more likely than not that the application of the sanction is discriminatory and persecutory. It is therefore inherently suspect and requires close scrutiny. In cases coming within the categories of race, religion and nationality, decision-makers should ordinarily have little difficulty in determining whether a sanction constitutes persecution of persons in the relevant category. Only in exceptional cases is it likely that a sanction aimed at persons for reasons of race, religion or nationality will be an appropriate means for achieving a legitimate government object and not amount to persecution.
>
> In cases concerned with political opinion and the membership of particular social groups, the issue of persecution may often be difficult to resolve when the sanctions arise from the proper application of enacted laws. Punishment for expressing ordinary political opinions or being a member of a political association or trade union is prima facie persecution for a Convention reason. Nevertheless, governments cannot be expected to tolerate political opinion or conduct that calls for their violent overthrow. Punishment for expressing such opinions is unlikely to amount to persecution. Nevertheless, even in these cases, punishment of the holders of the opinions may amount to persecution. It will certainly do so when the government in question is so repressive that, *by the standards of the civilised world*, it has so little legitimacy that its overthrow even by violent means is justified. One who fled from the regime of Hitler or Pol Pot could not be denied the status of refugee even if his or her only claim to that status relied on a fear of persecution for advocating the violent overthrow of that regime.[61] [Emphasis added.]

Thus where a law appears to discriminate for a Convention reason it is necessary to examine the circumstances to decide if either the law or its enforcement has a legitimate objective and whether it is appropriate and adapted to achieving that objective.

The legitimate purpose and appropriate and adapted test is invoked when a law, directly or indirectly, targets a person for a Convention reason. This test can be applied to save laws that discriminate for a Convention reason on their face or have the practical effect of doing so.

The main difficulty with the legitimate purpose and appropriate and adapted test is the uncertainty surrounding the meaning of several key terms. As discussed

60 Germov and Motta, *Refugee Law in Australia*, p. 235.

61 ibid., pp. 259–60. This approach was adopted more recently by McHugh and Kirby JJ in *Appellant S395/2002 v MIMA* [2003] HCA 71 (9 December 2003), [45], where in the context of a particular social group (homosexuality) claim, they stated 'if a person claims refugee status on the ground that the law of the country of his or her nationality penalises homosexual conduct, two questions always arise. First, is there a real chance that the applicant will be prosecuted if returned to the country of nationality? Second, are the prosecution and the potential penalty appropriate and adapted to achieving a legitimate object of the country of nationality? In determining whether the prosecution and penalty can be classified as a legitimate object of that country, international human rights standards as well as the laws and culture of the country are relevant matters. If the first of these questions is answered: Yes, and the second: No, the claim of refugee status must be upheld even if the applicant has conducted him or herself in a way that is likely to attract prosecution.'

below, phrases such as 'the standards of civilised society' and 'common humanity' do not provide meaningful guidance.[62]

15.4.4 Unsatisfactory state of existing law regarding nexus elements

Clearly, the concept of persecution is multifaceted. According to existing case law there are several essential defining elements of persecution. These elements include systematic and discriminatory conduct, motivation and a causal nexus between the harm and the grounds. Statutory requirements entrench the requirement that prosecution involves systematic and discriminatory conduct, and underline the fact that the causal connection between the grounds and the harm is such that a Convention ground must be the main reason for the harm. In addition, where the conduct stems from the application of a legal standard it is necessary to ascertain whether the law has a legitimate objective and is appropriate and adapted to achieving that objective.

The tests that have been developed for persecution are unsatisfactory. There is considerable uncertainty regarding its scope and meaning. This is not surprising, as many of the elements overlap, are poorly defined, and in some cases are simply obsolete.

The requirement that persecutory conduct be systematic – interpreted as non-random – lacks substance as a means for distinguishing persecution from forms of harm that do not constitute persecution. The only form of harm that it may exclude is accidental harm. Moreover, any form of harm that satisfies the 'for reasons of' requirement cannot possibly be random. The motivation requirement suffers from the same defect. Given that relevant motivations include acts of cruelty and kindness, one has exhausted most of the range of human motivations. Thus if harm is 'for reason of' a Convention ground, it cannot be as a result of an irrelevant motivation. The motivation requirement is redundant.

The overlap between the elements of persecution has resulted in only the loosest of distinctions being made between these elements. Indeed, at times they have been used as synonyms. As is noted by Germov and Motta:

> The High Court has frequently used the adjective 'discriminatory', 'selective' and 'systematic' to differentiate 'random' or 'non-discriminatory' harm from 'persecution' for the purposes of the Refugees Convention. They underscore the necessity for there to be the requisite 'nexus' – expressed by the phrase 'for reasons of' – between the harm feared and a ground mentioned in the Convention definition before the harm feared satisfies the requirement of 'persecution' for Convention purposes.[63]

62 For a recent discussion of the test, see *Minister for Immigration and Citizenship v SZNWC* [2010] FCAFC 157.

63 Germov and Motta, *Refugee Law in Australia*, p. 198. They have also stated that the notion of a motivation does not add anything to the context of persecution. This is particularly so because motivation does not always involve an element of antipathy of malice.

In our view, Germov and Motta touch on an important point here: that the requisite connection between the harm and the grounds is underpinned by a unifying concept that has not been expressly and clearly articulated by the courts. There is a single concept that, when fully understood, underlies this nexus. It is the concept of discrimination. Properly understood and applied it can make this area of the law coherent, and render the other elements constituting the nexus unnecessary. The notion of discrimination is also a means through which this area of law can be interpreted in its most favourable light from the point of view of asylum-seekers, thereby injecting principle and certainty into the law.

Discrimination as the sole criterion for the nexus between the harm and the Convention grounds can distinguish between prosecution and persecution and, in the process, make tests that have been developed in relation to this issue (that is, the law of general application and the legitimate and appropriate and adapted test) redundant. This is especially so in cases where harm is sanctioned by a law of a state. The reform proposal in the next section most pointedly applies to such situations. Its relevance to other forms of persecution – that is, where the conduct is not sanctioned by the manner in which a law is drafted or interpreted – is discussed in section 15.4.7.

15.4.5 A new unifying understanding: Discrimination as the touchstone where persecution stems from the operation or application of a law

15.4.5.1 The nature of discrimination

Discrimination is a universal concept.[64] The principle requires that like cases should not be treated differently and unlike cases must not be treated alike unless objectively justified. In essence, to discriminate is to treat people differently when they are similar in relevant respects, or to treat them similarly when they are different in relevant respects. That is, to discriminate is to treat someone differently without a relevant basis for that difference.[65]

In *Street v Queensland Bar Association*, Gaudron J stated:

> Although in its primary sense 'discrimination' refers to the process of differentiating between persons or things possessing different properties, in legal usage it signifies the

64 In this sense we are obviously referring to its meaning in a pejorative sense. The other sense of the word was noted by the High Court in *IW v City of Perth* [1997] HCA 30 (31 July 1997) 1, which made the following observations regarding the meaning of discrimination: '"Discrimination", as a matter of ordinary English, has quite distinct shades of meaning. Some of these lack the critical if not pejorative connotation the term has in human rights legislation. Thus, "discrimination" may identify the ability to observe accurately and make fine distinctions with acuity, good judgment or taste, as well as the making of unjust or prejudicial distinctions.'

65 A.F. Bayefsky, 'The Principle of Equality of Non-Discrimination in International Law', (1990) 11 *HRLJ* 1. In the Australian context the same definition has been adopted: see, for example, *Castlemaine Tooheys Ltd v South Australia* (1990) 169 CLR 436, 480, below. See also L. Katzner, 'Is the Favouring of Women and Blacks in Employment and Educational Opportunities Justified?', in J. Feinberg and H. Gross (eds), *Philosophy of Law* (4th edn) (Belmont CA, Wadsworth, 1991), p. 468.

> process by which different treatment is accorded to persons or things by reference to considerations which are irrelevant to the object to be attained.[66]

In *Castlemaine Tooheys Ltd v South Australia*, Gaudron and McHugh JJ stated:

> The essence of the legal notion of discrimination lies in the unequal treatment of equals, and, conversely, in the equal treatment of unequals.[67]

In the context of refugee law it is clear that the sort of discrimination that is prohibited is discrimination in terms of the Convention grounds. This is a point noted by Germov and Motta, who state that discriminatory conduct (in the context of refugee law) 'is the treatment of an individual differently on the basis of criteria that are not legitimate; in the case of the Refugees Convention, this means one of the reasons listed in the Convention definition'.[68] Thus a law discriminates (at least *prima facie*) for a Convention reason (directly or indirectly) where it operates disproportionately against people for a Convention reason. It will be discriminatory where it imposes additional burdens on people from particular races, nationalities, religions or political backgrounds or from particular social groups.

As noted above, discrimination can be direct or indirect. Direct discrimination is the easiest to identify. It occurs when the law or policy expressly applies only to a particular group. An example is a law prohibiting (only) black people from entering a park. Indirect discrimination occurs when the law or policy is neutral on its face, but in substance disproportionately excludes groups from enjoying certain advantages or imposes disadvantages on them.[69] For example, a law stating that 'pet owners are not permitted in parks' is neutral on its face, but indirectly discriminates if only one group in the community happens to be pet

66 The High Court in *IW v City of Perth* [1997] HCA 30 (31 July 1997) 1 made the following additional observations regarding the meaning of 'discrimination': 'In Australia, discrimination is also a constitutional concept. The terms "discriminate" or "discrimination" appear in various provisions of the Constitution, notably ss 51(ii), 102 and 117. Section 117 states: "A subject of the Queen, resident in any State, shall not be subject in any other State to any disability or discrimination which would not be equally applicable to him if he were a subject of the Queen resident in such other State." Section 51(ii) authorises the making of laws with respect to taxation "but so as not to discriminate between States or parts of States".' In *Street v Queensland Bar Association*, when dealing with s 117, Gaudron J said: 'Although in its primary sense "discrimination" refers to the process of differentiating between persons or things possessing different properties, in legal usage it signifies the process by which different treatment is accorded to persons or things by reference to considerations which are irrelevant to the object to be attained. The primary sense of the word is "discrimination between"; the legal sense is "discrimination against".' Further, in *Castlemaine Tooheys Ltd v South Australia*, a case concerned with the application of s 92 of the Constitution after *Cole v Whitfield*, Gaudron and McHugh JJ said: 'A law is discriminatory if it operates by reference to a distinction which some overriding law decrees to be irrelevant or by reference to a distinction which is in fact irrelevant to the object to be attained; a law is discriminatory if, although it operates by reference to a relevant distinction, the different treatment thereby assigned is not appropriate and adapted to the difference or differences which support that distinction. A law is also discriminatory if, although there is a relevant difference, it proceeds as though there is no such difference, or, in other words, if it treats equally things that are unequal – unless, perhaps, there is no practical basis for differentiation.' This passage deals with species of discrimination which elsewhere have been identified as 'direct' and 'indirect' discrimination. The succinct terms by which the fundamental precepts are explained in this passage have been eschewed by legislatures when framing human rights legislation (such as the Act). Language which is both complex and obscure and productive of further disputation has been employed.

67 (1990) 169 CLR 436, [8].

68 Germov and Motta, *Refugee Law in Australia*, p. 201.

69 S. Prechal, 'Combating Indirect Discrimination in the Community Law Context', [1993] *LIEI* 81, 83–4.

owners. This is a point also noted by the High Court. In *Street v Queensland Bar Association*, McHugh J stated:

> Not only can discrimination arise from the factual operation of the law; but it can arise just as readily from a law which treats as equals those who are different as it can from a law which treats differently those whose circumstances are not manifestly different.

It is important to note that there is no discrimination where there is a 'relevant basis' for marking out people for extra burdens. This underlines a fundamental aspect of the notion of discrimination and its logical converse, the notion of equality. The fact that different treatment alone does not constitute discrimination is a point that has been expressly noted by Gaudron J in *Street*: 'the primary sense of the word discrimination is "discrimination between"; the legal sense is "discrimination against"'.[70]

In refugee law, it is unclear in what sense of the term discrimination has been used. However, in this context, given that the concept has not been analysed in depth and the reliance by courts on concepts that inhere in the concept of discrimination, it is almost certain that it means 'discrimination between'.[71] In this sense, to discriminate means simply to treat someone differently (that is, to subject them to serious harm) for a Convention reason. Irrespective of the meaning that is currently attributed to discrimination in refugee law, a proper understanding of the term and application of it to refugee law makes the other elements of persecution superfluous. This argument is now developed in the context of articulating a test for determining the difference between prosecution and persecution.

15.4.5.2 Statement of the new test for the requisite nexus between the grounds and the harm

The starting point here is acknowledging that laws that inflict serious harm for a Convention reason are persecutory. The second point is that a law can target a person for a Convention reason in one of two ways. It can do so by adverting to the Convention reason on the face of the law or it can do so indirectly, by targeting people for a Convention reason as a result of the manner in which the law is applied.

Schematically, these premises can be laid out as follows:

(1) Does the law on its face impose an additional burden for a Convention reason?

(2) If the answer is 'no', it is necessary to examine if the practical effect of the law is to impose an additional burden on people for a Convention reason, either because the law selectively targets people for a Convention ground or because it operates disproportionately against people for a Convention ground.

(3) If the answer to both questions is 'no', the law does not constitute persecution.

70 *Street v Queensland Bar Association* [1989] HCA 53 (16 November 1989).

71 The one notable exception is in *MIMA v Ibrahim* [2000] HCA 55 (16 November 2000) at paras 29–30, per Gaudron J.

(4) If the answer to question 1 or 2 is 'yes', then the law will constitute persecution unless there is a relevant basis for causing serious harm to people for a Convention reason.

15.4.5.3 The notion of a relevant difference

Step 4 in the above list is the most complex. The notion of what constitutes a relevant difference has not been directly addressed, let alone settled, by the courts. A relatively uncontroversial aspect of the notion is that there must be a 'universal' reason for any permissible discrimination.[72] Wider moral theory informs us regarding what such a reason would be.[73]

According to Hayek:

> The requirement that the rules of true law be general does not mean that sometimes special rules may not apply to different classes of people if they refer to properties that only some people possess. Such distinctions will not be arbitrary, will not subject one group to the will of others, if they are recognised as justified by those inside and those outside the group . . . This does not mean that there must be unanimity as to the desirability of the distinction, but merely that individual views will not depend on whether the individual is in the group or not. So long as, for instance, the distinction is favoured by the majority both inside and outside the group, there is a strong presumption that it serves the ends of both. When, however, only those inside the group favour the distinction, it is clearly privilege; while if only those outside favour it, it is discrimination.[74]

As a crude guide to what constitutes a relevant distinction, Hayek's test has considerable merit. The most appealing aspects of it are that majoritism (both within and outside a group) is generally relatively easy to measure; and that it reflects the idea that our, even unreflective, moral notions are often correct. However, it cannot serve as the ultimate standard regarding the soundness of a relevant difference. People are not always good judges regarding whether an activity or proposal is in their self-interest, and morality is ultimately not a popularity contest. The ultimate test of what constitutes a legitimate interest must be informed by the moral theory that applies to govern all conduct. Previously, it has been argued that the most sound theory of morality is utilitarianism.[75] It follows that in relation to conferring benefits and burdens, a legitimate relevant difference is one that will serve to best promote net happiness. Rights-based theorists would

72 See J. Waldron, *The Law* (New York, Routledge, 1997), pp. 43–44. A judgment is universalisable if the acceptance of it in a particular situation entails that one is logically committed to accepting the same judgment in all other situations, unless there is a relevant difference. To state that moral judgments are universal entails that whenever one judges a certain action or thing (situation) as having a particular moral status, then one is logically committed to the same judgment about any *relevantly* similar action or situation. In this regard numerical differences are irrelevant. This refers to specific descriptions of the person, relation or situation. Thus the fact that a judgment relates to a particular person (such as John Smith), place (such as Melbourne), or relation (John's mother) is irrelevant. Also irrelevant are generic differences; tastes, preferences and desires. Likewise, whether a person is rich, poor or middle-class should not impact on the rights and protections that are bestowed on that person: J.L. Mackie, *Ethics: Inventing Right and Wrong* (New York, Viking Press, 1977), pp. 83–102.
73 Mackie, *Ethics: Inventing Right and Wrong*.
74 *Constitution of Liberty* (Chicago, University of Chicago Press, 1960), p. 154.
75 See, further, Chapter 18.

argue, no doubt, that a relevant difference is one that serves to promote the recognition of human rights. Irrespective of how the concept of relevant difference is defined, the important point to note for the purposes of this discussion is that the concept is universalisable and must be informed by the moral theory to which one subscribes. Given the large degree of overlap between rights-based theories and utilitarianism, in terms of the ultimate interests which are accorded to people,[76] it is doubtful whether the application of the relevant difference test from the respective perspectives would yield meaningfully different outcomes.

The ultimate question in this regard is when will a law which targets people for a Convention reason not be persecutory because there is a relevant reason for targeting such people? In the context of refugee law the notion of a relevant difference is complicated further by the concept of state sovereignty.

In order to advance this issue, a starting point is to consider what the case law offers on this matter. As noted above, the courts have not directly canvassed the issue of relevant difference – especially in the context of refugee law. However, the same notion has been discussed under the pretext of another doctrine: the legitimate objective and appropriate and adapted test.

15.4.5.4 The legitimate objective and appropriate and adapted test as a synonym for relevant difference

A full understanding of the meaning of discrimination reveals that the 'legitimate objective and appropriate and adopted' criterion is already incorporated within this notion. There will be no discrimination where there is a relevant reason for the different treatment, and a relevant reason will always exist where the law has a legitimate objective and is appropriate and adapted to achieving this. Thus a full understanding of the concept of discrimination requires one to consider not only if the law treats people differently but whether there is a relevant reason (that is, a justification) for this. The notions of relevant reason and the legitimacy/appropriate and adapted criteria are effectively synonymous.

The notion of legitimacy so far as the objectives that a nation state can pursue is ostensibly inimical to the concept of state sovereignty. As noted earlier, the law-making power of a state is plenary. Laws do not require a certain moral content to be valid. Despite this, in the context of refugee law, courts cannot avoid the issue of passing judgment on the legitimacy of law. The humanitarian objectives of the Convention compel such an analysis. This is made more palatable by the realisation that such analysis does not purport to impugn the validity of a law, although a finding that a law is persecutory can cast a pejorative spectre over the legal system of the violating country. Further, it is not the case that the interests protected by the Convention are absolute. Nation states are right to place fetters on, for example, the freedom to express one's political opinion, otherwise citizens would be entitled to express their political opinion by painting graffiti on private

76 See M. Bagaric, 'In Defence of a Utilitarian Theory of Punishment: Punishing the Innocent and the Compatibility of Utilitarianism and Rights', (1999) 24 *Australian Journal of Legal Philosophy* 95.

property and playing loud political messages or songs at all hours of the day and night.

In order to define legitimate state objectives, it may be best to start with a definition of illegitimate state objectives. Illegitimate objectives that stem from the Convention are obviously those that directly flout its terms and have no other purpose. Thus, laws will be illegitimate where they, for example, *aim* to suppress political opinion by inflicting serious harm on people and have no 'proper' rationale. In terms of identifying other illegitimate objectives, the starting point is to note that, given the diversity of human interests, the richness of human culture and the considerable weight that any moral theory must accord to (individual and group) liberty, a law can be improper only if it violates a fundamental norm. As noted in the above discussion of serious harm, the most important moral norm and the most basic human interest is the right to life. Thus a law or practice that has as its objective to destroy human life would be illegitimate. Beyond this, it can be argued that any other forms of interference with human interests that are invariably destructive of the human capacity to subsist would also be illegitimate.

Given the few limits that follow from the legitimacy objective, the appropriate and adapted test assumes extra importance in the context of laws that potentially subject people to serious harm. The essence of this requirement is embodied in the concept of proportionality.[77] The principle of proportionality is most prominent in the area of sentencing law. In its crudest and most persuasive form it is the view that the punishment should equal the crime. The proportionality principle strikes a strong intuitive chord, and probably for this reason is embodied not only in sentencing law, but also in many other areas of the law. As Fox notes, the notion that the response must be commensurate with the harm caused, or sought to be prevented, is at the core of the criminal defences of self-defence and provocation. It is also at the foundation of civil law damages for injury or death, which aim to compensate for the actual loss suffered, and equitable remedies, which are proportional to the detriment sought to be avoided.[78]

The focus in the context of refugee law should be on the types of harm that nation states should not be permitted to inflict on their citizens. In *Chen Shi Hai v MIMA* the High Court stated:

> Whether the different treatment of different individuals or groups is appropriate and adapted to achieving some legitimate government object depends on the different treatment involved and, ultimately, whether it offends the *standards of civilised societies* which seek to meet the calls of *common humanity*. Ordinarily, *denial of access to food, shelter, medical treatment and, in the case of children, denial of an opportunity to obtain an education, involve such a significant departure from the standards of the*

77 See *Castlemaine Tooheys Ltd v South Australia* [1990] HCA 1 (7 February 1990).

78 R.G. Fox, 'The Meaning of Proportionality in Sentencing', (1994) 19 *Melbourne University Law Review* 489.

> *civilized world as to constitute persecution*. And that is so even if the different treatment involved is undertaken for the purpose of achieving some legitimate national objective.[79] [Emphasis added.]

The concept of basic human needs is one that in our view merits some development. As noted in the above discussion of serious harm, in the hierarchy of human interests the most basic element is need, in the form of the conditions that are necessary for subsistence, and this should be the focus of the Refugee Convention. And, in considering the conditions that are necessary for human subsistence, there is little scope for debate – it is a matter of science, not sociology. Humans need food, water, shelter and clothing to survive. All other interests are contingent on the availability of these basic goods. Displaced persons who lack any of these goods to a point where it threatens their survival should be accorded refugee status. These interests aside, the other interests that merit protection are the right to liberty and physical integrity.

Thus in our view, measures that encroach on a person's capacity to subsist will normally violate the 'appropriate and adapted' requirement. It would be rare that a state objective is so important that placing the lives of citizens in peril is a proportionate and measured response to achieving the objective. In applying this standard, the other aspect of the proportionality test must also be applied. Thus harsher forms of treatment can be imposed on citizens where the harm sought to be prevented or the good that is pursued is high. This means that a law that prescribes mandatory life imprisonment for people who express their political opinion by carrying banners in the streets constitutes persecution, but the same punishment for people who express their political opinion by burning down the houses of their opponents may not be persecution.

15.4.6 A new test or unification of previous principles?

It is important to note that the approach suggested above does not involve a fundamental reinterpretation of 'persecution'. Rather it explains and unifies the meaning of 'persecution'. There are relatively few practical changes to the existing law that would flow from the proposed approach. As noted above, many of the existing aspects of persecution (such as causation and the legitimate and appropriate and adapted test) are already incorporated into the proposed model.

One change that at least ostensibly would follow from the proposed approach is that persecution would occur where a law disproportionately impacts on people of a certain race or ethnicity, or who belong to a particular social group or hold a certain political opinion, or who adhere to a certain religion. There is no requirement that the harm imposed should selectively target such people. This is not, however, a disadvantage of the suggested approach. There are several reasons for this.

79 *Chen Shi Hai v MIMA* [2000] HCA (13 April 2000).

First, as noted by Hathaway, it is notoriously difficult to ascertain the purpose for which a law is enacted and hence it is often meaningless to ask whether a law actually systematically targets a person. In nations with well-developed institutions of government, there is some scope for trawling through government debates to ascertain the objective of legislation. However, even in nations such as Australia, it has been suggested that the concept of coherent legislative intent is artificial.[80] Such difficulties are compounded many times over in relation to countries from which refugees most commonly originate. In most cases, they are third world countries where there are negligible opportunities for obtaining credible or cogent evidence regarding the objective of a law.

Moreover, the concept of discrimination inherently involves motivation and targeting. In this context, this is an objective test. Kirby J, in the context of discussing the meaning of 'discrimination' pursuant to the *Equal Opportunity Act 1984* (WA) in *IW v City of Perth*, noted:

> Against this background, it is unsurprising that the weight of authority supports the proposition that it is unnecessary for a complainant to show that the alleged discriminator intended to discriminate or set out with that motivation and purpose. Some doubts have been expressed concerning this opinion. Certainly, where the alleged discriminator is shown to have been actuated by a deliberate discriminatory purpose, that fact, if proved, will make the breach of the statute easier to establish. But much discrimination occurs unconsciously, thoughtlessly or ignorantly. It would subvert the achievement of the purposes of the Act if it were necessary for a complainant to establish that the alleged discriminator intended, or had the motive, to discriminate. All that need be shown is that the alleged discriminator has acted 'on the ground of', relevantly [in this case], impairment. That involves an objective characterisation of the discriminator's 'ground' for its conduct, for which subjective intention may be relevant but is not decisive.[81]

As discussed above, the real touchstone, and the only one, that is relevant to distinguishing between prosecution and persecution is the concept of discrimination. This has not been expressly acknowledged or accepted by relevant case law. However, an understanding of the concepts in this area of refugee law reveals that what the courts have been alluding to all along is no more than the concept of discrimination.

The concept of discrimination, when properly understood, unifies and explains most of the standards and doctrines that currently exist concerning the concept of persecution. It is submitted that discrimination is the only test for persecution that unifies all aspects of current persecution law, except for the 'motivation' requirement. However, given the manner in which this requirement has been interpreted (such that it does not require antipathy), this does not constitute a meaningful impediment to a unified approach to persecution.

80 For a contrary view, see M. Bagaric, 'Originalism: Why Some Things Should Never Change – or at Least not Change too Quickly', (2000) 19 *University of Tasmania Law Review*, pp. 173–204.
81 [1997] HCA 30 (31 July 1997).

15.4.7 Relevance of proposed test where persecutory conduct is not pursuant to legal standard

As already noted, the test stipulated above is most apposite to situations where the persecutory conduct is pursuant to the application or operation of a legal rule or principle. In particular, it provides a mechanism for distinguishing between prosecution and persecution. It may intuitively seem less appropriate in situations where an individual is being targeted for direct adverse treatment pursuant to a practice or policy of state authorities: for example, where security forces regularly detain and beat people from a certain ethnic group.

The proposed test does not require individuals to be selectively targeted. However, this does not reveal a shortcoming of the test in such circumstances. The notion of targeting or selectivity is in fact superfluous. This is because the concept of discrimination, as defined above, encompasses all circumstances where individuals are directly targeted by state agents, and also extends to situations where the mistreatment is less direct: for example where a person is denied welfare or food for a Convention reason.

15.4.8 Non-state agents: failure of state protection

An important aspect of persecution is that it does not necessarily need to be directly caused by agents acting for the state. Persecution can also occur where the state cannot or will not protect an individual from serious harm brought about for a Convention reason. Although section 91R(1)(c) refers to systematic and discriminatory conduct, the term 'conduct' has been interpreted very broadly by the High Court to include situations where authorities consciously elect not to prevent serious harm occurring to a person for a Convention reason.

The leading authority is *MIMA v Khawar*,[82] which involved the failure by police to enforce the law to protect a wife from being beaten by her husband because of systematic discrimination against women that was both tolerated and sanctioned by the state. A failure by a state to act, for discriminatory reasons, in circumstances where there was a duty to act, was found to convert serious non-Convention harm into persecutory conduct.

The converse also applies. The majority in *MIMA v Respondents S152/2003* held that where the persecutor is a non-state agent, the willingness and ability of a state to provide the requisite level of protection to its citizens will preclude a finding that an applicant fears persecution under the Convention.[83] Thus while 'protection' in Article 1A(2) is concerned with external protection, in a case involving non-state persecutors, internal protection from persecution by the authorities of a state is relevant to whether a person is unable or 'unwilling' to avail himself or herself of the protection of his or her home state. To this end, it is important to note that the appropriate level of protection (such that

82 [2002] HCA 14 (11 April 2002).
83 *MIMA v Respondents S152/2003* [2004] HCA 18 (21 April 2004).

an applicant's unwillingness to seek internal state protection is unreasonable) does not require the state to provide an assurance or guarantee of safety. In the majority judgment the court noted:

> If the Full Court contemplated that the Tribunal, in assessing the justification for unwillingness to seek protection, should have considered, not merely whether the Ukrainian government provided a reasonably effective police force and a reasonably impartial system of justice, but also whether it could guarantee the first respondent's safety to the extent that he need have no fear of further harm, then it was in error. A person living inside or outside his or her country of nationality may have a well-founded fear of harm. The fact that the authorities, including the police, and the courts, may not be able to provide an assurance of safety, so as to remove any reasonable basis for fear, does not justify unwillingness to seek their protection. For example, an Australian court that issues an apprehended violence order is rarely, if ever, in a position to guarantee its effectiveness. A person who obtains such an order may yet have a well-founded fear that the order will be disobeyed. Paradoxically, fear of certain kinds of harm from other citizens can only be removed completely in a highly repressive society, and then it is likely to be replaced by fear of harm from the state.[84]

The majority of the court further noted that 'no country can guarantee that its citizens will at all times, and in all circumstances, be safe from violence. Day by day, Australian courts deal with criminal cases involving violent attacks on person or property.'[85] The degree of state protection that is required is determined according to international standards. A country has a duty:

> to take reasonable measures to protect the lives and safety of its citizens, and those measures would include an appropriate criminal law, and the provision of a reasonably effective and impartial police force and justice system.[86]

15.4.9 Personal responsibility to avoid persecution

As discussed in Chapter 14, there are cases where individuals may be able to eliminate or minimise the chance of persecution by concealing certain traits (such as their religion or political sentiments) or modifying their conduct (for example, remaining discreet about their sexual orientation); on this issue, the High Court, in the case of *Appellant S395/2002 v MIMA*, has held that the fact that individuals can take steps to avoid coming to the notice of their persecutors does not disentitle them from refugee status.[87]

It is unclear to what extent this principle will be developed. It is unlikely that it will apply in an absolute manner, otherwise issues of personal responsibility and accountability will be removed from refugee determinations. In Western cultures people are expected to suppress certain desires, and an election not to do so which results in harsh sanctions is not usually viewed as constituting unfair

84 *MIMA v Respondents S152/2003* [2004] HCA 18 (21 April 2004), [28].
85 *MIMA v Respondents S152/2003* [2004] HCA 18 (21 April 2004), [26].
86 *MIMA v Respondents S152/2003* [2004] HCA 18 (21 April 2004), [26].
87 *Appellant S395/2002 v MIMA* (18 April 2003), [40], [80]. See also *Applicant NABD/2002 v MIMA*, which applied *Appellant S395/2002 v MIMA* in the context of religious persecution (as discussed in Chapter 14).

treatment. Thus we are expected to keep our clothes on in public, not have sex with children, not beat our spouses, vote only once and not mistreat animals. If we elect to act to violate such norms, we are held responsible for our choices.

As previously stated, the Convention is meant to offer protection to blameless people who are at risk of harm as a result of social and political circumstances beyond their control. It is not a visa mechanism for people who abdicate all notions of responsibility and elect to engage in conduct that they are aware will bring adverse attention from the authorities. Given that notions of blame and responsibility cannot be divorced from this context, it is likely that courts in the future will place limits on the type of characteristics or behaviour which individuals are not expected to modify or conceal. To this end, it may be that individuals are required to curtail all conduct to avoid persecution except that which would require extraordinary steps or result in them living oppressive existences. Many individuals regard their sexual orientation and religious convictions as defining aspects of their personhood. However, in most cases it may be less important, for example, to publicly express one's political preference.

16

Well-founded fear of persecution

16.1 Overview

The notion of a well-founded fear is one of the constituent elements of the definition of a refugee. In *Chan v MIEA* the High Court held that 'well-founded fear' has both a subjective and an objective element:

> The phrase 'well-founded fear of being persecuted' . . . contains both a subjective and an objective requirement. There must be a state of mind – fear of being persecuted – and a basis – well-founded – for that fear.[1]

It is important to emphasise that in determining whether a fear of persecution is well-founded the relevant point of inquiry is at the time when the decision is made, not at the point at which the applicant left his or her country,[2] and must take into account not the current situation but what is likely to occur in the reasonably foreseeable future.[3]

16.2 The subjective element

The subjective element focuses on the perceptions of the individual regarding the risk involved in returning to the relevant country. The applicants' personal beliefs regarding the dangers awaiting them in their country of origin are rarely a defining consideration in the determination of refugee status. The best evidence of what an applicant believes is obviously his or her express comments on the

1 [1989] HCA 62 (9 December 1989), [16].
2 [1989] HCA 62 (9 December 1989), [16].
3 *Minister for Immigration and Ethnic Affairs v Wu Shan Liang* [1996] HCA 6 (7 March 1996), [47].

subject matter. It is difficult to reject an applicant's claim that he or she fears persecution. This is especially so given that this belief does not need to have a rational basis. Nevertheless, in some cases a fact finder may be entitled to reject such an assertion on the basis that it is disingenuous. Examples are where the applicant voluntarily and regularly visits his or her country of origin or where there is absolutely no evidential basis for the fear.

The more contentious issue will normally be the objective fear.

16.3 The objective element

The objective element requires there to be a rational, factual basis for the fear. In *Chan v MIEA* Dawson J noted that 'whilst there must be a fear of being persecuted, it must not all be in the mind; there must be a sufficient foundation for that fear'.[4] The High Court held that a fear is objectively well founded if the evidence establishes that there is a 'real chance' of being persecuted.[5] The courts have used several terms and concepts to illuminate the meaning of 'real chance'. It has been noted that a real chance involves a substantial risk of persecution as opposed to a hypothetical or remote chance. The courts have not ascribed a statistical probability to size of the risk, but it is obvious that it can be less than 50 per cent and even no higher than 10 per cent. Mason CJ has stated that 'real chance':

> Conveys the notion of a substantial, as distinct from a remote chance, of persecution occurring. If an applicant establishes that there is a real chance of persecution, then his fear, assuming that he has such a fear, is well-founded, notwithstanding that there is less than a fifty per cent chance of persecution occurring.[6]

This interpretation fulfils the objects of the Convention in securing recognition of refugee status for those persons who have a legitimate or justified fear of persecution on political grounds if they are returned to their country of origin.

McHugh J has stated:

> The decisions in *Sivakumaran* and *Cardoza-Fonseca* also establish that a fear may be well-founded for the purpose of the Convention and Protocol even though persecution is unlikely to occur. As the U.S. Supreme Court pointed out in *Cardoza-Fonseca* an applicant for refugee status may have a well-founded fear of persecution even though there is only a 10 per cent chance that he will be shot, tortured or otherwise persecuted. Obviously, a far-fetched possibility of persecution must be excluded. But if there is a real chance that the applicant will be persecuted, his fear should be characterised as 'well-founded' for the purpose of the Convention and Protocol.[7]

4 [1989] HCA 62 (19 December 1989), [16].
5 [1989] HCA 62 (19 December 1989), Mason, CJ [12].
6 [1989] HCA 62 (19 December 1989), Mason, CJ [12]. See also *NAES v MIMA* [2004] FCA FC 79 (30 March 2004).
7 *Chan v MIEA* [1989] HCA 62; (1989) 169 CLR 379 F.C. 89/034 (9 December 1989), [35]. For more recent application of this test, see *VTAG v MIMIA* [2004] FCA 447 (16 April 2004).

A fear of persecution is not well founded if it is merely assumed or if it is mere speculation. In *SGKB v MIMIA*, the Full Federal Court noted that:

> In the *Minister for Immigration and Ethnic Affairs v Guo* (1997) 191 CLR 559 at 571–2, where six members of the Court (Brennan CJ, Dawson, Toohey, Gaudron, McHugh and Gummow JJ) said . . . No doubt in most, perhaps all, cases . . . the application of the real chance test, properly understood as the clarification of the phrase 'well-founded', leads to the same result as a direct application of that phrase . . . Nevertheless, it is always dangerous to treat a particular word or phrase as synonymous with a statutory term, no matter how helpful the use of that word or phrase may be in understanding the statutory term . . . A fear is 'well-founded' when there is a real substantial basis for it. As *Chan* shows, a substantial basis for a fear may exist even though there is far less than a 50 per cent chance that the object of the fear will eventuate. But no fear can be well-founded for the purpose of the Convention unless the evidence indicates a real ground for believing that the applicant for refugee status is at risk of persecution. A fear of persecution is not well-founded if it is merely assumed or if it is mere speculation. In this and other cases, the Tribunal and the Federal Court have used the term 'real chance' not as epexegetic of 'well-founded', but as a replacement or substitution for it.[8]

In *MZXSA v Minister for Immigration and Citizenship* [2010] FCAFC 123 the Full Federal Court recently endorsed the following summary of some of the pertinent aspects of the real chance test:

> 95 In *Minister for Immigration and Multicultural Affairs v Rajalingam* [1999] FCA 719; (1999) 93 FCR 220 Sackville J (with whom North J agreed) analysed the question of decision-making in migration cases. His Honour considered *Minister for Immigration and Ethnic Affairs v Wu Shan Liang* [1996] HCA 6; (1996) 185 CLR 259, *Minister for Immigration and Ethnic Affairs v Guo* (1997) 191 CLR 559 and *Re Minister for Immigration and Multicultural Affairs; Ex Parte Abebe* [1999] HCA 14; (1999) 197 CLR 510, for the purpose of addressing the requirement of whether an applicant for a protection visa has a well-founded fear of persecution. His Honour (at [60]–[67]) distilled a number of principles from those decisions, including the following:
>
> (a) There are circumstances in which the Tribunal must take into account the possibility that alleged past events occurred even though it finds those events probably did not occur. This is because the Tribunal must not foreclose reasonable speculation about the chances of a hypothetical future event occurring.
>
> (b) In this connection it is not always possible for the decision-maker to be satisfied as to whether alleged past events have occurred with certainty or even confidence. Therefore, if the Tribunal is uncertain as to whether an alleged event occurred, or finds that, although the probabilities are against it, the event might have occurred, it may be necessary to take into account the possibility that the event took place in considering whether the applicant has a well-founded fear of persecution.
>
> (c) Reasonable speculation may require the decision-maker to take into account the chance that past events might have occurred, even though the decision-maker thinks that they probably did not.
>
> (d) There is no reason in principle and nothing in the reasoning of the High Court in those cases that the Tribunal must express findings as to whether alleged past

8 [2003] FCAFC 44 (18 March 2003), [18].

events actually occurred in a manner that makes explicit its degree of convictional confidence that the findings are correct.

(e) Similarly there is nothing in the reasoning of the High Court which permits a Court exercising powers of judicial review to 'impute' to the Tribunal a lack of conviction or confidence in its findings of fact, such as to warrant a holding that the Tribunal should not or could not have relied on those findings to hold that the applicant's fear of persecution was not well-founded. To do so would be to engage in merits review.

(f) In general, the question whether the Tribunal should have considered the possibility that its findings of fact might not have been correct is to be determined by reference to the Tribunal's own reasons. If a fair reading of the reasons as a whole shows that the Tribunal itself had no real doubt that claimed events had not occurred, there is no warrant for holding that it should have considered the possibility that its findings were wrong.

96 As to the last of these principles, his Honour said (at [67]):

... Reasonable speculation as to whether the applicant had a well-founded fear of persecution does not require a possibility inconsistent with the [Tribunal's] own findings to be pursued. A 'fair reading' of the reasons incorporates the principle that the [Tribunal's] reasons should receive a 'beneficial construction' and should not be 'construed minutely and finely with an eye keenly attuned to the perception of error': *Wu Shan Liang*, at 271–272, quoting *Collector of Customs v Pozzolanic Enterprises Pty Ltd* [1993] FCA 456; (1993) 43 FCR 280, at 287. Only if a fair reading of the reasons allows the conclusion that the [Tribunal] had a real doubt that its findings on material questions of fact were correct, might error be revealed by the [Tribunal's] failure to take account of the possibility that the alleged events might have occurred (or the possibility that an event said not to have occurred did not in fact occur). If the fair reading allows of such a conclusion, the failure to consider the possibilities might demonstrate that the [Tribunal] had not undertaken the required speculation about the chances of future persecution.

16.4 Fear must be objective and subjective

As the law stands currently, both these elements of well-founded fear must be satisfied. Thus, a claim for refugee status will fail if either element is not satisfied. This is understandable where a case fails on the basis that an objective fear is lacking. However, it is curious that a claim will fail where there is an objective basis for the well-founded fear, but the applicant does not share this fear.[9]

There is no logical or normative reason for not providing protection to a person who is in danger simply because the person is not aware of the danger. This anomaly is to a large extent ameliorated by the fact that it is rare that an applicant will not be aware of the relevant danger. However, situations will arise where applicants, because of, say, a flawed assessment of current country information, incorrectly believe that a certain risk to their safety has subsided.

9 In *SDAQ v MIMIA* [2003] FCAFC 120 (30 May 2003) Cooper J, [19], stated that the issue of objective fear does not even arise if there is no subjective fear.

Although judicial authority expressly states that both elements of the well-founded fear must exist, none of the cases related to this issue involves situations where an applicant mistakenly no longer feared an objective risk, hence the principle mandating both elements is strictly *obiter dictum*. Faced with such a factual situation it is likely that a court will find that only an objective fear is necessary, and that the subjective component is, in fact, simply one consideration that is relevant to the existence of an objective fear. This view is supported by the fact that in the case of children and the mentally disabled, it is possible to impute a subjective fear.[10]

Some support for this view derives from comments by Dawson J in *Chan v MIEA*. In remarking on the emphasis on the subjective component of the test in the UNHCR handbook, his Honour stated:

> Perhaps the emphasis upon the subjective element in this view of the test was prompted by recognition of the fact that some member States of the Convention are reluctant to find an actual danger of persecution in another country for fear of damaging relations with that other country: see *Reg. v Home Secretary; Ex parte Sivakumaran* (1988) AC 958, at p. 998. But 'well-founded' must mean something more than plausible, for an applicant may have a plausible belief which may be demonstrated, upon facts unknown to him, to have no foundation. It is clear enough that the object of the Convention is not to relieve fears which are all in the mind, however understandable, *but to facilitate refuge for those who are in need of it*.[11] [Emphasis added.]

16.5 The relevant time at which risk is assessed and relevance of past events and 'sur place' claims

As noted above, the relevant time at which the fear must be assessed is at the time the decision is made, not when the applicant left his or her country or when the application for a protection visa is drafted or filed.[12] Thus, if an applicant is a refugee at the time of leaving his or her country, this will not necessarily be the case when his or her refugee status is assessed.

The fact that a person has previously experienced persecution does not necessarily mean that he or she is a refugee at the relevant time, as defined in the previous paragraph. However, as was noted by the Court in *MIEA v Guo*, past events often serve as a good guide to future events:

> The course of the future is not predictable, but the degree of probability that an event will occur is often, perhaps usually, assessable. Past events are not a certain guide to the future, but in many areas of life proof that events have occurred often provides a reliable basis for determining the probability – high or low – of their recurrence. The extent to which past events are a guide to the future depends on the degree of probability that they have occurred, the regularity with which and the conditions under which they have or probably have occurred and the likelihood that the introduction of

10 *Chen Shi Hai v MIMA* [2000] FCA (5 June 1997), [14].
11 [1989] HCA (9 December 1989), [16].
12 *Chan v MIEA* [1989] HCA 62 (19 December 1989), [17].

> new or other events may distort the cycle of regularity. In many cases, when the past has been evaluated, the probability that an event will occur may border on certainty. In other cases, the probability that an event will occur may be so low that, for practical purposes, it can be safely disregarded. In between these extremes, there are varying degrees of probability as to whether an event will or will not occur. But unless a person or tribunal attempts to determine what is likely to occur in the future in relation to a relevant field of inquiry, that person or tribunal has no rational basis for determining the chance of an event in that field occurring in the future. Determining whether there is a real chance that something will occur requires an estimation of the likelihood that one or more events will give rise to the occurrence of that thing. In many, if not most cases, determining what is likely to occur in the future will require findings as to what has occurred in the past because what has occurred in the past is likely to be the most reliable guide as to what will happen in the future. It is therefore ordinarily an integral part of the process of making a determination concerning the chance of something occurring in the future that conclusions are formed concerning past events.[13]

It follows that in deciding what is likely to happen in the future it is normally necessary to make an assessment of what happened in the past. If an applicant faced persecution when she or he left the country of origin, in the absence of any relevant change in circumstances the applicant will continue to be a refugee.[14] A relevant change will normally be in the form of changed social and political circumstances in the country of origin, which provide evidence that people with the profile of the applicant are no longer being persecuted.

The clearest example of this in recent years is the events in East Timor after the nation's vote for independence. In the 1990s, a large number of East Timorese (mostly of Chinese background) arrived in Australia, and claimed refugee status on the basis that they were being persecuted by the then-ruling Indonesian regime. There was strong evidence that this group had a well-founded fear of persecution and hence were refugees at the time they left East Timor.

However, in late 1999, the people of East Timor voted overwhelmingly in favour of independence. This initially triggered large-scale looting and killings by pro-Jakarta militias, backed by senior elements of the Indonesian military. As a result of world outrage at these events, UN peacekeeping troops arrived in East Timor approximately three weeks after the vote for independence. East Timor finally became independent in May 2002. On the path to independence, the controlling Indonesian army and the militia left or were expelled or fled from East Timor. This was made possible by the collective resolve of much of the international community, acting through the United Nations, which responded decisively to the killings in August and September 1999. The almost wanton killings, violence, looting and burning which occurred during this period ceased nearly instantly upon the arrival of the peacekeeping troops in late September 1999. The violence did not resume, and almost 'overnight' previously persecuted groups were no longer at risk of harm (for a Convention reason). As a result, almost all of the thousand or so East Timorese applications for protection

13 *Minister for Immigration and Ethnic Affairs v Guo* [1997] HCA 22 (13 June 1997). For application of this test, see *W221/01 A v MIMA* [2002] FCA 399 (12 April 2002).
14 *Chan v MIEA* [1989] HCA 62 (9 December 1989).

visas that were finalised after the intervention of UN forces were rejected by the Refugee Review Tribunal (RRT). This is despite the fact that many applicants were subjected to egregious types of mistreatment at the hands of Indonesian authorities.[15] This did not result in this group being required to leave Australia. Most applicants were ultimately granted humanitarian visas, partly in recognition of the many years they had spent in Australia.

Thus past events are a relevant, but not decisive, consideration in terms of whether or not an individual has a well-founded fear of persecution. Where political and social conditions have not materially changed since the applicant left his or her country, past events are a good guide to what is likely to happen in the future. Where there have been considerable changes, past events may be of virtually no relevance.

Accordingly, a person may not be a refugee at the time of determination, even though he or she was a refugee when leaving his or her country of origin. The opposite also applies – an applicant may not have been a refugee on leaving his or her country, but he or she may be a refugee at the time of determination. In such circumstances the person is known as a refugee 'sur place'. People who are outside their country of origin may become a refugee sur place as a result of changes in circumstances in their country or as a result of their own actions.

Changed circumstances in the country of origin include matters such as a new government which has a hard line towards people with a certain political or religious profile being installed. Changed personal circumstances include where a person while in the new country engages in conduct that provides him or her with a profile that is likely to result in adverse treatment if he or she returned to the country of origin. This includes conduct such as publicly denouncing the activities of the government in the country of origin or changing religions.

In relation to voluntary behaviour, there is obviously considerably scope for exploitation of sur place claims. For example, a person may be able to acquire a well-founded fear of persecution simply by making public comments contrary to the interests of the government in the country of origin. This is despite the fact that the person does not actually believe those comments.

To minimise the scope of exploitation, section 91R(3) was inserted in the *Migration Act 1958* (Cth) in 2001. It states:

> For the purposes of the application of this Act and the regulations to a particular person:
> (a) in determining whether the person has a well-founded fear of being persecuted for one or more of the reasons mentioned in Article 1A(2) of the Refugees Convention as amended by the Refugees Protocol;
>
> disregard any conduct engaged in by the person in Australia unless:
> (b) the person satisfies the Minister that the person engaged in the conduct otherwise than for the purpose of strengthening the person's claim to be a refugee within the meaning of the Refugees Convention as amended by the Refugees Protocol.[16]

15 For further background regarding the changes to East Timor, see RRT Reference: V01/14633 (13 January 2003); RRT Reference: V02/14784 (18 March 2003).

16 The constitutional validity of this section was upheld in *SAAS v MIMA* [2002] FCA 726 (11 June 2002).

Recently it was held that where an applicant engages in conduct that strengthens his or her refugee claim for several reasons, only one of which is to strengthen his or her claim, the conduct cannot be disregarded in determining the applicant's claim for a protection visa.

The case of *Minister for Immigration and Citizenship v SZJGV; Minister for Immigration and Citizenship v SZJXO* [2009] HCA 40 focused on a decision by the RRT to use evidence of respondents' involvement in Falun Gong activities in Australia to cast doubt on their claims. The High Court held that section 91R(3) did not prohibit adverse inferences being drawn about the legitimacy of refugee applications based on the conduct of applicants after they arrive in Australia. In reaching this conclusion French CJ and Bell J made the following observations regarding the operation and scope of section 91R(3):

> 1. The first respondents to these two appeals each applied unsuccessfully to the Minister for Immigration and Citizenship ('the Minister') for protection visas under the *Migration Act 1958* (Cth) ('the Migration Act'). They were also unsuccessful before the Refugee Review Tribunal ('the Tribunal') which affirmed the decisions. The Federal Magistrates Court dismissed their applications for judicial review of the decisions of the Tribunal. They succeeded, however, in persuading the Full Court of the Federal Court that the Tribunal had erred by taking into account, adversely to them, and contrary to s 91R(3) of the Migration Act, conduct in which they had engaged in Australia.
>
> 2. The first respondents' success before the Full Court turned upon the construction of s 91R(3) which provides:
>
> 'For the purposes of the application of this Act and the regulations to a particular person:
> (a) in determining whether the person has a well-founded fear of being persecuted for one or more of the reasons mentioned in Article 1A(2) of the Refugees Convention as amended by the Refugees Protocol; disregard any conduct engaged in by the person in Australia unless:
> (b) the person satisfies the Minister that the person engaged in the conduct otherwise than for the purpose of strengthening the person's claim to be a refugee within the meaning of the Refugees Convention as amended by the Refugees Protocol.'
>
> 3. The question posed by these appeals is whether s 91R(3) prohibits a decision-maker, in making the determination contemplated in par (a), from drawing inferences *adverse* to a visa applicant based on the applicant's conduct within Australia unless the condition referred to in par (b) is satisfied.
>
> 4. The factual and procedural history leading to these appeals and the background to the enactment of s 91R(3) have been set out in the judgment of Crennan and Kiefel JJ. The appeals should be allowed and orders made in the terms which they propose. Our reasons for coming to that conclusion depend primarily upon the construction of par (a).
>
> **The construction of s 91R(3)**
>
> 5. The construction of s 91R(3) begins with the ordinary and grammatical sense of the words having regard to their context and legislative purpose. That purpose in this case, as shown in the reasons of Crennan and Kiefel JJ, was to overcome the effects of decisions of the Full Court of the Federal Court in *Minister for Immigration*

and Multicultural Affairs v Mohammed and *Minister for Immigration and Multicultural Affairs v Farahanipour*. Those decisions concerned cases in which the applicant for a protection visa had deliberately engaged in conduct within Australia calculated to strengthen his claim for protection under the Refugees Convention by enhancing the risk of persecution if he were to be returned to his country of origin. In each case the Full Court held that although such bad faith conduct might well lead to adverse findings about an applicant's credibility, it did not automatically bar the claim for a visa which would have to be assessed by reference to Australia's obligations under the Refugees Convention.

6. Section 91R is concerned with the application of the criteria in Art 1A(2) of the Refugees Convention to determining whether a person is a refugee within the meaning of that Article and to whom Australia owes 'protection obligations' within the meaning of s 36 of the Migration Act. The first two sub-sections of s 91R are closely related. Section 91R(1) limits the range of circumstances in which apprehended harm will be characterised as persecution for the purposes of Art 1A(2). Section 91R(1)(b) requires that such persecution involve serious harm to the person and s 91R(2) sets out a non-exhaustive list of instances of serious harm.

7. Section 91R(3) stands apart from the two preceding sub-sections. Unlike them, it does not define limits to be applied, for statutory purposes, to the criteria in Art 1A(2). Rather it operates as an awkwardly framed command to the world by the use of 'disregard' in an imperative sense. Section 91S, which concerns 'membership of a particular social group' as an occasion of apprehended persecution in Art 1A(2), is drafted along similar lines. The command in s 91R(3) is clearly directed, although not expressly, to the Minister (and therefore to the Minister's delegates) determining applications for protection visas and to the Tribunal in reviewing such decisions. It is in its character as a command to administrative decision-makers that it must be construed. It is not directed to the courts, for the courts are not involved in determining such cases on their merits. But a court, upon judicial review, may be required to determine whether the command, where applicable, has been applied in accordance with its terms properly construed.

8. Section 91R takes its place in a legislative scheme providing means by which Australia can comply with its obligations as a Contracting State under the Refugees Convention. A necessary condition for the grant of a protection visa under the Migration Act is that the applicant is, relevantly, 'a non-citizen in Australia to whom the Minister is satisfied Australia has protection obligations under the Refugees Convention as amended by the Refugees Protocol'. The 'protection obligations' are not defined but refer to those of Australia's substantive obligations under the Refugees Convention, which can be characterised as protective in nature and imposed with respect to refugees as individuals. They include obligations concerning 'the status and civil rights to be afforded to refugees who are within Contracting States' conferred by Chs II–IV and those obligations imposed by Ch V (Arts 25–34). The substantive obligation of most immediate relevance to a refugee applying for a protection visa in Australia is that imposed by Art 33(1) of the Refugees Convention, which provides:

> 'No Contracting State shall expel or return ('*refouler*') a refugee in any manner whatsoever to the frontiers of territories where his life or freedom would be threatened on account of his race, religion, nationality, membership of a particular social group or political opinion.'

9. The legislative purpose of s 91R(3) as disclosed in the Second Reading Speech is to ensure that an applicant for a protection visa, in seeking to demonstrate a well-founded fear of persecution within the meaning of Art 1A(2), cannot place any reliance upon, nor gain any advantage from, conduct engaged in within Australia for the purpose of strengthening his or her claim to meet the criteria of classification as a refugee under Art 1A(2). Neither that purpose nor Australia's protection obligations under the Refugees Convention require that such conduct be disregarded where it is adverse to an applicant's credibility. Such a result would be irrational. A construction of s 91R(3) to avoid that result may properly encompass a departure from the literal or natural and ordinary meaning of the text. If the language be so intractable that it requires a word or words to be given a meaning necessary to serve the evident purpose of the provision, then such a course may be permissible as a 'realistic solution' to the difficulty. In the 12th edition of Maxwell's *On the Interpretation of Statutes* the approaches which can be taken in dealing with statutory language whose ordinary meaning is plainly at odds with the statutory purpose were explained:

> 'Where the language of a statute, in its ordinary meaning and grammatical construction, leads to a manifest contradiction of the apparent purpose of the enactment, or to some inconvenience or absurdity which can hardly have been intended, a construction may be put upon it which modifies the meaning of the words and even the structure of the sentence. This may be done by departing from the rules of grammar, by giving an unusual meaning to particular words, or by rejecting them altogether, on the ground that the legislature could not possibly have intended what its words signify, and that the modifications made are mere corrections of careless language and really give the true meaning.' [Footnote omitted.]

This approach is reflected in decisions of the courts of the United Kingdom. In *Inco Europe Ltd v First Choice Distribution*, Lord Nicholls of Birkenhead restated the need for the court to correct obvious drafting errors. He referred to the third edition of Cross' *Statutory Interpretation*:

> 'In omitting or inserting words the judge is not really engaged in a hypothetical reconstruction of the intentions of the drafter or the legislature, but is simply making as much sense as he can of the text of the statutory provision read in its appropriate context and within the limits of the judicial role.'

The limits of the judicial role, as pointed out by Lord Nicholls, require that the courts 'abstain from any course which might have the appearance of judicial legislation'. Three matters of which the court must be sure before interpreting a statute in this way were the intended purpose of the statute, the failure of the draftsman and parliament by inadvertence to give effect to that purpose, and the substance of the provision parliament would have made. The third of these conditions was described as being of 'crucial importance'. Otherwise any attempt to determine the meaning of the enactment would cross the boundary between construction and legislation.

10. The construction of s 91R(3) in accordance with its legislative purpose begins with a consideration of the nature of the ministerial determination with which par (a) is concerned. In this respect there are two ways of reading par (a). The first way is to read 'whether' as introducing alternatives in the sense of 'whether or not'. That reading would apply the command of the sub-section to all processes of reasoning which could lead to determinations favourable or unfavourable concerning the existence

of an asserted well-founded fear of persecution within the meaning of Art 1A(2). It accords with the natural and ordinary meaning of 'whether' as '[i]ntroducing a disjunctive dependent question or its equivalent expressing doubt, choice, etc between alternatives'. It would require the decision-maker to disregard, for all purposes relevant to a determination of the existence of a well-founded fear of persecution, any conduct engaged in within Australia, however probative of the falsity of an applicant's claim, unless the condition in par (b) were satisfied. The creation of false documents to support a claim would be an example of such conduct. Such an outcome is improbable and inconvenient to a degree that would be irrational.

11. The Solicitor-General of the Commonwealth submitted that the words 'in determining' in par (a) refer to a process undertaken after findings of primary fact have been made and said:

> 'So after all the facts are found once and for all, what the direction in the section requires is that conduct in fact engaged in by the person in Australia be disregarded, that means simply left out of account, in determining whether, which we would say means as a basis for determining that, such fear of persecution as a person may in fact have is to be characterised in terms of Article 1A(2) as well-founded.'

12. The proposition that s 91R(3) is concerned with the process of determination after the primary facts have been found does not meet the textual difficulty generated by the ordinary meaning of the word 'whether'. However, the Solicitor-General's submission does lead to consideration of an alternative construction, which is to read 'whether' as 'that': not introducing alternatives, but indicating only processes of reasoning leading to a favourable determination. The usage is awkward and probably reflects a misuse of the term 'whether' in par (a). But such misuse is not entirely without precedent. In this case, the substituted text corrects what would be an obvious drafting error were 'whether' to be construed according to its ordinary and natural meaning. On the alternative construction, par (a) hypothesises the existence of a chain of reasoning leading to a determination in favour of the applicant where that determination is based in whole or in part upon inferences drawn from conduct engaged in by the person in Australia. The command in s 91R(3) therefore requires that the decision-maker not apply any such chain of reasoning unless the condition in par (b) is satisfied with respect to the relevant conduct. We consider that to be the correct construction. It meets the purpose of the sub-section and avoids absurd results. Upon that construction the appeals must be allowed.

13. As to what is necessary to satisfy the condition in par (b), we agree with Crennan and Kiefel JJ that an applicant seeking to rely upon conduct engaged in in Australia must show that the conduct was not engaged in solely to strengthen his or her claim. By way of example, conduct in Australia may reflect a continued commitment by the applicant to religious practices followed or political opinions held and expressed in his or her country of origin. It could not be said to have been engaged in solely to strengthen the claim to be a refugee. It might then be relied upon by a decision-maker to infer prior commitment to a particular religious practice or political opinion in the country of origin.[17] [Citations omitted.]

17 Crennan and Kiefel JJ adopted a similar approach.

16.6 Relocation

A person is not a refugee if he or she can avoid persecution by relocating to another region in his or her country of origin. If a fear of persecution is localised, a person is not entitled to protection in Australia. Instead the person is required to relocate to another part of the country where the risk of persecution is not well founded. Australia's protection obligations do not crystallise until an individual has exhausted all reasonable avenues in his or her country to avoid persecution. As was noted in *SKFB v MIMA*:

> In *Randhawa v Minister for Immigration, Local Government and Ethnic Affairs*... the Full Court decided (at 440) that although the Convention definition of refugee does not refer to part or regions of a country, 'that provides no warrant for construing the definition so it would give refugee status to those who, although having a well founded fear of persecution in their home region, could nevertheless avail themselves of the real protection of the country of nationality elsewhere within that country'. As the Chief Justice (who delivered the leading judgment) said (at 441): 'If it were otherwise, the anomalous situation would exist that the international community would be under an obligation to provide protection outside the borders of the country of nationality even though real protection could be found within those borders.'[18]

However, it is important to emphasise that a person is not required to relocate at all costs. Relocation is only necessary where it can be reasonably undertaken by an individual. Once a well-founded fear of persecution for a Convention reason has been shown, 'a refugee does not also have to show a Convention reason behind every difficulty or danger which makes some suggestion of relocation unreasonable'.[19]

The principles relating to relocation were recently noted in *SZAZX v Minister for Immigration*:

> The principles applicable in relation to relocation are those determined by the Full Court of the Federal Court in *Randhawa v MILGEA* (1994) 124 ALR 265. As Black CJ stated at [13], the question is whether the applicant's fear is well founded in relation to his country of nationality, not simply the region in which he lived. The question is not to be approached in a narrow way. It is necessary to ask the further question of whether the applicant could relocate to another area of the country and whether he could reasonably be expected to do so on the basis that 'notwithstanding that real protection from persecution may be available elsewhere within the country of nationality, a person's fear of persecution in relation to that country will remain well-founded with respect to the country as a whole if, as a practical matter, the part of the country in which protection is available is not reasonably accessible to that person'. (At [14]) Further, 'If it is not reasonable in the circumstances to expect a person who has a well-founded fear of persecution in relation to the part of the country from which he or she has fled to relocate to another part of the country of the nationality it may be said

18 [2004] FCAFC 142 (25 May 2004) [17].
19 *Perampalam v MIMA* (1999) 84 FCR 274, 283–285.

> that, in the relevant sense, the person's fear of persecution in relation to that country as a whole is well founded.'[20]

The reasonableness proviso is thought to stem from the humanitarian underpinning of the Convention.

There are a large number of considerations that are relevant to determining if relocation is reasonable. In essence, the focus is on the degree of inconvenience that a person will face in relocating and the practical obstacles to survival and flourishing that are likely to be faced in the proposed region.

In *Al-Amidi v MIMA*[21] the court held that factors that are relevant to the reasonableness of relocation include the person's age and resourcefulness, the norms of civil and political rights, and familial and health considerations. Thus it follows that the more competent and capable the individual, generally speaking, the more likely it is that relocation will be reasonable.

The test for how much pain and inconvenience is necessary before a proposed relocation is not reasonable has not been articulated by the courts. However, in keeping with the definition of a refugee, logically it should amount to at least the 'serious harm' threshold (although there is no need for the harm associated with the relocation to have a Convention nexus). A lower level of inconvenience or pain would result in the principal protection obligations towards individuals being too readily thrust onto other nations, as opposed to the state in question.

20 [2004] FMCA 393 (16 July 2004), [15].
21 (2000) FCA (4 August 2000) [18]; *Al-Asam v MIMA* [2001] FCA 127 (23 February 2001); *Montes-Granados v MIMA* [2000] FCA 60 (4 February 2000).

17

Limits on protection of refugees – cessation, exclusion exceptions and protection by another country

17.1 Overview of exclusion, cessation and exceptions

The Refugees Convention sets out a number of circumstances where the protection obligations by states towards refugees are limited or expunged. The duty of states to protect refugees is limited in seven broad circumstances. These are set out in:

- Article 1C – which defines several circumstances where refugee status ceases to exist;
- Article 1D – which excludes from the Convention persons who receive protection from certain UN organs;
- Article 1E – which excludes persons who can obtain access to a third country;
- Article 1F – which excludes individuals who have committed specified criminal acts;
- Article 32 – which permits expulsion of a refugee where the refugee is a security danger;
- Article 33(2) – which permits expulsion where there are grounds to believe that the refugee has been convicted of a 'particularly serious crime'; and
- in addition to this, a person is not entitled to protection in Australia where he or she can receive protection in a third country.

The overarching rationale for the exceptions is that either the protection obligations to refugees only arise as a matter of last resort or a State's security interests trumps its obligations to needy foreigners.

Article 1C applies where refugee status has already been conferred and sets out the circumstances in which refugee status can be lost: that is, where refugee status *ceases*. The *exclusions* contained in Articles 1D to 1F relate to situations where a person has not yet been granted refugee status. Articles 32 and 33(2) are properly categorised as *exceptions*, in that they apply where refugee status has been conferred and operate to expunge a state's protection obligations on the basis of national interest. Where a person is eligible to receive protection in a third country, this is properly classified as an *exclusion*, since it justifies a state not conferring refugee status.

The circumstances in which a state's refugee obligations are limited do not frequently arise, so they are not considered at length in this book. Moreover, they are not central to the definition of a refugee. Rather, they are exceptions to the general principle that signatories to the Convention must provide protection to people who are at risk of persecution for a Convention reason.

The rationale for Articles 1C to 1E is not controversial. In essence, these Articles relate to situations where the refugee no longer requires protection. Consequently, only a brief descriptive account is provided of these provisions. Article 1F is more controversial. In these circumstances protection is required but not granted because of competing state security interests. After an overview of Article 1F, we provide an analysis of the operation of this provision.

17.2 Cessation: Article 1C

Article 1C relates to circumstances where a person who has been declared a refugee is no longer in need of protection due to changed circumstances. The rationale is that refugee law is concerned with protection, not migration, and protection should only be conferred as a matter of last resort. Once the threat to the refugee is obviated, so too are protection obligations of the other state. Article 1C provides:

> This Convention shall cease to apply to any person falling under the terms of section A if:
>
> (1) He has voluntarily re-availed himself of the protection of the country of his nationality; or
> (2) Having lost his nationality he has voluntarily re-acquired it; or
> (3) He has acquired a new nationality, and enjoys the protection of the country of his new nationality; or
> (4) He has voluntarily re-established himself in the country which he left or outside which he remained owing to fear of persecution; or
> (5) He can no longer, because the circumstances in connection with which he has been recognised as a refugee have ceased to exist, continue to refuse to avail himself of the protection of the country of his nationality;

(6) Provided that this paragraph shall not apply to a refugee falling under section A(1) of this Article who is able to invoke compelling reasons arising out of previous persecution for refusing to avail himself of the protection of the country of nationality;
(7) Being a person who has no nationality, he is, because the circumstances in connection with which he has been recognised as a refugee have ceased to exist, able to return to the country of his former habitual residence;
(8) Provided that this paragraph shall not apply to a refugee falling under section A(1) of this Article who is able to invoke compelling reasons arising out of previous persecution for refusing to return to the country of his former habitual residence.

Section 1C of the Convention only becomes relevant in circumstances where a person has already been recognised as a refugee.[1] The main situation where Article 1C becomes relevant is in relation to refugees who have been granted temporary protection visas, whose visa has expired and who wish to apply for a further protection visa application. The central point at issue is whether or not they are still refugees.

Sub-paragraphs (1) to (4) relate to situations that are personal to the refugee. The last two clauses relate to situations where there has been a relevant change to the country of origin, such that the risk to the refugee has dissipated. There has been little judicial consideration of section 1C.

17.2.1 Articles 1C(1)–(4) voluntary actions by refugee

Article 1C(1) applies to refugees who are outside their country of origin (for refugees who return to their country of origin the relevant provision is Article 1C(4)), but nevertheless voluntarily re-avail themselves of the protection of their country of origin. Protection means the establishment of normal relationships with the authorities in that country. It extends beyond the protection that can be offered by being physically present in the state and includes consular and diplomatic protection.[2] Other acts that can enliven this provision include an application for a re-issue of a passport or a residency permit or travelling internationally on the passport of the country of origin.[3] Visits to the country of origin, while not necessary, constitute very persuasive evidence that there has been a re-availment of protection.[4]

Article 1C(2) is self-explanatory. It applies to refugees who have lost their nationality and then voluntarily[5] re-acquire it. It is assumed that a person would not seek to re-acquire nationality if protection was not available to him or her in that country.

1 *Chan v MIEA* [1989] HCA 62 (9 December 1989).
2 UNHCR, *Handbook on Procedures and Criteria for Determining Refugee Status*, para 118.
3 UNHCR, *Note on the Cessation Clauses* (EC/47/SC/CRP.30, 1997), [12].
4 *Rezaei v MIMA* [2001] FCA 1294 (14 September 2001).
5 See UNHCR, *Handbook on Procedures and Criteria for Determining Refugee Status*, para 128.

Article 1C(3) applies where a refugee acquires a new nationality, and enjoys the protection of the country of that nationality. In such circumstances there is no need for protection in another country.

Article 1C(4) applies to refugees who re-establish themselves in the country of origin. This is obviously strong evidence that they do not feel at risk of persecution. A brief visit or return is not sufficient to enliven this provision. Re-establishment means that the refugee must take steps which indicate that he or she wishes to maintain a durable presence in the country of origin.

17.2.2 Articles 1C(5)–(6) changed country circumstances

Article 1C(5) and (6) apply to refugees with a nationality and stateless people, respectively, who because of changed relevant circumstances in the country of origin are no longer at risk. The operation of these provisions has recently been considered by an Australian court.

The interpretation and scope of Article 1C(5) remained unclear for several years, leading to divergent approaches by the Federal Court and the Federal Magistrates Court. The operation of 1C(5) was finally resolved by the High Court in *Minister for Immigration and Multicultural and Indigenous Affairs v QAAH of 2004*.[6] In that case, the High Court stated that the test in Articles 1C(5) and (6) is effectively the same as in 1A(2) – whether the applicant has a well-founded fear of prosecution for a Convention reason. This effectively renders Articles 1C(5) and (6) useless. The relevant parts of the decision of Gummow ACJ, Callinan, Heydon and Crennan JJ are set out below:

> (1) Because s 36 of the Act [*Migration Act 1958* (Cth)] refers to protection obligations under the Convention it is legitimate, in deciding whether those obligations arise, to look to such other provisions of the Convention as bear upon that question . . .
>
> (2) [T]he opening words of Art 1C(5), 'He can *no longer*', and the subsequent words, 'the circumstances . . . *have ceased to exist*', make it clear that the circumstances from time to time and not merely as a matter of history are the relevant circumstances, that is, that the 'status', as the Convention has it, of a person permitted to reside in an asylum country may change as circumstances in the country which he has left change. [Emphasis added.]
>
> (3) The opening words of Art 1C state that the 'Convention shall cease to apply to any person falling under the terms of [Art 1A]' if any of the following pars (1)–(6) apply. Accordingly, the language of Art 1C(5) is unambiguous and compels the same conclusion as the Act. The appellant's submission, that the cessation provision operates automatically according to its terms, and need not for its application be triggered by a request for a, or any particular kind of visa, although in practice such a request will ordinarily be the occasion for a visa consideration of a person's right or otherwise to continuing protection, should be accepted. This is the operation that Art 1C(5) has, and is the work that it has to do and for which Art 1A does not make provision.

6 [2006] HCA 53 (15 November 2006).

(4) In *R (Hoxha) v Special Adjudicator* the House of Lords (Lord Nicholls of Birkenhead, Lord Steyn, Lord Hope of Craighead, Baroness Hale of Richmond and Lord Brown of Eaton-under-Heywood) considered the relevant articles of the Convention without reference to any legislative framework for them in the United Kingdom. The argument for the appellant in *Hoxha* went a step beyond that accepted by the Full Court in the present case. The argument was that if, albeit without any formal determination of refugee status made at an earlier time, the applicant subsequently was shown to have fulfilled the criteria under Art 1A(2) at that earlier time, the applicant was to be treated as having been 'recognised' for the purposes of Art 1C(5). That argument was rejected by the House of Lords unanimously.

(5) Lord Brown's view that '[Art] 1C(5), a cessation clause, simply has no application . . . at any stage unless and until it is invoked by the State *against* the refugee in order to deprive him of the refugee status previously accorded to him' [Original emphasis.] is not inconsistent with the conclusion to which we have come. The authority of this Court is however to a different effect on the question of onus, as to which Lord Brown adopted a statement made at the Lisbon Conference: 'the asylum authorities should bear the burden of proof that such [benign] changes [of circumstances in the country of departure] are indeed fundamental and durable. The jurisprudence of this Court is that no burden of proof lies upon either party in Tribunal proceedings.'

(6) The first respondent argued that articles of the Convention other than those so far referred to support his submission that once he has been accepted as a refugee he must be taken to be a refugee for all times and purposes, stressing that Chs II, III and IV which are concerned with juridical status, employment and welfare in the country of asylum, and which confer upon a refugee many of the other conventional benefits of citizenship, including rights to hold property (albeit as an alien), of association, access to the courts, to work for remuneration, and to welfare, imply that a person, once recognized as being entitled to protection, effectively ceases to be a refugee, acquires a 'status' as an ordinary citizen, and may not be treated otherwise, or removed from Australia, or at least not removed unless and until the appellant establish relevantly changed circumstances in the first respondent's own or former country of residence.

(7) The argument would fail even if the Act left open unqualified recourse to the articles upon which the first respondent seeks to rely for the implication. Those articles do not purport to define a refugee either for all times or purposes or at all. Nor do they touch upon how a refugee is to be defined or accorded recognition as such, or to be entitled to continue to avail himself of protection. These matters are expressly and exhaustively the subject of Art 1 of Ch I. Such consequential rights as flow from recognition as a refugee and give effect to the extent that they do to the Convention, are the subject, in part at least, of the Act under which conditions of residence can be imposed, and of other legislation, including social security and industrial legislation enacted from time to time.

17.3 Article 1D

Article 1D provides:

> This Convention shall not apply to persons who are at present receiving from organs or agencies of the United Nations, other than the United Nations High Commission for Refugees, protection or assistance.

> When such protection or assistance has ceased for any reason, without the position of such persons being definitively settled in accordance with the relevant resolutions adopted by the General Assembly of the United Nations, these persons shall ipso facto be entitled to the benefits of this Convention.

Article 1D is of little contemporary relevance, applying to only a very small number of asylum-seekers. The history of the article shows that it was inserted to deal with Palestinian asylum-seekers following the partition of Israel following World War II. Palestinians were excluded from the Convention if they were receiving assistance from UN agencies other than the UN High Commission for Refugees. The UN Conciliation Commission for Palestine (UNCCP) and the UN Relief and Works Agency in the Near East (UNRWA) were established to assist Palestinians who were dislocated as a result of the establishment of Israel. The history, operation, scope and continued relevance of Article 1D were considered by the Full Federal Court in *MIMA v WABQ*.[7]

In *WABQ*, the court held that 'persons' means a class of persons, not particular individuals. Thus, even if an individual is not receiving assistance, he or she will be excluded by the first paragraph if he or she belongs to the class that is receiving assistance. The court also held that the term 'at present' refers to the circumstances when the Convention was signed (in 1951) and operates to identify the group or community to whom Article 1D would apply in 1951 and into the future. As an evidential matter the court found that Palestinians were receiving assistance in 1951 and hence the first paragraph in Article 1D operates to exclude Palestinians who were displaced by the partition of Israel.

However, the operation of the second paragraph, as a pragmatic matter, makes the first paragraph redundant – at least for the present time. The court in *WABQ* held that the second paragraph is also concerned with a class of persons rather than individuals and that it is sufficient if either protection or assistance has ceased for any reason in respect of the class (without their position being definitively settled) for the second paragraph to apply. In relation to Palestinians, if either protection or assistance has ceased in relation to this group, then Article 1D is not applicable and an asylum-seeker is entitled to have his or her application for a protection visa determined in accordance with the Convention. As a factual matter, it appears Palestinians are not receiving protection by a UN agency. As is noted in RRT decision (N03/47958):

> I find on the independent evidence before me that whether or not UNRWA ever did provide protection to Palestinians, it does not do so now. UNRWA provides assistance to stateless Palestinians, primarily in the areas of 'health, education, social and emergency aid' (Report from the Fact-Finding Mission to Lebanon, 1–8 May 1998, s. 5A–C, Danish Refugee Council and Danish Immigration Service, October 1998, RRT Library). When UNRWA was specifically asked by the Danish researchers for its view of the Article 1D clause and its scope, its head office in Gaza stated that:

7 [2002] FCAFC 329 (8 November 2002).

> [I]t is the UNRWA's clear understanding that its mandate does not extend to protection from persecution, but merely embodies a number of practical aid measures.
>
> Independent evidence shows that the UNCCP has not been formally abolished but seems to be largely inactive.
>
> Since independent evidence shows that the class of persons to which the applicant belongs does not enjoy protection from a relevant UN body, I find that the applicant is not excluded from the Convention.

Given that there is no evidence to suggest that the United Nations is seeking to increase the level of assistance to stateless Palestinians in the foreseeable future,[8] Article 1D is effectively an obsolete provision.

17.4 Article 1E

Article 1E states:

> This Convention shall not apply to a person who is recognized by the competent authorities of the country in which he has taken residence as having the rights and obligations which are attached to the possession of the nationality of that country.

As with Article 1D, this article has little if any practical relevance in Australia. It is designed to exclude from protection individuals who have de facto nationality in another country (not being the country from which they are fleeing). However, as is discussed in section 17.7 below, Australia does not have protection obligations towards people who enjoy the protection of a third country. If it is determined that an applicant enjoys the protection of a third country, it will be unnecessary to consider whether the authorities of the third country in which the individual has taken residence recognise that the individual has the rights and obligations which are attached to the possession of the nationality of that country.[9]

17.5 Article 1F

17.5.1 Overview of Article 1F

Article 1F states:

> The provisions of this Convention shall not apply to any person with respect to whom there are serious reasons for considering that:
>
> (a) he has committed a *crime against peace, a war crime, or a crime against humanity*, as defined in the international instruments drawn up to make provisions in respect of such crimes;

8 See L. Roffonelli, 'With Palestine, against the Palestinians', in US Committee for Refugees, *World Refugee Survey 2004*, 66.

9 For judicial analysis of the meaning and scope of Article 1E, see *MIMA v Thiyagarajah* [1998] 152 FCA (9 March 1998); *Nagalingam v MILGEA* (1992) NoWG 309 of 1992; *Rajendran v MIMA* [1998] 464 FCA (4 May 1998).

(b) he has committed a *serious non-political* crime outside the country of refuge prior to his admission to that country as a refugee;
(c) he has been guilty of acts contrary to the purposes and principles of the United Nations.

The UNHCR Note on the Exclusion Clauses provides that: The rationale for the exclusion clauses, which should be borne in mind when considering their application, is that certain acts are so grave as to render their perpetrators undeserving of international protection as refugees. Their primary purpose is to deprive those guilty of heinous acts, and serious common crimes, of international refugee protection and to ensure that such persons do not abuse the institution of asylum in order to avoid being held legally accountable for their acts. The exclusion clauses must be applied 'scrupulously' to protect the integrity of the institution of asylum, as is recognised by UNHCR's Executive Committee in Conclusion No. 82 (XLVIII), 1997. At the same time, given the possible serious consequences of exclusion, it is important to apply them with great caution and only after a full assessment of the individual circumstances of the case. The exclusion clauses should, therefore, always be interpreted in a restrictive manner.[10]

It is important to note that Article 1F only applies in relation to acts committed by an individual prior to entering the receiving state (unlike Articles 32 and 33, which apply in relation to acts committed in the receiving country). From the above it is apparent that there are two principal objectives underpinning Article 1F. The first is to exclude 'undeserving' people from the protective provisions of the Convention. The second is to ensure that individuals who have committed heinous acts cannot escape prosecution. A third objective is to protect the security interests of the receiving states.

The soundness of these objectives is considered following a brief examination of each of the subclauses. It is also important to note that there is significant overlap between the three subparagraphs. Often the one act, such as a war crime or a crime against humanity, would come within each subparagraph.

17.5.2 Article 1F(a) – crimes against peace, war crimes, and crimes against humanity

The meaning of 'crimes against peace, war crimes, and crimes against humanity' is evolving and is dealt with in a number of international documents.[11] The most striking feature of these crimes is the lack of specificity with which they are defined. Given the formless nature of the central terms in Article 1F and the rarity with which this article is invoked, the discussion below is limited to a brief overview. As will become apparent, there has been very little Australian judicial analysis of Article 1F.

10 30 May 1997.
11 These include the 1945 London Agreement and Charter of the International Military Tribunal (the Nuremberg Charter); the 1948 Genocide Convention; the Geneva Conventions of 1949 and the Additional Protocols of 1977; the Draft Code of Crimes Against Peace and Security of Mankind; the Statute of the ad hoc International Criminal Tribunals for the Former Yugoslavia; the Rome Statute of the International Criminal Court.

The meanings of most of the key phrases in Article 1F(a) are to be derived from international law. They are not defined in the Convention. As a result of the continually evolving and often vague nature of the international law and the fact that there does not exist a single international instrument or anything approaching a consensual opinion in relation to the key terms employed in Article 1F, there is no point in a book of this nature attempting to define the exact parameters of Article 1F. Given the vagueness of the terms and lack of authoritative commentary on the topic this task is indeed impossible in a text of any size.

The purpose of the discussion below is to suggest to readers the main issues relating to Article 1F. As noted below, there are a large number of international instruments dealing with some of the key terms, none of which constitutes a decisive account of the nature and scope of the relevant terms and concepts. We make no attempt to provide a systematic account of each of these documents. In elaborating on the meaning of certain international criminal offences, we rely heavily on the Rome Statute of the International Criminal Court. The definition of the relevant crimes in this instrument is not decisive of their meaning in the international law context. However, the Rome Statute is a useful guide because it is a recent international law instrument which is ratified by a large number of states,[12] and the definitions of the crimes stipulated in it were made in full knowledge of pre-existing international law jurisprudence.

17.5.2.1 Crimes against peace

An Australian court has not considered the meaning of 'crime against peace' at length and there is no internationally settled definition of the term.[13] It has been noted that the definition of a 'crime against peace' is in 'an uncertain state as a crime that an individual can commit'.[14] The UNHCR *Note on the Exclusion Clauses* (1997) provides that:

> According to the London Charter a crime against peace involves the 'planning, preparation, initiation or waging of a war of aggression, or a war in violation of international treaties, agreements, or assurances, or participation in a common plan or conspiracy for the accomplishment of any of the foregoing'. Given the nature of this crime, it can only be committed by those in a high position of authority representing a State or a State-like entity. In practice, this provision has rarely been invoked.[15]

This interpretation is significantly at odds with the literal meaning of the term. 'Peace' minimally refers to a situation where people enjoy a level of security whereby their physical integrity does not feel threatened. There are a large number of acts that can jeopardise the security of other citizens, some of which,

12 In November 2006, 106 nations had ratified the Rome Statute. There are 139 signatories. An important omission is the United States.

13 G. Gilbert, 'Current issues in the application of the exclusion clauses', in E. Feller et al. (eds), *Refugee Protection in International Law* (Cambridge & New York, Cambridge Univerity Press, 2003) 425, 434. For a cursory discussion of the term, see *SRYY v MIMIA* (2005) 147 FCR 1; *SZITR v MIMA* [2006] FCA 1759.

14 The UNHCR *Note on the Exclusion Clauses* (1997), at 15.

15 Para 11.

relatively speaking, constitute minor offences, such as a serious (random) assault. Such a literal approach to the term is not likely to be adopted by a court. However, given the lack of guidance on the matter it is not possible to predict with any confidence the manner in which this provision will be interpreted. It is an example of the problems that arise when aspirational sentiments underpin instruments which have legal effect.

17.5.2.2 War crimes

The term 'war crime' is defined in several international documents. However, there is no uniform definition. The matter has not been considered by an Australian court at length.[16] The UNHCR *Note on the Exclusion Clauses* (1997) provides that:

> Certain breaches of international humanitarian law constitute war crimes. Although such crimes can be committed in both international and non-international armed conflicts, the content of the crimes depends on the nature of the conflict. War crimes cover such acts as wilful killing and torture of civilians, launching indiscriminate attacks on civilians, and wilfully depriving a civilian or a prisoner of war of the rights of fair and regular trial.[17]

The most recent definition of 'war crimes' is found in Article 8(2) of the Rome Statute which lists 50 crimes (34 relate to international conflict and 16 apply in relation to non-international armed conflict). The definition is very lengthy. This can often lead to clarity and precision. However, unfortunately this is not the situation in the case of 'war crimes'. Many inexact and imprecise phrases are employed. In addition to this, many acts which do not involve violations of particularly important human interests are included.[18] We set out parts of the definition at some length to highlight the complexity and open-ended nature of this inquiry. We highlight the phrases which on this criteria (broadness or (relative) triviality) seem inapposite:

> For the purpose of this statute, 'war crimes' means:
> (a) Grave breaches of the Geneva Conventions of 12 August 1949, namely, any of the following acts against persons or property protected under the provisions of the relevant Geneva Convention:
> (i) Wilful killing; . . .
> (iv) Extensive *destruction and appropriation of property*, not justified by military necessity and carried out unlawfully and wantonly; . . .
> (vii) Unlawful deportation *or transfer* or unlawful confinement;
> (viii) Taking of hostages.
> (b) Other serious violations of the laws and customs applicable in international armed conflict, within the established framework of international law, namely, any of the following acts: . . .

16 For some cursory observations, see *SRYY v MIMIA* (2005) 147 FCR 1.
17 Para 12.
18 We accept that it is difficult to make a hierarchy of human interests, but we endeavour to make a partial ranking in Chapter 18.

(ix) Intentionally directing attacks against *buildings* dedicated to religion, *education, art, science or charitable purposes*, historic monuments, hospitals and places where the sick and wounded are collected, provided they are not military objectives; . . .

(xi) Killing or wounding *treacherously* individuals belonging to the hostile nation or army;

(xii) Declaring that no quarter will be given; . . .

(e) Other serious violations of the laws and customs applicable in armed conflicts not of an international character, within the established framework of international law, namely, any of the following acts: . . .

(ii) Intentionally directing attacks against *buildings, material*, medical units and *transport*, and personnel using the distinctive emblems of the Geneva Conventions in conformity with international law; . . .

(iv) Intentionally directing attacks against *buildings* dedicated to religion, *education, art, science or charitable purposes*, historic monuments, hospitals and places where the sick and wounded are collected, provided they are not military objectives; . . .

(ix) Killing or wounding *treacherously* a combatant adversary; . . .

Beyond this (non-authoritative list) list there is no agreed consensus on the meaning of 'war crime': 'as for war crimes, the various [international] statutes are equally divergent'.[19] The term 'war crime', nevertheless, is less vague than 'crimes against peace'. There is sufficient particularity and consensus associated with the term to make it possible to state with a large degree of confidence that an act is a war crime. However, given the lack of convergence regarding non-core acts coming within the term, uncertainty abounds regarding the full ambit of the phrase. However, one settled aspect relating to war crimes is that they can be committed by individuals or combatants.

17.5.2.3 Crimes against humanity

The UNHCR *Note on the Exclusion Clauses* (1997) provides that:

> The distinguishing feature of crimes against humanity, which cover acts such as genocide, murder, rape and torture, is that they must be carried out as part of a widespread or systematic attack directed against the civilian population. An isolated act can, however, constitute a crime against humanity if it is part of a coherent system or a series of systematic and repeated acts. Since such crimes can take place in peacetime as well as armed conflict, this is the broadest category under Article 1F(a).[20]

The term was most recently defined by Article 7(1) of the Rome Statute, which states:

1. For the purpose of this Statute, 'crime against humanity' means any of the following acts when committed as part of a widespread or systematic attack directed against any civilian population, with knowledge of the attack:
   (a) Murder;
   (b) Extermination;

19 Gilbert, 'Current issues in the application of the exclusion clauses', pp. 425, 437.
20 Para 13.

(c) Enslavement;
(d) Deportation or forcible transfer of population;
(e) Imprisonment or other severe deprivation of physical liberty in violation of fundamental rules of international law;
(f) Torture;
(g) Rape, sexual slavery, enforced prostitution, forced pregnancy, enforced sterilization, or any other form of sexual violence of comparable gravity;
(h) Persecution against any identifiable group or collectivity on political, racial, national, ethnic, cultural, religious, gender as defined in paragraph 3, or other grounds that are universally recognized as impermissible under international law, in connection with any act referred to in this paragraph or any crime within the jurisdiction of the Court;
(i) Enforced disappearance of persons;
(j) The crime of apartheid;
(k) Other inhumane acts of a similar character intentionally causing great suffering, or serious injury to body or to mental or physical health.

Article 7(2) provides definitions of 'attack directed against any civilian population'; 'extermination'; 'enslavement'; 'deportation or forcible transfer of population'; 'torture'; 'forced pregnancy'; 'persecution' (which in Article 7(2) is defined as 'the intentional and severe deprivation of fundamental rights contrary to international law by reason of the identity of the group or collectivity'); 'crime of apartheid'; and 'enforced disappearance of persons'.

Although not specifically stipulated in the Rome Statute as a crime against humanity (it is listed as a discrete offence), the crime of genocide is also a crime against humanity,[21] and in fact is perhaps the most widely accepted crime against humanity. Article 2 of the Genocide Convention and Article 6 of the Rome Statute define genocide as:

> Any of the following acts committed with the intent to destroy, in whole or in part, a national, ethnical, racial or religious group, as such: (a) Killing members of the group; (b) Causing serious bodily or mental harm to members of the group; (c) Deliberately inflicting on the group conditions of life calculated to bring about its physical destruction in whole or in part; (d) Imposing measures intended to prevent births within the group; (e) Forcibly transferring children of the group to another group.

Crimes against humanity can be committed in times of peace or war.[22]

17.5.3 Article 1F(b) – serious non-political crimes

Article 1(F)(b) states:

> The provisions of this Convention shall not apply to any person with respect to whom there are serious reasons for considering that:
> (b) he has committed a serious non-political crime outside the country of refuge prior to his admission to that country as a refugee;

21 Gilbert, 'Current issues in the application of the exclusion clauses', pp. 425, 435.
22 ibid.

The objective of Article 1F(b) is to protect the interests of the receiving state by excluding from it people who have committed serious offences.[23]

The UNHCR *Note on the Exclusion Clauses* (1997) provides that:

> This category [Article 1F(b)] does not cover minor crimes nor prohibitions on the legitimate exercise of human rights. In determining whether a particular offence is sufficiently serious, international rather than local standards are relevant. The following factors should be taken into account: the nature of the act, the actual harm inflicted, the form of procedure used to prosecute the crime, the nature of the penalty, and whether most jurisdictions would consider it a serious crime. Thus, for example, murder, rape and armed robbery would undoubtedly qualify as serious offences, whereas petty theft would obviously not. A serious crime should be considered non-political when other motives (such as personal reasons or gain) are the predominant feature of the specific crime committed. Where no clear link exists between the crime and its alleged political objective or when the act in question is disproportionate to the alleged political objective, non-political motives are predominant. The motivation, context, methods and proportionality of a crime to its objectives are important factors in evaluating its political nature. The fact that a particular crime is designated as non-political in an extradition treaty is of significance, but not conclusive in itself. Egregious acts of violence, such as those acts commonly considered to be of a 'terrorist' nature, will almost certainly fail the predominance test, being wholly disproportionate to any political objective. Furthermore, for a crime to be regarded as political in nature, the political objectives should be consistent with human rights principles. Article 1F(b) also requires the crime to have been committed 'outside the country of refuge prior to [the individual's] admission to that country as a refugee'. Individuals who commit 'serious non-political crimes' within the country of refuge are subject to that country's criminal law process and, in the case of particularly grave crimes, to Articles 32 and 33(2) of the 1951 Convention.[24]

This provision on its face is less open-ended than the paragraphs in 1F(a). However, a close reading reveals several complexities relating to this provision. The basic thrust is that individuals who commit crimes in their country of origin should be excluded from the Convention – to preserve the security of the receiving country. However, exclusion is not applicable in two circumstances: (i) where the crime is not serious; and (ii) where the crime is serious but it is a political crime.

We look at these issues separately.

17.5.3.1 When is a crime serious?

The meaning of 'serious crime' is unclear. However, the Full Federal Court in *Ovcharuk v MIMA*[25] made some general observations about the concept. The court noted that the notion of seriousness in the context of crime is culturally relative. Where an act is an offence in both the country of origin and the receiving

23 See *Dhayakpa v MIEA* (1995) No. WAG 134 of 1994 FED No. 942/95.
24 Para 14.
25 [1998] FCA 1314 (16 October 1998).

country, the seriousness of the crime is determined according to the values, customs and beliefs of the receiving country.[26]

There is little question that the criminalisation of conduct and the seriousness with which criminal conduct is regarded varies greatly depending on the state in question. This is a point highlighted in Chapter 15. Given the context-sensitive nature of crime and sentencing and the cultural relativity associated with decisions pertaining to crime and punishment, there is considerable merit in the view that receiving states should be permitted to define what they regard as a serious crime. The purpose of Article 1F(b) is to maintain the safety of the receiving state.

Moreover, an inability on behalf of the receiving state to set the boundaries of what constitutes a serious crime may discourage states from ratifying and observing the Convention. This, however, must be balanced against the fact that this approach provides considerable scope for manipulating the spirit of the Convention by setting the bar of seriousness too low, thereby excluding significant numbers of asylum-seekers. Added to this is the fact that the Convention is an international instrument and hence there should be a move towards adopting universal standards of criminality and seriousness.

In *Ovcharuk* it was doubted whether Article 1F(b) operates to exclude a person who has committed an act which is an offence in the receiving state but not in the country of origin. This is irrespective of the seriousness with which the conduct is regarded in the receiving country. Selling cocaine and having sex with children under 16 are regarded as very serious offences in Australia. However, they are not subject to criminal sanctions in some states. The court was of the view that Article 1F(b) implies that a crime must have been committed in order for the article to become operable. As a matter of fairness, this interpretation is sound. Article 1F(b) is principally concerned with protection, not punishment (and hence it does not matter that an applicant has already been punished for the crime).[27] People who engage in acts that are not criminal at the time at which they are committed do not, by so doing, evince a predisposition towards engaging in anti-social behaviour.

It is unclear whether there should be a degree of proportionality between the crime and the level of threatened persecution. The UNHCR *Guidelines on Exclusion*[28] state that in applying Article 1F(b), the worse the persecution feared, the more serious must be the crime committed. In the United States and Canada, this approach has been rejected on the basis that Article 1F is a hurdle requirement which an applicant must clear before being eligible for protection, but in some parts of continental Europe practice has included courts not excluding where there was a fear of persecution.[29] As noted in Chapter 15, the proportionality thesis has a strong doctrinal underpinning. However, in the context of Article

26 [1998] FCA 1314 (16 October 1998).
27 *Dhayapka v MIEA* (1995) No. WAG 134 of 1994 FED No. 942/95.
28 1 December 1996, para [53].
29 Gilbert, 'Current issues in the application of the exclusion clauses', pp. 450–51.

1F(b) it would appear that the balancing exercise has already been undertaken in the drafting of the subparagraph. In other words, it is felt that the commission of any serious non-political crime disentitles a person from the protection of another state.

17.5.3.2 Meaning of (serious) non-political crime

Section 91T(1) of the *Migration Act 1958* (Cth) defines 'non-political crime' for the purpose of Article 1F as a crime where a person's motives for committing the crime *were wholly or mainly non-political in nature.*[30]

Thus a crime will be considered political (and hence outside the scope of Article 1F(B)) where one of the motivations (though not necessarily the main motivation) was political in nature. This sets the bar for a political crime very low. However, this is subject to section 91T(3), which prescribes that offences listed in section 5 of the *Extradition Act 1988* (Cth) are non-political crimes. Section 5 states that a non-political crime is:

(a) an offence that is constituted by conduct of a kind referred to in:
  (i) Article 1 of the Convention for the Suppression of Unlawful Seizure of Aircraft, being the convention a copy of the English text of which is set out in Schedule 1 to the *Crimes (Aviation) Act 1991*; or
  (ii) Article 1 of the Convention for the Suppression of Unlawful Acts against the Safety of Civil Aviation, being the convention a copy of the English text of which is set out in Schedule 2 to the *Crimes (Aviation) Act 1991*; or
  (iii) paragraph 1 of Article 2 of the Convention on the Protection and Punishment of Crimes against Internationally Protected Persons, including Diplomatic Agents, being the convention a copy of the English text of which is set out in the Schedule to the *Crimes (Internationally Protected Persons) Act 1976*; or
  (iv) Article III of the Convention on the Prevention and Punishment of the Crime of Genocide, being the convention a copy of the English text of which is set out in the *Genocide Convention Act 1949*; or
  (v) Article 1 of the International Convention against the Taking of Hostages, being the convention of that title that was adopted by the General Assembly of the United Nations on 17 December 1979; or
  (vi) Article 1 of the Convention against Torture and other Cruel, Inhuman or Degrading Treatment or Punishment, being the convention of that title that was adopted by the General Assembly of the United Nations on 10 December 1984; or
  (vii) Article 3 of the Convention for the Suppression of Unlawful Acts Against the Safety of Maritime Navigation, a copy of the English text of which is set out in Schedule 1 to the *Crimes (Ships and Fixed Platforms) Act 1992*; or
  (viii) Article 2 of the Protocol for the Suppression of Unlawful Acts Against the Safety of Fixed Platforms Located on the Continental Shelf, a copy of the English text of which is set out in Schedule 2 to the *Crimes (Ships and Fixed Platforms) Act 1992*;

(b) an offence constituted by conduct that, by an extradition treaty (not being a bilateral treaty) in relation to the country or any country, is required to be treated

30 It should be noted that this overturns earlier authorities which predate s 91T and which stipulated that for a crime to be political, the sole or substantial motivation needed to be political.

as an offence for which a person is permitted to be surrendered or tried, being an offence declared by regulations for the purposes of this paragraph not to be a political offence in relation to the country or all countries;

(c) an offence constituted by:
   (i) the murder, kidnapping or other attack on the person or liberty; or
   (ii) a threat or attempt to commit, or participation as an accomplice in, a murder, kidnapping or other attack on the person or liberty;

(d) of the head of state or head of government of the country or a member of the family of either such person, being an offence declared by regulations for the purposes of this paragraph not to be a political offence in relation to the country; or

(e) an offence constituted by taking or endangering, attempting to take or endanger or participating in the taking or endangering of, the life of a person, being an offence:
   (i) committed in circumstances in which such conduct creates a collective danger, whether direct or indirect, to the lives of other persons; and
   (ii) declared by regulations for the purposes of this paragraph not to be a political offence in relation to the country.[31]

Thus a crime is non-political for the purposes of Article 1F(b) if the motive for committing it is *wholly or mainly* non-political. However, in relation to the crimes listed in section 5 of the *Extradition Act 1988* (Cth), the motivation is irrelevant; these crimes are deemed inherently non-political irrespective of the reason for which they were committed. The rationale for this is that certain crimes, those that seriously violate the safety, lives, or physical integrity of others, constitute a callous disregard of the interests of others and cannot even purport to be justified by the fact that they have a political motivation.

For serious crimes not excluded by section 5 of the *Extradition Act 1988* (Cth), the meaning of a non-political crime is an important issue. Section 91T(1) states that a crime is non-political where it is motivated *wholly or mainly by non-political considerations*. Thus, the crime will be political if it is motivated, at least in part, by political considerations. This leaves open the issue of what is meant by 'political'. The High Court in *Singh v MIMA*[32] stated that a political crime must be linked with a political objective, such as changing the government, or altering the practices or policies of those who exercise political power. Other relevant considerations include the target of the crime offence (that is, was it a government official or a person chosen at random?), the means used to commit the offence and whether or not the individual has links with an organisation and its objectives and purposes.[33]

The court stated that it is also relevant to consider the degree of proportionality between the crime and the political objective. If the harm caused by the crime is disproportionate to the ends sought it is easier to infer that the motive was other than political.

31 The Explanatory Memorandum accompanying the changes states that the reason for the amendment was that the courts set too low a threshold when determining the degree of political motivation necessary for a criminal act to fall outside the Article 1F exclusion clause: Migration Legislation Amendment Bill (No. 6) 2001, Explanatory Memorandum, [33].

32 [2002] HCA 7 (7 March 2002).

33 This part of the decision was not altered by s 91T of the *Migration Act 1958* (Cth).

The court did not provide an exhaustive definition of 'political crime'. Kirby J in *Singh* offered some insights regarding the complexity of such a task:

> 111. Various attempts have been made to define with greater exactitude the conduct that will take an applicant for refugee status outside the Convention even if, in some general way, the crimes in which that person was involved might have been linked in the offender's mind with some vague political purpose. Thus, if the crime concerned involved an 'atrocious act, grossly out of proportion to any genuine political objective', such that it could not reasonably be seen to be advancing a political objective, it might be classified as 'non-political'. Likewise, the infliction of indiscriminate violence; the 'open manifestation of anarchy'; the perpetration of 'acts of odious barbarism and vandalism'; the involvement in a 'rampage' of crime or sheer acts of terrorism, have all been excluded from the category of 'political crime'. Judges have vied with each other to invent new epithets for conduct that will take its perpetrator outside the Convention's protection. The debate about the subject has continued. It is not concluded . . .
>
> 120. Various ways were found to express this link between the subjective motivation of the offender and the mental element of the offence. However, as Lord Mustill pointed out in *T v Secretary of State for the Home Department*,[34] the gravity of the offence in question is already hypothesised by the requirement that the offence must be 'serious'. Its character cannot depend on the consequences that may follow, nor, as such, upon those that the offender intended. Whilst the object of the offender may therefore be relevant to the character of the particular offence, political motivation on the part of the offender does not convert every offence committed for such motives into a 'political' crime. Neither will some degree of personal motivation on the part of the offender necessarily exclude the offence from being a political one. A stable discrimen will not be provided by reference to whether the decision-maker approves or disapproves of the objectives of the offender.
>
> 121. . . . Decision-makers are entitled to guidance from this Court on how they should approach the task of characterisation of criminal conduct presented by a case such as the present. In my view, this much can be said. A person who is otherwise entitled to protection as a 'refugee' has, on the face of things, a high claim to that status. It is one written in Australia's own law. It also reflects obligations of international law, which Australia has accepted and by which it is bound. Even the existence of serious grounds for believing that he or she has committed a 'serious' crime will not disqualify a person from protection, if a proper view of the crime in question, looked at as a whole, is that it is 'political' rather than 'non-political' in character.
>
> 122. The motives for the crime are not conclusive as to its character. But because crime in most societies, including our own, ordinarily involves a mental element, the perpetrator's intention may well be relevant to the character of the crime. It may, for example, constitute a reason for classifying a crime, performed by a person who happens to be a member of a political movement, as 'non-political', if its purpose was mainly for extraneous, personal or selfish reasons. On the other hand, the mere fact that the crime has been committed by a person involved in a political movement, or during disorder associated with that movement, is not enough to warrant its classification as 'political' rather than 'non-political'. Neither does the existence of some degree of personal motivation necessarily warrant the classification of the offence as 'non-political.' The

34 [1996] UKHL 8.

sometimes complex array of motivations for any offence must be considered before a characterisation of the offence for the purposes of the Convention is determined.

> 123. Nor are the consequences of the crime in question, known or implied, determinative of its character. The history of liberation movements, and rebellion against autocratic, colonial and tyrannical governments, has witnessed too many instances of serious crimes, involving innocent victims, to permit a hard and fast exclusion of otherwise 'political' crimes because they had terrible outcomes. It is not possible, conformably with long-established case law, to exclude, as such, the crime of murder.
>
> 124. If the target of the crime is an armed adversary or armed agent of the State (such as a police officer or other public official), it is more likely that the crime should be classified as 'political', than if the target comprises innocent civilians, or if there is no particular target and just the indiscriminate use of violence against other human beings. In such cases it is open to the decision-maker, in the context of 'non-political crimes' in Art 1F(b) of the Convention, to conclude that the crimes are 'serious' but outside the scope of the protection for serious 'political' crimes.
>
> 125. In the context of a phrase used in an international treaty it would be inappropriate to apply to its elucidation doctrines developed peculiarly by the common law, either to exclude classification as 'political' by reference to notions of remoteness, or to inculpate persons on the basis of their indirect involvement in a joint criminal enterprise with others. On the other hand, where the achievement of 'political' objectives may be viewed as 'remote' from the conduct in question, this may just be another way of saying that the true character of the serious crime is 'non-political' rather than 'political'. The mere fact that the person did not actually 'pull the trigger' does not necessarily exculpate him or her from involvement in a 'serious crime' of the disqualifying kind.[35]
> [References omitted.]

Thus in addressing the issue relating to Article 1F(b) the approach is as follows. Article 1F(b) will apply where:

(i) the crime is serious; and
(ii) one of the motives for the crime was wholly or mainly non-political in nature; and
(iii) the crime is not one listed in section 5 of the *Extradition Act 1988* (Cth).

17.5.4 Article 1F(c) – acts contrary to the purposes and principles of the United Nations

Article 1F(c) excludes the protective provisions of the Convention for persons guilty of acts contrary to the purposes and principles of the United Nations. This calls into consideration the purposes and principles of the United Nations. Articles 1 to 4 of the *United Nations Charter* provide that:

> The Purposes of the United Nations are:
>
> 1. To maintain international peace and security, and to that end: to take effective collective measures for the prevention and removal of threats to the peace, and for the suppression of acts of aggression or other breaches of the peace, and to

35 *MIMA v Singh* [2002] HCA 7 (7 March 2002), [111]–[125]. See also *Ovcharuk v MIMA* [1998] 1314 FCA (16 October 1998).

bring about by peaceful means, and in conformity with the principles of justice and international law, adjustment or settlement of international disputes or situations which might lead to a breach of the peace;

2. To develop friendly relations among nations based on respect for the principle of equal rights and self-determination of peoples, and to take other appropriate measures to strengthen universal peace;
3. To achieve international co-operation in solving international problems of an economic, social, cultural, or humanitarian character, and in promoting and encouraging respect for human rights and for fundamental freedoms for all without distinction as to race, sex, language, or religion; and
4. To be a centre for harmonizing the actions of nations in the attainment of these common ends.

The scope, purpose and operation of Article 1F(c) have not been considered by an Australian court. There is also no agreed international approach to the scope and application of this provision. The little discussion or commentary that there is on the matter is speculative and not well informed. This is not surprising. The article is by its very nature open-ended, unclear and poorly defined. There is no clarity around the acts covered by Article 1F(c), or the agents who can commit them.

It has been pointed out that the UN Charter only applies to states, and hence a sound argument can be made that only people in very senior state positions can be guilty of acts contrary to the United Nations.[36] However, in *Pushpanathan v Canada (Minister of Citizenship and Immigration)*[37] it was held that the provision can potentially apply to all individuals.

Given the uncertainty surrounding the provision it is obviously open to abuse and manipulation by states. At least one state (the Netherlands) has indicated that it will not use the article – it feels that Articles 1F(a) and (b) provide ample scope for exclusion.[38] This is the approach which Australian lawmakers would be wise to follow.

This is another example of the problems that arise when law is driven totally by aspirational ideas. A particularly disconcerting aspect of Article 1F(c) is the self-indulgent, self-serving nature of the provision (bearing in mind that UN organs were centrally involved in drafting the Convention). It assumes that the purposes of the United Nations are beyond question and so noble that any person acting contrary to them should not be protected from persecution. The paragraph also assumes the perpetual existence of the United Nations; a notion which has been recently questioned due to the repeated failure of the United Nations to achieve its principal goal of securing international peace and security.[39] The most glaring example of the failure of the United Nations is its spectacular lack of success in preventing governments killing large numbers of their own people.

36 Gilbert, 'Current issues in the application of the exclusion clauses', p. 456.
37 [1998] 1 SCR 982.
38 See Gilbert, 'Current issues in the application of the exclusion clauses', p. 457.
39 This is an issue that has been questioned. See for example J Morss and M Bagaric, 'If we can't have Global Democracy, let's all be Americans: injecting principle into the international law-making process' (2006) 15 *Transnational Law & Contemporary Problems* 1, pp. 217–42.

The United Nations has been in existence for over 60 years, so it is not too early to draw a line through its forms and make an informed decision regarding its competence. In a nutshell, the United Nations aims to make the world a more peaceful place and to increase the level of human flourishing. Has it achieved this aim? Certainly, the world is in absolute terms not a peaceful place. More than 170 million people have died in internal conflict alone since World War II.[40] This is more than double the number of deaths in both 'great wars'. During this period there have also been dozens of wars between states.

Of course there is no firm evidence that the alleged failings of the United Nations have directly contributed to this unhappy state of affairs. Supporters of the United Nations will no doubt charge that while the state of world disrepair is significant, it would have been far worse if the United Nations had not been in existence. It could tenably be suggested that because of the United Nations we at least have not had a World War III, and that there are some signs that peace and security in the world are improving.

It is not possible to definitively determine the correctness of either of these conflicting views. To do so would require a comparison of two parallel worlds, one being the present state of affairs (where the United Nations has operated for over 60 years); the other being identical in all respects except for the absence of the United Nations. We cannot play any such imaginary game, but this does not preclude us from making an assessment of the performance of the United Nations. All that needs to be asked is: 'Is the current state of affairs as far as world peace and global human flourishing acceptable?'

This is the approach taken by voters at domestic elections. When voters decide whether or not to re-elect an incumbent government, they are not paralysed into inaction by claims that a bad economic situation, for example, would have been worse had the opposition been in power. Rather they look at the current state of affairs and pass judgment on whether or not it is acceptable. In relation to this all-important question as far as the United Nations is concerned, the answer would appear to be no. The human deprivation and misery that continues to abound in a world is highlighted by the fact that 13 000 people die every day from hunger. Of course this state of affairs is largely a result of geopolitical and domestic matters beyond the direct control of the United Nations. The United Nations has no direct authority over the internal matters or the foreign policy of the United States, for example, but it does have the capacity to have an indirect impact.

The failings of the United Nations are so great that one of us has suggested that it should be abolished.[41] In any event, it is beyond question that its principles are not universally supported, let alone upheld, and its activities are not approved of by all.

40 UN Development Programme, *Human Development Report 2002: Deepening Democracy In A Fragmented World* (Oxford, OUP, 2002), 6.
41 M. Bagaric, *Future Directions in International Law and Human Rights* (Melbourne, Sandstone Academic Press, 2007).

17.5.5 Evidential issues and the scope of individual liability

Prior to critiquing the provisions of Article 1F it is important to emphasise that in order for Article 1F to be invoked there is no necessity that an individual must have been convicted of a relevant act. It is sufficient for there to be 'serious reasons for considering' that an individual has committed a relevant act or crime. This means simply that there must be 'strong evidence' in support of the relevant contention. It is sufficient if the 'material before the decision-maker demonstrates that there is evidence upon which it could reasonably and properly be concluded that the applicant committed the alleged crime'.[42] However, it seems that the weight of evidence does not need to be such as to satisfy the normal criminal standard of proof (beyond reasonable doubt), nor even the civil standard (balance of probabilities).[43]

There is no question that individuals can be responsible for crimes proscribed by international law. The notion of secondary or derivative liability, which is also employed in domestic criminal law,[44] has also been adopted into international law. Article 25 of the Rome Statute states:

> 2. A person who commits a crime within the jurisdiction of the Court shall be individually responsible and liable for punishment in accordance with this Statute.
> 3. In accordance with this Statute, a person shall be criminally responsible and liable for punishment for a crime within the jurisdiction of the Court if that person:
>   (a) Commits such a crime, whether as an individual, jointly with another or through another person, regardless of whether that other person is criminally responsible;
>   (b) Orders, solicits or induces the commission of such a crime which in fact occurs or is attempted;
>   (c) For the purpose of facilitating the commission of such a crime, aids, abets or otherwise assists in its commission or its attempted commission, including providing the means for its commission;
>   (d) In any other way contributes to the commission or attempted commission of such a crime by a group of persons acting with a common purpose. Such contribution shall be intentional and shall either:
>   (i) Be made with the aim of furthering the criminal activity or criminal purpose of the group, where such activity or purpose involves the commission of a crime within the jurisdiction of the Court; or
>   (ii) Be made in the knowledge of the intention of the group to commit the crime;
>   (e) In respect of the crime of genocide, directly and publicly incites others to commit genocide;
>   (f) Attempts to commit such a crime by taking action that commences its execution by means of a substantial step, but the crime does not occur because of circumstances independent of the person's intentions. However, a person who abandons the effort to commit the crime or otherwise prevents the completion of

42 *Arquita v MIMA* [2000] FCA 1989 (22 December 2000). See also *SRYY v MIMIA* (2005) 147 FLR 1.
43 *Arquita v MIMA* [2000] FCA 1989 (22 December 2000). See, further, *VWYJ v MIMIA* [2006] FCACF 1.
44 For a discussion of the relevant principles, see M. Bagaric and K. Arenson, *Criminal Laws of Australia: Cases and materials* (Melbourne, OUP, 2004), Ch. 13.

the crime shall not be liable for punishment under this Statute for the attempt to commit that crime if that person completely and voluntarily gave up the criminal purpose.

There are a number of defences available for some crimes. Broadly they are similar to the defences available under Australian domestic criminal law, including self-defence, duress, mental incapacity, mistake. There is also the defence of 'superior orders' that is available in the case of certain international crimes. Articles 31 to 33 of the Rome Statute set out the principal defences:

Article 31 Grounds for excluding criminal responsibility

(1) In addition to other grounds for excluding criminal responsibility provided for in this Statute, a person shall not be criminally responsible if, at the time of that person's conduct:
   (a) The person suffers from a mental disease or defect that destroys that person's capacity to appreciate the unlawfulness or nature of his or her conduct, or capacity to control his or her conduct to conform to the requirements of law;
   (b) The person is in a state of intoxication that destroys that person's capacity to appreciate the unlawfulness or nature of his or her conduct, or capacity to control his or her conduct to conform to the requirements of law, unless the person has become voluntarily intoxicated under such circumstances that the person knew, or disregarded the risk, that, as a result of the intoxication, he or she was likely to engage in conduct constituting a crime within the jurisdiction of the Court;
   (c) The person acts reasonably to defend himself or herself or another person or, in the case of war crimes, property which is essential for the survival of the person or another person or property which is essential for accomplishing a military mission, against an imminent and unlawful use of force in a manner proportionate to the degree of danger to the person or the other person or property protected. The fact that the person was involved in a defensive operation conducted by forces shall not in itself constitute a ground for excluding criminal responsibility under this subparagraph;
   (d) The conduct which is alleged to constitute a crime within the jurisdiction of the Court has been caused by duress resulting from a threat of imminent death or of continuing or imminent serious bodily harm against that person or another person, and the person acts necessarily and reasonably to avoid this threat, provided that the person does not intend to cause a greater harm than the one sought to be avoided. Such a threat may either be:
      (i) Made by other persons; or
      (ii) Constituted by other circumstances beyond that person's control.

Article 32 Mistake of fact or mistake of law

1. A mistake of fact shall be a ground for excluding criminal responsibility only if it negates the mental element required by the crime.
2. A mistake of law as to whether a particular type of conduct is a crime within the jurisdiction of the Court shall not be a ground for excluding criminal responsibility. A mistake of law may, however, be a ground for excluding criminal responsibility if it negates the mental element required by such a crime, or as provided for in article 33.

Article 33 Superior orders and prescription of law

1. The fact that a crime within the jurisdiction of the Court has been committed by a person pursuant to an order of a Government or of a superior, whether military or civilian, shall not relieve that person of criminal responsibility unless:
   (a) The person was under a legal obligation to obey orders of the Government or the superior in question;
   (b) The person did not know that the order was unlawful; and
   (c) The order was not manifestly unlawful.
2. For the purposes of this article, orders to commit genocide or crimes against humanity are manifestly unlawful.

17.5.6 Analysis of Article 1F

As discussed above, there are several objectives underpinning Articles 1F(a) and (c). The soundness of the objectives and the extent to which they are achieved by these paragraphs is questionable.

The first objective is simply to ensure that the 'undeserving' are not granted protection. There is a natural human tendency to not bestow benefits upon the non-virtuous:

> The principle that wrongdoers deserve to suffer seems to accord with our deepest intuitions concerning justice.[45]

> As individuals we have a wholly proper desire to seek revenge when wrongs are inflicted on us: as a society we demand that constituted authority punish those who unjustifiably inflict injury on others or otherwise act in ways we think are wrong.[46]

There are several problems applying this in the context of the Convention. First, for the acts listed in Article 1F it is not necessary that the applicant has been found guilty of the proscribed conduct. A much lower standard of proof is adequate. Thus a certain hardship (denial of protection) can be imposed for what is merely speculated to be a transgression. Moreover, a fundamental aspect of any non-primitive system of punishment is that the punishment should, at least roughly, fit the crime. As we saw in Chapter 15, this is known as the principle of proportionality. Serious violations of this principle bring into disrepute the integrity of the relevant system of law. This is despite the somewhat culturally relative nature of offence seriousness. It is for this reason that much of the world was appalled at the sentence of death by stoning handed down to a Nigerian woman for adultery in late 2003.[47]

There is no evidence that the principle of proportionality is sensibly incorporated in Article 1F. In this regard, it is important to emphasise that denial

45 J. Kleinig, *Punishment and Desert* (The Hague, Martinus Nijhoff, 1973), p. 67. See also D.J.B Hawkins, 'Punishment and Moral Responsibility', in S.E. Grupp (ed.), *Theories of Punishment* (Bloomington IN, Indiana University Press, 1971), p. 13, where he asserts that at the pre-reflective level it seems to be assumed that a guilty act deserves punishment.

46 H.L. Packer, 'Theories of Punishment and Correction: What is the Function of Prison?', in L. Orland (ed.), *Justice, Punishment, Treatment: The Correctional Process* (New York, Free Press, 1973), pp. 183, 184.

47 This sentence was ultimately overturned following international condemnation by an appeals court: 'Court spares Nigerian woman stoning death for adultery', 26 September 2003: www.nupge.ca/news2003/n26se03a.htm.

of protection always constitutes a significant hardship to the individual, given the serious harm threshold that must be crossed to be eligible for protection. The operation of Articles 1F(a) and (c) means that a state is entitled to send an individual back to his or her country of origin, in some cases to face almost certain death, for something as trifling as the fact that there is reason to believe the individual has made 'improper use of a flag of truce' or destroyed or seized the enemy's property, or for committing an offence of indeterminate nature as an offence against peace or acting contrary to the purposes of the United Nations.

The deficiencies stemming from the vague and aspirational nature with which the paragraphs are drafted and the overlapping nature of many of the provisions are such that Articles 1F(a) and (c) can be held out as brilliant examples of law-making and drafting at its most confused and inadequate. This is one of the reasons for there being virtually no domestic consideration of these paragraphs. Refugee law would be substantially improved if these two provisions were simply ignored. In practice this is already the case; however, to prevent the possibility of abuse in future, legislation should be drafted declaring that these paragraphs will not be utilised in Australian domestic law.

Article 1F(b) has a sounder justification. It is prefaced on the rationale that people who commit a serious crime may do so again and hence endanger the security of others. Ostensibly this appears to be justifiable. However, empirical evidence shows that prior serious criminality is a poor indicator of how an individual will behave in the future – most people who commit a serious offence do not re-offend in a similar manner.[48] Nevertheless, the deficiencies associated with it are not as pronounced as with the other paragraphs. Moreover, Article 1F(b) is broad enough to encompass most of the conduct to which paragraphs 1F(a) and (c) appear to allude.

17.5.7 Expulsion: Articles 32 and 33

Articles 32 and 33 apply where a person has already been granted refugee status and permit the receiving country to expel the refugee in certain circumstances.[49] Article 32 states:

> (1) The Contracting States shall not expel a refugee lawfully in their territory save on grounds of national security or public order.
> (2) The expulsion of such a refugee shall be only in pursuance of a decision reached in accordance with due process of law. Except where compelling reasons of national security otherwise require, the refugee shall be allowed to submit evidence to clear himself, and to appeal to and be represented for the purpose before competent authority or a person or persons specially designated by the competent authority.
> (3) The Contracting States shall allow such a refugee a reasonable period within which to seek legal admission into another country. The Contracting States reserve

48 Bagaric, *Punishment and Sentencing: A Rational Approach*.
49 See *Ovcharuk v MIMA* [1998] 313 FCA (1 April 1998), where it was stated that Article 33 deals with 'post admission refugees'.

the right to apply during that period such internal measures as they may deem necessary.

Article 33 provides a general prohibition against refoulement and an exception to this. It provides:

(1) No Contracting State shall expel or return ('refouler') a refugee in any manner whatsoever to the frontiers of territories where his life or freedom would be threatened on account of his race, religion, nationality, membership of a particular social group or political opinion.
(2) The benefit of the present provision may not, however, be claimed by a refugee whom there are *reasonable grounds for regarding as a danger to the security of the country* in which he is, or who, having been convicted by a final judgement of a *particularly serious crime*, constitutes a danger to the community of that country.

Section 91U of the *Migration Act 1958* (Cth) defines the term 'particularly serious crime' for the purpose of Article 33(2). It states:

(1) For the purposes of the application of this Act and the regulations to a particular person, Article 33(2) of the Refugees Convention as amended by the Refugees Protocol has effect as if a reference in that Article to a particularly serious crime included a reference to a crime that consists of the commission of:
    (a) a serious Australian offence (as defined by subsection (2)); or
    (b) a serious foreign offence (as defined by subsection (3)).
(2) For the purposes of this section, a serious Australian offence is an offence against a law in force in Australia, where:
    (a) the offence:
        (i) involves violence against a person; or
        (ii) is a serious drug offence; or
        (iii) involves serious damage to property; or
        (iv) is an offence against section 197A or 197B (offences relating to immigration detention); and
    (b) the offence is punishable by:
        (i) imprisonment for life; or
        (ii) imprisonment for a fixed term of not less than 3 years; or
        (iii) imprisonment for a maximum term of not less than 3 years.
(3) For the purposes of this section, a **serious foreign offence** is an offence against a law in force in a foreign country, where:
    (a) the offence:
        (i) involves violence against a person; or
        (ii) is a serious drug offence; or
        (iii) involves serious damage to property; and
    (b) if it were assumed that the act or omission constituting the offence had taken place in the Australian Capital Territory, the act or omission would have constituted an offence (the Territory offence) against a law in force in that Territory, and the Territory offence would have been punishable by:
        (i) imprisonment for life; or
        (ii) imprisonment for a fixed term of not less than 3 years; or
        (iii) imprisonment for a maximum term of not less than 3 years.

Articles 32 and 33 do not revoke refugee status where it has been granted. Rather they remove the duty of the receiving country to not expel or refouler refugees. Pursuant to Articles 32 and 33 there are in fact four circumstances when a refugee can be expelled:

(i) where the refugee constitutes a danger to national security;
(ii) where the refugee constitutes a danger to public order;
(iii) where the refugee is a danger to security of the country; and
(iv) where the refugee has been convicted of a particularly serious crime and constitutes a danger to the community of that country.

It is unlikely that the third requirement adds anything to the first two. In relation to the last situation, case law pre-dating section 91U held that the mere commission of a particularly serious offence does not necessarily mean that the person constitutes a danger to the community.[50] This is no doubt correct given that many people who commit serious offences do not do so again.[51] Thus, where a refugee commits a particularly serious offence, to consider if Article 33(2) applies it is then necessary to take another step, and from an examination of all the circumstances of the offence and the personal circumstances of the offender make an assessment of whether or not the refugee is a danger to the community. Section 91U does not seem to change this approach: it merely sets out the definition of one limb of this inquiry.[52]

A curious aspect of section 91U is that it also extends to offences committed overseas. Given that Article 33(2) is confined to acts committed in the receiving country, this seems to go beyond the terms of the Convention. It has been suggested that perhaps the explanation for the presence of the foreign offence element is to accommodate situations where a refugee who is receiving protection commits an offence while travelling overseas and then returns to the receiving country.[53]

17.6 Country of reference and effective protection in another country

As previously noted, in order to be a refugee the person must be outside the country of his or her nationality or (where the person has no nationality) outside his or her country of former habitual residence.

50 In *A v MIMA* [1999] FCA 227 (16 March 1999), [3], the court noted: 'The principal statement of exclusion is "who constitutes a danger to the community". The phrase "having been convicted . . . of a particularly serious crime" adds an additional element, but it is not expressed as if that additional element swallowed up the principal statement. This aspect of the drafting is perhaps made clearer when attention is directed to the first alternative contained in the provision, that "there are reasonable grounds for regarding [the person] as a danger to the security of the country in which he is". The whole provision is concerned with perils represented by the refugee, either because of a threat to the security of the country, or because of a danger to its community.'

51 See Bagaric, *Punishment and Sentencing: A Rational Approach*.

52 See also Germov and Motta, *Refugee Law in Australia*, p. 453.

53 ibid.

The second paragraph in Article 1A(2) provides that:

> In the case of a person who has more than one nationality, the term 'the country of his nationality' shall mean each of the countries of which he is a national, and a person shall not be deemed to be lacking the protection of the country of his nationality if, without any valid reason based on well-founded fear, he has not availed himself of the protection of one of the countries of which he is a national.

Thus, where a person has more than one country of nationality, he or she is not a refugee unless he or she cannot obtain protection in any of those countries.

The term 'country' has a narrower meaning in the context of 'country of nationality' than 'country of former habitual residence' (in the first paragraph of Article 1A(2)). Only a sovereign state can grant nationality, so in the first context it refers to regions that meet the criteria for statehood under international law. According to Charlesworth and Chinkin, the criteria for and incidence of statehood are: a permanent population, a defined territory, government, and capacity to enter into relations with other states.[54] An incident of statehood is the capacity to make laws regarding nationality. Thus in order to determine if a person is a national of a state it is necessary to consider the domestic laws of the state.

In *Tjhe Kwet Koe v MIEA*[55] the court found that in the second context, 'country' means a region that need not have the capacity to grant nationality, but is the region where the person resides.

This was cited with approval in *Leung v MIMA*:

> In *Koe*, Tamberlin J at 296 said: The objective of the Convention is to provide a practical humanitarian solution to the problems of refugees. It should be interpreted with this objective in mind. Individuals should not be denied the protection of the Convention by an unnecessarily narrow reading of the definition of 'refugee'. It is not appropriate to conclude that an applicant has no recourse under the Convention simply because his or her 'country' of former habitual residence happens to be a colony or other entity that is not an independent sovereign state.[56]

Thus it can be a colony or other region that is not an independent state. This broader definition is in keeping with the aim of the Refugees Convention: that is, to protect persons in real fear of persecution.

In order to constitute a former habitual residence, it is necessary for the applicant to at least have de facto residence in the region. The relationship between the person and the state should be analogous to that between a citizen and his or her country of nationality. However, in *Taiem v MIMA*[57] it was noted that in order for a region to be a 'country of former habitual residence' it is not necessary that the applicant has a right to re-enter that region. Where a person has more than one 'country of former habitual residence', it is not necessary to

54 H. Charlesworth and C. Chinkin, *The Boundaries of International Law* (Manchester, Manchester University Press, 2000), pp. 124–34.
55 [1997] 912 FCA (8 September 1997).
56 [2001] FCA 1691 (3 December 2001), [17].
57 [2001] FCA 611 (25 May 2001), [14].

establish that they fear persecution in more than one of those countries in order to be a refugee.

In *Al-Anezi v MIMA*, it was held:

> A person who has a nationality, who has left the country of nationality owing to persecution for a Convention reason and is, as a result of a fear of such persecution, unwilling to return or is unable to avail himself or herself of the protection of that country, remains a refugee no matter in how many intermediate countries he or she may have resided and however many of them may correctly be described as countries of former habitual residence. It would be surprising if a stateless person who, owing to a well-founded fear of persecution for a Convention reason, had left (was outside) a country of former habitual residence and was unable or, due to such a fear, unwilling to return to that country, ceased to be a refugee merely because of subsequent habitual residence in another country in which he or she had no fear of persecution. That the Convention definition does not have that surprising result is precisely what the UN Handbook says: a stateless person may have more than one country of former habitual residence; he or she may have a fear of persecution in relation to more than one of them; but the definition does not require that he or she satisfy the criteria in relation to all of them; rather, if the person satisfies the criteria in relation to one of those countries (I do not think 'determined to be a refugee' should be taken as requiring some earlier formal assessment) the person's status is not affected by a 'further change to his country of habitual residence'. That reasoning in the Handbook is supported by the Travaux Préparatoires of the Convention: see Rishmawi at 424–427.[58]

This approach appears to be inconsistent with the outcome where an applicant has more than one country of nationality. The inconsistency is somewhat ameliorated by the fact that in order to qualify as a country of former *habitual* residence the applicant must have spent a considerable amount of time in that region recently, whereas nationality can simply be a formal status. It is rare that a person will have more than one habitual residence. It is further ameliorated by the third country protection doctrine, to which we now turn.

17.7 Third country (or effective) protection

Under the doctrine of 'third country protection', a nation is not obliged to assist a person defined as Convention refugee in situations where protection is available in a safe third country.[59] This doctrine is sourced in both the common law and statute.

At common law, even if a person meets the definition of a refugee under section 36(2) of the *Migration Act 1958* (Cth), Australia is not compelled to protect that person in circumstances where 'effective protection' can be obtained in a

58 [1999] FCA 355 (1 April 1999), [24].
59 'Safe third country' means any country other than that where the person is fleeing from and any country other than that where the person is seeking asylum. See *Thiyagarajah v MIMA* [1997] FCA 1494 (19 December 1997). A country need not be a party to the Convention in order to be a safe third country: *Patto v MIMA* [2000] FCA 1554 (2 November 2000), [36].

'safe third country'. A failure by Australia to protect such a person will not result in a breach of Article 33 of the Convention.[60] As is noted by Germov and Motta, this doctrine does not derive from the express wording of the Convention. It is based on a certain interpretation of Articles 33(1) and 1A(2). As noted previously, the main obligation under the Convention, which stems from Article 33(1), is not to refoule a person to a country in which they have a well-founded fear of persecution. There is, supposedly, no breach of this prohibition where the individual can obtain protection from refoulement to the country in relation to which he or she has the fear of persecution by travelling to another (safe) third country. In considering whether effective protection can be obtained in the third county, the standard that is applied is the same as under Article 1A(2); that is, whether or not they have a well-founded fear of persecution for a Convention reason.[61]

Complementing the common law doctrine of effective protection are subsections 36(3)–(7) of the *Migration Act 1958* (Cth).[62] These provide that Australia is not obliged to protect non-citizens who have failed to take all possible steps to avail themselves of a right to enter and reside in a safe third country. The statutory provisions apply only to persons who apply for protection visas on or after 16 December 1998, whereas the common law effective protection doctrine applies in all cases where protection visas are sought, irrespective of the application date. The statutory provisions are narrower than the doctrine of effective protection at common law.

17.7.1 Common law

In *MIMA v Thiyagarajah*[63] it was held that there is no conclusive test to determine what is meant by 'effective protection'; however, several factors are considered by the courts when deciding whether or not effective protection exists. One factor is whether the refugee applicant can gain access to the safe third country in question.[64] In order for this to be satisfied, it is not necessary that the individual has a legally enforceable right to enter the third country. Moreover, effective protection is not dependent on a person having a legal right to permanent residence.[65] It is enough to show that the third country would consider the claims of the refugee applicant in accordance with the Convention. Hence, a right to temporary residence may meet the effective protection test in some situations.[66]

If an applicant is not permitted to enter a third country, effective protection cannot be established. Moreover, the third country itself must not be a place where the applicant's life and freedom will be endangered. To determine whether

60 *Thiyagarajah v MIMA* [1997] FCA 1494 (19 December 1997).
61 For further commentary, see Germov and Motta, *Refugee Law in Australia*, pp. 463–70.
62 It has been made clear that these legislative provisions do not codify the common law: see, for example, *V856/00 A v MIMA* [2001] FCA 1018 (3 August 2001).
63 *Thiyagarajah v MIMA* [1997] FCA 1494 (19 December 1997).
64 *Thiyagarajah v MIMA* [1997] FCA 1494 (19 December 1997).
65 *MIMA v Gnanapiragasam* [1998] FCA 1213 (25 September 1998).
66 *MIMA v Gnanapiragasam* [1998] FCA 1213 (25 September 1998).

or not the third country is safe, it must be asked whether the applicant has a well-founded fear of persecution for a Convention reason in the third country.[67] The central consideration is whether or not there is a real chance that the person may be refouled by the third country to a country where the person faces a real risk of persecution.[68]

It is often difficult to determine if in fact an individual does have the capacity to enter a third country. This will ultimately turn on the laws, protocols and practices (which often involve the exercise of a considerable degree of discretion) of the third country. Hence, in many cases it will be difficult to make a confident assessment regarding the issue of effective protection elsewhere. It has been suggested that a flexible approach ought be taken in relation to the effective protection doctrine.[69] The doctrine has been applied in a wide range of circumstances and usually arises when the refugee applicant has some previous connection to a third country, but having such a connection is not a precondition to the doctrine being invoked.[70]

In *Patto v MIMA*[71] French J set out the following, non-exhaustive, propositions in relation to the protection obligations assumed by Australia under Article 33 of the Convention in its application to persons who travel to Australia via a third country or who have links with a third country:

1. Return of the person to the third country will not contravene Article 33 where the person has a right of residence in that country and is not subject to Convention harms therein.
2. Return of the person to the third country will not contravene Article 33, whether or not the person has right of residence in that country, if that country is a party to the Convention and can be expected to honour its obligations thereunder.
3. Return of the person to a third country will not contravene Article 33 notwithstanding that the person has no right of residence in that country and that the country is not a party to the Convention, provided that it can be expected, nevertheless, to afford the person claiming asylum effective protection against threats to his life or freedom for a Convention reason.

17.7.2 Statute

A statutory form of third country protection was introduced in December 1999. As noted above, statutory third country protection may only be applied to refugee applications lodged after 16 December 1999.

67 *Thiyagarajah v MIMA* [1997] FCA 1494 (19 December 1997): 'Under Article 33 the "well-founded fear" test which applies under Article 1A(2) should be applied'.
68 If there is a real chance that this may occur, then effective protection could not be said to exist: see *V872/00A v MIMA* [2001] FCA 1019 (3 August 2001).
69 See, for example, *Al-Rahal v MIMA* [2001] FCA 1141 (20 August 2001); *Al Toubi v MIMA* [2001] FCA 1381 (28 September 2001).
70 See *NAEN v Minister for Immigration & Multicultural & Indigenous Affairs* [2003] FCA 216 (19 March 2003).
71 [2000] FCA 1554 (2 November 2000), [37].

The changes to *Migration Act 1958* (Cth) are as follows:

> 36(3) Australia is taken not to have protection obligations to a non-citizen who has not taken all possible steps to avail himself or herself of a right to enter and reside in, whether temporarily or permanently and however that right arose or is expressed, any country apart from Australia, including countries of which the non-citizen is a national.
>
> (4) However, if the non-citizen has a well-founded fear of being persecuted in a country for reasons of race, religion, nationality, membership of a particular social group or political opinion, subsection (3) does not apply in relation to that country.
>
> (5) Also, if the non-citizen has a well-founded fear that:
> (a) a country will return the non-citizen to another country; and
> (b) the non-citizen will be persecuted in that other country for reasons of race, religion, nationality, membership of a particular social group or political opinion;
>
> subsection (3) does not apply in relation to the first-mentioned country.

Section 36(3) differs from effective protection at common law in that it requires a legally enforceable[72] right to both enter and reside in the third country.[73] A non-legally enforceable right to enter the third country is not sufficient to enliven section 36(3): otherwise an applicant would be required to apply to all countries where it could be reasonably expected that he or she would be granted an entry visa or temporary residence.[74]

However, like effective protection at common law, a refugee applicant under section 36(3) need not have visited or lived in the country in relation to which effective protection is being considered.

Once it has been determined that a refugee applicant has the requisite rights referred to in section 36(3), what must next be considered is whether the non-citizen has taken all possible steps to avail himself or herself of a right to enter and reside in a third country. The scope and operation of the statutory and common law third party protection was summarised in *NAGV of 2002 v Minister for Immigration & Multicultural & Indigenous Affairs*:[75]

> The principle is that Australia does not owe protection obligations to a person who has acquired effective protection from persecution for a Convention reason in a third country and who is not at risk of being sent from that country to the country in respect of which a fear of such persecution is well-founded. The concept was explained by von Doussa J (with whom Moore and Sackville JJ agreed) in *Thiyagarajah v MIMA* (1997) 80 FCR 543 at 562:
>
>> It is not necessary for the purpose of disposing of this appeal to seek to chart the outer boundaries of the principles of international law which permit a Contracting State

72 See, for example, *N1045/00A v MIMA* [2002] FCA 1546 (19 April 2002), [31]; *Applicant C v MIMA* [2001] FCA 229 (12 March 2001).
73 See *WAGH v Minister for Immigration & Multicultural & Indigenous Affairs* [2003] FCAFC 194 (27 August 2003), [66].
74 *Applicant C v MIMA* [2001] FCA 229 (12 March 2001). See further, Germov and Motta, *Refugee Law in Australia*, pp. 473–75. In *SZMWQ v Minister for Immigration and Citizenship* [2010] FCAFC 97 it was held that 'In order for an individual to have the right to enter and reside a country pursuant to s 36(3), there is no requirement that the individual must also have the right to social welfare in that country.'
75 [2002] FCA 1456 (27 November 2002), [13]–[16].

> to return an asylum seeker to a third country without undertaking an assessment of the substantive merits of the claim for refugee status. It is sufficient to conclude that international law does not preclude a Contracting State from taking this course where it is proposed to return the asylum seeker to a third country which has already recognised that person's status as a refugee, and has accorded that person effective protection, including a right to reside, enter and re-enter that country. The expression 'effective protection' is used in the submissions of the Minister in the present appeal. In the context of the obligations arising under the [Convention], the expression means protection which will effectively ensure that there is not a breach of Art 33 if the person happens to be a refugee.

> The principle may apply where the visa applicant is entitled to residence in the third country for reasons other than the grant of refugee status; *Rajendran; MIMA v Gnanapiragasam* (1998) 88 FCR 1. It also applies where, as a matter of practical reality, he or she is likely to be given effective protection even in the absence of a legally enforceable right to enter and live in the third country; *Applicant C* at [21]–[22], *Kola* at [63]. Effective protection involves the person not only being permitted to remain in the third country without risk of persecution for a Convention reason but also not being at risk of being refouled to his or her country of origin. In deciding whether the principle applies it is necessary to abjure any rigid standard of applicability and concentrate on the circumstances of each applicant and the practical consequences of sending that person to the third country; *Applicant C* at [22], *Kola* at [63]; see also *Al-Zafiri v MIMA* [1999] FCA 443 at [26] per Emmett J approved in *MIMA v Al-Sallal* [1999] 94 FCR 549 at 558.
>
> As I summarised it in *Applicant C* at [65], the combined effect of the principle of effective protection and s 36(3)–(5) is that Australia does not owe protection obligations under the Convention to:
>
> (a) a person who can, as a practical matter, obtain effective protection in a third country; or
>
> (b) a person who has not taken all possible steps to avail himself or herself of a legally enforceable right to enter and reside in a third country.

It follows that the effective protection principle in section 36(3) is narrower than – and is in fact totally subsumed by – the broader doctrine at common law. Every factual situation that comes within the scope of section 36(3) will also come within the common law doctrine. It may be contended that this effectively makes the statutory principle redundant. However, this is not necessarily the case. As was noted at the start of this section, the common law effective protection principle does not stem from the express words of the Convention. It arises from an interpretation of interaction between Articles 33 and 1A(2) of the Convention. This approach is by no means beyond question. The fact that an applicant has the capacity to apply for refugee status or reside in another country does not necessarily mean that Australia should be permitted to 'circumvent' its principal obligation under the Convention. Shuttling a person who has left a persecutory environment to another uncertain fate is arguably at odds with the humanitarian underpinning of the Convention. Thus section 36(3) creates a legislative 'insurance policy' against the risk that the courts will overturn the common law effective protection doctrine. To this end, it is noteworthy that the High Court has not considered the soundness of the common law doctrine.[76]

76 Moreover, the Full Federal Court in *NAGV of 2002 v Minister for Immigration & Multicultural & Indigenous Affairs* [2002] FCA 1456 (27 November 2002) doubted the (logical and normative) correctness of the doctrine, but continued to apply it in deference to the doctrine of precedent. For some cursory observations by the High Court, see *NBGM v Minister for Immigration and Multicultural Affairs* [2006] HCA 54.

18

Time for a fundamental rethink: Need as the criterion for assistance

18.1 Overview: Time to stop paying homage to the Convention and to fix it

As noted in Chapter 11, the definition of a refugee was first advanced about 60 years ago. At the international law level, it has remained (effectively) unchanged during this period. Likewise at the domestic law level, although as we have seen the definition has been subject to relatively minor statutory modifications.

The Refugee Convention has been ratified by well over 100 nation states and is one of the most important and successful international humanitarian documents. In Australia, the refugee issue is of widespread social and political importance. It is perhaps the most emotive and divisive social issue of our time. This level of interest in refugee issues was greatly heightened in 2001 when the Australian Parliament introduced legislation and border control mechanisms to prevent asylum-seekers entering Australia without a visa. This polarised public opinion and resulted in a groundswell of action from many people, including many current and former refugees, which in turn led to the establishing of many refugee and asylum-seeker support organisations. The preparedness of so many individuals in the community, and so many community groups, to assist asylum-seekers is, like any altruistic act, commendable.

The issue was reignited in 2010 when the number of asylum-seekers arriving by boat increased dramatically following the decision of the government to abandon temporary refugee visas. The manner in which the government processed refugees and the rights accorded to them became a key theme of the 2010 federal election. In this chapter we provide a normative evaluation of the Convention. Is the document morally sound? This may seem to be a curious question to raise in relation to a document which has been so effective in securing protection for millions of people. We accept that protecting blameless people is an admirable objective. However, we believe that the objective can be markedly improved if the Convention definition (at least at the domestic level, if international consensus is unattainable) is altered to cure the main defect with the existing document – its discriminatory nature. In this chapter we suggest how the Convention can be improved.

We contend that the definition of a refugee is flawed – fundamentally so in at least one very important respect: the Convention grounds (race, religion, nationality, membership of a particular social group and political opinion) are unduly narrow and ultimately arbitrary. The only manner in which refugee law can be made non-arbitrary is to remove the Convention grounds as the cornerstone of the definition and instead base the definition on the concept of deprivation and need, not the *reason* for the need. As has been previously noted, 'the great issues of our day transcend party, region, religion and sex'.[1] In a nutshell, the basic premise of this chapter is that a person who will die from starvation due to a drought deserves refugee status more than one who risks being imprisoned for venting his or her political opinion.

18.1.1 Refugee law – not humanitarian law – is the appropriate vehicle for change

Before turning to substantive matters, we briefly discuss why the changes that we are foreshadowing are better placed in the context of refugee law than within broader notions of humanitarian international (or domestic) law. There are two central reasons for this. First, the Convention has gained widespread acceptance. According to Hathaway, the Convention definition of 'refugee' is of singular importance because it has been subscribed to by more than 100 nations and is the only refugee accord of global scope. Many nations have also chosen to import this standard into their domestic legislation as the basis upon which asylum and other protection decisions are made.[2]

Second, while refugee law is (almost) mandatory, international humanitarian principles are largely discretionary. As noted in Chapter 15, refugee law is one of few areas of international law where the needs of the individual trump the needs of sovereign states. It is essentially based upon what a country can do for an individual, unlike migration law, which is based on the opposite – what the individual can do for the country. Thus recognition that a person falls within a class of people called 'refugee' allows the rights of that person to override the capacity of a nation to exclude people from its borders. This is no minor victory. Nations zealously guard their borders. A key manifestation of any nation's sovereignty is its capacity to control the entry of people. All sovereign nations

1 J. Jackson, 'Measuring Human Rights and Development by one Yardstick', (1985) 15 *Ca W Intl L J* 453 at 456–60.
2 Hathaway, *The Law of Refugee Status*, p. v.

steadfastly believe that they have the right to determine who can enter their land. This is an unquestioned aspect of sovereignty – both at the international and at the domestic law level. The refugee exception to this aspect of national sovereignty is not absolute. However, in reality, once countries do ratify the Convention they do not repudiate it.[3]

Thus the Convention is important because it is the one universal, humanitarian international treaty that offers some guarantee that the fundamental rights of desperate people will be safeguarded. By and large, most nations observe their obligations under the Convention: 'The Refugee Convention stands out as a measure that offers substance and "teeth" to the concept of internationally recognised human rights.'[4] As is noted by Hathaway, the fact that a state which has jurisdiction over a refugee automatically owes that person core rights (especially protection against non-refoulement) is the strength of refugee law: 'it ensures that few refugees fall through the cracks of the protection regime'.[5] However, there is no room for complacency in this regard. As has been noted recently by the United Nations, the costs associated with hosting large numbers of asylum-seekers, in addition to security concerns, have resulted in 'the Convention's provisions [being] more respected in their breach than their adherence'.[6]

18.1.2 The implications of finite international compassion – proper targeting of refugees critical

A significant expansion of the Convention grounds would greatly liberalise the international people movement (assuming continued adherence to the Convention), thereby eroding an important aspect of the concept of sovereignty. This would ultimately diminish the relevance of the concept of a nation state. If, for example, a refugee was defined as a 'person who believed that he or she was not permitted full opportunity to flourish in their country of birth', the likely result would be a massive transference of the world's population. It should, of course, also be noted that the concept of breaking down national borders is not a new one.[7] There are certainly many appealing aspects to the idea. It could enhance the liberty of all people and lead to a more just distribution of resources – not only food, medicine and clothing but also education and employment. However,

3 Some countries even have a right of asylum written into their constitutions: see S. Collinson, *Beyond Borders: Western European Migration Policy Towards the 21st Century* (London, Royal Institute of International Affairs, 1993), p. 65.

4 M. Crock, *Immigration and Refugee Law in Australia* (Sydney, Federation Press, 1998), p. 163.

5 J.C. Hathaway, 'Refugee Law is Not Immigration Law', *World Refugee Survey 2002* (Arlington VA, US Committee for Refugees and Immigrants [USCRI], 2002), p. 43.

6 United Nations, Executive Committee of the High Commissioner's Programme, *Note on International Protection*, 13 September 2001, p. 5. The breaches range from situations where individuals are refouled or where borders are closed to refugees, to violence against refugees. For comments regarding future challenges to the problem confronted by refugees, see W. Maley, 'A Global Refugee Crisis?', in W. Maley et al., *Refugees and the Myth of the Borderless World* (Canberra, Department of International Relations, Australian National University [ANU], 2002), p. 1. See, further, Chapter 15.

7 See, for example, Morss and Bagaric, 'If we can't have Global Democracy, let's all be Americans: injecting principle into the international law-making process'.

it is not something that is likely to occur in the near future – if at all. Given that nations will continue to place strict controls on who enters their land and only grant asylum to a finite number of people, it is important that that they do so on a rational and coherent basis. Thus there are two important threshold assumptions that we make in this chapter.

The first is that nations will continue to exist and tightly control people movement across their borders. The history of human civilisation over the past century or so shows that this assumption has a solid platform. The second assumption is that nations have limited sympathy for those in need – were it otherwise, a strong case could be mounted for a more expansive refugee definition. As is noted by Collinson:

> two linked assumptions appear to underlie almost all current debates on the issue of migration and refugee flows in Western Europe. First, there is the assumption that immigration poses a threat . . . Second, it is assumed that Western Europe lacks the capacity to cope with any further immigration, whether it be in demographic, economic, social or political terms.[8]

She adds: 'the international community . . . is not infinitely generous. An obligation . . . to protect refugees, and the needs of refugees themselves, will in practice always be balanced against the political and economic interests and concerns of potential asylum states.'[9] Amnesty International has described refugee protection as the 'black spot' in the European Union's rights ambitions,[10] and is deeply concerned that 'the focus of the European Union's asylum policy is overwhelmingly on how to keep refugees out, rather than how to protect effectively people fleeing from war, civil upheaval and grave human rights abuses'.[11] The international community's finite level of preparedness to absorb refugees is supported by refugee numbers, which show a remarkable level of consistency over the past decade or so, although there has been a decline in the past two recorded years mainly as a result of an unprecedented number of voluntary repatriations. Figures from the US Committee for Refugees and Immigrants show the number of refugees and asylum-seekers from 1999 to 2008:

1999: 14 100 000
2000: 14 500 000
2001: 14 900 000
2002: 13 000 000
2003: 11 900 000
2004: 11 500 000
2005: 12 000 000
2006: 13 948 800

8 S. Collinson, *Beyond Borders: Western European Migration Policy Towards the 21st Century* (London, Royal Institute of International Affairs, 1993).
9 ibid., p. 60.
10 Amnesty International EU Office, Press Release, *Asylum Seekers in Europe: The Real Story Amnesty International Launches Europe-Wide Campaign*, 25 September 2001: www.amnesty.org.
11 ibid. See also G. Goodwin-Gill, 'The International Protection of Refugees: What Future?', (2000) 12 *International Journal of Refugee Law* 1.

2007: 14 047 300
2008: 13 599 900.[12]

Sidetracking for one moment, it is interesting to note that despite the level of criticism that the Australian government has received for its refugee policy and practices over the past few years, on the basis of contribution per capita, Australia is the 15th most substantial donor country to international refugee aid agencies. In absolute terms, it is the 13th most generous donor country. On per capita terms, the 10 most generous countries are Luxembourg, Norway, Sweden, Denmark, Liechtenstein, Ireland, the Netherlands, Finland, Switzerland and Monaco. The United States is 14th on the list.[13]

Australia is in fact the most generous country on earth in terms of resettling refugees who do not come to its shores. There is no obligation on countries to bring refugees to their shores. Australia is one of the few nations that proactively engages in this process. The top five nations and the ratio of settled refuges to host country population are Australia (1: 2400); Canada (1: 3100); Sweden (1: 4200); United States (1: 5100); and Norway (1: 5300).[14]

The key proposition being argued in this chapter is that the five Convention grounds should be removed. They are arbitrary and hence discriminatory: there is no relevant basis for giving preferential treatment to a person who is 'persecuted' because of his or her political or religious beliefs as distinct from a person who suffers serious harm for economic or other non-Convention reasons. Also, why should a person's eligibility for asylum be contingent upon whether there are sufficient others who also engage in like conduct? That is, what is so special about belonging to a group that ought to more readily stimulate the international community's sympathy gland? The only way to treat people equally in this respect is not to focus on the *reason* for the persecution, but *the extent of the need* for asylum. The only universal criteria for sympathy and compassion are *need and pain*. Thus it follows that state assistance and protection should be accorded to those most bereft of the resources and opportunities that are preconditions to human survival and flourishing. This raises difficult questions about the hierarchy of human needs and wants. We suggest that the most important needs are food, shelter, security of person and liberty. People who are denied these should be considered refugees – irrespective of the reason for the deprivation.

We discuss this issue at length in section 18.3. In section 18.4, to avoid the charge that it is easy to criticise but harder to offer constructive reform suggestions, we spell out the definition of 'refugee' that we believe should be adopted. In the process we stipulate the implications that this has for other aspects of the definition as it currently stands. For example, our definition makes redundant the notion that a causal nexus must exist between the grounds and the reason for the persecution.

12 US Committee for Refugees and Immigrants, *World Refugee Survey 2009* (2009), 4.
13 ibid., 28.
14 ibid., 29.

18.1.3 History of Convention inevitably resulted in flawed definition

The deficiency in the Convention definition is not surprising given that, as we saw in Chapter 12, the definition was formed in an ad hoc manner by various UN groups, initially to help only refugees fleeing from Europe as a result of the devastation caused by World War II. It was based on expedience rather than principle, and reflects the economic and political interests of the powerful Western states that drafted it rather than the needs of displaced persons. Not only is the definition unsatisfactory today; it was equally so at the time of drafting.

Further, as has been noted:

> the Convention definition of refugee has made less sense as the nature of refugee flows has changed and as numbers have risen. Since 1980, refugee movements have been more likely to be the result of civil wars, ethnic and communal conflicts and generalised violence, or natural disasters or famine – usually in combinations – than individually targeted persecution by an oppressive regime.[15]

By retaining the current definition of 'refugee' in the Convention, this situation will not, and indeed cannot, change.

18.2 The problem with the Convention grounds

As we saw in Chapter 14, the Convention grounds have been interpreted broadly.[16] However, despite this we believe that the Convention still falls well short of being able to achieve the ultimate objective of refugee law and policy. As we have noted earlier, refugee law is the one area of international law where ratifying parties accept that the needs of the individual trump those of the state. Given this, it is appropriate that human need should form the lynchpin of refugee law.

No matter how broadly the grounds are interpreted, the Convention would still not act as a vehicle to assist those experiencing the greatest degree of deprivation. The main defect with the Convention is that the grounds do not come close to identifying the minimum conditions necessary for human subsistence. The right to express which political party or political ideology one prefers, for example, is of little use unless one has food and shelter. Further, it is regrettable (if not offensive) that all that is important in a person's life can turn on the interpretation of a concept as unclear as 'particular social group'.

This leads us to a more pervasive and fundamental problem with the Convention. Not only is it not based on a needs criterion, it is not based on *any* overarching

15 Millbank, *The Problem with the 1951 Refugee Convention*.

16 However, it has been noted by the United Nations, Executive Committee of the High Commissioner's Programme, *Note on International Protection*, 13 September 2001, at 23, that 'a certain tendency over recent years to restrict the application of the 1951 Convention refugee definition within narrow confines has continued in a number of countries around the world, although there have been positive signs in certain jurisdictions'. The states which supposedly give a narrow interpretation to the Convention were not named.

principle at all. There is no underlying rationale which unifies the grounds and justifies why they are of greater importance than other human concerns. As a result – blind allegiance to the Convention aside – a causal connection between persecution and a Convention ground does not provide a normative reason for compliance with the Convention. Absent an explanation for why the Convention grounds are more important than other human interests, the Convention definition of 'refugee' is arbitrary and ultimately discriminatory – it gives a preference to those falling within the grounds on the basis of an irrelevant difference. In light of universal principles governing the commitment to all humankind, why should any state be concerned about complying with the Convention? The answer is that from the normative perspective (that is, international law obligations aside), relatively speaking it should care very little – sending money to the starving in Africa would be a far better use of resources. As Goodwin-Gill has noted, given the narrow framework of the Convention, which was not intended to provide for universal refugee solutions, it 'is remarkable . . . that the 1951 Convention still attracts both ratifications and support among States from all regions'.[17]

18.3 An alternative definition

18.3.1 Universal moral standards should underpin the new definition

The only way the Convention can be reformed to circumvent such criticisms is to select universal needs of humankind as the cornerstone for refugee status. We accept that there is a large grey area concerning the hierarchy of resources that are necessary for human subsistence. As we discuss shortly, things like the right to a certain level of education and health care are in the grey area, but this should not prevent us making definite judgments in the black and white areas.

The new definition should appeal to universal sociological and normative considerations in order to be persuasive at the level of international discourse. Fortunately, these inquiries are linked. Morality, by definition, is the ultimate set of principles by which we should live, and more particularly includes the principles that dictate how serious conflict should be resolved. Given that morality is the ultimate principle that governs our conduct, in order for it to be relevant, it must promote the ultimate human aim. This follows from the constraints of psychological reality. If the ultimate principle guiding our conduct fails to reflect our ultimate desire, it would become redundant very quickly. As a sociological fact, moral theory must be tailored to accord with basic human needs and interests, and sets the ultimate standard by which human need should be evaluated and defined.

17 Goodwin-Gill, *The Refugee in International Law*, p. 297.

18.3.1.1 Overview of moral theory

Broadly, there are two types of normative moral theories. Consequential moral theories claim that an act is right or wrong depending on its capacity to maximise a particular virtue, such as happiness. Non-consequential (or deontological) theories claim that the appropriateness of an action is not contingent upon its instrumental ability to produce particular ends, but follows from the intrinsic features of the act. Thus the notion of absolute (or near absolute) rights, which now dominates moral discourse, is generally thought to sit most comfortably in a non-consequentialist ethic. The ramifications that these theories have for defining the interests that are relevant to refugee status will now be discussed.

18.3.1.2 New approach not contingent on acceptance of particular moral theory

The foregoing analysis suggests that the avoidance of pain and suffering should be the touchstone for refugee status. It is further suggested that this follows from adopting the most persuasive normative ethic. For those who refuse to accept that there is such a concept as universal objective morality,[18] it is important to emphasise at this point that a case for the definition of 'refugee' we propose can yet be mounted so long as one is willing to accept either of the following premises: (i) as a sociological imperative, the minimisation of pain and suffering ought to be the first priority of a civilised society; or (ii) refugee law should eradicate arbitrary choices and adhere to the principle of equality (or non-discrimination).

Readers who are dismissive of the prospect of an objective morality are encouraged to directly proceed to section 18.7.

18.3.2 Deontological rights-based theories underpinning the new definition

If one adopts a non-consequentialist rights-based moral theory as the starting point, the process for refugee reform would involve three broad steps: selecting the rights the people have, identifying those that are the most important and then linking these into the definition of 'refugee'. Unfortunately, as we shall see, this process breaks down at the first two steps.

18.3.2.1 The influence of rights-based theories

A rights-oriented framework for refugee law would be in keeping with international moral discourse over the past half century or so. Since World War II, there has been an immense increase in 'rights talk',[19] both in sheer volume and

18 One of us has previously argued that there are such things as objective universal norms: see M. Bagaric, 'A Utilitarian Argument: laying the foundation for a coherent system of law', (2002) 10 *Otago Law Review* (NZ) 163.

19 See T. Campbell, *The Legal Theory of Ethical Positivism* (Aldershot, Dartmouth Publishing, 1996), pp. 161–88, who discusses the near universal trend towards Bills of Rights and constitutional rights as a focus for political choice. In 'rights talk' I also include the abundance of declarations, charters, bills, and the like, referred to below, that seek to spell out certain rights. There were numerous declarations, and the like, of rights

in the number of supposed rights. The rights doctrine has progressed a long way since its original modest aim of providing 'a legitimisation of . . . claims against tyrannical or exploiting regimes'.[20] As Campbell points out:

> The human rights movement is based on the need for a counter-ideology to combat the abuses and misuses of political authority by those who invoke, as a justification for their activities, the need to subordinate the particular interests of individuals to the general good.[21]

There is now, more than ever, a strong tendency to advance moral claims and arguments in terms of rights.[22] Assertion of rights has become the customary means to express our moral sentiments: as Campbell also says, 'there is virtually no area of public controversy in which rights are not to be found on at least one side of the question – and generally on both'.[23] There is no question that 'the doctrine of human rights has at least temporarily replaced the doctrine of maximising utilitarianism as the prime philosophical inspiration of political and social reform'.[24] And as has been previously noted, 'refugee protection is no exception to [the] deployment of the language of rights'.[25]

The influence of rights-based theories is demonstrated by the sheer number of international human rights instruments that are now in existence. The main three are the Universal Declaration of Human Rights (the UDHR);[26] the International Covenant on Economic, Social and Cultural Rights (the ICESCR);[27] and the International Covenant on Civil and Political Rights (the ICCPR).[28] There are dozens of rights that are prescribed in one form or another by at least one of these documents. These include what can be described as basic protections, such as the right to life,[29] liberty and security of person,[30] and to be free from torture or cruel, inhuman or degrading treatment or punishment.[31] Then there are more vague rights, such as the right to the economic, social and cultural rights indispensable for one's dignity and the free development of one's personality,[32]

prior to World War II, such as the *Declaration of Independence of the United States* (1776) and the *Declaration of the Rights of Man and Citizens* (1789), but it is only in relatively modern times that such documents have gained widespread appeal, recognition and force.

20 S.I. Benn, 'Human rights – For Whom and For What?', in E. Kamenka and A.E. Tay (eds), *Human Rights* (Melbourne, Edward Arnold, 1978), pp. 59, 61.

21 T. Campbell, 'Realizing Human Rights', in T. Campbell et al. (eds), *Human Rights: From Rhetoric to Reality* (New York, Blackwell, 1986), pp. 1, 13.

22 Almost to the point where it is not too far off the mark to propose that the 'escalation of rights rhetoric is out of control': L.W. Sumner, *The Moral Foundation of Rights* (Oxford, OUP, 1987), p. 1.

23 ibid.

24 H.L.A. Hart, *Essays in Jurisprudence and Philosophy* (Oxford, Clarendon Press, 1983), pp. 196–7.

25 B.S. Chimni, 'Globalization, Humanitarianism and the Erosion of Refugee Protection', (2000) 13 *Journal of Refugee Studies*, pp. 243, 251. See also G. Goodwin-Gill, 'Asylum 2001 – A Convention and a Purpose', (2001) 13 *International Journal of Refugee Law*, pp. 1, 8, who states that we turn to human rights to fill out the grey areas in refugee law.

26 10 February 1948, entered into by Australia on that day.

27 4 January 1976, entered into by Australia on 10 March 1976.

28 23 March 1976, entered into by Australia on 13 November 1980. Australia has also ratified (in September 1991) the *First Optional Protocol to the ICCPR* which makes it possible for complaints to be made to the UN Human Rights Committee.

29 UDHR, article 3 and ICCPR, article 6.

30 UDHR, article 3 and ICCPR, article 9.

31 UDHR, article 5 and ICCPR, article 7.

32 UDHR, article 22 and ICESCR, articles 9 and 15.

and the right to be free from the arbitrary interference with one's privacy, family, home or correspondence and attacks upon one's honour and reputation.[33] There are also some so-called rights which are probably best placed on a wish list, such as the right to rest and leisure,[34] and the right to a standard of living adequate for the health and wellbeing of oneself and one's family, including food, clothing, housing and medical care and necessary social services.[35]

18.3.2.2 The absence of a foundation of rights

Despite the dazzling veneer of deontological rights-based theories, and their influence on present-day moral and legal discourse, one of us has previously argued that when examined closely, such theories are unable to provide persuasive answers to central issues such as: what is the justification for rights? How can we distinguish real from fanciful rights? Which right takes priority in the event of conflicting rights?[36]

Such intractable difficulties stem from the fact that contemporary rights theories lack a coherent foundation. Campbell has argued against certain rights-based theories on the basis that they are unable to provide a satisfactory account of the relationship between concrete rights (rights that provide a justification for political decisions by society in general) and more fundamental rights ('background rights') from which concrete rights are supposedly derived.[37] However, in our view an even more fundamental flaw with rights theories is that there is no defensible virtue that underpins the background interests from which narrower rights claims can be derived.

When examined closely, it emerges that the concept of non-consequentialist rights is vacuous at the epistemological level. It has been argued that attempts to ground concrete rights in virtues such as dignity, integrity or concern and respect are unsound because to resort to such ideals is arbitrary and leads to discrimination against certain members of the community (for example, those with severely limited cognitive functioning) or speciesism (the systematic discrimination against non-humans).[38]

Ultimately, a non-consequentialist ethic provides no method for distinguishing between genuine and fanciful rights claims and is incapable of providing

33 UDHR, article 12 and ICCPR, article 17.

34 UDHR, article 24 and ICESCR, article 7(d).

35 UDHR, article 25 and ICESCR, article 11. It does not end there. In addition to this, Australia has entered into or voted for numerous other specific human rights instruments such as the: Declaration on the Rights of Mentally Retarded Persons; Declaration on the Rights of Disabled Persons; Convention on the Elimination of all Forms of Discrimination Against Women; Convention Relating to the Status of Refugees; Protocol Relating to the Status of Refugees; Declaration on the Rights of the Child; Convention on the Rights of the Child; Discrimination (Employment and Occupation) (ILO Convention 111); International Convention on the Elimination of all Forms of Racial Discrimination; Declaration on the Elimination of all Forms of Religious Intolerance; and the Convention Against Torture and other Cruel, Inhuman and Degrading Treatment or Punishment.

36 M. Bagaric, 'In Defence of a Utilitarian Theory of Punishment: Punishing the Innocent: the Compatibility of Utilitarianism and Rights', (1999) 24 *Australian Journal of Legal Philosophy* 95, 121–43; Bagaric, *Sentencing and Punishment: A Rational Approach*, Ch. 4.

37 T. Campbell, *Justice* (London, Macmillan, 1988), 199, p. 54.

38 See for example, M. Tooley, 'Abortion and Infanticide', in Singer (ed.), *Applied Ethics*, pp. 69, 70–71. See also P. Singer, 'All Animals are Equal' in P. Singer (ed.), *Applied Ethics*, p. 215.

guidance regarding the ranking of rights in the event of a clash. Not surprisingly then, all sorts of dubious rights claims have been advanced. Thus we have a situation where people are able to – with a straight face – urge interests such as 'the right to a tobacco-free job', the 'right to sunshine', the 'right of a father to be present in the delivery room', the 'right to a sex break',[39] and even 'the right to drink myself to death without interference'.[40] Novel rights continue to be asserted. A good example is the claim by the former Australian Prime Minister John Howard (in the context of the debate concerning the availability of IVF treatment to same-sex couples or individuals) that 'each child has the right to a mother and father'. In a similar vein, in light of the increasing world oil prices, it has been declared that this violates the 'right of Americans to cheap gasoline'. In England, the Premier League has been accused of violating the right of football club supporters to an FA Cup ticket.

More than 30 years ago, Hart said of rights theories:

> It cannot be said that we have had . . . a sufficiently detailed or adequately articulated theory showing the foundation for such rights and how they are related to other values. Indeed the revived doctrines of basic rights are . . . in spite of much brilliance still unconvincing.[41]

Nothing has happened to diminish the force of this objection.

18.3.2.3 Explanation for the appeal of rights-based theories

We may seem to be unduly dismissive of rights-based theories and paying inadequate regard to the considerable moral reforms that have occurred against the backdrop of rights talk over the past half century. It cannot be denied that rights claims have been an effective lever for social change. As Campbell correctly notes: the discourse and the theories have provided 'a constant source of inspiration for the protection of individual liberty rights'.[42] For example, recognition of the right to liberty resulted in the abolition of slavery, and more recently the right of equality has been used as an effective weapon by women and other disempowered groups seeking greater employment and civil rights (such as the right to vote).

We also do not seek to question that there is an ongoing need for moral discourse about rights: 'whether or not . . . rights are intellectually defensible or culturally tolerant, we do have a need for them, at least at the edges of civilisation and in the tangle of international politics'.[43]

However, we do not believe that *deontological* rights-based moral theories (with their absolutist overtones) are capable of providing answers to questions about the existence and content of proposed rights. This view could obviously be

39 These examples are cited by J. Kleinig, 'Human Rights, Legal Rights and Social Change' in Kamenka and Tay (eds), *Human Rights*, pp. 36, 40.
40 S.I. Benn, 'Rights', in P. Edwards (ed.), *Encyclopedia of Philosophy* (New York, Macmillan, 1967), vol. 7, p. 196.
41 Hart, *Essays in Jurisprudence and Philosophy*, p. 195.
42 T. Campbell, *The Legal Theory of Ethical Positivism*, p. 165.
43 ibid.

criticised on the basis that if non-consequentialist rights are fanciful, then how does one account for the significant changes to the moral landscape for which they have provided the catalyst?

There are several responses to this. First, the fact that a belief or judgment is capable of moving and guiding human conduct says little about its truth – the widespread practice of burning 'witches' is a case in point. Second, at the descriptive level, it is probably the case that the intuitive appeal of rights claims and the absolutist and forceful manner in which they are expressed has been normally sufficient to mask fundamental logical deficiencies associated with the concept of rights. Claims couched in the language of rights seem to carry more emotive punch than equivalent claims grounded in the language of duties. For whatever reason (perhaps the necessarily egocentric nature of rights discourse), the claim that 'I have a right to life' appears to resonate more powerfully than the assertion that 'You have a duty not to kill me.' In effect, the much-criticised[44] meta-ethical theory of emotivism, which provides that morality is a set of utterances which express one's attitude with the aim of influencing the behaviour of others, seems to provide at least a partial explanation for the influence of rights-based discourse.

Finally, and perhaps most importantly, we do not believe that there is not any role in moral discourse for rights claims. Simply, as is discussed below, we believe that the only manner in which rights can be substantiated is in the context of a consequentialist ethic.

In any event, given the vacuousness of non-consequentialist rights-based moral theories at the epistemological level, it would not be instructive to attempt to formulate a hierarchy of human interests of the basis of such theories. Given that such rights are not ultimately founded on broader determinate notions, it is simply not tenable to ascertain whether, for example, the rights to liberty and property are more or less important than, say, the rights to health care and welfare, or even the right to privacy.[45]

18.3.3 Consequentialist underpinning to new definition – the preferred approach

A more promising tack for constructing and justifying a ladder of human needs is to ground the analysis in a consequentialist ethic. The most popular consequentialist moral theory is utilitarianism. Several different forms of utilitarianism have been advanced. In our view, the most cogent (and certainly the most influential in moral and political discourse) is hedonistic act utilitarianism, which provides that the morally right action is that which produces the greatest amount of happiness or pleasure and the least amount of pain or unhappiness. This theory

44 For example, see G.L. Warnock, *Contemporary Moral Philosophy* (London, Macmillan, 1982), pp. 24–26.
45 The limits of rights discourse in the refugee domain is also noted by N. Nathwani, 'The Purpose of Asylum', (2000) 12 *International Journal of Refugee Law*, pp. 354, 365–67, who believes that if all human rights violations were taken seriously, States could not pursue their restrictive immigration policies.

selects the avoidance of pain, and the corollary, the attainment of happiness, as the ultimate goals of moral principle.

Unlike the Convention grounds, pain and happiness are not arbitrary. In the context of identifying non-arbitrary criteria for moral concern (in this case the argument was directly addressed to the moral status of animals), Bentham noted that:

> The day may come when the rest of the animal creation may acquire those rights which never could have been withholden from them but by the hand of tyranny. The French have already discovered that the blackness of the skin is no reason why a human being should be abandoned without redress to the caprice of a tormentor. It may one day come to be recognized the number of legs, the villosity of the skin, or the termination of the os sacrum are reasons equally insufficient for abandoning a sensitive being to the same fate. What else is it that should trace the insuperable line? Is it the faculty of reason, or perhaps the faculty of discourse? But a full-grown horse or dog is beyond comparison a more rational, as well as more conversable animal, than an infant of a day or a week or even a month, old. *But suppose they were otherwise, what would it avail? The question is not, Can they reason? nor Can they talk? but Can they suffer?*[46]
>
> [Emphasis added.]

Suffering, unlike political opinion or belonging to a group, is not arbitrary. It is the converse – it is universal. Capable of being felt by all; and desired to be avoided by all. Quite simply, the desire to avoid suffering[47] is the sentiment felt most strongly by all people at all points in history and across all cultures. Why should this then not form the criteria for international compassion? We can think of no logical reason.[48] In light of this, the international humanitarian community needs to be dragged (albeit in some cases, kicking and screaming) towards fundamentally changing the focus of the Convention to reflect this.

18.3.3.1 Interlude – criticisms of utilitarianism

Linking the proposed change to an overarching moral theory provides it with the soundest possible justification. We are aware that utilitarianism has received a lot of bad press over the past few decades, resulting in its demise as the leading normative theory. Considerations of space and focus do not permit us to fully discuss these matters, but there is sufficient room to summarise the responses that one of us has made to the most common criticisms of utilitarianism.

The main general argument against utilitarianism is that because it prioritises net happiness over individual happiness, it fails to safeguard fundamental

46 J. Bentham, *Introduction to the Principles of Morals and Legislation* (New York, Hafner, 1948 [1789]), Ch. 17.

47 For a view that the notion of necessity should underpin refugee law, see Nathwani, 'The Purpose of Asylum'. However, Nathwani does not expand on what sorts of rights or interests the violating of would fall within the scope of the necessity rationale.

48 Goodwin-Gill raises the suggestion that violations of human rights which are a result of deliberate harm are perhaps more egregious and hence of greater 'value' than other forms of deprivations: G. Goodwin-Gill, 'Asylum 2001 – A Convention and a Purpose', (2001) 13 *International Journal of Refugee Law* 1. He does not develop this point. It is one with which we obviously disagree – a person who dies of starvation is no less dead than one who is killed by a bullet.

individual interests. As a result of this, it has been argued that in some circumstances utilitarianism leads to horrendous outcomes, such as punishing the innocent[49] or compelling organ donations where the donations would maximise happiness by saving the lives of many or assisting those most in need.[50] It has even been argued that there is no place for individual rights or interests in a utilitarian ethic.

18.3.3.2 Horror scenarios not that bad

On closer reflection, however, many of the appalling conclusions utilitarianism supposedly commits us to do not *really* allow one to argue that any theory which approves of such outcomes must necessarily be flawed.[51] The horror scenarios which it is claimed utilitarians are committed to are in fact consistent with the decisions we as individuals and societies as a whole have readily made and continue to make when faced with extreme and desperate circumstances. Once we come to grips with the fact that our decisions in extreme situations will be compartmentalised to desperate predicaments and will not have a snowball effect and serve to henceforth diminish the high regard we normally have for important individual concerns and interests, we find that when placed between a rock and a hard place we do and *should*, though perhaps somewhat grudgingly, take the utilitarian option. In the face of extreme situations we are quite ready to accept that one should, or even must, sacrifice oneself or others for the good of the group.[52]

However, what we actually *do* does not justify what *ought* to be done. Morality is normative, not descriptive in nature: an 'ought' cannot be derived from an 'is'.[53] Still, the above line of reasoning is telling because the force of the horrendous-consequences criticism lies in the fact that it supposedly so troubles our moral consciousness that all of utilitarianism must be dismissed on the basis that such an outcome is so horrible that 'there must be a mistake somewhere'.

18.3.3.3 Utilitarian rights

Further, it is important to note that it has been argued that rights do in fact have a place in a utilitarian ethic, and that it is only against this background that rights can be explained and their source justified. Utilitarianism provides a sounder foundation for rights than any other competing theory. For the utilitarian, the

49 H.J. McCloskey, *Meta-Ethics and Normative Ethics* (The Hague, Martinus Nijhoff, 1969), pp. 180–81. A similar example to McCloskey's is provided in E.F. Carritt, *Ethical and Political Thinking* (Oxford, Clarendon Press, 1947), p. 65.

50 R. Nozick, *Anarchy, State, and Utopia* (New York, Basic Books, 1974), pp. 206–07.

51 The distinction we are making between intuitive moral judgments and those formed after due reflection is similar to that made by R.M. Hare between intuitive and critical levels of moral thinking: see R.M. Hare, *Moral Thinking: Its Levels, Methods and Point* (Oxford, OUP, 1981).

52 See Bagaric, 'In Defence of a Utilitarian Theory of Punishment: Punishing the Innocent: the Compatibility of Utilitarianism and Rights', where a number of examples of society readily sacrificing individual lives for the good of the group are given.

53 This has been used as an argument against a naturalistic view of morality. However, see C.R. Pigden, 'Naturalism', in P. Singer (ed.), *A Companion to Ethics* (Oxford, Basil Blackwell, 1991), pp. 421, 422–26, where he points out that this phenomenon simply reflects the conservative nature of logic – you cannot get out of it what you do not put in.

answer to the question 'why do rights exist?' is simple: recognition of rights best promotes general utility.[54] Their origin accordingly lies in the pursuit of happiness. Their content is discovered through empirical observations regarding the patterns of behaviour which best advance the utilitarian cause. The long association between utilitarianism and rights appears to have been forgotten by most. However, over a century ago it was Mill who proclaimed the right of free speech, on the basis that truth is important to the attainment of general happiness and truth is best discovered by its competition with falsehood.[55]

Difficulties in performing the utilitarian calculus regarding each decision make it desirable to ascribe to people certain rights and interests, which evidence shows tend to maximise happiness[56] – even more happiness than if we made all of our decisions without such guidelines. Rights save time and energy by serving as shortcuts to attaining desirable consequences. By labelling certain interests as rights, we are spared the tedious task of establishing their importance as a first premise in practical arguments.[57] There are also other reasons why performing the utilitarian calculus on each occasion may be counterproductive to the ultimate aim. Our capacity to gather and process information, and our foresight, are restricted by a large number of factors, including lack of time, indifference to the matter at hand, defects in reasoning, and so on. We are quite often not in a good position to assess all the possible alternatives and to determine the likely impact upon general happiness of each alternative. Our ability to make the correct decision will be greatly assisted if we can narrow down the range of relevant factors in light of predetermined guidelines. History has shown that certain patterns of conduct and norms of behaviour, if observed, are most conducive to promoting happiness[58]

Thus utilitarianism is well able to explain the existence and importance of rights. It is just that rights do not have a life of their own (they are derivative, not foundational), in contrast to all deontological constructs. However, this is not a criticism of utilitarianism; it is rather a strength, since it is farcical to claim that any right is absolute. Another advantage of utilitarianism is that only it provides a mechanism for ranking rights and other interests. In the event of a clash, the victor is the right that will generate the most happiness.

54 According to Mill, rights reconcile justice with utility. Justice, which he claims consists of certain fundamental rights, is merely a part of utility. And 'to have a right is . . . to have something which society ought to defend . . . [if asked why] . . . I can give no other reason than general utility': Mill, 'Utilitarianism', pp. 251, 309. Campbell, in *The Legal Theory of Ethical Positivism*, pp. 161–85, also proposes a reductive approach to rights, but underlying his rights thesis is not utilitarianism, but rather (ethical) positivist ideals. Ethical positivism is also discussed in T. Campbell, 'The Point of Legal Positivism', in T. Campbell (ed.), *Legal Positivism* (Aldershot, Dartmouth Publishing, 1999), p. 323.

55 Mill, 'Utilitarianism', pp. 141–83.

56 These rights, however, are never decisive and must be disregarded where they would not cause net happiness (otherwise this would be to go down the rule of utilitarianism track).

57 See J. Raz, *Morality of Freedom* (Oxford, Clarendon Press, 1986), p. 191. Raz also provides that rights are useful because they enable us to settle on shared intermediary conclusions, despite considerable dispute regarding the grounds for the conclusions.

58 See M. Bagaric, *How to Live: Being Happy and Dealing with Moral Dilemmas* (Lanham MD, University Press of America, 2007). Ch 2.

18.3.4 Ramifications for a new definition

18.3.4.1 Repeal of grounds

The logical upshot of the above discussion is that the notion of Convention grounds becomes redundant. This will cause many refugee lawyers and human rights proponents to recoil – Convention grounds have been part of refugee law for over 50 years. However, unless proponents of the grounds can provide a justification for continued adherence to them (tradition does not suffice), they are logically committed to overhauling them – or they risk facing being accused of Convention worship. In this regard, we note that 50 years is a very short period in the context of human history and even though the changes we are proposing are quite radical, they are less ambitious than the Convention was at the outset.

Further, although human rights proponents have not previously been so bold as to recommend the changes advocated here, it seems that there is some movement towards support for them. One of the fashionable reform proposals in refugee literature at present is that women should be recognised as a 'particular social group'.[59] We agree, and add that men should also be recognised as a 'particular social group'. The effect of this would be that being a member of the human species is the sole criterion that marks one out as being worthy of compassion. The *reason* for one's pain and destitution is not cardinal – pain and destitution suffice. The focus then turns on the notion of persecution: in particular, what sort of deprivation is significant enough to warrant international assistance?

18.3.4.2 Hierarchy of human interests – life and liberty as fundamental

In terms of the exact changes that are appropriate, a Convention based on the concept of need would focus on the conditions that are necessary for human subsistence. As noted in Chapter 15, at the core there is little scope for debate here – it is a matter of science, not sociology. Humans need food, water and shelter and clothing to survive. All other interests are contingent on the availability of these basic goods. Displaced persons who lack any of these goods to a point where it threatens their survival should be accorded refugee status. These interests aside, there are also other interests that seem to be a precondition for human existence. They consist of security of person (in the context of physical autonomy) and freedom from arbitrary deprivation of liberty. Access to education, minimum standards of health care and property rights would seem to be on the next level. Other rights then follow, such as the right to one's political opinion, privacy and so on.

18.3.4.3 Where to draw the line?

At what point the refugee line should be drawn is unclear. However, as noted in Chapter 15, the most important consideration in this regard is the willingness

59 See, for example, N. Kelley, 'The Convention Refugee Definition and Gender-Based Persecution: A Decade's Progress', (2002) 13 *International Journal of Refugee Law* 559; M. Falcon, 'Gender Based Persecution', (2002) 21 *Refugee Survey Quarterly* 133. See, further, Chapter 14.

of the international community to take in needy foreigners. The greater the preparedness, the higher the point at which the line should be drawn. However, as was discussed earlier, the desire to help comes in finite doses. Given this, it is important to properly target those who are assisted – every spot taken by a refugee is one less that remains available. While an expansive definition of refugee law may seem to be the most humanitarian approach to take, ultimately it may be the least desirable. Such a definition could lead to a situation of people dying of starvation, so that others can enjoy a university education or express their political views. In our view, given that a choice must be made, we would prefer to feed the hungry each time.

Thus we would limit assistance to people whose lives are in peril as a result of lack of food, water or shelter, or who have a real fear of having their physical integrity or liberty violated. This, effectively, means that the principal right recognised in the proposed definition is the right to life. The only concession we would make to confining assistance to threats to life is to recognise the importance of personal liberty, which while not fundamental to the right to life, is essential for human beings to attain any semblance of fulfilment. The importance of liberty to the human species is reflected by the fact that deprivation of it constitutes the gravest form of punishment that is inflicted by Western cultures on wrongdoers (apart from many parts of the United States, where capital punishment is still sanctioned).

As noted in Chapter 15, it is ultimately undesirable to adopt a broad approach to the type of harm that qualifies for refugee assistance. Courts and other legal bodies (no doubt well intentioned) may appear to be assisting the refugee cause by expanding the type of harm that qualifies for assistance, and viewed narrowly this is no doubt the case – the people who come within the expanded definition are granted access to the relevant nation state. However, at this point good intention and good consequences part company as a result of a failure to acknowledge the fact that nations have a very limited appetite for desperate foreigners. This only seems to be getting worse: 'the international refugee regime still saves lives, of course. But given the world's increasingly tight fisted treatment of uprooted people, this is an anniversary fit for sober reflection not celebration.'[60] It follows that, given the scarcity value and preciousness of refugee places, the kind thing to do is not to expand the range of human interests that are recognised under the Convention, but in fact to do the opposite. The interests should be narrowed to ensure, as far as possible, that the refugee places are occupied by those in greatest need.

A related point is that while an expansive definition of 'serious harm' appears to be consistent with the humanitarian underpinnings of the Convention, it is ultimately misguided because it verges on merging refugee law and immigration law. As we have noted, refugee law is not about equalising the international playing field so far as the capacity for people to flourish is concerned; it is about

60 J. Drumtra, 'The Year in Review', in US Committee for Refugees, *World Refugee Survey 2001* (2002), pp. 14, 16. See also UNHCR, 'The Asylum Dilemma', in *The State of the World's Refugees 1997–98* (1998), p. 182.

assisting those in greatest need. The definition we advance in the following section seeks to avoid such confusion.

18.4 The preferred definition

18.4.1 Proposed definition

In light of the above discussion we suggest that the definition of 'refugee' in the Convention should be amended as follows:

> A refugee is a person who owing to:
> (i) the fact that his or her life is in peril as a result of lack of food, water or shelter; or
> (ii) a well-founded fear of having his or her physical integrity or liberty violated;
> is outside the country of his or her nationality and is unable to avail himself or herself of the relevant resources or protection of that country; or who, not having a nationality and being outside the country of his or her former habitual residence, is unable or unwilling to return to it.[61]

Critics may take issue with the wording or exact drafting of the definition. Nevertheless it is important that future debate on the matter maintains a level of perspective. By this we mean that the discussion should focus on the substance of the definition and not on the grey issues that invariably arise in definitions. No doubt it will be difficult to determine with exactness what level of food shortage will come within the scope of the definition, but we have every confidence that such teething problems are not insurmountable.

18.4.2 The concept of persecution is made (effectively) redundant

It is important to note that the proposed definition not only removes the grounds, but also impacts on other important aspects of the definition. Most notably, it makes the amorphous concept of persecution almost redundant. As the definition currently stands there are several requirements that stem from the notion of persecution. First, as was discussed in Chapter 15, the persecution must involve harm beyond a certain threshold. This requirement has been (effectively) retained but the notion of harm has been significantly tightened – confined to threats to life and liberty.

The second aspect of persecution is that it must be in the form of systematic and discriminatory conduct. This is no longer relevant: once being hungry to the point of near starvation is sufficient, which means that potentially a whole nation

61 This has some similarities with the UN definition of 'internally displaced people': 'persons who have been forced to flee their homes suddenly or unexpectedly in large numbers, as a result of armed conflict, internal strife, systematic violations of human rights or natural or man-made disasters, [and who are within the territory of their own country]': *Analytical Report of the Secretary-General on Internally Displaced Persons* (E/CN 4/19992/93, 14 February 1992), paragraph 17.

may cross a border in search of food is not a barrier to assistance, discrimination is not necessary.

Third, the persecution must have an official quality, in the sense that it is caused by government authorities or officially tolerated or uncontrollable by the authorities of the country of nationality. This requirement remains relevant only in relation to limb (ii) of the proposed definition. Fourth, as the law currently stands, persecution implies an element of motivation to inflict harm on the part of those who persecute. This is now obviously redundant. As is the final requirement, which is the existence of a formal nexus between the grounds and the harm. Pursuant to our model it is not necessary that the persecution feared must be attributable to a Convention ground.[62]

18.5 Concluding remarks

The Refugee Convention is a poorly drafted document. It has a humanitarian overtone, but is devoid of an overarching justification. Its greatest failing is that it prioritises 'sexy' interests – such as the right to project one's political opinion – over basic human needs. The fact that an applicant's cause of distress must be linked to the specific grounds in the definition – that is, persecution due to race, religion, nationality, membership of a particular social group or political opinion – renders the Convention unnecessarily and unjustly restrictive. It bars people whose lives are unbearable because of war, famines, drought and earthquakes from receiving protection under the Convention. The current definition ignores the human interests that are most essential for survival. In light of this, it is time to reform the definition of 'refugee' so that the world's collective compassion is targeted more directly at those who are suffering the greatest degree of deprivation.

18.5.1 Practical obstacles to reform

We accept that the practical difficulties of changing the Convention definition are considerable, not least among them being the logistic difficulty of possibly reconvening an international refugee Convention for the purpose of adopting proposed amendments.[63] However, these difficulties should not prevent the necessary amendments from being made. The area is too important to ignore and we should change the definition in order to provide the most just outcome to the neediest people. Further, the problems with amending the definition are

62 In Australia, the persecution feared need not be *solely* attributable to a Convention reason. However, persecution for multiple motivations will not satisfy the relevant test unless a Convention reason or reasons constitute at least the essential and significant motivation for the persecution feared: *Migration Act 1958* (Cth), s 91R(1)(a). See Chapter 15.

63 See, further, M. Zan, 'Refugees and the International Refugee Convention: Some issues, reform proposals and realistic constraints', *Malaysian Law News*, April 1996, 23.

not nearly as significant as those involved in its initial drafting and its gaining acceptance in the international community.

It has been suggested that 'because refugee law is, after all, the creation of largely self-interested nation states, it may ultimately prove impossible to define access to asylum more generously than as we know it today'.[64] We do not disagree with this. This chapter, however, is not about generosity. It is about perspective, raising international awareness about the things that are central to people's lives and redefining the term 'refugee', not to increase the pool of candidates who fit within the criteria, but to target those most in need.

For the Convention to retain the high level of acceptance that it has in the international community, it is important that it not be regarded as arbitrarily selecting certain human needs as worthy of state protection, while ignoring even more important needs. Absent a wholesale definitional change along the lines proposed in this chapter, the Convention will ultimately be regarded as a discriminatory document, unless a justification can be given for preferring the interests protected in the Convention to other interests (in particular the ones discussed in this chapter). We believe that this is not possible. To this end, we note that the risk that the Convention (in its current form) may diminish in importance has not been lost on others: Hathaway notes that 'as contemporary protection concerns become increasingly distinct from those of post-war Europe, the risk of Convention definition becoming a mere legal anachronism is real'.[65]

18.5.2 The proposed definition is not a complete solution

We acknowledge that from a humanitarian perspective the definition we propose is still somewhat deficient. To qualify for state assistance, a needy person must still be outside his or her country of nationality. In terms of qualifying for state assistance, why should it matter, it can be fairly asked, whether a starving person happens to hobble over a border or not? Either way, that person's life is in peril. Further, international borders are simply arbitrary invisible lines in terrain. In terms of being entitled to assistance, we agree that the hungry should obtain assistance irrespective of which side of a border they are on.[66] However, one immutable aspect of the term 'refugee' (that is, one of the denotations of the word) is that the person is displaced from his or her abode. While from a

64 Hathaway, *The Law of Refugee Status*, p. 233.
65 ibid., p. 232.
66 We agree that there is a desperate need for greater international protocols concerning the treatment of the internally displaced, as is noted by 'refugees have an international agency and legal structure to turn to for protection and assistance. The internally displaced have nothing comparable': R. Cohen, 'Protecting the Internally Displaced', in USCR, *World Refugee Survey 1996*, pp. 20, 23. The definition we advance does not impose any obligation on the states whose actions arguably create or cause the refugee influx into other countries. The Convention has been criticised on this basis, with some jurists arguing that principles of state responsibility should be used to draft international legal rules that would make a state internationally responsible for creating massive refugee movements by its actions (say human rights violations) within its borders. Although a preventive approach of this kind is attractive in theory, the fact that state sovereignty remains so important in the current international climate suggests that there would be a strong resistance to 'interference in internal affairs' by states. Hence, such a proposal is perhaps too idealistic right now.

humanitarian perspective this has no relevance, it is a defining aspect of refugee law. As Kimminich said as long ago as 1962, 'Alienage is inherent in the concept of refugee.'[67]

The same cannot be said in relation to the grounds – they are simply the reason for the alienage. As is noted by Hathaway:

> We commonly refer to persons who have been forced to flee to another region of their country as refugees. We normally assume that a person who is prepared to abandon her home, her family, her security is a refugee . . . We recognise the logic of escape from natural disasters, or from generally oppressive political regimes as much as from the possibility of persecution.[68]

In a similar vein, Collinson states that 'in popular usage, the term "refugee" has a broad meaning, signifying a person fleeing any one of a wide range of life-threatening conditions, including war, famine, natural disaster, oppression, persecution or massive human rights abuses'.[69]

The reform proposals we have suggested in this chapter do not purport to be a solution to the international humanitarian problems – not by a long way. If adopted, what they would do is make the Convention, the most widely accepted international humanitarian law, fairer by offering protection to those in the greatest peril. We do not question that if these changes are adopted there would remain a pressing need to increase the level of obligation that states have towards providing assistance to states whose citizens are denied the basic needs for life: this needs to change from an aspiration to an obligation. A needs-based underpinning to the Refugees Convention may provide momentum towards such an end.

67 Nathwani, The Purpose of Asylum', p. 367, citing Otto Kimminich, *Der Internationale Rechtsstatus des Fluchtlings* (Köln, C. Heymann, 1962).
68 Hathaway, *The Law of Refugee Status*, p. v.
69 Collinson, *Beyond Borders: Western European Migration Policy Towards the 21st Century*, p. 59.

19

The determination and review process for migration and refugee decisions

19.1 Merits review

An administrative review tribunal 'stands in the shoes of the original decision-maker'. It reconsiders an administrative decision with the objective of making the correct or preferable decision based on the facts before it, and in accordance with the applicable law. It is axiomatic to merits review that an administrative review tribunal has power to substitute its decision for that of the original decision-maker.

Primary decisions about migration and refugee visa applications are made under the *Migration Act 1958* (Cth) by the Minister for Immigration or DIAC officials acting as the Minister's delegates. Subject to a few exceptions mentioned below, those decisions are subject to merits review by the Migration Review Tribunal (MRT), the Refugee Review Tribunal (RRT) or the Administrative Appeals Tribunal (AAT).

19.2 Decisions reviewable by the MRT, RRT and AAT

The MRT reviews decisions to refuse visas to applicants in Australia (other than protection visas); decisions to refuse visas to overseas applicants who have an Australian sponsor, nominator, or close family member; decisions to cancel visas within Australia; and decisions concerning certain business nominations and sponsorships.[1]

1 See *Migration Act 1958* (Cth), s 338.

Decisions to refuse or cancel protection visas in relation to applicants in Australia are reviewed by the RRT.[2] That tribunal has no jurisdiction to review refugee decisions that are made offshore, including those made in relation to asylum-seekers who arrived in parts of Australia that have been excised from the migration zone and have been held on various islands.[3] Nor does it have jurisdiction to make decisions on humanitarian or compassionate grounds if those grounds are not related to the Refugees Convention.

The AAT reviews decisions to refuse protection visas or to cancel protection visas on criminal and character grounds, including the basis of exclusion under Articles 1F, 32 or 33 of the Refugees Convention; decisions to order the deportation of a non-citizen convicted of certain crimes; and decisions to refuse or to cancel visas on the basis that the non-citizen does not pass the character test. In addition, it reviews decisions to cancel business permits or visas.[4]

In *Plaintiff M61/2010E v Commonwealth of Australia; Plaintiff M69 of 2010 v Commonwealth of Australia*[5] the High Court held that applicants who are assessed as part of the offshore processing regime (after arriving at Christmas Island by boat) are entitled to procedural fairness and hence can have their assessments reviewed by courts.

The High Court rejected the submissions by the government that the assessments and administrative reviews (which were undertaken by independent contractors) conducted in relation to applicants who are part of the offshore processing regime were an exercise of non-statutory executive powers and hence there was no obligation to accord applicants procedural fairness and otherwise act according to the law.

The High Court noted that in processing the applications, the Minister decided to consider exercising powers conferred under the *Migration Act 1958* (Cth). This process affected the rights of the applicants, in particular their freedom from detention, and hence the agents making the assessments were required to act according to the law. The consequence of this decision is that applicants who are part of the offshore processing regime are also entitled to have their assessment decisions reviewed by the courts. At the time of writing this book, the government had yet to announce a processing system for offshore applicants.

19.3 Judicial review

Decisions made by the MRT, the RRT, the AAT and now those reviews conducted in relation to offshore applicants are subject to judicial review by the Federal Magistrates Court, the Federal Court and the High Court. In reviewing an administrative tribunal decision, a court is not concerned with the merits

2 *Migration Act 1958* (Cth), s 411.
3 See Chapter 13, 'Onshore applications'.
4 *Migration Act 1958* (Cth), ss 134 and 501.
5 [2010] HCA 4.

of the tribunal's decision but with the question of whether the tribunal has made an error of law. The general principles for challenging administrative determinations, especially in the refugee context was recently summarised by the High Court in *Minister for Immigration and Citizenship v SZJSS*,[6] as follows:

> 23. General principles governing the limited role of the courts in reviewing administrative error have long been identified. As Mason J observed in *Minister for Aboriginal Affairs v Peko-Wallsend Ltd*, 'mere preference for a different result, when the question is one on which reasonable minds may come to different conclusions' is not a sufficient reason for overturning a judicial decision upon a review. Further, Brennan J said in *Attorney-General (NSW) v Quin*:
>
> > 'The merits of administrative action, to the extent that they can be distinguished from legality, are for the repository of the relevant power and, subject to political control, for the repository alone.'
>
> 24. In 1989 with the codification of migration policy the Migration Act was amended significantly. At that time, judicial review of migration decisions was conducted under the *Administrative Decisions (Judicial Review) Act* 1977 (Cth) ('ADJR Act').
>
> 25. Grounds for review under s 5(1) of the ADJR Act include the ground that 'the making of the decision was an improper exercise of the power conferred' by the relevant enactment. Section 5(2) provides that the reference to 'an improper exercise of a power' includes a reference to 'failing to take a relevant consideration into account', 'an exercise of a power that is so unreasonable that no reasonable person could have so exercised the power', and 'any other exercise of a power in a way that constitutes abuse of the power'. Section 5(2)(f) identifies as a ground for review 'an exercise of a discretionary power in accordance with a rule or policy without regard to the merits of the particular case'. Section 6 provides further statutory grounds for review of conduct related to the making of decisions, which include a ground that the making of the proposed decision would be an improper exercise of power conferred by the relevant enactment.
>
> 26. In *Khan v Minister for Immigration and Ethnic Affairs*, Gummow J considered a migration appeal brought in 1987, when such appeals were decided under the ADJR Act. His Honour construed an improper exercise of power as including a reference to an exercise of a discretionary power in accordance with a rule or policy, without regard to the merits of a particular case. His Honour found that in considering all relevant material placed before him, the Minister's delegate was required to 'give proper, genuine and realistic consideration to the merits of the case and be ready in a proper case to depart from any applicable policy'.
>
> 27. On 1 September 1994, Pt 8 of the Migration Act was introduced. The new Pt 8 scheme for judicial review differed significantly from the provisions of ss 5 and 6 of the ADJR Act; it contained provisions which sought to exclude judicial review of migration decisions on numerous grounds, which included the grounds of failing to take relevant considerations into account and a breach of the rules of natural justice. Whilst recognising that statutory limits were then prescribed which bore upon the construction of improper exercise of power, in *Minister for Immigration and Multicultural Affairs v*

6 [2010] HCA 48.

> *Yusuf*, McHugh, Gummow and Hayne JJ observed that jurisdictional error may include ignoring relevant material in a way that affects the exercise of a power.
>
> 28. It is sufficient for present purposes to note that from October 2001, Pt 8 as discussed above was repealed and replaced with the current Pt 8, including the privative clause provisions of s 474 [which is discussed below], which do not protect decisions involving jurisdictional error or oust the jurisdiction conferred by s 75(v) of the Constitution.

The *Migration Act 1958* (Cth) contains cumbersome provisions for the 'handing down' of RRT and MRT decisions that have been the subject of judicial review.[7] In the case of *Inderjit Singh v MIMA*, the Federal Court found that an RRT decision is not finalised until the decision is 'handed down'.[8] In that case, the RRT had signed its decision on 28 March 2000 and informed the applicant that it had made a decision that would be handed down on 14 April 2000. On 13 April 2000, the applicant submitted relevant material to the RRT which was not considered by the RRT member. On the basis of section 430B(4), which provides that '[t]he date of the decision is the date on which the decision is handed down', the court found that the RRT had 'erred in law in considering itself *functus officio* when it was not', and that it had ignored relevant material submitted to it on 13 April 2000 without a lawful reason.[9]

The decision of the Federal Court in *Inderjit Singh* can be contrasted with another decision of the Federal Court concerning a decision of a primary decision-maker, in which the court found that a draft decision record, undated but signed by a DIAC delegate and sent to a superior officer for review was, in law, a finalised decision for the purposes of section 65(1) and section 67 of the Act.[10]

The judiciary does not have jurisdiction to review decisions of the Minister not to exercise, or not to consider the exercise of, the Minister's power under section 37A(2) or (3) (altering the period of validity of a safe haven visa); 48B (allowing a further protection visa application); 72(1)(c) (determining a person to be an 'eligible non-citizen'); 91F, 91L and 91Q (relating to permitting visa applications that would otherwise not be valid); and 345, 351, 391, 417 or 454 (substituting negative decisions of merits review tribunals).[11]

19.4 Original jurisdiction of the High Court

Section 75(v) of the Australian Constitution confers original jurisdiction on the High Court in all matters in which a writ of mandamus or prohibition or an injunction is sought against an officer of the Commonwealth. This means that the High Court has original jurisdiction to review decisions of members of the

7 *Migration Act 1958* (Cth), ss 368A and 368B in relation to the MRT and ss 430A and 430B in relation to the RRT.
8 [2001] FCA 73 (Merkel J).
9 [2001] FCA 73 (Merkel J), [51].
10 *VHAF v MIMA* [2002] FCA 1243.
11 See Chapter 10, 'Ministerial Intervention'.

MRT, the RRT, the AAT and the body conducting offshore determinations against which such remedies are sought. The Commonwealth Parliament cannot enact legislation to restrict the High Court's jurisdiction under section 75(v).

19.5 Background to enactment of privative clause

When the federal government's migration policy was codified in the *Migration Act 1958* (Cth) in 1989, judicial review of administrative decisions was conducted under the *Administrative Decisions (Judicial Review) Act 1977* (the ADJR Act). However, successive governments perceived that some members of the judiciary were engaging in merits review of tribunal decisions under the ADJR Act. On 1 September 1994, Part 8 of the Act was introduced as a result of the *Migration Reform Act 1992* (Cth). Part 8 contained provisions that sought to exclude judicial review of decisions of the Immigration Review Tribunal (the precursor to the MRT) and the RRT[12] by the Federal Court on grounds that included a breach of the rules of natural justice;[13] *Wednesbury* unreasonableness;[14] taking irrelevant considerations into account;[15] and failing to take relevant considerations into account.[16]

The federal government's motivation in seeking to restrict judicial review was bluntly explained by the then Minister for Immigration:

> There are people who are intent on bypassing the established categories of entry into this country. Some do this by trying to avoid immigration processing altogether by arriving in Australia without authority. The boat people are a good example. Owing to weaknesses which have been inherent in our migration laws for many years, these people are often successful. Many manage to stay here, even though they do not fall within the specific visa categories, which is the only lawful way to enter and stay in Australia. At the very least, many manage to delay the substantive decision on their case and, as a consequence, their departure, by using the courts to exploit any weaknesses they can find in our immigration law. This must stop . . .
>
> The Reform Bill proposes significant extensions to the current system for review of migration decisions. Credible independent merits review will ensure that the Government's clear intentions in relation to controlling entry to Australia, as set out in the Migration Act, are not eroded by narrow judicial interpretations. Under the Reform Bill, the following people who are adversely affected by a decision will be entitled to independent merits review: onshore refugee claimants; onshore cancelled visa holders, except those cancelled at the border; onshore applicants for a visa, except those detected at the border; and an Australian sponsor of an offshore applicant for a visa . . .
>
> As I have indicated, the Government wishes to make the application of the legal concepts of migration decision making predictable. Judicial review rights for decisions on the grant or cancellation of a visa will be set out in the Migration Act. Judicial review will only be possible after the applicant has pursued all merits review rights or where

12 See *Migration Act 1958* (Cth), s 475(1).
13 *Migration Act 1958* (Cth), s 476(2)(a).
14 *Migration Act 1958* (Cth), s 476(2)(b) and see *Associated Provincial Picture Houses v Wednesbury Corporation* [1948] 1 KB 223 at 230.
15 *Migration Act 1958* (Cth), s 476(3)(d).
16 *Migration Act 1958* (Cth), s 476(3)(e).

> merits review is not available. Grounds for review will include failure to follow the codified decision making procedures set out in the Act. As the codified procedures will allow an applicant a fair opportunity to present his or her claims, failure to observe the rules of natural justice and unreasonableness will not be grounds for review.[17]

Ironically, Part 8 has been described in retrospect as 'the engine room of the 1990s for the growth and extension of administrative law principles in Australia'.[18]

Part 8 was the subject of judgments by the High Court in *Abebe v Commonwealth*[19] and in *MIMA v Eshetu*.[20] In *Abebe*, the High Court found that it was within the power of the Commonwealth Parliament to restrict the Federal Court's jurisdiction to review tribunal decisions by the provisions of Part 8 of the Act. A month after that judgement, the High Court decided in *Eshetu* that section 420 of the Act[21] did not override section 476(2)(b) so as to enable judicial review of tribunal decisions by the Federal Court on the ground of *Wednesbury* unreasonableness;[22] nor did it enable judicial review by the Federal Court for a breach of the rules of natural justice.[23]

Section 430(1) of the *Migration Act 1958* (Cth) requires the tribunal to prepare a written statement setting out its decision, the reasons for its decision, the findings on any material questions of fact, and references to evidence on which the findings were based. In the case of *MIMA v Yusuf*,[24] the High Court held[25] that a failure by the RRT to comply with section 430(1) of the Act[26] was not a ground for judicial review by the Federal Court under Part 8.[27] Nevertheless, the judgment of McHugh, Gummow and Hayne JJ indicated, somewhat cryptically, that judicial review would be available on broader grounds derived from 'jurisdictional error' under general law:

> 'Jurisdictional error' can thus be seen to embrace a number of different kinds of error, the list of which, in the passage cited from *Craig*, is not exhaustive. Those different kinds of error may well overlap. The circumstances of a particular case may permit more than one characterisation of the error identified, for example, as the decision-maker both asking the wrong question and ignoring relevant material. What is important, however, is that identifying a wrong issue, asking a wrong question, ignoring relevant material or relying on irrelevant material in a way that affects the exercise of power is to make an error of law. Further, doing so results in the decision-maker exceeding the authority or powers given by the relevant statute. In other words, if an error of those types is made, the decision-maker did not have authority to make the decision that

17 Commonwealth, *Second Reading Speech*, Migration Reform Bill 1992, House of Representatives, 4 November 1992, 2620 (Gerry Hand, Minister for Immigration, Local Government and Ethnic Affairs).
18 John McMillan, 'Judicial Restraint and Activism in Administrative Law', [2002] *Federal Law Review* 12.
19 (1999) 162 ALR 1.
20 [1999] HCA 21(13 May 1999).
21 *Migration Act 1958* (Cth), s 420 provides that the RRT is to provide 'a mechanism of review that is fair, just, economical, informal and quick' and that it 'must act according to substantial justice and the merits of the case'.
22 *MIMA v Eshetu* [1999] HCA 21(13 May 1999), [48] (Gleeson CJ and McHugh J) and [74] (Gaudron and Kirby JJ), and see above n 6.
23 *MIMA v Eshetu* [1999] HCA 21(13 May 1999), [77] (Gaudron and Kirby JJ).
24 (2001) 206 CLR 323.
25 Kirby J dissented.
26 *Migration Act 1958* (Cth), s 430(1). In *Minister for Immigration and Citizenship v SZLSP* [2010] FCAFC 108 the court provided a summary of the obligations of the RRT pursuant to *Migration Act 1958* (Cth), s 430.
27 See further, below, the discussion in *Minister for Immigration and Citizenship v SZMDS* [2010] HCA 16.

was made; he or she did not have jurisdiction to make it. Nothing in the Act suggests that the Tribunal is given authority to authoritatively determine questions of law or to make a decision otherwise than in accordance with the law.

No doubt full weight must be given to s 476(3) and the limitations which it prescribes in the construction of improper exercise of power in par (d) of s 476(1). Equally, however, it is important to recognise that these limitations, unlike those prescribed by s 476(2), are limitations on only one of the grounds specified in s 476(1). All this being so, there is no reason to give either par (b) or par (c) of s 476(1) some meaning narrower than the meaning conveyed by the ordinary usage of the words of each of those paragraphs. In particular, it is important to recognise that, if the Tribunal identifies a wrong issue, asks a wrong question, ignores relevant material or relies on irrelevant material, it 'exceeds its authority or powers'. If that is so, the person who purported to make the decision 'did not have jurisdiction' to make the decision he or she made, and the decision 'was not authorised' by the Act.

Moreover, in such a case, the decision may well, within the meaning of par (e) of s 476(1), involve an error of law which involves an incorrect interpretation of the applicable law or an incorrect application of the law to the facts as found. That it cannot be said to be an *improper* exercise of power (as that expression is to be understood in s 476(1)(d), read in light of s 476(3)) is not to the point. No doubt it must be recognised that the ground stated in par (e) is not described simply as making an error of law. The qualification added is that the error of law involves an incorrect interpretation of the applicable law or an incorrect application of the law to the facts as found. That qualification emphasises that factual error by the Tribunal will not found review. Adopting what was said in *Craig*, making an erroneous finding or reaching a mistaken conclusion is not to make an error of law of the kind with which par (e) deals. That having been said, the addition of the qualification to par (e) is no reason to read the ground as a whole otherwise than according to the ordinary meaning of its language. If the Tribunal identifies a wrong issue, asks itself a wrong question, ignores relevant material or relies on irrelevant material in such a way as affects the exercise of its powers, that will very often reveal that it has made an error in its understanding of the applicable law or has failed to apply that law correctly to the facts it found. If that is so, the ground in s 476(1)(e) is made out.[28] [Footnote omitted.]

In interpreting *Yusuf*, it has recently been held that a failure to comply with section 430 can in fact constitute a jurisdictional error. In *Minister for Immigration and Citizenship v SZLSP*[29] the Full Federal Court rejected an appeal by the Minister regarding a Federal Magistrates' decision quashing an RRT refusal for a protection visa. The respondents were Chinese nationals who claimed to be Falun Gong practitioners; this claim was rejected by the RRT. The Federal Magistrate found that the RRT failed to disclose the source of information in its reasons and thus asked the wrong question, which constituted a jurisdictional error. In reaching its conclusion, Kenny J made the following comments (Rares J agreeing; Buchanan J dissenting):

28 *MIMA v Yusuf* [2001] HCA 30 (31 May 2001), [82]–[84]. See Rebikoff, '*MIMA v Yusuf*: One Door Closed, Another Opened?', (2001) 29 *Federal Law Review* 453.
29 [2010] FCAFC 108.

43. During the hearing of the matter, as noted earlier, much attention was given to the inferences that might be drawn from the transcript. Any inferences to be drawn from the transcript regarding the Tribunal's approach must, however, be consistent with the reasons the Tribunal has actually provided, and those reasons must be read in light of the Tribunal's obligations under s 430 of the Migration Act. As Gleeson CJ said in *Minister for Immigration and Multicultural Affairs v Yusuf* [2001] HCA 30; (2001) 206 CLR 323 ('*Yusuf*') at 330 [5], '[w]hen the Tribunal prepares a written statement of its reasons for decision in a given case, that statement will have been prepared by the Tribunal, and will be understood by a reader, including a judge reviewing the Tribunal's decision, in the light of the statutory requirements contained in s 430' . . .

45. In argument on the appeal, counsel for the Minister was asked to address the possibility that the Tribunal had failed to comply with s 430(1)(d), i.e., that there was 'evidence or . . . other material' against which the Tribunal evaluated the first respondent's answers, but which was not referred to in the written statement prepared by the Tribunal. In the Federal Magistrate's reasons, and, to some extent, in the argument before us, the assumption was made in light of the transcript that this was the case. For the reasons explored below, including that the Tribunal is presumed to have been cognizant of s 430(1), this assumption may not be justified. These reasons flow from the authorities interpreting s 430 and, in particular, from the High Court's judgment in *Yusuf*.

46. In *Yusuf*, the High Court construed s 430(1)(c) as simply obliging a Tribunal to set out the findings which it had actually made. The Court rejected the position that the provision imposed an obligation to make findings on particular questions of fact that are objectively 'material': see *Yusuf* 206 CLR at 330–32 [5], [9]–[10] per Gleeson CJ and 346 [68] per McHugh, Gummow and Hayne JJ (with whom Gleeson CJ agreed); see also 337–38 [33]–[34] per Gaudron J and 392 [217] per Callinan J. The absence of a finding on a particular question of fact in the Tribunal's reasons did not mean that the Tribunal had failed to set out the finding, but that it had not made a finding on the question at all. The Court therefore held that an alleged violation of s 430(1)(c) was not in itself a ground for jurisdictional error: *Yusuf* 206 CLR at 348–49 [75] . . .

48. Nonetheless, *Yusuf* indicates that s 430 plays an important role in ensuring that administrative decision-makers do not exceed their jurisdiction . . .

49. Gummow ACJ and Kiefel J recently considered the function of s 430 in *SZMDS*. Their Honours explained that '[m]any of the leading authorities in [the High Court] in which administrative decisions were challenged concerned legislative regimes in which there was no counterpart of s 430 of the [Migration] Act', and administrative decision-makers were therefore not required to provide a statement of the reasons for their decisions: *SZMDS* at 266 ALR at 375 [34]. When such decisions 'presented an inscrutable face', error could often only be inferred from the circumstances surrounding the decision: *SZMDS* 266 ALR at 375 [34], citing *Avon Downs*. Gummow ACJ and Kiefel J observed that s 430's requirements obviate 'the necessity for a process of divination undertaken in the earlier authorities dealing with other legislation': *SZMDS* 266 ALR at 376 [36].

Application of authorities

50. Although the transcript of the interview became the focus of the Minister's argument at the hearing of the appeal, the Court's analysis must begin with what the reasons reveal

about the Tribunal's decision. The fundamental difficulty in this case is that there is no reference in the Tribunal's reasons to any material on which it based its finding that none of the first respondent's answers were 'correct' and the first respondent therefore knew 'almost nothing' about Falun Gong belief. Taking the Tribunal's reasons on their face, it appears that the Tribunal arbitrarily decided the first respondent's answers were 'wrong' without any logical basis to do so. Had there been any 'evidence or . . . other material' on which the Tribunal's finding regarding the first respondent's knowledge was based, the Tribunal, aware of its obligations under s 430(1)(d), would presumably have referred to it. The inference arises that the Tribunal's decision was not based on findings or inferences of fact grounded upon probative material and logical grounds. The question is whether the Court should draw this inference, or the contrary inference that the Tribunal's finding was logically based on probative material to which it has not referred in the reasons.

51. The former inference (i.e., as to the absence of probative material or logical grounds) arises squarely from the principle enunciated in *Yusuf* that reasons are prepared in the context of s 430 and must be read in light of that section's requirements. However, a comment of Gleeson CJ in *Yusuf* raises the questions whether a reviewing court should always draw this inference in circumstances like the present and, if not, when should the court draw the other inference. Gleeson CJ's comment was that '[t]here may be cases where it is proper to conclude that the Tribunal has not set out all its findings' (206 CLR at 332 [10]), without indicating what factors might distinguish such cases. The same reasoning would indicate that there may be cases where it is proper to conclude that the Tribunal has not referred to the evidence on which its findings were based (though the Tribunal had such evidence). His Honour noted that it was not suggested in the matters before the Court then that the Tribunal had made a finding which it failed to set out, adding that the consequences of such a failure were not in issue.

52. In their joint judgment, McHugh, Gummow and Hayne JJ did not directly address the possibility raised by Gleeson CJ. Their Honours' reasons indicate, however, that a reviewing court should be wary of inferring lightly that the Tribunal has made a finding that it has not set out: see *Yusuf* 206 CLR at 346 [68]–[69]) (or, relevantly in the present case, has relied on unknown evidence or other material to which it has not referred). Their Honours emphasized that the purpose of s 430 was to ensure that an aggrieved party can identify with 'certainty' why the Tribunal decided as it did, and that a reviewing court is informed of the same thing. Similarly, although Gaudron J did not address Gleeson CJ's suggestion directly, her Honour's reasons discuss the inference to be drawn in terms that would not appear to allow for variation. Gaudron J explained that 'if in its written statement setting out its decision, the Tribunal fails to refer to or fails to make findings with respect to a relevant matter, **it is to be assumed, consistently with the clear directive in s 430 of the Act**, that the Tribunal has not regarded that question as material': see 206 CLR at 338 [37] (emphasis added) . . .

54. The Court's function is, of course, to review *decisions* for jurisdictional error, and not to review reasons. There may be cases where what appears on the face of the Tribunal's reasons to be a jurisdictional error is shown by the record before the reviewing court to be merely a failure to comply with s 430. Such a failure does not constitute jurisdictional error. In the case of a failure to comply with s 430, the appropriate course for an aggrieved applicant is to seek an order compelling the Tribunal to comply with

its obligations under s 430. The ensuing written statement may or may not reveal jurisdictional error: cf *Re Minister for Immigration and Multicultural and Indigenous Affairs; Ex parte Palme* [2003] HCA 56; (2003) 216 CLR 212 ('*Ex parte Palme*') at 224–25 [41]–[46] per Gleeson CJ, Gummow and Heydon JJ; and *Kennedy v Australian Fisheries Management Authority* [2009] FCA 1485; (2009) 182 FCR 411 at 435 [70] per Tracey J.

55. In a case such as the present, it will always be possible to speculate that the Tribunal has relied on absent and unidentified probative material, but it will rarely be possible to establish that fact with any degree of confidence. In the ordinary course of things, a reviewing court is bound to consider, consistently with s 430, that what purports to be the Tribunal's written statement under s 430 sets out what were in fact the reasons for the Tribunal reaching the decision set forth in that statement; the findings set out therein are the findings the Tribunal actually made and considered material to its decision; and the evidence and other material referred to therein is in fact the evidence and material on which the Tribunal based those findings. To do otherwise would transform judicial review into an exercise in divination of the sort s 430 was designed to avoid. Considering the function of s 430, a reviewing court should not depart from this approach unless there is a sound reason to do so. I conclude that there is no such reason here . . .

60. Ultimately, as noted earlier, the choice here is between an inference that material to which the Tribunal did not refer and which does not appear in the record was not part of the material on which the Tribunal based its finding regarding the first respondent's knowledge, and an inference that unidentified material, not mentioned in the Tribunal's written statement and not in the record, provided a basis for the Tribunal's finding. Having regard to s 430, the first inference is self-evidently stronger than the second, notwithstanding that counsel for the Minister argued for acceptance of the second inference . . .

72. . . . Under the circumstances of the present case, the respondents have met their burden. On the face of the Tribunal's written statement, the Tribunal's conclusion that the first respondent's answers were not correct was not grounded in probative material and logical grounds. That is, the statement does not disclose any material by reference to which a rational decision-maker could have evaluated the first respondent's answers; no such material can be found in the record; and no other logical basis justifies the Tribunal's finding. In these the circumstances, it is appropriate to infer that the Tribunal's decision-making was arbitrary and irrational such as to constitute jurisdictional error. In support of validity, the Minister could only speculate as to the nature and existence of purportedly probative but unidentified and unidentifiable material, an approach antithetical to that of s 430 of the Migration Act. Accordingly, the Federal Magistrate did not err in finding jurisdictional error.

A new judicial review scheme for visa-related decisions was introduced in October 2001. The old Part 8 judicial review scheme was repealed and replaced by Parts 8 and 8A. During the second reading of the Migration Legislation Amendment (Judicial Review) Bill 2001 (Cth), the then Minister for Immigration detailed the reasons why the Federal Government sought to insert a privative clause into the Act:

The bill gives legislative effect to the government's longstanding commitment to introduce legislation that in migration matters will restrict access to judicial review in all but exceptional circumstances. This commitment was made in light of the extensive merits review rights in the migration legislation and concerns about the growing cost and incidence of migration litigation and the associated delays in removal of non-citizens with no right to remain in Australia.

The bill introduces a new judicial review scheme for decisions made under the Migration Act relating to the entry to, and stay in, Australia of non-citizens of Australia. The key mechanism in the new scheme is the privative clause provision at new section 474. The privative clause, and the related provisions, will replace the existing judicial review scheme at Part 8 of the Migration Act. Unlike the existing scheme, the new judicial review scheme will also apply to the High Court and not just the Federal Court.

The privative clause does not mean that access to the courts is denied, nor that only the High Court can hear migration matters. Both the Federal Court and the High Court can hear migration matters, but the grounds of judicial review before either court have been limited . . .

Counsels' advice was that a privative clause would have the effect of narrowing the scope of judicial review by the High Court and of course the Federal Court. That advice was largely based on the High Court's own interpretation of such clauses in cases following the seminal High Court case of Hickman in 1945. The privative clause in the bill is based on a very similar clause in Hickman's case.

The High Court has not since, despite opportunities to do so, repudiated the Hickman principle as formulated by Justice Dixon in Hickman's case. Indeed, that principle was described as 'classical' in a later High Court case.

Members may be aware that the effect of a privative clause such as that used in Hickman's case is to expand the legal validity of the acts done and the decisions made by decision makers. The result is to give decision makers wider lawful operation for their decisions, and this means that the grounds on which those decisions can be challenged in the Federal and High Courts are narrower than currently.

In practice, the decision is lawful provided:

- the decision maker is acting in good faith;
- the decision is reasonably capable of reference to the power given to the decision maker – that is, the decision maker had been given the authority to make the decision concerned, for example, had the authority delegated to him or her by the MIMA, or had been properly appointed as a tribunal member;
- the decision relates to the subject matter of the legislation – it is highly unlikely that this ground would be transgressed when making decisions about visas since the major purpose of the Migration Act is dealing with visa decisions; and
- constitutional limits are not exceeded – given the clear constitutional basis for visa decision making in the Migration Act, this is highly unlikely to arise . . .

Under the reforms in this bill, unlike today, there will be no advantage in sidestepping the Federal Court and going straight to the High Court in its original jurisdiction. This is because the same grounds of review will apply in either the Federal Court or the High Court. It will be open to the High Court to remit all matters to the Federal Court if it wishes. It cannot do so today under the current judicial review scheme because of the disparity between the High Court's original jurisdiction and that of the Federal Court.[30]

30 Commonwealth, *Second Reading Speech*, Migration Legislation Amendment (Judicial Review) Bill (Cth), House of Representatives, 26 September 2001, 31559 (Philip Ruddock, MIMA).

19.6 Privative clause

The new scheme does not prevent applications from being made to review courts, but seeks to restrict the available grounds on which judicial review may be sought. The provisions for judicial review that are now set out in Part 8 of the Act include section 474.[31] Section 474(2) defines a 'privative clause decision' as:

> . . . a decision of an administrative character made, proposed to be made, or required to be made, as the case may be, under this Act or under a regulation or other instrument made under this Act (whether in the exercise of a discretion or not), other than a decision referred to in subsection (4) or (5).

Section 474(1) of the Act provides that a privative clause decision:

> (a) is final and conclusive; and
> (b) must not be challenged, appealed against, reviewed, quashed or called into question in any court; and
> (c) is not subject to prohibition, mandamus, injunction, declaration or certiorari in any court on any account.

The constitutional validity of the privative clause was unsuccessfully challenged in the High Court case of *S157/2002 v Commonwealth*.[32] However, the High Court interpreted the privative clause narrowly, and found that it did not apply to judicial review of decisions affected by jurisdictional error.[33] In a joint judgment, Gaudron, McHugh, Gummow, Kirby and Hayne JJ stated that a breach of the rules of natural justice would constitute jurisdictional error under section 75(v) of the *Australian Constitution* (Cth).[34]

The judicial review ground of 'natural justice' has been the focus of attention for reform. Despite a procedural code being included in the Act, in *Re MIMA; Ex parte Miah*,[35] the court found that the code had not clearly and explicitly replaced the common law or natural justice 'hearing rule'. The *Migration Legislation Amendment (Procedural Fairness) Act 2002* (Cth) was subsequently enacted so that specified codes of procedure (such as subdivision AB of the *Migration Act 1958* (Cth)) exhaustively replace the 'hearing rule' in natural justice.

In *Re MIMA; Ex parte Applicant S20/2002*,[36] McHugh and Gummow JJ left open the question of whether *Wednesbury* unreasonableness could constitute

31 Inserted into the *Migration Act 1958* (Cth) by *Migration Legislation Amendment (Judicial Review) Act 2001* (Cth) which came into effect on 2 October 2001.
32 [2003] HCA 2 (4 February 2003).
33 See *S157/2002 v Commonwealth* [2003] HCA 2 (4 February 2003), [87] (Gaudron, McHugh, Gummow, Kirby and Hayne JJ). In *Minister for Immigration and Citizenship v SZNPG* [2010] FCAFC 51 it was held that unsound reasoning by the RRT does not constitute an error of law and the dealing with corroborative evidence in a perfunctory manner did not constitute a jurisdictional error. See also, *Minister for Immigration and Citizenship v SZNSP* [2010] FCAFC 50.
34 *S157/2002 v Commonwealth* [2003] HCA 2 (4 February 2003), [45]. See also *MIMA v SGLB* [2004] HCA 32 (17 June 2004).
35 [2001] HCA 22 (3 May 2001).
36 [2003] HCA 30 (17 June 2003).

jurisdictional error in this context.[37] Nevertheless, their Honours considered the scope of jurisdictional error in the context of the appellant's claim that the RRT's decision had been affected by jurisdictional error because it 'was illogical, irrational, or was not based on findings or inferences of fact supported by logical grounds'. In the course of their reasons for dismissing the appellant's claim on this basis, their Honours distinguished between discretionary decisions and decisions concerning findings of fact essential to the exercise of jurisdiction:

> ... the Minister urged the rejection of the appellant's claims to relief under s 75(v) of the Constitution and that this be done by treating distinctions between legal and factual errors as providing the decisive discrimen. The Minister submitted that the 'ultimate' question for the Tribunal was its satisfaction (or lack of it) respecting the appellant's well-founded fear of persecution for a Convention reason, whereas at the 'lower level' there were questions of 'primary fact'. Further, it was submitted that (i) want of logic in making findings of such primary facts does not constitute an 'error of law' and (ii) the presence of an 'error of law' is essential for a finding of jurisdictional error for s 75(v) ...
>
> In *Re MIMA; Ex parte Lam*, we emphasised that the distinction between jurisdictional and non-jurisdictional error which informs s 75(v) manifests the separation between the judicial power and the legislative function of translating policy into statutory form and the executive function of administration of those laws. In this Australian constitutional setting, there is added significance to the point that the English common law courts 'always disowned judicial review for error of fact' and 'jurisdictional fact review proceeds on the basis that it is a jurisdictional error of law for someone to exercise public power in the absence of a jurisdictional fact'.
>
> These considerations militate against acceptance of the Minister's submissions. On the other hand, they also caution against the introduction into the constitutional jurisprudence attending s 75(v) of broader views of the scope for consideration of factual error in 'appeals' on questions of law which are created by statute, or in legislatively created systems of judicial review. There, what is engaged are principles of statutory, not constitutional, construction.[38] [Footnote omitted.]

The distinction between jurisdictional and non-jurisdictional error was most recently considered by the High Court in *Minister for Immigration and Citizenship v SZMDS*,[39] where it was held that:

> **Jurisdictional error**
>
> 16. Of the distinction between jurisdictional and non-jurisdictional error in the setting of the Australian Constitution, Justice Selway, writing extrajudicially, said:
>
>> 'Notwithstanding the difficulty, indeed often apparent artificiality, of the distinction, it is a distinction between errors that are authorised and errors that are not; between acts that are unauthorised by law and acts that are authorised. Such a distinction is inherent in any analysis based upon separation of powers principles.'
>
> 17. In *Plaintiff S157/2002*, Gaudron, McHugh, Gummow, Hayne and Kirby JJ said:

37 [2003] HCA 30 (17 June 2003), [67]. It is now assumed that this can constitute a basis for appeal: see, for example, *SZOFZ v Minister for Immigration and Citizenship* [2010] FCA 1288.
38 *Re MIMA; Ex parte Applicant S20/2002* [2003] HCA 30 (17 June 2003), [53] and [59]–[60].
39 [2010] HCA 16.

> 'Because, as this Court has held, the constitutional writs of prohibition and mandamus are available only for jurisdictional error and because s 474 of the Act does not protect decisions involving jurisdictional error, s 474 does not, in that regard conflict with s 75(v) of the Constitution and, thus, is valid in its application to the proceedings which the plaintiff would initiate.'

18. The constitutional jurisdiction has its origins in the control exercised by the English courts to prevent administrative authorities exceeding their authority or neglecting their duties. The execution of the laws made by the Parliament was seen as an aspect of the executive power. There was no distinct concept of public administration as developed in some civilian systems. In the English system the 'jurisdictional fact' was an appropriate marker for the enforcement of legality; how much further the field for judicial review of administrative action extended remained a matter of debate.

19. It is in this setting that the statement of general principle by Brennan J in *Attorney-General (NSW) v Quin* is to be understood. His Honour said:

> 'The duty and jurisdiction of the court to review administrative action do not go beyond the declaration and enforcing of the law which determines the limits and governs the exercise of the repository's power. If, in so doing, the court avoids administrative injustice or error, so be it; but the court has no jurisdiction simply to cure administrative injustice or error. The merits of administrative action, to the extent that they can be distinguished from legality, are for the repository of the relevant power and, subject to political control, for the repository alone.'

20. In his work *Administrative Law*, Professor Paul Craig describes jurisdictional facts as those relating to the existence of the power of a public body over the relevant area and continues:

> 'The statutory conditions thus laid down may be factual, legal or discretionary in nature. A classic factual precondition is that a person should be of a particular age to qualify for a benefit; a simple legal stipulation is provided by the meaning of the term employee; a discretionary precondition is where the statute provides that if a minister has reasonable grounds to believe that a person is a terrorist then he may be detained. Claims of factual error can arise in all three types of case. It might be argued that the agency simply got the applicant's age wrong because it confused the applicant with a different person. It might be claimed that the agency misapplied the legal meaning of the term employee to the facts of the applicant's case. It might be contended that the minister did not on the facts have sufficient material to sustain a reasonable ground for believing that the applicant was a terrorist.'

The criterion for attraction of the jurisdiction of the decision maker in deciding an application under the Act for a protection visa is not expressed in terms of 'fact' as simply understood. Rather, as explained earlier in these reasons, the Act fixes upon a criterion of 'satisfaction' as to the existence of a certain state of affairs respecting the status of the applicant.

21. In that regard, a statement of principle by Lord Wilberforce made in 1976, before the tectonic shifts in English public law which occurred in later decades, is of first importance. In *Secretary of State for Education and Science v Tameside Metropolitan Borough Council*, his Lordship said of a provision conditioning the power of the Secretary of State to act upon satisfaction as to a certain state of affairs:

'The section is framed in a "subjective" form – if the Secretary of State "is satisfied". This form of section is quite well known, and at first sight might seem to exclude judicial review. Sections in this form may, no doubt, exclude judicial review on what is or has become a matter of pure judgment. But I do not think that they go further than that. If a judgment requires, *before it can be made*, the existence of some facts, then, although the evaluation of those facts is for the Secretary of State alone, the court must inquire whether those facts exist, and have been taken into account, *whether the judgment has been made upon a proper self-direction as to those facts*, [and] whether the judgment has not been made upon other facts which ought not to have been taken into account.' (Emphasis added.)

22. The essence of the case upon which the first respondent succeeded in the Federal Court was that in attaining the satisfaction required by the Act, the RRT did not make its judgment upon a proper self direction as to the inferences to be drawn from its rejection of the factual account given by the first respondent.

23. In Australia, as Basten JA recently observed, the principles applicable where the jurisdictional fact is a state of satisfaction or opinion are traced back to the use by Latham CJ in *R v Connell; Ex parte The Hetton Bellbird Collieries Ltd* of the terms 'arbitrary, capricious, irrational' as well as 'not bona fide' to stigmatise the formation of an opinion upon which a statutory power was enlivened. Subsequently, for the Supreme Court of Canada, Iacobucci J spoke of decision making upon an assumption which had no basis in the evidentiary material or which was contrary to the overwhelming weight of that material, and also of decisions based upon a contradiction in the processes by which conclusions were reached or upon the drawing of inferences which were not properly open.

24. A decision upon jurisdictional fact which has these characteristics is treated as a failure to exercise jurisdiction. There has been a purported exercise of public power in the absence of the necessary jurisdictional fact.

25. These considerations have added significance where the law in question is made by a legislature of limited powers. Thus, in Australia a jurisdictional fact may also be or include a constitutional fact. An example would be a criterion of liability that required the satisfaction of a non-curial decision maker that a propositus answer the description of a trading or financial corporation formed within the limits of the Commonwealth. If that satisfaction were not examinable on judicial review, the result, as the *Australian Communist Party v The Commonwealth* teaches, would be that the legislation could rise higher than its constitutional source. These considerations apply in the present case. No doubt, the first respondent being an alien, a Pakistani national, the Act applies to him as a law with respect to that alienage. But the answer to the question posed by ss 36 and 65 as to the application of the definition of 'refugee' determines whether in its operation upon the first respondent the Act also is supported as a law with respect to external affairs.

26. In England the distinction between jurisdictional and non-jurisdictional facts has fallen into deep disfavour and broader notions of the scope of judicial review have been developed and applied by the English courts. The submissions for the Minister by the Commonwealth Solicitor-General in significant measure sought to discourage any such development by this Court in applying s 75(v) of the Constitution.

27. In *Re Minister for Immigration and Multicultural and Indigenous Affairs; Ex parte Lam* there was some consideration of the difficulties in Australia with the recent English authorities respecting review on the ground of 'abuse of power' through the alteration of policy to frustrate unfairly the 'legitimate' expectations of the individuals seeking

review. No such ground was relied on by the first respondent. Nor does the present case require consideration of a doctrine of proportionality to review the exercise of a discretion where there is lacking an appropriate relationship between ends and means.

28. Still less is this the occasion to consider the development in Canada of a doctrine of 'substantive review' applied to determinations of law, of fact, and of mixed law and fact made by administrative tribunals. Of substantive review, the Supreme Court of Canada recently said:

> 'The current approach to judicial review involves three standards of review, which range from correctness, where no deference is shown, to patent unreasonableness, which is most deferential to the decision maker, the standard of reasonableness *simpliciter* lying, theoretically, in the middle. In our view, it is necessary to reconsider both the number and definitions of the various standards of review, and the analytical process employed to determine which standard applies in a given situation. We conclude that there ought to be two standards of review – correctness and reasonableness.'

It may, however, be noted that the Supreme Court was not dealing with a system of judicial review created by statute, such as a counterpart of the ADJR Act. Rather, in Canada 'the inherent power of superior courts to review administrative action and ensure that it does not exceed its jurisdiction stems from the judicature provisions in ss 96 to 101 of the *Constitution Act* 1867'.

29. The determination of this appeal turns on the application of the doctrine of jurisdictional error, implicit in s 75(v) of the Constitution, to a legislative criterion expressed in terms of the satisfaction of the RRT.

30. Writing after the decision in *Tameside*, Professor Craig said:

'The general approach now is for the courts to require that a minister produce reasonable grounds for his action, even where the jurisdictional fact is subjectively framed.'

31. In *Television Capricornia Pty Ltd v Australian Broadcasting Tribunal*, Wilcox J carefully, and with respect correctly, distinguished a 'no evidence' ground respecting the existence of a jurisdictional fact, from the more debatable question (which does not arise in this appeal, as counsel for the first respondent stressed) of defective fact finding as an independent ground of judicial review, or as indicative of an 'error of law' within the meaning of the ADJR Act.

The importance of reasons

32. Professor Wade wrote that a system of judicial review which cannot cope with crucial questions of fact necessarily is seriously defective. In Australia that deficiency is alleviated by requirements in various laws, notably s 13 of the ADJR Act and its progeny in State legislation, for the obtaining of reasons for the decision. Section 430(1) of the Act is such a provision. Its operation in the present dispute is to lay out, more clearly than otherwise would be the case, the field upon which these operate the considerations mentioned, for example, by Lord Wilberforce in *Tameside* and Latham CJ in *Connell*.

33. Section 430(1) obliged the RRT, in making its decision, to prepare a written statement setting out its decision (par (a)), its reasons for the decision (par (b)), the findings on any material questions of fact (par (c)) and referring to the evidence or any other material on which those findings of fact were based (par (d)). The obligation is to set out the findings on what the RRT considers to be material questions of fact; this focuses

upon the thought processes of the decision maker, and may disclose jurisdictional error.

34. Many of the leading authorities in this Court in which administrative decisions were challenged concerned legislative regimes in which there was no counterpart of s 430 of the Act. The decisions at stake in those cases presented an inscrutable face. Thus, in *Avon Downs Pty Ltd v Federal Commissioner of Taxation*, s 80(5) of the *Income Tax Assessment Act* 1936 (Cth) required the taxpayer company, if prior losses were to be allowed deductions, to satisfy the Commissioner of the state of its voting power on the last day of the year of income. No reasons were given by the Commissioner for the disallowance of the taxpayer's objections to its assessment. In that context Dixon J explained the circumstances in which the conclusion of the Commissioner was liable to review by the court. Likewise, the inadequacy of the material before the decision maker may support an inference that the decision maker has applied the wrong test or was not 'in reality' satisfied of the requisite matters or from the absence of reasons the court may infer the absence of any good reason.

35. On the other hand, of provisions such as s 430, it was said in *Wu Shan Liang* that the reasons are meant to inform and, upon judicial review, are not to be scrutinised in an over-zealous fashion. In that case, where the refugee status of the respondent was at stake, the Court said of the use by the decision maker of the term 'speculative':

> 'The word "speculative" in the context in which it appears need not amount to a denial of the delegates' function of assessment of future chances of persecution. Rather, the word might equally have been used to refer to the probative force of the material before the delegate.'

36. Here the RRT did give reasons in response to the requirement of s 430(1). The issue is whether, having regard to those reasons and without the necessity for a process of divination undertaken in the earlier authorities dealing with other legislation, the RRT fell into jurisdictional error to attract the remedy provided by the Federal Court.

SGLB

37. The ascertainment of the relevant jurisdictional error, if there be one, must fix upon the treatment of the requirement mandated by s 65 of the Act that the decision maker be 'satisfied' that there is 'satisfied' the criterion that the applicant is one to whom the decision maker is satisfied under s 36(2)(a) that Australia owes protection obligations.

38. In dealing with that question two distinctions must be made. They are foreshadowed in what has been said earlier in these reasons. The first is that the first respondent does not assert any general ground of jurisdictional error of the kind disfavoured by Mason CJ where there were alleged deficiencies in what might be called 'intra-mural' fact finding by the decision maker in the course of the exercise of the jurisdiction to make a decision. The apprehensions respecting 'merits review' assume that there was jurisdiction to embark upon determination of the merits. But the same degree of caution as to the scope of judicial review does not apply when the issue is whether the jurisdictional threshold has been crossed. There the imperatives are the separation of powers considerations to which Justice Selway referred.

39. The second distinction concerns attacks upon the exercises of discretionary power which are said to be unreasonable in the sense attributed to *Associated Provincial Pictures Houses Ltd v Wednesbury Corporation*. The concern here is with abuse of power

in the exercise of discretion, again on the assumption that the occasion for the exercise of discretion had arisen upon the existence of any necessary jurisdictional facts. Confusion of thought, with apprehension of intrusive interference with administrative decisions by judicial review will be avoided if the distinction between jurisdictional fact and other facts then taken into account in discretionary decision making is kept in view.

40. It was against this background that, when considering s 65 of the Act in *Minister for Immigration and Multicultural and Indigenous Affairs v SGLB*, Gummow and Hayne JJ said:

> 'The satisfaction of the Minister is a condition precedent to the discharge of the obligation to grant or refuse to grant the visa, and is a 'jurisdictional fact' or criterion upon which the exercise of that authority is conditioned. The delegate was in the same position as would have been the Minister (s 496) and the Tribunal exercised all the powers and discretions conferred on the decision-maker (s 415).
>
> The satisfaction of the criterion that the applicant is a non-citizen to whom Australia has the relevant protection obligations may include consideration of factual matters but the critical question is whether the determination was irrational, illogical and not based on findings or inferences of fact supported by logical grounds. If the decision did display these defects, it will be no answer that the determination was reached in good faith.'

However, it should be remarked that what is characterized as the 'critical question' should not receive an affirmative answer that is lightly given. It may be noted that the outcome in *SGLB* and in *Applicant S20/2002* was to deny the presence of jurisdictional error. This reflected the approach upon judicial review earlier expressed in *Wu Shan Liang* to which earlier reference has been made.

41. Similar reasoning to that found in *SGLB* has been applied by the Full Court of the Federal Court in *WAIJ v Minister for Immigration and Multicultural and Indigenous Affairs*, which in turn was followed in authorities including the decision of Gordon J in *SZLGP v Minister for Immigration and Citizenship*, upon which Moore J particularly relied in the present case.

The Minister submitted that there was no occasion for a redetermination by the RRT, as ordered by the Federal Court. This was because the above line of authority should be disowned, essentially for the apprehended fear of 'merits review'. But, as indicated in these reasons, that submission should be rejected. It gives insufficient weight to the importance of s 75(v) of the Constitution in ensuring that the legislative expression of jurisdictional facts in terms of satisfaction or opinion of a decision maker does not rise higher than its source.

The most illuminating aspect about the above commentary is its rambling, non-committal nature, which is underpinned by the reluctance of the court to provide anything approaching clear guidance about the distinction between jurisdictional and non-jurisdictional error. The High Court is at the apex of the Australian legal system and has a duty to clarify the law, especially in relation to important legal issues that centrally affect the welfare of people and which are regularly litigated. The judges on the High Court are aware of this function. The distinction between jurisdictional and non-jurisdictional is a vague issue, but conceptually it is not difficult to define principles demarcating the distinction.

The High Court presumably elected not to in order to keep vague the distinction and thus preserve ample scope to make result-orientated judgments in this area.

The High Court has not conclusively decided whether jurisdictional error may arise where a tribunal fails to make its own inquiries of certain facts. However, if such a doctrine exists it would only be in the most limited of situations. In *Minister for Immigration and Citizenship v SZIAI*,[40] at [23]–[25], it was held:

> The proposition which may emerge from *Prasad* has not been the subject of full consideration in this Court, whether in litigation under the ADJR Act, or any other statutory regime or under s 75(v) of the Constitution. Some observations by Mason CJ in *Chan v Minister for Immigration and Ethnic Affairs* have been taken as an indication of a need for decision-makers to make inquiries in relation to claimed changes in the political circumstances in the home country of a person seeking protection as a refugee. However, the legal consequences of a failure to inquire were not discussed in that judgment. In *Minister for Immigration and Ethnic Affairs v Teoh*, Mason CJ and Deane J accepted the correctness of the approach in *Prasad* in 'an appropriate case'. *Teoh* was not such a case as reliance was not placed on the ground of review under the ADJR Act which was considered in *Prasad*. McHugh J also made reference to *Prasad* and other Federal Court decisions to similar effect. But, like Mason CJ and Deane J, he found them inapplicable in *Teoh*. In *Abebe v The Commonwealth*, Gummow and Hayne JJ rejected a submission that the Tribunal in that case should have made further inquiries. They did so on the basis that '[n]o plausible and possible line of inquiry was suggested'. They did not think it necessary to consider the premise of the submission, namely that the Tribunal was under an obligation to make further inquiries. Nor was it necessary to consider the limits of so-called *Wednesbury* unreasonableness.
>
> Mason CJ and Deane J in *Teoh* also rejected the proposition that failure by a decision-maker to initiate inquiries could constitute a departure from common law standards of natural justice or procedural fairness. It is difficult to see any basis upon which a failure to inquire could constitute a breach of the requirements of procedural fairness at common law . . .
>
> Although decisions in the Federal Court concerned with a failure to make obvious inquiries have led to references to a 'duty to inquire', that term is apt to direct consideration away from the question whether the decision which is under review is vitiated by jurisdictional error. The duty imposed upon the Tribunal by the Migration Act is a duty to review. It may be that a failure to make an obvious inquiry about a critical fact, the existence of which is easily ascertained, could, in some circumstances, supply a sufficient link to the outcome to constitute a failure to review. If so, such a failure could give rise to jurisdictional error by constructive failure to exercise jurisdiction. It may be that failure to make such an inquiry results in a decision being affected in some other way that manifests itself as jurisdictional error. It is not necessary to explore these questions of principle in this case.

Recently, the High Court, in a decision which represents the high-water mark of judicial creativity, has read down another provision that aims to limit natural

40 [2009] HCA 39.

justice to visa applicants, including offshore applicants who are entitled to appeal decisions. In *Saeed v Minister for Immigration and Citizenship*[41] the High Court found that an offshore applicant from Pakistan for a Skilled – Independent Visa (subclass 175) was entitled to natural justice in that she was entitled to be made aware of adverse information that was relied upon by the decision-maker to reject her application. Section 51A of the *Migration Act 1958* (Cth) was inserted specifically to limit the operation of the natural justice role. It states that the provisions in the Act are an 'exhaustive statement of the requirements of the natural justice hearing rule'. The court noted that in the Second Reading Speech the Minister stated:

> 'Therefore, the purpose of this [B]ill is to make it expressly clear that particular codes in the Migration Act do exhaustively state the requirements of the natural justice or procedural fairness hearing rule.
>
> This will have the effect that common law requirements relating to the natural justice or procedural fairness hearing rule are effectively excluded, as was originally intended.'

And:

> 'In conclusion, these amendments are necessary to restore the [P]arliament's original intention that the Migration Act should contain codes of procedure that allow fair, efficient and legally certain decision making processes that do replace the common law requirement of the natural justice hearing rule.'[42]

Despite this, the intention of the section was circumvented by the court, by relying on two principles. First, it stated:

> As Gummow J observed in *Wik Peoples v Queensland*, it is necessary to keep in mind that when it is said the legislative 'intention' is to be ascertained, 'what is involved is the "intention *manifested*" by the legislation'. Statements as to legislative intention made in explanatory memoranda or by Ministers, however clear or emphatic, cannot overcome the need to carefully consider the words of the statute to ascertain its meaning.[43]
>
> [Emphasis in original.]

Second, the court noted that:

> 1. In *Coco v The Queen* it was said, with respect to fundamental rights, that '[t]he courts should not impute to the legislature an intention to interfere with fundamental rights'. The same may be said as to the displacement of fundamental principles of the common law. In *Coco v The Queen* Mason CJ, Brennan, Gaudron and McHugh JJ said:
>
>> 'Such an intention must be clearly manifested by unmistakable and unambiguous language. General words will rarely be sufficient for that purpose if they do not specifically deal with the question because, in the context in which they appear, they will often be ambiguous on the aspect of interference with fundamental rights.'[44]

41 [2010] HCA 23.
42 *Saeed v Minister for Immigration and Citizenship* [2010] HCA 23 at [30].
43 *Saeed v Minister for Immigration and Citizenship* [2010] HCA 23 at [31].
44 *Saeed v Minister for Immigration and Citizenship* [2010] HCA 23 at [58].

Thus it follows that offshore applicants are entitled to comment on adverse information, and that a decision-maker must then take into consideration those comments in determining their visa application. For a recent decision regarding the scope of the obligation of the MRT to provide adverse information to applicants, see *Minister for Immigration and Citizenship v Kumar*.[45]

19.7 Ministerial intervention

Under sections 345, 351, 391, 417, 454 and 501J of the *Migration Act 1958* (Cth), the Immigration Minister has the power to substitute, for a decision made by one of the review tribunals,[46] a decision that is more favourable to the visa applicant(s), if he or she considers it is in the public interest to do so. That is, ministerial intervention is contingent on an applicant having undergone a merits review procedure. The relevant sections provide that it is a non-compellable power and the Minister has no obligation to consider a request for intervention. Policy is that the power will only be exercised in 'unique or exceptional circumstances'.[47] Such circumstances are considered most likely to arise in the light of international human rights conventions and other circumstances where compassion may be required.

19.8 Commentary on current state of judicial review of migration and refugee decisions

In light of such judgments by the High Court, it is hardly surprising that judicial review of migration and refugee decisions is seen as being 'undertaken in a climate of doctrinal ambiguity'.[48] McMillan has also made the following observations on de facto merits reviews being undertaken by the Federal Court:

> Immigration litigation is thus an area of special challenge. On any objective view it has been handled by the Federal Court in a customary judicial fashion by the assiduous application of legal method. That said, the role of the Court has not been free of difficulty. In an earlier article I wrote that a problem of 'judicial merits review' and 'judicial overreach' has patterned the work of the Court for more than a decade. The problem, indisputably, has not been pervasive, and can be traced to a small minority of judgments. Unquestionably, too, the Court is alert to the emergence of such a trend, particularly in a court of nearly fifty members in areas as vexed as review of deportation and refugee decisions: in a very public way members of the Court have confronted and discussed the dangers of judicial merits review in judgments and extra-curial writings.

45 [2009] HCA 10.
46 The former Migration Internal Review Office (MIRO – ceased operation on 31 May 1999); the former Immigration Review Tribunal (IRT – ceased operation on 31 May 1999); the Migration Review Tribunal (MRT – commenced operation on 1 June 1999); the Refugee Review Tribunal (RRT); and the Administrative Appeals Tribunal (AAT).
47 MSI No. 386, 14 August 2003, s 4.2.
48 MSI No. 386, 14 August 2003, s 4.2, at n 14.

> Yet, the problem is real, and it persists. It illustrates an underlying theme of this paper, that exceptional, one-off and single judge decisions of a court often have greater impact in defining the dynamics of a legal system than the large body of consistent and less-talked about jurisprudence.[49] [Footnote omitted.]

And in defence of the complex task confronted by judges in reviewing migration and refugee decisions, Sackville J has referred to one factor that has contributed to tensions between the judiciary and the executive as:

> . . . the reliance by Parliament on repeated legislative amendments to overturn unwelcome judicial decisions or to curtail the scope of judicial review, without proponents of the legislation appreciating the profound difference between their subjective intentions and the intention to be attributed to Parliament by the courts when applying well established techniques of statutory interpretation.[50] [Footnote omitted.]

Legislative provisions for determining visa applications create some inherent tensions. Applicants have more or less unlimited rights to seek judicial review, irrespective of parliamentary attempts to curtail their grounds of review and, from their point of view, their chances of success. Applying for a protection visa is often a last resort for people who cannot make a valid application for any other visa and is, therefore, open to abuse, even if only by a few applicants.

In addition, some people who have genuinely compelling grounds for remaining in Australia but do not meet any visa criteria can only have genuine consideration of their claims by the Minister (rather than delegates or tribunal members), but must first proceed through the merits primary application and review procedures. This takes time and is an apparent waste of the determination process, but it is a legitimate exercise and is permitted and encouraged by the legislation.

No doubt there will be continuing friction between Parliament and the judiciary as some politicians view some judges as intervening in the fact-finding process, notwithstanding that the vast majority of judicial review decisions uphold the determinations made by administrative decision-makers. The review system may be cumbersome, drawn out and expensive, and it can create anomalies, such as long-term detention for applicants seeking judicial review (along with their children). It could be streamlined and may also be open to abuse by some applicants but, as it currently operates, it ensures that applicants are able to exhaust a comprehensive legislative scheme to make their cases.

49 ibid.
50 'Refugee Law: The Shifting Balance', [2004] 26 *Sydney Law Review* 37.

Index

For EU product safety concerns, contact us at Calle de José Abascal, 56–1°,
28003 Madrid, Spain or eugpsr@cambridge.org.

www.ingramcontent.com/pod-product-compliance
Ingram Content Group UK Ltd.
Pitfield, Milton Keynes, MK11 3LW, UK
UKHW020901231025
464099UK00017B/256
* 9 7 8 1 1 0 7 6 2 3 2 7 9 *